Two Living Traditions

Essays on Religion and the Bible

Two
Living
Traditions

Essays on Religion and the Bible

by Samuel Sandmel

HEBREW UNION COLLEGE · JEWISH INSTITUTE OF RELIGION

Wayne State University Press · Detroit 1972

Published simultaneously in Canada
by the Copp Clark Publishing Company
517 Wellington Street, West
Toronto 2B, Canada.

Library of Congress Catalog Card Number 72-173919
International Standard Book Number 0-8143-1460-0

Library of Congress Cataloging in Publication Data
Sandmel, Samuel.
   Two living traditions.
   Includes bibliographical references.
   1. Judaism—Relations—Christianity—Addresses,
essays, lectures. 2. Christianity and other
religions—Judaism—Addresses, essays, lectures.
3. Theology—Addresses, essays, lectures.
I. Title.
BM535.S217   1972   200'.1   72-173919
ISBN 0-8143-1460-0

To F.F.S.
Many daughters have done virtuously,
but thou excellest them all.
PROVERBS 31:29

contents

foreword

SAMUEL SANDMEL'S WORK stands firmly on two feet, ancient Judaism and early Christianity. But his numerous books and articles deal with the whole wide range of Judaism and Christianity, not only with the brief centuries when Christianity was being born from its mother religion. He is familiar with the scholarly literature that bears on both. Studying their interrelations—their common convictions and their differences—requires detailed and accurate understanding, even when controversy beclouds the ancient issues; and this is what Dr. Sandmel provides.

Impartial scholarship is hard to come by, but it offers one of the few ways out of the thickets of controversy, old and new. It is the prelude to genuine understanding. Neither Christians nor Jews can be content with simply reiterating the accumulated traditions of the past, even though both will bring forth treasures of religious insights from the works of their forefathers. Making use of the insights of scholarship, they will incline toward "dialogue" rather than toward controversy—especially if controversy means no more than reiteration. What counts is the determination to be fair and honest.

The Christian Gospels, like such documents as the Sayings of the Fathers, came out of, and reflected, a growing body of tradition. In fact, all ancient literature that rested on tradition has the same kind of foundation. With Dr. Sandmel we try to push behind the written documents to the living tradition beyond them. We find, then, a variety of convictions and practices in these ancient religions. Even though we may disregard and reject some of them and reinterpret others, the variety enriches the wealth of religious experience and offers a freedom of living insight into its still vital growth. The Bible provides a priceless variety of living utterance, and inspiration old and new.

The glowing enthusiasm and the knowledge and insight of such a biblical scholar as the author of these essays will open the door for many a grateful reader.

Frederick C. Grant

prefatory note

THESE ESSAYS, AS will be noted, have appeared in a variety of places. When they appeared, the manner of notation, punctuation, and the like, conformed to the practices or regulations of the journals where they appeared. To bring these now into some uniformity has entailed a chore of considerable detail. I record my deep thanks to my student, Mr. David Wortman, and especially to Miss Sandra Yolles and Mrs. Barbara Woodward of Wayne State University Press, for the combination of a keen eye and a dedicated spirit. As in other things I have written, I could scarcely have proceeded from the handwritten manuscript through the typescript without my unique secretary, Mrs. Sam November.

I am deeply grateful to the various publishers who have graciously given permission to reproduce articles that have appeared previously in periodicals and books. The sources are listed on the first page of each essay. In every case the publishers have responded to my request promptly, graciously, and generously.

S. S.

1

The Jewish Scholar and Early Christianity *

I PROPOSE IN this paper, to raise some general and some specific issues related to the Jewish scholar and his study of Christian documents.

It is by now platitudinous to set forth the purpose of research scholarship as the impartial search for the truth. Few, if any, will disagree with this statement, or, more precisely, few will disagree with its intent. However, there will be those who will want to add a factor, that of relevancy, on the contention that disinterested, impartial research is mere antiquarianism, and that clearly either humanistic benefit must emerge from the research, or else the research is meaningless. Such abstract desiderata could float in mid-air and none would be the worse or better for them; but when they are applied to the *ad hoc* problem, then the issue can be raised in this way; if Christian scholarship is designed to enhance the Gospels, must Jewish scholarship be designed to denigrate them? If Jewish scholarship is designed to enhance rabbinic literature, must Christian scholarship be designed to denigrate it? When the question is put in some such way, the answers become obvious; it thereby becomes patent that no danger is greater to scholarship than the attitude that some direct, proximate, and demonstrable benefit must arise from research. It follows that Jewish scholarship on the Gospels has as its mission the learning of what is most nearly correct, and the clear and impartial exposition of what has been learned. The impartial scholar must not allow the long centuries of mutual Jewish and Christian antipathies to becloud his judgment or warp his perspective, and he must consciously and

* This article first appeared in *Jewish Quarterly Review*, 75 (1967): 473–81.

deliberately face the likelihood that the possibilities of warped judgment exist in all of us.

Two major barriers impede the Jewish scholar from attaining fullest objectivity, the one active and the other reactive. By active barrier I have in mind the impulse among us Jews even in the twentieth century to vindicate what Jews thought and believed in the first. I describe it as active in the sense of a laudable and spontaneous sense of identification with the Jews of that long past era, and the inadvertent distortion that can possibly emerge from that sense of identification. I would allege, for example, that my natural bent for enjoying Midrash is neatly balanced by a bent for not enjoying Paul; and all that I am here saying is that I must take conscious care to prevent my warm inclination toward the halaka from bringing me to a misunderstanding of Paul. Similarly, my affinity for rabbinic subtleties must not deter me from understanding the nuances of the subtleties of Christian literature. At stake here is that intangible element, loyalty, the most commendable of all human traits. Yet loyalty to preconceptions is not comparable in any sense to loyalty to the truth, and it is this latter loyalty which must command the scholar. My friends to whom I am loyal need not be perfect, as I need not be perfect to bask in their loyalty to me; my loyalty to rabbinic Judaism need not lead me to ascribe to it a perfection, that is a freedom from any blemish, which it cannot have. I find it possible to feel a loyalty to men who possess human foibles, and to lack a warmth toward other men who have fewer and less serious foibles. My innate sense of identification with the ancient rabbis must not lead me to misunderstand, and to portray wrongly, the early (and later) Christians with whom I do not have this sense of identification.

But, by contrast, the reactive barrier is much more difficult to cope with, at least specifically for me. While on the one hand I can find much to admire in Paul (without sharing his sense of his religious achievement), I admit that I find myself responding with antagonism to his aspersions of the Torah. Yet in the case of Paul, and in the case of the authors of the Gospels, I find it relatively easy to maintain a certain reactive calmness, as if I am prone to regard their expressions hostile to Jewishness and Jews as products of an age when religious amity and toleration were not even dreamed of. But it is infinitely more difficult for me to take in stride the hostilities to Judaism which have disfigured substantial segments of modern Christian scholarship in its dealing with Judaism. I do not here have in mind the mere inaccuracies, inexactitudes, and unintentional misinterpretations and distortions; I have in mind, rather, the arrogant condescension, the pretentious superiority, and the self-congratulatory banalities which I encounter in some scholarly literature. My focus, if I am to be understood, is on the work of Christian scholars, and not on the work of the pious who write half-learnedly for the edification of the faithful; here too I can react, but this kind of writing is outside my bent and the scope of the present consideration.

My experience has been that the best Christian scholars are the freest of these blemishes and some are completely free. The more there are such blemishes, the least is the total scholarship admirable. Difficult as I sometimes find it to avoid feeling a sharp resentment, I am often able to come to the conviction, which I believe is the right one, that even here the issue is not so much Jewish and Christian disposition, as it is the issue of good scholars and of poor ones. The errors in the scholarship can be exposed in the arena of public notice, as in journals and in books, and such exposure, set forth calmly and tellingly, is legitimately a function of scholarship. What I must guard against, however, is permitting the reactive in me to elicit a counterbalancing untruthfulness. For example, it is not my obligation to the Pharisees to guard their reputation from the assessment of them in some lamentable Christian scholarship; my obligation is to the truth and to sound scholarship, not to the Pharisees. I must not distort Pharisaism affirmatively simply because some Christian scholars distort it negatively.

Outsiders to traditions normally find it much easier to describe the externals of belief and practice than to weigh, assess, and appreciate the inherent values as they are felt internally. What is more complicated than the wish of a Jewish scholar to try to learn accurately what the death of Jesus on the cross meant and means to Christians? It is a fact of history that our Jewish forebears, and even we Jews today, have been called Christ-killers. How difficult it is for a Jew to traverse beyond self-defense and enter into comprehension! And, assuming that a Jewish scholar has tolerably well traversed the defensive, how can he achieve an understanding of a set of theological doctrines alien to his own suppositions?

As to the crucifixion and alleged Jewish responsibility, I do not hesitate to say that I expect little relationship between the results of historical scholarship and popular attitudes; I do not believe that the one deeply affects the other. To my mind, the alleged Jewish responsibility is something for Christians to wrestle with their consciences about; it is an unsuitable subject for Jewish apologetics. As to the scholarship by Jews on the matter, I must comment that all too often Jewish scholars have bypassed the Christian scholarship on the Gospels and have trespassed directly into the Gospels themselves, with the result that very often Jews have attributed to the Gospels a historical reliability which Christian scholars do not. The consequence has been that Jews have "refuted," supposedly in the realm of scholarship, what is actually not contended there. For example, the question of the Jewish right to impose capital punishment, denied in John 18:31, is on the one level a matter of correctness; but on the second, and perhaps more important level, there is the question of how and why that passage got into the Gospel. There is a difference between an amateur understanding of Christian literature, and a professional one; and I am sometimes aghast at the amateurishness of Jewish scholars in Christian literature. One sometimes suspects that the New Testament has, as it were, become a *kosher* field, but Christian scholarship seems to remain *traif*. How otherwise can one account for the almost fundamentalism of some Jewish scholars when they approach the Gospels and New Testament literature?

Is it, perhaps, that issues of delicacy arise unconsciously? Is it that Jewish scholars feel that to apply the process and results of higher criticism to the New Testament is a prerogative only of Christians, and that Jews must abstain from it? Or, can one say again that the issue here is not Jewish or Christian but the issue of good and poor scholarship? How often Jews cite from Joseph Klausner, as if he were a repository of penetrating Christian scholarship! The fact is that Klausner barely trespassed over the borders, and he who knows only Klausner knows precious little of Christian scholarship.

To the scholar, early Christianity seems like a jigsaw puzzle; more than half of the pieces are missing, and it is possible that pieces from other puzzles have gotten into the box. There is no such thing as what liberal Christians a generation ago described as the "simple Gospel." Sheer complexity, utter complicatedness describe the birth and early development of Christianity. There are on record nimble solutions of the problems, and nimbleness is the warmest invitation to error. The "facts" about Jesus, the disciples, Paul, the church in the Diaspora are elusive; when these stray facts are arrayed schematically, one may occasionally gain a speculative insight. But there remains the ineluctable truth that what we do not know about early Christianity exceeds what we know, and not all that we know is assured and unmistakable. The exaggerations about the Dead Sea Scrolls should be interpreted as the end product of the desperateness to go beyond the small quantity of "fact," and even beyond the challengeable factuality of what we know. Even those of us willing to date the Scrolls in the age, approximately, of early Christianity, deceive ourselves if we suppose that they clarify Christian origins; rather, they make the problems even more complicated, for the range of possible combinations in Jewish life at that time is broadened and it is the more difficult to pinpoint the specifically Christian. There lies before scholarship the unending task of understanding better the documents and artifacts and art that we already have. Let the contribution of the Scrolls be interpreted as at most this—that they have taught us how relatively little we have known.

As to the figure of Jesus, about whom in the past 150 years Jews in abundance have written voluminously, there is this one comment I select here out of much more that could be said. It is to invite attention to a strange variation in the writings by Jewish scholars. One might lead into this by noting that East European Jewish laymen have ordinarily assumed that Jesus was "theirs," not "ours," while in the United States a growing number of laymen seem to regard him as "ours," not "theirs." The variation which I have in mind is found among Jewish scholars, too; and if scholars have not made Jesus *fully* "ours," by comparison with the way in which Paul is invariably "theirs," Jesus is by contrast *very often* "ours." I do not have in mind here the closing paragraphs of Klausner's *Jesus of Nazareth* (New York, 1925) or Wolfson's essay "How the Jews Will Reclaim Jesus" (published as a preface to the second edition of Jacobs, *As Others Saw Him*, New York, 1925); I have in mind, rather, a certain fuzziness, if that is the word, which intrudes into Jewish scholarship when the scholar finds it necessary to mention him. I write this with the fullest sympathy, and not critically, for the figure of Jesus is for Jewish scholars the acme of delicacy. The scholar wishes to avoid bad taste; he recognizes that the Christian's Jesus has a sanctity which the Jew simultaneously does not share but which he wants to respect. To what extent can he speak appreciatively of Jesus without seeming to compromise his convictions, and how can he express his convictions and still discuss Jesus with what he hopes Christians will recognize as respect?

17

The fact needs to be faced that there is a very small number of Jews who still today want the tone of Jewish writing on Jesus to be derisive and destructive; this fact can be supported both from the general press and from the abusive letters which come to those who venture into the field.

It does not seem to me that there is any solution for this problem of "fuzziness." My own academic, personal conclusions may or may not be influenced by a wish to avoid this pitfall, for it is my belief that the reliable data about Jesus are too small to justify any sound opinion about him, and I suppose that the amount of opinion I have expressed about Jesus is quantitatively the least among those Jews who have written in this area. Perhaps I have been guided unconsciously by two principles which might be articulated in this way, first, that Jewish scholarly laudation of Jesus, however generous it may seem to Jews, is niggardly in comparison with Christian laudation of him, for to Jews Jesus is never more than a mortal, fallible man; and, second, I have tried, as it were, even in writing about Jesus to forget it is Jesus I have been writing about, for thus paradoxically I have tried to invest him with neither superhuman virtues nor subhuman defects, but to approach him in the way that any historical person can be approached, this in the light of the available documents as these documents lend themselves to normal historical scrutiny. The standard to which one should aspire here too is scholarly responsibility, and if one has done his best to meet this standard, then the approval or disapproval by the partisan and the unscholarly are simply the normal experience of the scholarly writer. As to "theirs" or "ours," I have found a helpful clarification in certain analogies; for example, John Wesley, the "founder" of Methodism, was himself not a Methodist, but a priest in the Church of England, from which church, after Wesley's time the Methodist Church emerged. Jesus, to my mind, is neither wholly "ours," nor wholly "theirs."

Lastly, letters that have come to me have not only scorned my particular efforts, but have suggested that the entire enterprise, even if it were pursued properly (as the correspondents might define propriety) is not legitimate. I have a certain sympathy with this view, for it often rests on a dismay resulting from the imprudence, the irresponsible utterances of writers unhampered by scholarship. Yet it has seemed to me that there are two major considerations which make the enterprise legitimate. One of these is external to the issue; I have in mind here the circumstance that since we Jews no longer live in a ghetto insulated from the stream of Western thought, Jesus and Christianity inevitably swim into our ken, and therefore our participation in

Western culture implies a need to encounter all of its facets. But the internal reason is to my mind the persuasive one: scholarship is at best when it is as broad and as complete as possible. The able student of the Second Jewish Commonwealth would not dream of ignoring the Apocrypha, the Pseudepigrapha, or Josephus, or Philo, or the appropriate rabbinic literature. The New Testament and other very early Christian writings in their own way throw light on that same period. Willfully to ignore these writings is willfully to abstain from completeness. If these are not to be ignored, then they ought to be studied in the normal way in which scholars study, namely, by the use of the lower and higher criticism, by the use of archaeology, linguistics, the history of religions, and so forth. Indeed, the New Testament writings are not only not irrelevant, but they relate most relevantly to the study of the Judaism of the age of the Second Commonwealth. The matter, indeed, can be turned around, for not only is it legitimate for the Jewish scholar to have recourse to these materials, it is illegitimate for him not to.

History, linguistics, etc., are the *sine qua non* of scholarly equipment. Normally, however, the greatest necessary endowment remains unlisted in the monographs. This endowment is *sechel,* plain, ordinary common sense. Useful everywhere, it is nowhere more useful than in the Jewish study, direct or indirect, of early Christianity.

Antiquarianism and Contemporaneity: The Relevance of Studies in Religion*

NTIQUARIANISM" AND "CONTEMPORANEITY" are terms that seem to me to apply to the diverse role of the scholar and the teacher, especially in significant aspects of the field of religion. I use "scholar" for want of a better word. The difficulty is its frequent sense of an accolade, with the consequence that though I secretly think that I am a scholar, it is unbecoming for me to say so about myself. By "scholar" I mean a professional student; a scholar in that sense I certainly am. As such, I have been engaged for several decades in studying an ancient period, and in that sense I am distinctly an antiquarian. On the other hand, I earn my livelihood as a teacher.

As a scholar, it is my task to know the restricted period I have chosen to specialize in as thoroughly and objectively as possible. As a teacher, I am expected to abstract some portion of what I have learned and to convey it tolerably clearly and accurately to students who have not yet had the opportunity to match my specialization. As a scholar, I am supposedly the master of, or at least well-versed in, a field; as a teacher, I am an intermediary between that field and my students.

Why have I recurrently felt, but now increasingly feel, an acute tension between these two roles? Why do I sense that they are obliquely different, or at some junctures antithetical? And what is the implication of my being in religious disciplines, and not in literature, economics, or philosophy?

* This article is adapted from a paper delivered before the 1966 Annual Meeting of the American Academy of Religion in Chicago, October 20–23, 1966. Reprinted with permission from *The Journal of the American Academy of Religion*, Vol. 35, No. 4 (Dec. 1967).

First, as to scholarship, what troubles me is that the older I get, the more I find myself with growing problems about professional, specialized scholarship. I can quote the ideal, that scholarship is an affirmative contribution to the totality of man's knowledge. The bits and pieces of tiny research, or a large volume of broad research, are justified in light of this noble definition. Moreover, scholarship represents the objective search for truth. We professionals take this business about the totality of man's knowledge and the search for truth to be axioms, and therefore none of us dares to challenge them. Even I do not, for when I am pushed into a corner, I will defend such propositions with all my available vigor. But I need to confess the growth within me of a certain skepticism and I begin to toy with a suspicion that they can be clichés and sacred cows.

The explosion in learning is a real problem to me. Books, articles, and monographs have proliferated beyond my ability to keep up with them. Hence, I need some principle of selectivity as to what to read, or else my personal learning can turn into a matter of the merely sporadic, the hit or miss. Unhappily, I can scarcely choose what not to learn unless I learn enough about it to be sure I do not need to learn it at all. Though I have no idea of how to construct any such principle, certain matters have become clear to me, initially in a negative sense. For example, multitudinous footnotes and interminable bibliography progressively impress me less and less. Having guided Ph.D. dissertations, I personally insist on an annotated bibliography, and not merely a list which includes books never consulted; I want the candidate to specify the major element that he learned from every book he includes. As for footnotes, I find myself looking not so much for the authority behind a statement as for the aptness, the penetrating quality, and the intrinsic merit in the statement. Footnotes and bibliography are merely the mechanics of scholarship, and scarcely its substance, but I fear that this elementary fact remains unknown or unheeded.

I know that I still have a deep thirst for scholarship, but I am worried about my subjective distinction between what I regard as true scholarship and what I do not so regard. Is the distinction based upon quantity? Do I introduce considerations of quality, of relevancy, to justify the margin of difference between what I can read and the larger quantity I cannot read? I try to account to myself for the growth in me of this somewhat capricious distinction. I attribute its origin to a contention years ago by a teacher in my own Ph.D. program. A linguist, whose horizons had even then seemed to me often bounded by dispensable refinements in the terminology of Semitic grammar, he asserted to me three times in the name of his own professor that one should have no concern about the meaning of a document, but only about the philological phenomena in it. On first hearing this, I considered it to be an only moderately successful *bon mot;* on the second hearing, I took it to be a whimsey or crotchet and no more than that; on the third hearing, I was shocked to discover that my professor was in dead earnest. Here, then, is the implication that scholarship is a pursuit completely detached. I can no longer accept this supposition, or regard this sort of thing as true scholarship.

Moreover, I recall all too vividly my own contributions to the totality of man's knowledge, and also of man's errors. For example, for some six or seven years I taught the Graf-Wellhausen hypothesis, firmly believing in its reliability. I knew all about JEDP. Entirely on my own, I came to question this assured result of scholarship, and thereafter to doubt it, and finally to reject it. What can I say to those students who learned from me what I now consider to be wrong?

Again, what shall I say about those years in which I, with other Bible men, parroted the standard observation that the Tübingen School of F. C. Baur consisted of Hegelians and espoused thesis, antithesis, and synthesis? And yet, I—like them?—had never read Hegel. How could I understand nineteenth-century German Protestant biblical scholarship without understanding the intellectual streams, secular and religious, of the nineteenth century? Was it not a waste in my Ph.D. program that I was compelled to retake beginning Aramaic, this after a very rich background in both grammar and texts? Was not modern intellectual history a more necessary tool for my chosen field of antiquarian biblical studies? (I have tried to remedy this deficiency.)

My own personal problem grows even more acute in that I cannot resist the impulse to go outside my specialty, simply because my present needs and interests drive me there. For example, I have become greatly attracted by Protestant German pietism, and also by the "salon" period of German-

Jewish history; moreover, I am profoundly interested in modern Christian-Jewish relations. Any time I spend in these is subtracted from what I might devote to my specialty, where, to repeat, I cannot achieve total mastery anyway, even were I to dedicate every moment to it.

Further, I own up to some personal sense of disquiet. Having seen all sorts of scholars at all sorts of institutions, I observe how many are literate only in their fields, and illiterate outside them. I see how my own specialization tends to push me too to such illiteracy, and I know how arduously I must struggle against this. I cannot relish a vision of myself enslaved to such illiteracy, and certainly not if I am to teach students. I do not believe that I can teach them from a framework of lack of acquaintance of them. If I am to be the intermediary between a body of learning and a body of learners, I have obligations as pressing in the one direction as in the other. I am certainly entitled to those moments when, as a scholar, I converse with fellow-scholars in the language of scholarese, and eavesdropping students are on those occasions left out in the cold. I am not only entitled to such moments of the fullest technicalities, I require them for constancy of growth in my own learning. But I must know the minds and the hearts of those I teach, and I must to some extent read what they read and hear the music to which they listen. So I find myself caught in the unsolvable problem of adequate time, aggravated by the fear that some who read these words may wrongly infer that I am trying to sanction shabby learning. Of course, I should never be willing to do that.

It is a very real and serious problem to me that I can know my students only approximately, and that, even though I know my field well, I cannot know it completely; and all this while nevertheless serving as an intermediary between the two *as if* I know them both beyond what is in fact the case. I fall back, of course, on the platitude that process is as important as substance, and therefore that conveying a subject I know less than perfectly to students I know less than completely, I am, through the mere act, pushing the students to achieve their own existential response to a tolerably acceptable entity. I know no better answer, but I have to confess that the answer fails to satisfy me.

If there is any difference between the teacher-scholar in religion and the teacher-scholar in other fields, it is in the circumstance that the stakes are higher. By and large, the teacher-scholar of English is an enthusiast for his field, and seeks to bring his students to a keener and finer appreciation of literature, and especially to move them from a juvenile or youthful approach into a mature one. He encounters students with some knowledge and either no opinions or possibly vague ones, and a few students with good knowledge and perhaps firm opinions or sometimes opinions that are too firm. He proceeds to induct his students into an acceptance of new opinions or else a revision of older ones, by an exposition of more and better facts of relevancy (such as an author's date, environment, and the like), and then moves on into the area of appreciation, either carrying the student along with him or failing to do so. The primary criteria beyond the facts are largely those of subjective opinion, of taste; yet these are matters of luxury, not of necessity, in the life of the student. But for the teacher of religion, the immediate difference is precisely one of necessity, of consequence. While the teacher of religion may in all earnestness stipulate that he, too, is at least partially in the realm of opinion, the students seem to me to prefer to suppose that he is also in the realm not alone of fact but of truth. We might put it that the teacher of literature is looked to for truthful taste, but the teacher of religion for tasteful truth. On many a campus there is a clear separation of the religious ministry from the professor. The impression exists that the campus ministers are apologists, special pleaders, but that we who are scholar-teachers are impartial custodians of objective verities. As a result of this distinction, we possess, in an academic setting, the advantage of appearing to be able, like the scholars in other branches of the humanities, to describe our work as an impartial quest for truth. The students, however, prefer to believe that we have gone far beyond this mere quest, and can and must convey to them the result, the successful accomplishment of the search. They are mistaken about us, but we will never manage to persuade them of this—simply because our field is religion.

The circumstance that we seek to teach maturity insures that we face more profoundly than others in the humanities the reality of the childhood instruction our students have had either formally in denominational daily or weekend schools, or alternatively no instruction but only a set of uniformed suppositions. The issue, it must be clear, is not that of moving fundamentalists to modernism, as it was perhaps in the college and university work of a generation ago. The mature fundamentalist teacher, or the mature liberal teacher, even in teaching like-minded students, discovers that maturity in studies in religion is not a stage into which a student progresses readily, but more often represents no less than a direct collision, a setting of childhood suppositions over and against maturer ones. Our scholarship, whether we are liberal or conservative, pious or impious, devout or cynical, involves some certain facts we cannot withhold. To exemplify, it is a fact that there are two endings to the Gospel of Mark, both of which are deemed spurious by most modern scholars of all religious persuasions; it is a fact that in the Septuagint, Jeremiah is about a seventh shorter than in the Hebrew, while both Daniel and Esther are longer. Certain numbers of students seem to have a zeal for learning these "destructive" facts; a tiny minority seems to me to prefer the view that the upsetting items are not really facts but only our misguided crotchets. But, to proceed now to generalize, we as scholars possess factual data that some of our worthy students are bent on resisting or distorting. Again without regard to our denominations or partisanships, the more facts we have, that is, the better scholars we are, the more we can find ourselves unintentionally athwart some of our students. All too often it is simply in the nature of things that progression to maturity in the study of religion connotes movement from certainty to uncertainty—a progression that can seem paradoxical.

Out of these circumstances there arises, so it seems to me, a disposition in some students of which a scholar must take account. Such students do not share fully in the enthusiasm that I have for the mastery of the ancient languages, or for the detailed, minute study of a concept as I prescribe it. These students seem to me to want a mere distillation, an instantaneous conclusion— though they imply, of course, that some day they will have the time and the patience to go through the laborious process. My requirements regarding the facts that they must learn appear to them as personal idiosyncrasies, or as examples of the inevitable tyranny of the classroom. They comply, but often only grudgingly. Yet I cannot allow the predilections of students to persuade me to accept that facet of their attitude which I allege is a disinterest in scholarship sometimes approaching disdain. I will not, in the misguided supposition that it will please students, cease to be a scholar.

Having said this, I face a clear issue as a teacher-scholar. My field is Bible. The biblical literature harbors such elements as theophanies, revelations, miracles, incarnation, and resurrections, and the literature itself has historically been credited with a supernatural origin. Our students represent either those who tacitly or openly have rejected supernaturalism or who, accepting it, usually are unaware of the gap between their supernaturalism and that of the biblical literature. It is ridiculously easy for a scholar to adopt the stance that his obligation ends once he has adequately described the biblical form of supernaturalism, and that he need make no comment on the relationship of this supernaturalism to minds of today. But what does he do as a teacher? Can he really retain that neutral stance? The personal views of the teacher can range from full supernaturalism, through demythologized supernaturalism, into a pure naturalism. His reliability as a scholar can remain, at least theoretically, wherever he stands in this range, but is it not inevitable that his personal viewpoint will influence at least the overtones of his teaching? Is he not in some sense implicitly expected, not by the authorities of his institution, but by the very nature of his discipline, to address himself to the meaning or meanings of supernaturalism even to naturalistic students?

I confess to an inability to see my way out of the array of problems inherent in this situation, problems largely absent from other humanistic fields. The issue seems to me as nearly unsolvable when teacher and student work on more or less common bases as when they present an unbounded range of diversity. I do not know what to prescribe beyond the obvious counsel that the teacher has the right to his personal attitude, and that he ought to observe the fullest intellectual honesty.

Would we not agree that a teacher ought to teach with conviction? But does not the supernaturalism of and in the Bible raise issues of diverse and contradictory convictions? To be sure that I am clear, I do not mean to suggest that it is the function of the teacher to be doctrinaire in some way that he elects. I only state that even in a pluralistic society, with its multiplicity of denominations and a wide range in the students respecting supernaturalism, it is in some way on the agenda that the factor of supernaturalism be more than the mere pigeonhole into which we stuff the ancient supernaturalism, as if, to change the metaphor, we can simply sweep it under the carpet. And this problem is probably more acute for a rationalist like me than for my less rationalist colleagues. The supernaturalism of and in the Bible is a fact, and I am obligated to handle it. I can do this easily as a scholar, but, frankly, I do not know how to do it as a teacher.

To restate my personal problem, I insist to the students on being a scholar; I insist, respecting scholarship, that I am first and foremost a teacher. The teacher in me must live in the scholar in me. The scholar in me must live in the teacher in me. I must always relate my materials to my students. I believe that I owe them whatever modest guidance I can give them. I must not think for them, but I am obligated to help them think. Were I forced to choose between neglecting some of the scholarship and neglecting some of my students, the choice for me would be easy: my students come first.

I am not saying that antiquarianism is wrong. I am saying only this: that mere antiquarianism has become more and more alien to me personally. Unless there is some segment, some aspect, some nuance in scholarship that in some way is related to contemporaneity, then scholarship smacks to me of futile mental exercises. To my mind a qualifying phrase needs to be added to that stock phrase I quoted before, about contributing to the totality of knowledge. Total knowledge cannot be a detached, hypostasized, Neo-Stoic, ethereal wisdom. No, total knowledge has to be related to man. When learning is unrelated to man, it is useless. I hold this to be true for all fields of learning. But I believe that it is an inescapable urgency for the scholar in the field of religion. I would not prescribe that the teacher of religion must be "constructive"; there has to be room in our society even for destructiveness. Through his scholarship, the teacher may compound the student's predicament, rather than easing it. But impinge on the student by his scholarship he must, and he must do so with deliberate intention. My own teacher to the contrary, the meaning of an ancient document is important. The inevitable question must never completely disappear: What can the document mean to living men?

Is it true that these problems are beyond solution? For me, I think they are. What then? For me, the consequence is that I must learn to live with unsolvable problems. But I will not willingly delude myself into supposing that they do not exist.

The Evasions of Modern Theology *

W HAT IS THE state of theology today? The recent years have witnessed in the United States an unprecedented upsurge in theological interest; names such as Tillich, Barth, Niebuhr, Buber and Bultmann have become known beyond the confines of the professionals. But there are some bases for questioning the value and, indeed, the validity of modern theological writing.

Theology is a special discipline, and the writer, even though he is a professor of Bible in a theological school, can qualify as no more than an amateur. My interest in modern theology can be considered akin to that of the intelligent layman, that mythical person, and my competency no greater. When he assesses the modern theological works that he has read, he inevitably emerges with some negative judgments. At any rate, I do.

Let it be clear that theology is a discipline of primary importance to the human spirit. Such is the case now quite as much as it was in the Middle Ages, when theology was universally acknowledged to be the queen of sciences. In those days, theology was the discipline that synthesized and

* This article first appeared in *The American Scholar*, 30 (1961): 1–14.

integrated all the other branches of learning. The fields to be learned had not yet become so vast and intricate as to preclude a single individual's amassing all the then known sciences. The polymath of today learns, as the etymology can show, many things, but not all. The encyclopedist of bygone centuries learned not many things, but everything. The twelfth-century Maimonides bequeathed to us in addition to theological writings—treatises on medicine, astronomy and law. The medieval theologian learned what there was to know, and then arrayed it in topics as part of a total world view.

A working definition can be helpful in distinguishing between religion and theology. Let us define religion as the spontaneous, intuitive, unmeditated experience of a person. Theology, on the other hand, is the effort to explain, to justify, or to analyze in universal terms what the individual has experienced. We are in the domain of religion, for example, when we observe a person praying, whether in dire straits or in happy circumstances. When we ask, What is prayer? and give a systematized answer, then we have moved into the domain of theology.

The primary characteristics of theology, then, are analysis, explanation, synthesis, and system.

A distinction between theology and philosophy would go along the following lines. Theology attempts to explain the experienced phenomena of religion, whereas philosophy is not bound to such experienced phenomena, but may represent a completely free and totally theoretical speculation. Indeed, in the Middle Ages, philosophy was one of the many disciplines that were handmaidens to the queen theology; philosophy, then as now, was relatively free from any antecedent commitment, while theology was never completely free from it. Philosophy was that tool by which, in the highest realms of dialectic, the theologian tested his assertions or conclusions. And finally, theology was always in some sense religious, whereas philosophy has always been in some sense secular.

The contribution of Spinoza in particular, and modern science and philosophy in general, has been to challenge the royal position of theology, to dethrone her and set philosophy in her place. This was especially the case in Protestant and Jewish circles. Theology, banished even from the court, changed from being the discipline above all disciplines to something lesser.

A balanced appraisal should deter us from unfairly blaming theology for the diminution of its status. The discovery of America, colonization, the new mercantilism, the incipient nationalisms, indeed, the beginnings of the death knell of feudalism—all these combined to channel the thinking man into areas, if not completely new, at least now possible to approach and assess in a new way.

There began at that time a process that amounts to a reversal of the direction taken in the Greek world. The historians of philosophy have noted correctly that prior to the conquests of Alexander the Great and of the Romans, Greek philosophy, which we call Hellenic, was largely social in character. How shall a city be governed? What are just laws? Who is best suited to rulership? But the conquest and occupation by the conquerors, first the Macedonians and then the Romans, made it futile or even silly to ask these questions. Thereupon the direction of philosophy changed, and a higher individualism arose. The new questions, in what we call Hellenistic philosophy, were these: How shall I act, now that I have no voice in the government of the city? How can I live in inner freedom, in view of the injustice of the laws? How shall I conduct myself relative to those rulers whom I have not chosen but who govern me? Hellenic philosophy before Alexander the Great presupposed a relatively free society; Hellenistic philosophy after Alexander addressed itself to individual salvation.

The same process, but exactly in reverse, characterized the transition from the Middle Ages to modern times. The pre-Alexander questions were now asked again, in only slightly different form. Issues of political theory came to a new relevancy when men were on the verge of fashioning democratic governments and institutions. With some considerable logic, there was a progression from arguments about democracy as mere political theory to democracy in western Europe and then to theories of so-called social democracy in the period after the Industrial Revolution. The discipline of economics before, during, and after the Industrial Revolution genuinely impinged on man's daily life.

In medieval theology and philosophy such areas as political theory and ethics were aspects of the larger concerns. When despotism began to recede, and mercantilism to grow, these areas began to emerge as separate disciplines. In the eighteenth century Hume not only wrote the *Natural History of Religion* and *Dialogues Concerning Natural Religion,* but also *Political Discourses.* Adam Smith first wrote his *Theory of Moral Sentiments* (1759) and seventeen years later his *An Inquiry into the Nature and Cause of the Wealth of Nations.* Thomas Malthus, who wrote *An Essay on the Principles of Population* (1798) and *Principles of Political Economy* (1820), was once a curate in the Church of England.

We call the period of the end of the eighteenth and the beginning of the nineteenth century the Age of Enlightenment. The leading motif was reason, even among those like Hume and Kant who argued for the limited relevancy of reason. A glance at the state of Bible studies among Protestants at this time is illuminating. In the Old Testament, the rich resources of comparative Semitic languages were now catalogued and synthesized. The Five Books of Moses were beginning to be assessed as aggregates of documents assembled at various ages, all of which were judged to be later than Moses. In the New Testament the wealth of the classic Greek and Roman civilizations and of rabbinic Judaism were marshalled for the Gospels to undergo study like any other documents from the past. There were those who held that Jesus was a man of highest and finest qualities, whose essential humanity was concealed by the legends and what they considered the theological absurdities in the Gospels. The Psalms were estimated to be other than a collection of proof-texts, and the Song of Songs ceased to be the allegory either of God's love for Israel or Christ's love for the Church and became instead erotic poetry.

History had previously been something of a fine art, much as the Greeks had estimated it. With Hegel, one began to talk about thesis, antithesis, and synthesis, and with Ranke history embarked on its career as a science, the recording of facts as they were.

Thus, the situation of theology was affected not only by the development outside its precincts of disciplines once within it, but also by the attacks on traditional religion, whether hostile, as in the case of Voltaire and Thomas Paine and the deists, or friendly, as in the case of the Bible scholars.

The religions in the West came to be divided into three domains. One of these consisted of the group that tried to remain untouched by the currents of new discoveries and new developments, a group characterized by the respectable term "fundamentalist." By and large, the fundamentalist attitude can be put this way: religion is an unchanging norm to which everything else must conform and adjust.

The other two groups were notably affected by the external developments.

The two, however, are marked off from each other by differences in the extent of their hospitality to that which is novel and external, and the extent of their fidelity to the religious tradition. The conservative has aimed to preserve the religious tradition as much unchanged as modern times will allow. The liberal for the most part has welcomed change. The fundamentalist theologian, by virtue of ignoring what is new, has had no need to come to terms with it.

The conservative and the liberal faced challenges in the nineteenth century that can be typified, or even in a sense summarized, by three names, Charles Darwin, Karl Marx, and Sigmund Freud. The twentieth century was to add the name of Einstein; it was to present the challenges of two World Wars, the Russian Revolution, atomic bombs, and sputniks.

The query that I put is this: When the intelligent layman feels himself confronted by some need or desire to shape his own personal platform, does he not openly or tacitly have in his mind, in his frame of reference, the changes wrought in the last century in science, in society, in the understanding of the individual?

What light can come to him from reading the modern theologian? The answer is discouraging.

Has modern theology sought to communicate to the ordinary intelligent person? Has it tried to vie in the market place of ideas with those movements characterized by Darwin, Freud, Marx and Einstein? Or has it instead developed into the property of a coterie of specialists who can communicate, if at all, only with each other?

Theology or, more precisely, theologians have in our day misconceived their role. They have allowed the discipline that should have attempted to synthesize all the others, from Darwinian biology through nuclear physics, to descend into mere denominational apologetics. Three examples will illustrate and support the contention that modern theology has evaded its responsibility of confronting the modern world.

The first is somewhat complex. It can best be approached by recalling the term "Social Gospel." When nineteenth-century New Testament scholarship, so ably summarized by Albert Schweitzer in his study, *The Quest of the Historical Jesus,* tried but failed to recover the Jesus of history, an earnest and even high-minded thinker, Walter Rauschenbusch, conceived of him as a social reformer. Thereby a sanction was found for interpreting Christianity as a vehicle for social reform. Social Gospel was at its height from about 1890 to 1910; students of political science will remember that this was the period when the words "Christian" and "Socialist" or "Christian" and "Democratic" were joined to form the names of European political parties. Inherent in the Social Gospel was the conviction that since religion needed to have some relevancy to life, one should translate his religious convictions into concrete and specific aspects of social action. I confess to admiring the proponents of the Social Gospel even though I must say that it is shabby New Testament scholarship that makes Jesus a social reformer. To be more precise, it is poor learning that condenses such conceptions as the Incarnation, the Atoning Death, and the Resurrection into the oversimple idea of social reform. I do not think it is too relevant to accuse the exponents of the Social Gospel, as some do, of shallowness in their expectation of bringing Utopia into being in the near future. The Social Gospelites were no more wrong than Victor Hugo and other "meliorists" of the time.

But the reaction on the continent of Europe, after World War I refuted the Social Gospelites and the meliorists, was in the first place to deny that religion has anything to do with conduct, and in the second place to assert that what man needs is—here I use a technical term—a "spiritual" (German, *pneumatisch*) approach to Scripture. In the view of the "pneumatics," the disciplines of philology, comparative religion, anthropology, and historical studies were worthless. Respecting the contention that religion has nothing to do with conduct, a mere glance at the records of Judaism and Christianity will provide instantaneous refutation. The issue is not whether one believes or disbelieves in the revelation of God to Moses at Sinai, or whether one believes in or doubts the Virgin Birth of Jesus. It is, rather, that the documents authoritative to Judaism and Christianity make it plain that the sequel to the act of religious faith is a set of obligatory social practices and concerns. To put it in another way, the following is true of both Judaism and Christianity: the essence of religion is man's relation to God, but the substance is man's social conduct. The "spiritualizers" betrayed not only Moses and Jesus, but also Paul, to whom they appealed because he said that legislation could not achieve proper conduct, but that proper motivation could.

33

In their confusion, the pneumatics have preferred to believe that this meant Paul was uninterested in conduct.

A tendency somewhat like that which produced the "pneumatics" in biblical scholarship has produced neo-orthodoxy in modern theology. As the name implies, the conclusions are traditional, but the bases for reaching them quite at variance with orthodoxy.

The neo-orthodox movement is not all of one piece. Not all modern theology can be called neo-orthodox; indeed, it is characteristic of neo-orthodox theologians to feel insulted if they are so labeled. Neo-orthodoxy has, however, influenced the present trend in theology by properly finding fault with the over-optimism of the "liberal" period. But curiously enough, neo-orthodoxy does not usually reject, as did the pneumatics, the rugged, iconoclastic biblical scholarship known as higher criticism that had been one of the props of the liberals in their view of the evolutionary character of religion. Indeed the neo-orthodox have espoused it.

Out of neo-orthodoxy there has come a broader tendency that seems to me to be a motif in much of modern theology. In assessing man, modern theology often finds fault with him for glorifying himself instead of God, and ascribes to his "sin" the perpetual crises in history. Man and his sin— not man, but *man and his sin*—is the preoccupation of modern theology.

After assuring us of man's sin, the theologians have moved on to tell us of man's helplessness. Indeed, modern theology has so emphasized man's helplessness that one wonders what, if anything, a man can do or should do. There is a little ditty, which appeared in the *Journal of Theological Studies,* that burlesques the neo-orthodox view of man's lack of capacity:

> Sit down, O man of God!
> His Kingdom He will bring
> Whenever it may please His will;
> You cannot do a thing!

Man is properly the subject of a theological essay. But one wonders if we are not witnessing a pendulum swing in the way the theologian treats this subject. The liberals prior to World War I were extreme in their optimism about man's capacity to improve himself. We see now in modern theology a total denial of any capacity in man. Have we not simply moved from one extreme to its opposite? Moreover, has the modern theologian fashioned his view of man's sin and helplessness out of the data afforded by modern psychology, or has he simply rushed to traditional terms, in defiance of what has been learned, however imperfectly, about man?

It seems to me when I read the theologians that they are talking not about man but about particular men. It seems to me that I must recognize that certain men are indeed arrogant and that certain men are indeed without capacity, and that certain human efforts are often doomed either to total failure or partial failure. Yet somehow I wish that the theologians were not quite so self-satisfied, complacent and condescending in their denunciation of the arrogance of man.

The second example of the evasion of responsibility by theology stems from Freudian psychology and from the discipline of psychiatry. Herein lies an unsurpassed concentration on the question, What is man? Few questions have agitated thinkers and writers from time immemorial as frequently and profoundly as this question. The Psalmist and the author of Job and indeed the author of Genesis all have opinions to set forth.

In the field of theology, the concern about man—who and what he is—normally is considered a subdivision known as anthropology, a term that overlaps, but is considerably different from anthropology as one of the disciplines offered in the modern university, usually in the humanistic or social sciences.

Does man possess free will, or does he not? Does divine providence amount to sheer determinism, so that man is without freedom or moral choice? Is free will so fully man's possession as to eliminate providence?

Various answers to these age-old questions are to be found in ancient religious writings. By and large Christianity and Judaism have bequeathed two different and opposing views of the nature of man. The emphasis in Christianity, by way of Paul, Augustine and Calvin, has been on man's poor estate; in Judaism, the emphasis has been on man's high estate. (I use the word "emphasis" to allow room for the overlapping in the respective views, and to concede that Christianity and Judaism have harbored counterbalancing views.) The definition of the nature of man has consequences for the total theology that comes to be constructed.

While Christianity and Judaism differ in the definitions of sin and of righteousness, they both use these two terms, as it is right that they should, for in revealed religion one necessarily distinguishes between sin and righteousness. But basic to Freudian psychology is the distinction not between sin and righteousness but between sickness and health. For example, is homosexuality sin or sickness?

Psychiatry is a secular science, theology is not. The view of man that the psychologist comes to may directly contradict the view bequeathed by traditional religion. While in a given *ad hoc* situation the minister of religion and the psychiatrist may find areas of cooperation, they do not and cannot start from the same premises.

But there has been such a spate of books on peace of mind and peace of spirit and on confident living because religionists have abandoned their premises—in part deliberately, and in part unconsciously. The deliberate abandonment has been on the part of theologians who are receptive to modern science and willing to exchange Genesis for Darwin. The unconscious abandonment appears in the departure from religion into secularism. It is to the credit of certain Roman Catholics that they have discerned the boundary clearly and have refused to cross it. It is with the "liberals" that one can quarrel on this point.

In large measure the modern theologians have justified their departure from religion to secularism by adopting a process that to me is most discouraging. It consists of using some term traditional in religion, of divesting it of its pristine meaning by defining the term in a sense consistent with modern science, and then of using the term in the pristine way. I can find it admirable in a Christian to say that he believes in the Virgin Birth, or in an ex-Christian to say that he disbelieves. But when a theologian informs me that the Virgin Birth is not to be taken literally, but is simply a term that essays to express the ineffable, and then proceeds to treat the Virgin Birth as though he believes in it literally, I confess I am not moved to admiration. At the best, these ancient terms now become mere slogans, catchwords that seek from religious antiquity an authority and sanction to which in the reinterpreted sense they are not entitled. At the worst, these reinterpreted terms raise seriously the question of the intellectual integrity of the users. It is startling to read or hear that the New Testament and rabbinic literature are the best textbooks in psychiatry. It is astonishing to read that

Jesus was the greatest psychiatrist of all times. What I am here alluding to has become commonplace.

If theology is unorthodox, then it is entitled to grapple with the question of whether the traditional religious anthropology is right, and modern psychology wrong, or if psychology is right and the traditional religious anthropology wrong. And it is not too grievous a wrong for unorthodox religion to reinterpret traditional terms. What is wrong is to reinterpret the terms in an unorthodox way, and then use them in an orthodox way, as if they have not been reinterpreted.

Has modern theology come to grips with the contentions of modern psychology? I believe that it has not. As is demonstrated by the Social Gospel, which I admire, and by the "spiritualizing" exegesis, which I do not, and by the adoption of modern psychology, whose claim to being a science sometimes troubles me, modern theology has failed to conceive its task as that of mastering the disciplines as they are properly understood, and then of integrating and synthesizing them. Instead, modern theology has toyed with bits and pieces.

The third example of an evasion of its responsibility by modern theology is illustrated from the pursuit usually called "the philosophy of history." Herein, in my judgment, lies the worst evasion of all.

The Judaism and Christianity of ancient times looked at the events in history so as to see in them the workings of God; it was a distinctive approach, and at variance with the Greek. The Greek tried to penetrate to the essence of reality by an analysis of the nature of the physical universe; the Hebrew or the Christian, on the other hand, felt and believed that the events of history disclosed God, for events did not blindly happen, but were rather planned for and executed by the Deity or through his will. A modern return to the view that God is revealed in history was obviously incumbent upon those modern theologians who said that the faith of the Bible must be returned to. But whereas an Amos or an Isaiah or a Jeremiah or a Second Isaiah did not shrink from declaring that world empires, such as that of the Assyrians, were only pawns in the hands of the Deity, the modern theologian does not have the boldness to make so plain a statement. Indeed, to digress briefly, many a theologian who feels impelled to support his contention by citations from Scripture does violence to it. The pedant in me has too often been offended by selective citation, by verses wrested out of context and by an oversimplification that pushes me to the brink of despair. I read about the biblical view of man, as though there is no difference between the author of Leviticus and Paul; the biblical view of history, as though there is no difference between the Deuteronomic authors and the author of Job. One can record it as a universal rule that when a theologian attributes one and only one view to Scripture, he is falsifying.

It holds true, again, that an effort to find one single theme as the reflection of all Scripture is scarcely tenable. An ancient rabbi, Hillel, once defined the essence of Scripture as the Golden Rule, but he had the honesty to add that there was much left over that merited learning. In modern writings the effort to make the Bible relevant usually involves putting the Bible into a Procrustean bed—and we know what happened to those who were welcomed into it. Modern theologians never demonstrate the continuing relevancy of the Bible; they only make assertions in a way so clumsy as to be self-refuting.

Let us revert to the philosophy of history. A typical recourse of theologians has been to declare that history has a meaning only if it is viewed from a special perspective. I quote from Christopher Dawson: "It is difficult, perhaps even impossible, to explain the Christian view of history to a non-Christian, since it is necessary to accept the Christian faith in order to understand the Christian view of history." (Mr. Dawson does not state which version of the Christian faith.)

The end result of contentions such as this is the development among theologians of a position that supposes that a distinction can be made between history on the one hand and "trans-history" on the other. As applied specifically to Christianity, trans-history is apparently a period both prior to the Incarnation and subsequent to the Ascension, while history is the period of the Incarnation. Such a view, without regard to its tenability, is not a universal approach, for its contentions are without meaning to non-Christians, such as Mohammedans, Buddhists, and Shintoists, who chance to be a large portion of the modern world.

As to its tenability, I would comment, as I have indicated, that in the Bible there is set forth on many, many pages the conviction that God is revealed in history. The Bible knows nothing of trans-history, and, indeed, the very idea is one hundred and eighty degrees removed from what the Bible says. It is the shabbiest kind of learning that dares to call trans-history biblical. And since the word is mongrel, for "trans" is Latin and "history" is Greek, a supposedly better term, "metahistory," is offered. It too is not biblical.

Is trans-history or metahistory an explanation, or is it an evasion? Does trans-history meet the contention of a secular historian who writes: "To maintain that God reveals Himself in what is usually called 'history,' in the history of international crime and mass murder, is indeed blasphemy." [1]

Does the modern theologian enter the arena of the intellectual combat with the secular historian? Is he grappling with a genuine issue, and setting it into a convincing array of ideas and propositions? Or does he simply abandon the field to his adversary?

In my judgment the modern theologian is guilty of evasion.

And, I would add, the theologian is at this point throwing away even the bare possibility of communicating with the layman, for to most of us the word "history" has had a particular import; the word "trans-history" seems to me to be more a barrier to, than a vehicle of, communication.

Trans-history is only one example of how theologians play with words. They are adept at inventing new words (such as "kairitic," from the Greek *kairos* for time), or at distorting a word, such as "eschatological," or at using common words in a sense known only to the user. Some theologians seem to find it obligatory to create a special vocabulary.

It is not a valid argument against theology that it deals with difficult concepts. But it is a valid contention that modern theologians unnecessarily increase the difficulty through their abuse of the dictionary. I am willing, even eager, to understand them. But should they not feel some need to communicate, some need to write with clarity, some disposition to shape what they have to say in such a way that form does not effectively obscure content?

I am disturbed even more by the substance of modern theology than by its manner. The tour de force, even if it is perceptive and poetic, seldom has lasting power; the clever and the cute do not succeed in providing a lasting satisfaction. Yet these are the terms necessary for appraising the works of even such men as Reinhold Niebuhr, Martin Buber, Paul Tillich, Karl Barth, and Rudolf Bultmann.

Niebuhr is to my mind the most admirable practical religionist of our day. My strictures are, of course, at his writings—as in *The Nature and*

Destiny of Man—and not at his person. His writings abound in nimble and misleading generalizations about the scriptural "view"; and he constantly proceeds so to reinterpret his generalizations that they lose even their remote connection with Scripture. He deals, often brilliantly, with corollaries of unproved theorems.

I know of no sequence of incomprehensible sentences and paragraphs as abundant and recurrent as in Martin Buber's essay, "Dialogue," in his *Between Man and Man.* And when one has struggled and perhaps understood Buber, where is one? At rock bottom fundamentals, or in quasi poetry, suspended in mid-air?

Paul Tillich belongs to the illustrious lines of the allegorists. Allegory is the device of applying a capricious meaning to aspects of a traditional text in replacement of the natural meaning. The Stoics had tried to raise Homer's earthy tastes to a heightened eminence by allegorizing him; Greek Jews, such as Philo, and Christians, such as Clement of Alexandria and Origen, adapted the Stoic method to Scripture, especially to its troubling passages. Mr. Tillich's book, *The Dynamics of Faith,* is primarily a series of allegorical definitions of "faith," "doubt," "holy," "the cross," and the like. Whatever of substance he has to say is recurrently obscured by his allegorisms, but there is little substance in the allegorisms themselves.

In justice to Karl Barth, the eminent Swiss theologian, it must be admitted that his many writings are seldom aimed at the layman. He presents a blend of the thinker and the exhorter, and he uses an abundance of paradox, as though paradox possesses some mystic capacity to transcend itself. He is the most difficult of all to read. I find in him passionate restatements of the old, not confrontations of the new.

The German Rudolf Bultmann is, in my judgment, the greatest New Testament scholar of this age. He is the leading exponent of "demythologizing." Briefly, demythologizing implies that although the basic Christian message is valid, the New Testament, unhappily, couches it in mythological terms; modern man must demythologize the basic Christian convictions, especially about the history of Jesus. The end product seems to many of us to result in the vanishing of Jesus, so that one wonders about the validity ascribed to a Christian message from which Jesus has vanished. We students are reminded of an early heresy called docetism, "seemingness," which changed Jesus from a supposed historical reality into an alleged apparition.

I want the theologian to enlighten me on what I should think and what I should do. I want him to grapple with Darwin, and Freud, and Marx, and atomic power, in the public arena where I can look on—and this I do not find him disposed to do.

I still read theologians. But more and more I find startlingly little substance or relevancy.

4

Mass Crime and the
Judeo-Christian Tradition *

Defenders of religion are by no means unaccustomed to having thrown up to them questions about the existence or perseverance of evil in the world. Often in reply we resort to an excursus on the history of questions of theodicy in the Judeo-Christian tradition, a device which demonstrates the antiquity and recurring nature of the problem and which permits us, if we are so inclined, to evade a direct answer. We cite Job to illuminate the problem in the personal realm, and Habakkuk in the international; these citations, of course, by no means exhaust the range and depth of the inquiry as it has been made. We can go on to rehearse various viewpoints revolving about the figure of Satan, which embroider the history of the question of evil: whether that putative figure was genetically vested with the ability to occasion evil; whether he had this authority because God had temporarily delegated it to him; or whether he seized the authority in a rebellion against God and established his satanic rule on earth until such time as God's kingdom would come.

Less evasively, a more direct religious answer from of old—if it is an answer—can be cited, or paraphrased, or rephrased. It is simply to say that man does not know why evil exists, but that the religious man has faith that the existence of evil in no way reduces or compromises, eternally, God's omnipotence and justice. The righteous man, not understanding why evil exists, abides by that faith in God—or, to quote Habakkuk in Habakkuk's context, "the righteous man lives in his faith." (Many homilies have been based on that verse, even though they distort its original intent.)

* This article first appeared in *The Minnesota Review*, 3 (1963): 220–227.

A subsidiary answer, perhaps designed to buttress such faith in God, is to declare that man lacks the capacity truly to discern evil and good. Thus, we read in Genesis that Joseph's brothers feared, after Jacob's death, that Joseph would repay them for the evil they had done him. Joseph said to them: "Am I in God's place? You designed evil against me; God intended it for good, so as to keep alive many people." Interesting as such a view may be, it does not escape from being a manipulation of words, for it "solves" the problem of evil by, in effect, denying its existence.

Again, in answer, Job contended, in a good many passages, that there is no relationship between conduct and fate, thus denying an opinion frequent in Deuteronomy that obedience to God brings reward and disobedience, punishment; later Jewish and Christian thinkers, sharing Job's observation that the righteous suffer and the unrighteous prosper, arrived at the opinion that such inequities were transitory, and that in a future age, or after an individual's death, the inequities would be corrected. The Gospel story of the Rich Man and Lazarus, and similar sentiments in the ancient rabbis, postpone to the world to come the righting of injustices in this world. In such views evil is not denied as it was in Joseph's story; rather, its existence is conceded, but its perpetrators are assured that they will ultimately pay the requisite price.

National immorality, as exemplified by certain kings of Israel such as Jeraboam and Ahab, is invariably denounced in Scripture; international immorality, on the part of world conquerors such as Assyria and Babylon, is scored; and in later apocalyptic literature (Daniel and the Revelation of John) there are assertions that the Greeks and, in turn, the Romans would know God's wrath, and, having sown the seeds, would reap a rich harvest of punishment.

The Judeo-Christian tradition, thus, has opposed mass crime. But its various explanations of evil underscore how often mass crime has dotted history. This later was the case in ancient Israel and in the Judean state in late pre-Christian times. It has also been the case in Europe after the triumph of Christianity in the fourth century and throughout its ascendancy, until the Age of Enlightenment at the end of the eighteenth century, better, until the Russian Revolution of 1917. During all these sixteen centuries whole nations internally have been hosts to injustice and violence, and externally to hostilities and wars, latterly to scientific modes of killing, while their religion was ostensibly opposed to it. At least the European and American participants have all been nominally Christian; but it should be clear that the history of

Christian nations is little different from that of the Hebrew nations of Israel and Judah, or from that of the Jewish Maccabean or Herodian kingdoms; and my personal partisanship for the infant state of Israel cannot lead me to exempt it from the necessarily all-embracing list.

The fact must be recognized without evasion or rationalization that the Judeo-Christian ethics and morals have not been decisive elements in the conduct of affairs either by groups or by nations. It is to a religionist a disconcerting recognition; but it is far better to admit the fact than to be, or pretend to be, blind to it. Accordingly, our inquiry cannot be whether Judeo-Christian ethics and morality are indecisive, but rather what it is that makes them indecisive. We shall, in due course, refer to the nature of their influence even when it falls short of being decisive.

It must be clear that Judeo-Christian ethics are asserted, or at least have usually been asserted to be divine in origin. Whether through a Mosaic legalism and its rabbinic extensions as in Judaism, or in illumination through the Holy Spirit, apart from laws, as Paul urged, and as Christendom has believed, the view was consistent that the requirements and standards were the products of revelation, and were not the conclusions derived from society's experience and its wisdom. Were it not the case that divine revelation was the assumed source of the standards, then the acute problems in theodicy would never have dotted the history of biblical thought, for basic in every formulation of the theodicy has been the question, "why does the omnipotent God, who gave standards, permit the flouting of His divine will?" This divine origin of ethics and standards makes the problem before us more acute, for it is easier to understand the Greek tyrannos, unaware of trespassing a god's will, than a Judeo-Christian who could scarcely deny an awareness.

We deal, then, with the incomplete effectiveness of Judeo-Christian morality. It has had two forms: morality accompanied by awareness, but also by unctuous indifference, and hence unconscious hypocrisy; or else, by awareness and also deliberate disobedience, and hence the direct challenge to God.

But what is it about the Judeo-Christian morality that has made it a factor so often to discount?

Three considerations seem to me to explain this. In the first place, the enforcers even of the divine have been human, indeed all too human, and hence the divine character of the ethics has necessarily seemed remote or evanescent to anyone prompted to disregard it. Thus, for example, the motif is frequent in the Book of Judges that disobedience to God prevailed at that time because "there was no king in Israel; each man did what was right in his own eyes." Judges is a prologue to Samuel (wherein first Saul and then David, his replacement, is crowned) and Kings; Samuel-Kings, in the correct judgment of modern scholars, is a review of what monarchy meant to Israel, but in two editions. The first of these terminated with Josiah (626–608 B.C.), who is called the greatest of kings, and this edition lauded monarchy as a tool of God. But Josiah died in battle, and his immediate successors were conquered and exiled by the Babylonians, so that Josiah represents not the acme of kingship, but the prelude to its debacle. The second edition of Kings provided interpolations, such as I Samuel 8, 10, 17–21, 12, which scorned monarchy.

Monarchy gave way (about 520 B.C.) to theocracy. The accounts of the subsequent high priests of Judea, related by Josephus, disclose conditions as chaotic as those which recurred in the medieval papacy, of rivalry, manipulation, purchase, and murder. We religionists often seem oblivious to the circumstance that our heritage from our sacred literature is irreligion as well as religion. The human advocates or enforcers of divine law or standards were often the worst offenders. In the case of invading nations, the challenge was repeatedly thrown up to God: "Where are You? Why do You tolerate this?" Could not the inference be that God Himself abstains from intervening, and that His vicars are self-appointed, and safely to be ignored?

Or else, perhaps the example of King Manasseh could lead a Bible reader to a wrong conclusion. In Kings we are told that Manasseh was both wicked and also one who reigned a very long time, a circumstance that should never have arisen if conduct and fate were connected. The later Book of Chronicles was troubled by Manasseh's undeservedly long reign, but justified it by attributing to him in his old age a repentance with which Kings is unacquainted. The Greek translation, even later, goes a step further by citing Manasseh's supposed prayer of repentance which neither Kings nor Chronicles know.

The danger which lurks in religion in any doctrine of repentance is the inference that repented conduct is the equivalent of unbrokenly fine conduct; hence one may act with license, provided that he make sure that he gets around to repenting in time.

The combination of the frailities of God's vicars and of the rewards for repentance can well have obliterated from the minds of men prone or destined to seize leadership the deterrents which may have been present (vividly or latently) in their minds that it was God they were disobeying when they acted ignobly.

Secondly, religion in its organized form has not always shrunk from adopting profane means for achieving a religious goal. The issue here is not that of the occasional venal Jewish high priest or Christian pope, but rather the resort by organized religion under moral leaders to mass murder—witness what Christians did to Jews and Mohammedans in the Crusades, or Catholics to Protestants at Saint Bartholomew's Eve, or Protestants to Papists in England and in the colonies. The persecutors of Christians have often been Christians. When religion has adopted irreligious means, it has given an implicit sanction to them.

During World War II, a song swept our country called "Praise the Lord and Pass the Ammunition." It glorified a chaplain who took up arms. I was at that time a Naval Chaplain and I recall clearly the dismay among us chaplains that our status as noncombatants was flagrantly compromised, if it was true that that chaplain had made himself a combatant. Some of us were even saddened by the popularity of the song, that implied a broad public approval of this disreputable act. But even those of us who remained strictly noncombatants—were we not in putting on a uniform giving some kind of approval to an effort, however necessary, that was scarcely consistent with religious ideals? In the history of the Judeo-Christian tradition there are too many examples, too distinctly etched, wherein organized religion has espoused irreligion as a tool, or even as an objective.

Third, and most important, is the fact that ideal religion by its essential nature possesses an admirable inherent weakness: the lack of power to cope with the determined offender. In illustration, the ancient rabbis apotheosized the Decalogue, especially "Thou shalt not kill." In this vein they declared that a Sanhedrin that over a period of thirty years sentenced one criminal to death was a group of murderers. Fine. Yet they bequeathed a dictum which has diverted most of us Jews from pacifism: "If one comes to kill you, kill him first." Scholars have noted that in Matthew there are injunctions against resistance to evil; perhaps Christians will forgive me if I comment that

Christendom has seldom been faithful to this injunction. (Other passages in Matthew are completely at variance with nonresistance.)

The dilemma for religionists is that strict abiding by ethics and morals exposes them to the caprices of the self-seeking, of the would-be tyrant, or of the depraved. Should religionists wish merely to defend their bodies, merely to defend and not to counterattack, they must abandon what they cherish most. To kill to avert being killed is still to kill, is still to violate "Thou shalt not kill."

There is a striking analogy in this regard to the weakness inherent in democracy, which must tolerate even the effort to destroy it, or else it must resort to undemocratic means to counter the effort. As we all know, the fascist or communist can utilize the fruits of democracy (free speech, the right peacefully to assemble, etc.) as steps in a process to subvert or even end the democracy.

The tragedy for religionists is the frequency with which an awful dilemma has presented itself. We confront choices between the bad and the worse, whereas as religionists we are committed to the good. Had we any choice but to fight Hitler? I cannot, even today, see a viable alternative then available. Had Roosevelt any choice after Pearl Harbor? Have police any choice when an armed man goes berserk?

No one will deny the lofty character of religious ethics and ideals. But what happens when a man, or a group of men, or a nation sets itself against them, and proposes to carry through some violent design? Even if the history of kings and priests were a better one than it is, and even if organized religion had an unblemished record, religious ideals would be, in themselves, a powerless tool to cope with determined, overt evil.

The history of human events and of nations is less that of men of peace and rectitude than it is of usurpers, dictators, and conquerors. When a man or a nation determines to scorn what Amos, or Hillel, or Jesus, or Francis of Assisi, or Israel of Miedzyboz, or Thomas Jefferson have lived and preached, the recollections of their lives and of their preachments are insufficient armor to withstand physical onslaught.

If the wicked determine to embark on some venture, moral people must either wait patiently for God and meanwhile succumb; or else they can resist by utilizing the same evil tools which the wicked use. Once moral people do the latter, they may even delude themselves into denominating the evil tools as moral ones.

I do not think that it will be denied that religious principles can be and are decisive in the choices made by an individual. This is the case even when we note that motives can be mixed and that self-interest can be intertwined with religious motivation. The point to be made is that acuteness of religious motivation in the individual can be blunted or even destroyed in that individual in his service in such as national and international affairs. It is not unusual for a nation of moral individuals to espouse, nationally, immoral objectives and procedures. I have in mind not only the politician-statesman who in his deeply personal affairs is honest but in public affairs devious, but also the implied approval which seems to exist in diplomacy that a lie on behalf of one's country is no lie, and that double-dealing for one's nation is admirable. Often duplicity goes under the name of political realism. While in the case of the individual, religious principles should point to the great concerns of humanity, in the case of nations, national self-interest comes to be the overriding concern. Indeed, it is the rare nation which has even a horizon of a concern beyond self-interest.

It seems to me the inherent strength and weakness of American foreign policy is that it has almost uniquely ranged moral intentions alongside national self-interest. Perhaps as a rich nation we alone have been able to afford the luxury of moral purpose. But our generosity in the Marshall Plan and other forms of foreign aid have transcended mere opportunism. Yet our sincerity has often gotten us into difficulties. Were we only realists, we would have encouraged and even abetted France, England, and Israel in the Suez debacle; as moralists, not only did we not abet them, but we above all were responsible for the lugubrious outcome. How moral was Nasser that we should have used a moral basis to save him?

Such instances can be multiplied, though, of course, I am by no means suggesting that our skirts have been entirely clean. And I am not making my own inference from mere events about the existence of a moral tone in American foreign policy, but rather hearkening back to an address on precisely this topic by Adolph Berle, then Assistant Secretary of State, given at the University of North Carolina early in World War II, which articulated the moral bases of American foreign policy. I do not for a moment maintain that this moral aspect is directly a product of religious conviction, for I would concede its secular tone. What I am saying is that, granted that religious principles have been less than decisive, they have not been completely impotent or completely without influence.

Yet all the foregoing cannot exempt a religious man from confronting the problem of what a man of faith is to make of a world in which mass slaughters occur. Out of the confrontation some answers have been offered which seem to me no answers at all. For example, it is no answer to say that in the light of mass crimes men must all the more emphasize the moral and ethical traditions of the prophets. I say that this is no answer, though I yield to no one in admiration for and loyalty to those traditions. But even the secular man, concerned for the welfare of mankind, can argue for a greater adherence on the part of men to high norms. The question, however, in religious terms, is not what is incumbent on man, but rather what it is that God is doing.

A second answer is implied in certain neo-orthodox theologians. These distinguished between what is *geschichtlich* and what is *historisch*. I trust that I do not do violence to their view, which seems to run as follows: What is *geschichtlich* is the bare account of the events of the past; what is *historisch* is that which the eyes of faith discern either behind the events or over and above them. The bare events are natural; there is, however, a power *beyond the events,* which by faith can be discerned. Thus, that the Hebrews were enslaved in Egypt and were liberated under Moses is *geschichtlich;* that it was God who liberated the Hebrews is *historisch.* The release from Egypt, then, was a natural event, but that it was God who occasioned the release is a supernatural belief. Such theologians seem to separate the natural from the supernatural, and such is their right; but they distort greatly when they apply this pattern to the Bible, for in Scripture God *supernaturally* controls *natural* events.

49

Not only is this theological approach an evasion, but its net effect is to etch most sharply the problem which the religious man faces, especially when the irreligious or the anti-religious challenge him. For it must be clear that even in revealed religion it is usual to ascribe revelation to the ancient past. Traditional Judaism is a religious system based on a theory of pristine revelations, which in the tradition are explicitly described and fully detailed. Traditional Christendom expressed the view that the Jewish revelation was the prologue to a more recent revelation of God in Christ: plain, explicit, and detailed—but by our day even this event has come to be ancient.

The modern heirs are guardians of values in a revelation bequeathed from the past; we are scarcely ourselves the recipients of present revelation in plain, explicit and detailed form. I know of no responsible priest, rabbi, minister, or of any theologian who makes the claim that God is telling him what God is doing or will do. Perhaps there are rural enthusiasts who make the claim, but certainly the claim never emerges from responsible religious leaders today. And if the claim were to be made, would the claimant be believed?

We religious people ought to muster the strength of our honesty and admit to the secular impotence of our Judeo-Christian tradition. We ought also to admit the lamented truth that we do not know what God is doing because He does not tell us—or, at least, He has not told us. We can afford to make these damaging admissions not only because truth urges that we should, but also because our survival as religionists depends on the strength that we genuinely possess.

I am not sure that this strength is sufficient to insure our survival. It is quite conceivable that secular man can become wise enought to learn to live in peace and to avert mass suicide via nuclear war. But such a survival would not automatically ensure the survival of religion.

The issue, at least for me, is that certain things I regard as values are quite secular; but certain values—indeed those that I think the highest—I regard as religious in that they stem from what have come to be my tacit or, occasionally, explicit beliefs. I term these religious not particularly because I think I am prepared to hold on to them tenaciously, for I concede that the irreligious can be quite as tenacious as I might possibly be. I call them religious simply because they appeal to me as emerging from that which remains with me even when my experience, and sophistication, and my studies of *Religionsgeschichte,* have prompted me to cast off this or that part of the heritage bequeathed to me.

I can make no claim to having a knowledge of God or of His ways. I can only say this: there are convictions I possess which emerge after inner self-struggle. I cannot assert that I understand events. I confess to frequent despair about them. I confess that religionists have said things glibly and that the glibness has offended me. But there abides within me some emotional, instinctive sense of that which I am persuaded is obligatory on me, and which transcends my logic and my learning and my experience. Some may perhaps dismiss this as mere romanticizing, or as mere sentimentality; but to me it is a reality.

I think that I am this way not because of catastrophes, but in spite of them. My mood at times is like that of the Hasidists in the ghetto who called God to stand trial because of His harshness to His people, and, since in the Hasidic view God is omnipresent, obviously He was there when He was tried.

I cannot explain what, if anything, God is doing. I also cannot explain to myself what I am doing, except in terms of my basic beliefs.

I confess to great uneasiness about such things as the Nuremberg trials and the Eichmann trial. Having no competence in law, I find that I am not sure whether it was legal machinery or military triumph which dictated the trials. It was, to my understanding, the victors and not a previously duly constituted international tribunal which tried and convicted the men who, I agree, were criminals. Since I am a Jew who was already mature at the time of Hitler's rise to power, I believe that I will never completely recover from the trauma of Hitlerism. In the same vein, I have no word to say on behalf of Adolph Eichmann. Yet despite the legal briefs I have read, I am uneasy that the criminal stood trial in a political entity, Israel, which did not exist when he committed his crimes and the laws of which he consequently did not directly violate. (I detest the judicial decision to execute him; I would have preferred that he be sentenced to life imprisonment in an insane asylum.)

In both the Nuremberg and Eichmann trials, it seems to me that I discern

51

vengeance and not simply pure justice. By no stretch of the imagination can human vengeance be justified as consistent with Judeo-Christian principles, if that tradition takes itself seriously.

The result of these trials (and note that I do not speak in behalf of the Nuremberg convicts or Eichmann) is that national policies have not avoided the punitive, and that desire for revenge has been a national tool. Our American policy included participation in the Nuremberg trials; the state of Israel is Jewish, not pagan.

Do these trials contribute to international morality (in the way that proponents of punition argue that the death penalty has a deterrent effect)? Or will they, in time, provide the precedent whereby any nation or group of nations may invoke opportunistic bases for disposing of those it wishes revenge on? I do not know the answer; I say only that I am uneasy about the trials. I wish, and have wished, that Germans, and not their conquerors, had tried and convicted the German war criminals. I have wished that West Germany, not Israel, had tried Eichmann.

Mass crime, obviously, is inconsistent with the best in Judeo-Christian tradition. That a case for retaliation can be made is conceded; we call it justice. But retaliation is religion at its worst, not at its best, and, outside the realm of religion, is retaliation an effective tool for ending, definitively ending mass crime? Or does it simply prolong and increase grievances which, in turn, demand and produce endless successions of retaliation? Retaliation is as much a violation of Judeo-Christian principles as is mass crime.

5

Reflections on the Problem of
Theology for Jews *

I N THE PAST two decades in the American Jewish community there
has developed an insistent and persistent demand for a theology. The nature of this demand may possibly be illustrated, and even have
begun, with a review article by Irving Kristol in *Commentary* in 1947 of
Rabbi Milton Steinberg's *Basic Judaism*.[1] Steinberg's book is a popularly
written but responsible exposition of the meaning and the forms of Jewish
rites and ceremonies. The dissatisfaction of the *Commentary* reviewer lay in
his insistence that Steinberg had abstained from a genuinely fundamental
inquiry into theological matters, had instead confined himself to, or at least
shaped his book by, ceremonies and customs, and that however lucid and
correct he might have been, his approach was quite inadequate to the times
—superficial and glaringly deficient when contrasted with the penetrating
and profound inquiries of, let us say, a Niebuhr and a Tillich. It was intimated that what Jews needed, and wanted, was a theological inquiry into
Judaism analogous to that of Christians.

Thereafter a number of Jews emerged who began to write about Judaism
in a way analogous to that of Christians, primarily Protestants. Paradoxically,
the Jewish writer Martin Buber had had, antecedently, a rather notable
impact, but almost exclusively upon Protestants; now, Jewish writers began
to inquire into the possible relevancy of Buber for Jews.

* This article first appeared in *The Journal of Bible and Religion,* 33 (1965): 101–121.

Not all Jews welcomed the development of this theological interest. Three possible reasons for such disinterest may be guessed at. First, the genre of Protestant theological writing is relatively absent from the immediate Jewish past, with the result that however loyally such Jews were now writing, they seemed to their opponents to be embarking on something totally alien to the essence of Judaism. These opponents were in a sense unwitting disciples of Erasmus and hence averse to the imitative scholasticism which was thought to inhere in theology. Second, the Protestant writers fitted into that amorphous category of "neo-orthodoxy"; by and large, Jews had been in the "liberal" camp, even if their commitment was Conservative or Traditional. Such Jews shared the liberal Protestant suspicion or disdain of neo-orthodoxy, often just as instinctively and intuitively as Protestants and seldom as learnedly. To state this in another way, such Jews had been direct or indirect disciples of Rauschenbusch, Royce, Hayden, Ames, Brightman, and Whitehead, and like their Protestant opposite numbers they resisted the reemergence of traditional concepts and phrases apparently long abandoned. In the first case the theological was resisted as though it were recognizably alien, and in the second case as though, while recognizably within the commonwealth, it was nevertheless irrelevant in the sense of being outmoded.

The third reason for the resistance may be associated with the fact that some Jewish writers, principally Will Herberg, went beyond regarding Niebuhr and Tillich as exemplars whose admirable profoundity should be emulated, and proceeded to use these men as if they were mentors for Judaism itself. It was alleged—correctly in my estimate—that Herberg was importing into Judaism materials from Christian writers which were as incongruous with Judaism as they were congruent with Christianity. This allegation focused upon the thought as well as upon the phraseology, for there is a distinction between a phrase which is borrowed in its usual meaning and a phrase borrowed but invested with a different meaning. It was charged against Herberg, for example, that his *Judaism and Modern Man* (1951) was an assessment of Judaism from a Protestant, not a Jewish, viewpoint. Enough petty errors dot Herberg's book to have bred the oft-made accusation of Herberg's incompetence in Judaism (as if the trival errors amounted to that!), and hence there were those who concluded, rather strangely, that it was the author's putative incompetency in Judaism which occasioned the misdirected Protestant approach. Herberg's signficant deficiencies in that book were, to my mind, a combination of unacquaintance with important aspects of Jewish literature and his failure to understand that the vocabularies of different religions, however common their words may be, often connote quite different things. Yet it is my opinion that Herberg succeeded despite his failure, for while his book bristles with inaccuracies of substance, he managed to propel his opponents into the very area where he had moved and where he was trying to move Jews. To his critics, it seemed that Herberg could be set aside, but these opponents were going to have to face beyond him the issues which they complacently felt they could ignore in him. (Herberg could in the 1960s perform the useful chore of recasting his book in the light of the just criticisms made of it, for his first-rate mind comes to the fore when he thinks instead of debates, and he seems to have learned very richly.)

Though I am not unlearned in Judaism, I am untrained in theology and little trained in philosophy, and hence I am in something of the same position as that of a dramatic critic who cannot himself write a play, but reacts to the plays he sees. There is in my mind a sense of good clarity on some of my negative reactions to Jewish theological writings; moreover, along with the negative, I have some reservations and anxieties relating to matters common to a diversity of Jewish writings. Less clear, admittedly, is the affirmative prescription which I would suggest, yet it is perhaps well enough defined in my mind to risk expressing it.

Let me begin with the negative and the critical.

There is to my mind an abiding issue for Jews in the distinction drawn above between Tillich and Niebuhr as exemplars and these men as direct mentors. Furthermore, the strange situation of Buber, the Jew influential on Christians and negligibly influential on Jews, poses a problem which needs either solution or at least clarification.

I would take it that the Jews of our day are not going to be parochial in their reading; hence, they will know Niebuhr, Tillich, et al. This is excellent; they should know these men. Yet the insights which a Jew might thereby gain can come to be blurred if he borrows without adapting, if he simply parrots the insights without understanding some obligatory distinctions. To me, the distortion which the figure of Martin Buber leads to seems to lie in the assumption of some Jews that a certain community of theological concern between Jews and Christians amounts to a total overlap. Requisite distinctions all too often fail to be made; and since theology contains not only thought but also slogans, both tend to be borrowed with a noticeable recklessness. Against all this, it must be insisted that certain matters which are problems in Christian theology are not problems in Jewish theology, and, indeed, that there is a certain characteristic homogeneity and consecutiveness in Jewish thought which is necessarily absent from Christian thought. That abused term "polarity" has much less relevance to Judaism than to Christianity, for paradox inheres in Christianity in a way which is not the case in Judaism. For Jewish writers simply to borrow Christian theological phrases and motifs and transfer them into Judaism is unsound in methodology and can only result in acute misinterpretation. This is a topic which seems to me to cry for exploration.

Professor W. D. Davies makes this comment regarding the substance of his book, *The Setting of the Sermon on the Mount:* "Historical as is its [the study's] intention, therefore, it is hoped that it may not be without significance theologically." That significance would appear to be "whether in the matter of Gospel and Law, the gulf fixed in the subsequent life of the Church between Protestant and Roman Catholic, Lutheran and Calvinist, cannot be bridged in terms of the wholeness of the New Testament." [2] Mr. Davies's wish to bridge this gulf between Gospel and Law indirectly makes relevant the question of the role of the Law of Moses in the great schism between Judaism and early Christianity.

The antiquarian aspect of the matter with which Davies wrestles is the antithesis—at least a surface one—between the views of Paul and the implication of the Sermon on the Mount. Paul, so we may say, regarded the Law of Moses as an outmoded and deficient vehicle for the attainment of righteousness, and as even an obstacle to that attainment, precisely because it was *law.* Certainly on the surface, the author of Matthew portrays Jesus as enunciating a new law in the Sermon on the Mount. I have twice used the word "surface" as a means of alluding to an interpretation of the Sermon on the Mount which utterly denies its legalistic character and which sees in it no conflict with Paul's views. This interpretation seems to me to represent the view of the great majority of Christian scholars. That minority which regards the Sermon as Christian legalism includes a few scholars who construe it as a direct retort to, or a purposed modification of, Paulinism; for, since Matthew's Gospel was written after Paul's time, this lateness of composition could account for a post-Pauline view of Jesus as speaking in a context of post-Pauline concerns.

Since the evidence is both incomplete and unclear, the historical problem which is raised here is beyond definite solution. Perhaps the schematic view is tenable that Paul's abrogation of the Law led after his time to a neutralization of his extreme position—this by a subsequent enfranchisement of law, provided it was the law of Jesus and not that of Moses. Even if this schematization is not tenable, what is beyond denial is the surface antithesis, and in none of the ingenuities which have reconciled the apparent divergencies has there been a failure at least to touch on the surface disparities. Yet it seems to me as someone outside the Christian tradition that the Christian theologian, particularly among Protestants in our own day, feels the need to treat of law and non-law either as a direct antithesis or, contrariwise, to depict the two as not antithetical. In Jewish Scripture and later Jewish thinking law and non-law are not antithetical. [3] To see the way in which Christians treat the issue of law and non-law can broaden the perspective of the modern Jewish theologian. But to transfer into Judaism even the overtone of the antithesis can result only in distorting the nature of Judaism.

Paul did not pose the antithesis of law and faith as one of equal elements. In Pauline thought the antithesis is accordingly that of an inferior to a superior. In Paul's view, first there was faith, as in Abraham's time, then a descent into law through Moses, and finally an abandonment of law and a return to faith through the revelation in Christ. It is therefore a common Christian theological motif to set the law pejoratively in contrast with faith. A proper estimate of law and faith in Judaism would, however, regard them as intertwined and inseparable, and not susceptible to a pejorative contrast. To see how alert and acute Christian minds treat faith and law can enrich Jewish theological writing, but to treat law and faith in Judaism in the way Christians treat them can only distort Judaism.

In Christianity the contrast between law and faith is often expressed in the form of a distinction between "works" and "faith." The definition of "works" in this contrast involves the aggregate of individual acts as required by or suggested in the Law. Perhaps the distinction, if any, between law and works might be that whatever may have been the affirmative qualities in the Law in its period of validity from Moses to Christ, man by his nature must fail to acquire even its limited benefit because he cannot unerringly execute the Law's requirements. To put this in a slightly different way, the Law is a less effective way of attaining righteousness than faith is, but even to the extent of the Law's limited effectiveness, man is debarred from acquiring that effectiveness through either individual acts or an aggregate of them. Paul argues, probably from his own experience, that man *cannot* observe the Law, and he illustrates this contention in his confession that what he wills to do he does not do. The futility of trying but failing in works combines with the limited utility even of success to prove for Paul the total bankruptcy of works. Moreover, since works are acts which a person does, any reliance on works for attaining righteousness would imply that man has the capacity for the attainment even without God's aid. Paul's conviction, to the contrary, is that man simply cannot attain righteousness on his own.

Whatever one moves out of and away from in order to attain righteousness is "sin," and in this sense sin is the opposite of righteousness. In Paul's view righteousness is a state, a condition; and so is sin. The divine act which enables man to move from sin to righteousness, from one condition to another, is "atonement." For Paul, the death of the Christ constitutes the atonement which would make possible this movement on man's part. Christ's death was an act of grace on God's part, for here was the alternative to man's inability to attain righteousness through his own actions. While in the normative Jewish formulations "sin" is at times an abstraction, this is so in the sense of the totality of individual sins. The usual Jewish view regards sin as a single act, and holds that for the aggregate of sins, large or small, man can make atonement and God can forgive. In the Christian sense, man is a sinner powerless to make atonement, and therefore dependent on God's grace. The individual act, the individual sin is only a manifestation of an antecedent sin which is "sinfulness," and sinfulness is man's condition prior to his having been redeemed.[4] In Paul's context, works (that is, what man does) and grace (what God does) are set in antithesis. Judaism has not seen them in this way; as in its view of law and faith, it has regarded works and grace as supplementary to each other. A usual Christian understanding of grace is the result of viewing it from the standpoint of an extreme antithesis of works versus grace; when a Jewish theologian views grace as totally the negative of works, in this way he is setting in *opposition* what Judaism formulated as *apposition*.

I do not here imply that the view of Paul is the total view of Christianity. I am quite aware that the Epistle of James argues—probably obliquely against Paul—that preeminent as is faith, it is meaningless without works. I am also aware of views in Christendom which rotate around sin as an individual act —as for example, the distinction set forth in First John between mortal and venial sins. I am aware as well of the attitude in the Epistle to the Hebrews which can be put in this way, that once a man has received grace and then falls from it, he cannot be restored to it. In view of this awareness I would go on to emphasize the relevant point that the terms "sin," "repentance," "atonement," and "grace" have connotations in Christianity which are different from their connotations in Judaism.

Again, the Christian view that man cannot attain righteousness through his own actions leads quite naturally to the question of which men are to receive grace. Obviously, man's inability to do anything toward righteousness absolves him of responsibility (if only theoretically), but also requires some such idea as providence or predestination in order to explain the way in which divine grace is administered. Furthermore, if it is predestination which accounts for man's receipt or non-receipt of grace, then he scarcely has the capacity for choice, the capacity of free will. The age-old dilemma between predestination or providence, on the one hand, and choice, on the other hand, never comes to a solution. To emphasize providence at the expense of choice is to absolve man of moral responsibility; to emphasize free will at the expense of providence is in effect to rule God out of man's life. By and large the Jewish Bible attributes free will to man: "Behold I have set before you this day life and good, death and evil . . . and you must choose life . . ." (Deut. 30:15, 19). The rabbinic halaka similarly attributes to man the capacity to choose. On the other hand, divine providence is made explicit in the Bible so often as to require no documentation, and is probably of the same implied importance in rabbinic literature, though the absence of historical narrative in the latter genre may account for its not having as highly explicit a place. The "resolution" of the dilemma of providence and free will, attributed to Rabbi Akiba (50?–132) is simply a restatement that both of these exist; it is no resolution at all. In Christian thought the preference doctrinally was for providence, for predestination—as in Paul, Augustine, and Calvin. Pelagius taught free will in the same epoch as Augustine, and was declared a heretic; the same thing happened with Arminius in the age of Calvin. Christian writers have declared that Christianity, especially Catholicism, is described more accurately as semi-Pelagian than as Augustinian, and such may well be the case. Yet the contrast seems legitimate that in the Christian approach providence is dominant and free will recessive, while in Judaism free will is dominant and providence recessive.

Judaism, unencumbered by the Augustinian-Pelagian type of conflict, seems to have felt little need to explain in detail and profoundly the nature of man in order to clarify his lack of free will. On the other hand, anthropology has been a topic of central importance in Christian theology. The point in the present context is not that of the substance of Jewish and Christian thought about man, but of the great difference in the relative attention to the topic together with the reason for Jewish inattention.

Certainly Jews have been a God-intoxicated people. Yet I have the hunch that Judaism has been more humanistic than Christianity, and Christianity more overtly theistic than Judaism. These words can lead to misunderstanding, and out of context can be damagingly quoted. Hence, it is well to add that the contrast is not one of the profundity of the belief in God, but only one of the ways in which the motifs of man's task and God's task are expressed in the two religions. The high place of halaka (which might be translated as "works") in Judaism has implied a high place for human obligation; whereas the repeated Christian motif that works do not bring a man to salavation tends to lower man's voluntary obligation. Once again the modern Jewish theologian can gain in depth and understanding by reading what Christian theologians write about man, free will, and providence; however, to transfer into Judaism the substance of the Christian approach is to distort Judaism.

Yet even more basic is the need to distinguish sharply between the connotation of "Torah" in Judaism and the connotation of "law" among Christians. I have contended elsewhere that in the Greco-Roman world as in our world, to render "Torah" by *nomos* or "law" is to distort the sense of the word.

"Torah" means something akin to revelation (only in passages from P does it mean a "regulation"). For Jews, Torah was an all embracing body of revelation which *included* Law, with that Law divine in origin. *Nomos,* "law," robs the term of its connotative fullness and implies a bare legalism distinctly at variance with the Jewish understanding of Torah and of legalism. Moreover, Paul assigns the origin of the Law to the "angels" (those commentators who believe he means "demons" may be right) with the implication that its origin is not strictly from God, and hence that the Law is a second-rate matter. In light of the different ring of the term, it is not difficult to understand why "law" (and "works") should have a pejorative ring in Christianity but an affirmative ring in Judaism. Once more, Jewish thinkers can find some light in discerning what Christian thinkers say about law and about works. But the Jew ought to understand that since the definitions and premises are different, the inferences and corollaries must be different.

A consequence of the Christian attitude toward law is that since Christian Scripture comprises the Old Testament as well as the New Testament, much in the latter is concerned with cancelling out a great deal that is in the former. The Laws of Moses are canonical to Christians, but so are Galatians and Romans. From one standpoint Christians have had to wrestle with the issue of whether the New Testament was a rupture of the Old Testament, or in direct continuity with it. To put this another way, does the Christian Gospel cancel the Law, or does the Law develop unbrokenly into the Gospel? (Luke appears to sanction this latter contention.) If Christians had followed Marcion and other gnostics in jettisoning the Law, they would not have confronted the need of trying to set Law and Gospel into some alignment with each other. Instead, Christianity has to try to find some overarching motif which can bring the disparities and even the antitheses into some semblance of unity. That is, Christianity, having broken the thread, feels the need to assert that the thread is unbroken; hence, the theological term *Heilsgeschichte,* "salvation history," which makes an assertion about the unity of the Old and the New Testaments. In this Christian sense the term is of no meaning to Judaism, for, from the latter point of view, the laws of Scripture were to undergo, not cancellation as in Christianity, but expansion and proliferation in the rabbinic literature. That is, having refrained from breaking the thread, Jews feel no need to raise the question of whether or not the thread is broken. Moreover, "salvation" in the Christian sense is alien to Judaism, wherein there is some focus on God as a savior, but no rabbinic

61

term which remotely resembles what Christians mean by "salavation." Jews may be enlightened and stimulated from reading about *Heilsgeschichte,* but they have little occasion to import the term.

Yet still another difference must command our attention. However difficult it may be to make distinctions respecting the magnitude of miracles, there is a difference between the Jewish idea of revelation, as at Sinai, and the Christian idea, as in the revelation of God in Christ. By and large, Jewish thought has considered the revelation at Sinai quite reasonable and rational and quite consistent with the God who acts in history. On the other hand, that Jesus met death and apparent defeat (Christian thought asserts the triumphant nature of the events) accounts for the theme in Christianity that the revelation of God in Christ is an irrational, incredible matter, acceptable to faith but not to reason. Paul speaks of the "foolishness of God" which is "wiser than men" (I Cor. 1:25), and Tertullian says, perhaps in extremes, that "I believe, because it is absurd; . . . it is certain, because it is impossible." The term used with considerable prominence in current Christian writings for this situation of the supposed credibility of the unbelievable is "paradox." That paradox is involved in the key concept of Christian thought would naturally lead to its reappearance elsewhere, so that paradox is necessarily endemic to that thought. The reverse of this is the case in Judaism, for no matter how incredible some modern Jews may find Sinai to be, Judaism has always proceeded on the basis of the credibility of the believable, not the credibility of the unbelievable. Much of Jewish thought of even our day, especially in the United States, is little more than a restatement of Moses Mendelssohn's rationalism, produced in an age of rationalism. Much of Jewish thought, especially in the United States, is inhospitable to the Kantian and post-Kantian movements even when it is aware of them (usually it is not). Perhaps this is why a Søren Kierkegaard seems often to befuddle American Jews, and a Martin Buber is more warmly received among Christians than among his co-religionists. Perhaps the Jewish resistance to a Franz Rosenzweig is also part of this Jewish bent toward the rational, the reasonable. Jewish theological writing has been impoverished, so it seems to me, by its resistance to post-Kantian philosophy; nevertheless, the method followed by some Jewish writers to transfer themes of paradox inevitable in Christianity into analogous themes in Judaism is a wrong one. The central paradox of Christianity leads there to corollary paradoxes. For example, there is a certain richness in the Christian view that the Incarnation represents the irruption of eternity within time. I am not as sure, however, that there is a comparable richness in the Christian distinction between history on the one hand and metahistory or suprahistory on the other hand, for I am of the opinion that these terms do not represent thinking quite as much as they do its absence. Moreover, I confess to being aghast at the way in which eschatology, that is, what is to happen within history at the end of history, has been transformed into a nonhistorical transcending of history. In Judaism, traditionally it is history which God controls, and not metahistory.

The preceding comments add up to little more than the conclusion that Jewish theology ought not be, and is not, a series of analogies to Christian theology. But if our discussion thus far has been in negatives, it is surely appropriate to ask: What, affirmatively, ought Jewish theology be?

The answer—if there is an answer—necessarily inquires into the general nature and purpose, or purposes, of theology. The curricula of Christian theological schools contain a series of limiting adjectives: "historical," "dogmatic," "practical." The dictionary defines theology as "the science of divinely revealed truths." I confess to an inability to define theology in a way that I think would be broadly acceptable. For purposes of communication, and communication alone, let me define Jewish theology as a conceptuo-philosophical and systematic exposition of Jewish beliefs and teachings. By this definition I should hope immediately to move the discussion beyond the equally important, but here irrelevant, matters which are dealt with in the *Shulhan Aruk* and its pale derivatives which describe Jewish ceremonies.

My reading elicits doubts and anxieties which seem to need confronting. Thus, for example, can the task of theology be merely descriptive? Does it suffice to describe what Jews have believed and what some or all appear still to believe? Or must theology go on to set forth as persuasively as possible the credibility of what was, or is, believed? Is theology aimed to deepen the faith of Jews who already believe, or to bring to belief those Jews who have found a basis for disbelief? Is it designed to translate ancient beliefs into modern categories of thought (if and where this can be done), or is it supposed to restate the ancient beliefs with a profound indifference to modern thought? At what point does the issue of intellectual honesty arise? Is it theology's legitimate task, when reinterpreting ancient beliefs, to use traditional phrases and formulas, even where reinterpretation is faithless to the plain meaning of these old expressions?

I raise these questions because while I recognize sympathetically the great thirst among Jews for a Jewish theology, it is not entirely clear to me exactly what such Jews are thirsting for. I have the impression, which I recognize as unflattering, that some want not theology but theologizing—as if some gain is to be derived merely from turning a simple idea into polysyllabic words, and as if a doubted or rejected belief automatically becomes accepted once it is framed theologically. I have an impression, also unflattering, that some Jewish writers, like their Christian counterparts, are more bent on fashioning slogans than on disciplined thought, and that they sometimes try to do quasi-philosophical chores without a thorough mastery of, or even good acquaintance with, modern philosophy.

But to take the thirst as earnestly as I believe and know it to be felt, I ask, is this need for a theology a wish for organized and systematic thought, that is, for form; or is it as much a wish for content? Is theology to make Judaism comprehensible on its own terms? If so, fine. I hope its objective is more than merely to vie chauvinistically with the great achievements of Christian theology. Yet I must also ask, and in all earnestness, is this wish for a theology apt to be satisfied by theology? Does the wish represent a desire for a carefully formulated exposition of items of Jewish belief, or something quite different: a desire for persuasion to belief? Is it an inquiry for its own sake, or one which serves an ulterior purpose? Is it not conceivable that a carefully, even an eloquently, formulated exposition, and one that is sound and responsible, may fail to clarify for the skeptic the bases for his continuing and increasing skepticism? One may comment inoffensively that there is often this difference between Jewish and Christian theological writings: the Christian writings seem to be trying to deepen the religiosity of their readers, while the Jewish writings seem to be trying to justify religiosity to those who lack it. The tone of the Bishop of Woolwich's *Honest to God*,[5] with its iconoclasm and untraditionalism, is very much uncharacteristic of Christian writings; yet *Honest to God* has seemed to me to be wondrously congruent to the mentality of skeptical Jews. While *Honest to God* certainly impinges on matters of theology, in no sense is it a systematic, unified exposition of the wide range of Christian convictions. It is a tract for the times, with only a limited number of themes, and it appears often to espouse positions diametrically opposed to usual Christian positions. A work of earnestness, though not of profundity (even when it raises profound questions), it contributes quite as much to a dissolution of aspects of traditional Christian attitudes as to their justification. Do Jews who desire a theology wish to know the content of the belief they already have, or do they want to be brought from skepticism to belief via systematic exposition? To what audience is Jewish theology to be addressed: believers or skeptics? Can one piece of writing serve for more than one audience? It is rare if it can.

Furthermore, how far beyond mere definition must Jewish theology go if it is to be theology and not merely a catechism? How long should a chapter be which discusses faith in its Jewish sense? A sufficiently staccato exposition could conceivably meet the need in a single page. Or if the theologian proceeded to embellish the theme, he could go on endlessly, especially if he felt so inclined, to cite the countless biblical and postbiblical embroideries, a project which would at the best sharpen the exposition and at the worst blunt it through a plethora of supporting evidence. The point at issue in this question of proportion necessarily relates to the problem of the audience and the scope of the work undertaken. Christian, and especially Protestant, theology very often represents an inner, closed group whose members talk communicably to each other but incommunicably when a nontheologian, including a Christian believer, tries to read them. Does the expressed wish for a Jewish theology mean a desire that there arise among Jews a similar cadre, a highly erudite in-group which will discuss within its own circle, employing all the requisite technicalities, the broad and fine points of theology? Or is it possible that the wish is more modest, that it seeks some modern equivalent, changed or unchanged, of Maimonides' Thirteen Principles? Do we merely desire a Jewish counterpart to the Thirty-nine Articles of the Church of England, that is, a brief summary of the content of faith, condensed and distilled? Or is something else sought? My hunch is that Jews are seeking two things which are related but on different levels. On the one level, they are looking for a list of articles of Jewish faith which they can and will accept; only thereafter do they desire an embellishment of these items by recourse to the citation of historical precedents. My impression is that Jewish thinkers tend to by-pass the first of these things—not through deliberate evasion, but through assuming that writer and reader have antecedently met on that level. Perhaps this may be put more strikingly: Jews in abundance are looking for religion, not for theology; they are looking for what they may be willing to believe, not for an embroidery of themes prior to acceptance.

Jewish thinkers have every reason to deplore the broad illiteracy of Jews in Jewish lore and learning. These thinkers often err, though, in interpreting this illiteracy as total. They seem to be unaware of the high cultural attainments of Jews in our day in areas outside the Jewish disciplines. The writing of many Jewish thinkers is either disdainful of the illiterate or reckless of the obligation to carry the reader along with the author.

The broad Jewish audience of non-technicians includes so many minds, and so many hearts, as to be in its own way a multiple audience, with the consequence that it imposes a tremendous burden on any writer who tries to address it. In this connection, it seems to me that there is a significant failure of minds to meet, that the broad Jewish public is looking for beliefs to hold, while Jewish thinkers are providing them with admirable expositions of beliefs they do not hold. If this is true, what is the task of Jewish theology?

The desire for a Jewish theology appears to me to include a demand for some unifying principle or principles which will bind together the disparate aspects of Jewish experience: social anti-Semitism; the satisfying or unsatisfying aspects of Jewish philanthropy; the contentment in, or discontent with, the synagogue and the rabbinate; and a concern for that elusive thing, Jewish destiny. And this desire seems to be at least related to the wish for a religious confrontation, for some religious security. Here, too, the wish is legitimate, but again it seems to me to be something different from what I would understand by theology. Obviously, a search for a unifying principle has a relationship to theology, but again it is oblique to, rather than identical with, the substance of theology, unless it is itself a theologically-formulated conclusion to a responsible and broad and deep theological inquiry.

Still another anxiety troubles me. It is my opinion that were some Jewish theologian to produce a work on Jewish theology which would not elicit a single dissent from among his colleagues and would be written with faultless clarity and great eloquence, his work would still fail to meet the desire for religious certainty. It might succeed in very large measure in persuading the Jewish mind. But would it thereby speak to the Jewish heart? Only if it succeeded in attaining the relevancy that a guide of conduct, a guide to action ought to have. Historically, Jews have much more often asked what they ought to do than what they ought to believe. It is significant that the same Maimonides who wrote the theological *Guide to the Perplexed* also wrote a classic compendium of the halaka. Jews, it seems to me, will always want a companion piece to a work of theology; they will always want counsel in what they are to do. And they will want this counsel to be made specific for them—even when they are determined not to accept it. Christian theology, with its emphasis on faith over and against law, can abstain from the specific; when and if Jewish theology abstains in this way, it appears instinctively to Jews as irrelevant. The point is that Jews have wishes related to religion which theology is scarcely apt to satisfy, for theology is conceptual, not programmatic.

That I raise these questions unquestionably reflects some reservations and apprehensions which I seldom find would-be Jewish theologians meeting. For example, I own to a negative response to modern and unconscious allegorizing; as a specialist in Philo, I am perhaps oversensitive to investing religious terms with capricious meanings. The objection here is not to new meanings, but to capricious ones. Especially do I find myself both puzzled and dismayed by the way in which the word "existentialism" is used as if it is an abracadabra; this is an objection not to existentialism, but to a condition which I think I detect that the term is a sanction for irresponsible utterance. Far from opposing existentialism, I welcome it as a resource, just as I welcome that abundance of modern philosophy which seems to me to remain largely absent from Jewish theology. But theology cannot be the métier for the merely fluent, for those who are merely intellectual adventurers. The combination of knowledge and of thinking, and then of relevancy is to my mind an inescapable necessity. I mention relevancy, for I see no purpose in mere antiquarianism or in a revived scholasticism which can be as meaningless to our age as was medieval scholasticism to the sixteenth-century humanists. There is no doubt in my mind that the need in our time for competent Jewish theologians is more urgent than the great need for technical scholars in the Jewish disciplines. But only by a generous definition can homiletical or inspirational writings, highly commended as they are, be classified as theological. And important as sociological writings are, they are only related to theology; they are not substitutes for it. Historical writing is perhaps related even more than sociological writing, but it is still not the same thing as theology. Thus, nationalism is a necessary topic in Jewish theology, in a way that the statistics of the migrations to Israel are not; Zionism is not co-extensive with theology.

I have the suspicion that difficult as is the task of Jewish theology, it is easier than that of Christian theology. Reform Judaism, Reconstructionism, and old-line Conservative Judaism (as distinct from its present-day, near interchangeability with American Orthodoxy) have a more rigorous task than Orthodoxy in that they must simultaneously espouse the traditional and justify the untraditional. Nevertheless, they do not have to struggle with the antitheses which beset Christianity. But, on the other hand, this very struggle in Christianity has unquestionably enhanced and enriched the range and profundity of the Christian theologies, and I suspect that Jewish theology will inevitably remain more restricted and possibly appear bare by comparison. If I am right in attributing a more organic humanism to Judaism in contrast to Christianity, then Jewish theology will necessarily lack the counterpart of themes such as those Reinhold Niebuhr has eloquently pursued: man's sin of pride, and the discrepancy between Western humanism's meaning of the dignity of man and the Christian view of man. I wonder too whether there could ever be Jewish counterparts of Karl Barth and Dietrich Bonhoeffer. Christianity recurrently feels a need to set itself over and against Western man, "secular" man. On the other hand, while Jewish thought can have reservations about man's neglect of God, and in that sense about his secularism, it does not have the same urgency totally to disown Western man.

I also have the suspicion that Jewish theology cannot, and will not, exhibit the range of topics, and the clash within them, found in Christian theology. Perhaps this inevitability respecting the future accounts for the surprise of the past, that while Jews since the Emancipation have produced eminent philosophers, eminent religious scholars, and brilliant homileticians, they have produced precious few theologians. We have provided men who have done good work on theological themes, but not a single first-rate systematic theologian. Insofar as I can explain this strange phenomenon to myself, it seems to stem also from a failure properly to understand what theology must be. For example, while philosophy, as such, may challenge at the same time that it inquires, theology does not challenge; it accepts and then probes in depth. Philosophy may be relatively neutral, but theology must be partisan. Philosophy can accept demolition as its goal, but theology is the explanation of what is antecedently affirmed.

It seems to me inescapable that theology must necessarily be scholarly. It can inquire into concepts only when these are responsibly understood; shabby scholarship can lead only to shabby theology. But theology is more than "foot-note scholarship," for it is inquiry into meaning and connotation, into significance and relevancy. The scholar who is not also immersed in philosophy—this is my own situation and my own disqualification from theology—cannot be a theologian, and the philosopher who is merely a dabbler in scholarship cannot be a theologian. Dilettantism is admissible (if it is) in aesthetics and in history, but never in theology. For theology is quite a serious business. It presupposes antecedent training, serious academic work, relentless thinking, and an unabated drive to understand and to explain and relate. The audience for theology can be only theologians. For others (the dilettante, the fluent, the merely clever) homiletics or popularization must suffice.

Is it possible, then, that the nature of Judaism destines it to a perpetual lack of an encompassing theology? Are theological *writings* (Buber, Rosenzweig, Heschel, et al.) the most we can expect—sporadic, "occasional" pieces in the sense in which rabbinic *responsa* were sporadic, "occasional," and *ad hoc*—but never a *total theology*? Or is it possible that even Christian theology in our day will tend to become occasional, rather than total? As an outsider to Christianity, I believe there is a trend in that direction.

Yet, without meaning to play with words, Jewish theology, as I see it, is Jewish theology only when it is simultaneously Jewish and also theology.

6

The Jewish Community and the Outside:
The Christian Community *

M Y PAPER DEALS with two somewhat different, yet quite related, matters: one, the inner problems of the Jews in the United States in relationship to the outside world in general, and two, in relationship to Christians and the Christian religion in particular.

For our purposes, I shall emphasize the religious strands of the issues that confront us, even though the sociological and all that that cumbersome word implies has its own specific weight, and will get some attention, though scarcely enough. Respecting the sociological, for example, much of the inner change and the need for adjustment by Jews stems from the circumstance that there is in the immediate background of most American Jews a vivid and recent East European heritage. There our existence was in the confines of the ghetto, usually in a small village, often alluded to today by the Yiddish word *shtetel*. The key word in any description of this ghetto existence was "isolation."

Our forebears lived in countries in which they did not speak the language of the land, but maintained instead that form of a German dialect plus a mixture of Hebrew and Slavic which we call Yiddish. Government regulations limited the trades and occupations which Jews could pursue. In the nineteenth and early twentieth centuries, various grudging concessions toward partial political and economic rights were received by Jewish communities in various places, including some special arrangements such as

* Previously unpublished, a draft of this paper was read at a symposium at Great Neck, New York, April 14, 1968. (Permission for publication, prior to and apart from the publication of the symposium, has been granted by Rabbi Jacob Philip Rudin of Great Neck.)

the granting of minority national rights in some states, including Poland.

In general—and to telescope matters—the Jewish communities in Europe constituted enclaves within countries, but these enclaves were isolated from the usual and normal developments in those lands. Economic repression was such that when religious persecution became acute, these two combined to compel Jews in large numbers to migrate to the Western world.

The first immediate result was the disappearance of the legal, compulsory isolation of Jews. We can point to two examples of this change. The difference in language vanished with great speed, for Jews promptly adopted the languages of the Western countries. Second, in the European ghettos of our fathers or grandfathers public education was denied us, and we Jews developed our system of education conducted almost entirely without reference to the content and the interest and the inclinations of the general education. The curriculum in the East European ghetto was Bible, Talmud, and the Commentators, and not geometry, mathematics, economics, and the like. My father was prohibited from attending the public schools in Eastern Europe where he was born. I was compelled to attend the public schools here where I was born.

In moving to the Western world, our fathers or grandfathers made a journey of something like thirty days, but traversed something like four hundred years. The abrupt end to isolation in terms of language and education brought Jews from Eastern Europe into the stream of Western culture, though certain sociological factors continued to constitute, or to effect, a pale reflection in this country of the European ghetto life, namely, in the residential segregation of Jews or in the voluntary congregation of them. Nevertheless, Jews became participants in the stream of Western culture to which antecedently they had been completely alien.

Shakespeare and Beethoven and Charles Darwin abruptly became part of our cultural inheritance. One sociological by-product was a diminution of the breadth and intensity of Jewish education. There has also been an erosion of individual Jews away from the Jewish community, for the lure of Western culture has been such that some Jews, consciously or unconsciously, have felt themselves impelled to make a choice—as if between irreconcilable alternatives—whether to be carriers of Judaism on the one hand, or only carriers of Western culture on the other.

What we must discover now is what the state of religion has been in this Western culture and what the impact has been on the Jewish religion and on its communicants as a consequence of the new situation. If, for example, the movement from the East European ghetto to the freedom of the Western world had been in a context in which religion in the Western world was monolithic, or else if the Christian context in the Western world had remained abidingly traditional, then our experience would have been quite different from what it was.

The fact is that we have encountered in the Western world a religious situation that is very chaotic from two standpoints. The first is the very obvious one of the diversity in the forms of Christian religion in our time, ranging from Roman Catholicism to the various shadings of Protestantism. The major impact on Jews in our generation, however, has come much more from the second factor, namely, that the Jewish people entered the stream of Western culture at a time when there has been and there abides an intense upheaval, a near chaos in the Christian religion as a consequence of tremendous intellectual developments.

The antecedents of this chaotic situation within Christendom can be traced back to the age of the Renaissance, to a period, indeed, well before the Protestant Reformation of the sixteenth century. In the eleventh and the twelfth centuries, when the great universities were founded, sanctioned, and supported by Christians, the ancient culture of the Greeks and Romans was reborn, and slowly the forerunners of such modern disciplines as astronomy and chemistry and history arose. The universities slowly became centers in which the doctrines and tenets of the Church, which was the patron of the universities, began to be challenged.

In astronomy, Copernicus and Galileo challenged the Church's understanding of the biblical story of creation and the origin of the world, and of the centrality of the earth in the solar system. In history, certain documents which justified the authority of the Church on the basis of privileges given to it by the Emperor Constantine in the fourth century were alleged by individual Roman Catholic scholars to be spurious documents, to be forgeries. In biology, the development of the microscope paved the way for the challenge to the origin of life as it is depicted in the opening chapters of Genesis.

Accordingly, even prior to the upheaval we call the Protestant Reformation, there had arisen a class of individual scholars who were not clerics, but who were men of learning and to whom historians have given the name "humanists." The Christian humanists, even before the Protestant Reformation, were coming to conclusions that were in opposition to the traditional views of the Church. Necessarily the issue was destined to arise, in one form or another, as to whether or not the individual humanist was free to pursue his discipline to whatever conclusions his balanced judgments brought him, or whether he needed, instead, to bend his conclusions to conform with the antecedent opinions of the clerics. Quite curiously, the most celebrated instance of such an issue prior to the Protestant Reformation began in a Jewish context with the so-called Reuchlin affair. In the city of Cologne about 1510, a Jewish *meshummad* ("apostate") made the allegation to some monks that the rabbinic literature contained secret disparagement of Jesus and of Christianity.

To understand what is meant by "secret," we must remember that the scattered handful of passages in the rabbinic literature mentioning Jesus had already been censored out. This new allegation held that allusions in the rabbinic literature to so-called Sadducees, Boethusians, and *Minim* were not denunciations of dissident Jews of the ancient rabbinic age, but rather were secret denigrations of Christians and Christianity. On that basis, the clerics appealed to the city officials to gather the Jewish literature and to burn it.

The Jews protested that these passages were allusions to ancient Jewish marginal sects or sectaries. They protested to the city officials against the seizure and burning of the Jewish literature. There lived in Cologne a pious Roman Catholic humanist, Johannes Reuchlin, a scholar in Hebrew. The city officials asked this Hebrew scholar to make his survey of the Jewish literature and to give his judgment as to whether or not these passages were, in reality, anti-Christian. When Reuchlin completed his broad survey, he declared that the passages were not anti-Christian.

Immediately, the Jewish context of the matter disappeared and the issue now arose as to whether or not a scholar like Reuchlin needed to bend his scholarship to please church officials. I would suppose that in all the history of what we call "academic freedom," there was no instance quite as spectacular as the Reuchlin Affair, for it spread throughout Europe, and there were enlisted on the side of Reuchlin the abundance of free scholars who saw in the Reuchlin Affair a threat to their own freedom of scholarship. The greatest scholar of that day, the Dutchman Erasmus, took up the cudgels on behalf of Reuchlin and wrote a satire against the ignorance of church officials which bore the title "In Praise of Folly." Both Reuchlin and Erasmus were pious Roman Catholics.

There was next a development of this sort that, in the age subsequent to the Protestant Reformation, humanism and its free pursuit of learning ceased to be wholly within the Church and began to make its way outside of it. This movement was accentuated by the celebrated case of Galileo, who

73

in 1616 was condemned at Rome for embracing the Copernican theory of the solar system and forced to recant. While the Catholic Church had power over the Italian Galileo, it no longer had power in the northern lands that had become Protestant, with the consequence that the Galileo Affair strengthened the resolve of the humanists and thereby pushed them even further in the assertion of their right to free inquiry.

In the meantime, the character of the universities began to change. Whereas they had been primarily what we would call today, divinity schools, they now tended to become centers of broad learning. And there began to develop those disciplines which are still the heart of the university.

The chief profound issue in the Protestant Reformation—there were many issues that were not profound—rested on the question of whether religious authority lay in Scripture as Protestants contended, or whether it lay in the Church as the Roman Catholics contended. Those Protestant scholars who worked in Scripture utilized their deep scriptural knowledge for the purpose of denying the claims of the Catholic Church. The true Christianity, according to these Protestants, was the Christianity found in the Gospels, the Christianity found within the Scripture. And the Catholic Church was deemed to be one great and grand digression and error.

There was, however, a turn which in retrospect seems inevitable, from that point at which free scholarship contested only the reliability of Roman Catholic or Protestant claims, to a next step in which free people began to contest the very claims of Christianity itself. This challenge to the claims of Christianity took place, as it were, on two fronts. The one front is best summarized in the word "rationalism," the reliance upon reason. It was argued that the new learning had created standards of correctness and incorrectness, or to put it differently, of truth or falsity. Scripture is full of miracles, and to the eighteenth-century mind, miracles were inconsistent with reason, and with nature. Therefore, miracles were incredible, false.

Again, the new view arose, and ultimately became a part of what we call deism, that the specific, historic claims of Christianity, namely, that God had revealed himself first to Abraham and then to Moses and the Prophets, and ultimately in the Christ Jesus, were acceptable only if these claims could be proved rationally and historically, and through investigation. That is to say, the special claims of Christianity to possess a history of supernatural revelation could be maintained, if at all, only if Christianity could come up with the historical evidences for the truth of the contention. The deists were quite content to believe that religion was a universal manifestation of man, and in that sense, a rational religion was agreeable to man. Such a religion would be a natural one, arising from the understandable yearnings of men. A historical religion such as Christianity, on the other hand, had to justify itself by proving its historical case.

There was no lack of efforts on the part of Christians of the time to adduce what seemed to them to be the evidences of reliable history: the particular tack that was pursued was to try to prove that the Bible was correct, not so much theologically as historically. The debates were on questions like the following: Did creation begin with Adam and Eve? Where did Cain, the only child of Adam and Eve after the death of Abel, get the wife whom, according to Genesis, he married? Did God become Jesus incarnate as the Fourth Gospel asserts? Did Jesus turn water into wine? Was Jesus actually resurrected? The point we emphasize here is that the debate went on against the background of whether or not such material could either be confirmed or denied by historical research.

In the interest of this historical pursuit, there arose a new facet of biblical learning, namely, the effort to be precise about the Bible rather than merely traditional. We must here confine ourselves to the book of Genesis and to the Gospels. The tradition of Christians and Jews had long recognized that there were passages in Genesis which were seemingly in contradiction of one another. Indeed, the important notice was already made back in the days of the ancient rabbis and of Philo that there are in the Five Books of Moses two different names for God: one the name that we ordinarily call "Yahwe," or "Jehovah," and the other that we call in Hebrew, "Elohim."

Modern Pentateuch scholarship began in the eighteenth century with the work of the French physician Jean Astruc, in his new notice of this phenomenon of the two names. Astruc explained the divergency in the divine names on this basis: that Moses, who had written Genesis, had utilized sources more ancient than his time, and that one source had used the word "Yahwe" and the other source had used the word "Elohim." Astruc maintained that Moses had written Genesis. Before the time of Astruc, traditional scholars were able to reconcile the difference implied in the two names for God. For example, the ancient rabbis did it in a beautiful way: When you read "Elohim" in Scripture, that means God, with an emphasis on God as judge. When you read "Adonoi" (Yahwe), the emphasis is on God as merciful. And if you think of man, how can he have any chance of being righteous before God on a strictly legal basis? It is only if the judge is merciful that man has the chance for forgiveness. In this way rabbis were able to reconcile the use of these two divine names. Somewhat similar is the case of Philo of Alexandria. Before Astruc, the problems in Scripture were handled by ingenious harmonization and clever interpretation which satisfied the moment but which later often fell short of being taken seriously.

After Astruc's time (Astruc published his book in 1753) the scholarship proceeded further, and, to the matter of the recognition of the real divergency in the divine names, there was now added the momentous contention that it was not Moses at all who had written the Five Books of Moses. This scholarship went on to become specific about matters which were dealt with more generally about a century earlier by Spinoza. Spinoza had published his "Tractatus Theologico Politicus" in 1670, and there he had argued that the real author of the Five Books of Moses was not Moses but Ezra. We can take the date of Moses as somewhere around 1250 B.C. But the date of Ezra is somewhere around 450 B.C., long after the time of Moses. Spinoza said it was this Ezra who had compiled the Five Books of Moses. Spinoza did not fill in the particulars; the scholarship after Astruc did.

Just as soon as you add these two things together: (1) that there are irreconcilable divergencies in Scripture and (2) that it was not Moses who wrote the Five Books of Moses, you come to the threshold of the biblical scholarship of the Western world which was nurtured at the end of the eighteenth century, and which in the nineteenth century emerged to almost universal acceptability. That is to say, respecting the older effort to prove Christian contentions by means of historical research, the end result of the effort was that the inherited contentions of traditional Christianity were set aside.

We must remember, of course, that there always were and always will be those adherents of traditional religion who will find a basis for denying those results of biblical scholarship which have displeased them. The reality must be faced, though, that the biblical scholarship which I have so briefly alluded to won the day in the nineteenth century, and has continued to prevail in the leading universities and seminaries in the Protestant Western world.

In the press for an intermediate position between the traditional Christian view of Scripture and the scholarly iconoclasm, there is one man who perhaps is worth citing. Paulus, a German scholar who flourished around 1810, felt that he could reconcile the miracles of history with the temper of the modern age of reason by eliminating the miraculous. For example, he explained Jesus' walking on the water on the basis that Jesus walked on a sand bar that was invisible to the disciples. Paulus was on an intermediate position in that it treated the miraculous as though it was a common human experience, and by doing violence to the Bible managed to "affirm" history. But still the extremes of modernism versus traditionalism went on.

A particular blend of modern untraditional scholarship and of rationalist philosophy expressed itself in the movement called Unitarianism, which has much more ancient roots than merely the end of the eighteenth century. In the history of Christianity there has been endless speculation on the relationship between the divine Christ and God, and while the main line of traditional Christian thought has been to equate the Christ and God, there has been a minor strand which has been insistent on some difference and distinction. Toward the end of the eighteenth century the minority view took the form of a new Unitarianism, which in essence asserted that there was a vast difference between the Christ and God, and even went to the point of saying that Jesus was only a man, gifted beyond all men in history, but still only a man. The same modes of inquiry that had already been made into Genesis were applied to the differing material of the Gospels.

There are four Gospels in the New Testament: Mark, Matthew, Luke, and John. Three of them overlap to a considerable degree. They are called the Synoptic Gospels. You can see them at a glance if you publish them in parallel columns. The fourth of the Gospels, John, largely goes its own way.

How reliable are these Gospels for the history of Jesus? This was the question Protestant Bible scholars raised in the eighteenth century. In the nineteenth century they began to give answers with respect to the documents themselves, seeking to answer such questions as who wrote them, when and where and how and why, and whether each Gospel was an independent account, or whether some of the Gospels borrowed material from other Gospels, and questions of that kind. Involved in these newly raised questions was the issue of Church tradition, for the Church had long ago held that at least two of the Gospels, Matthew and John, were composed by eyewitnesses. Mark was held to be a recording by the secretary of the apostle Peter, who had presumably witnessed the events.

The new scholarship, in the first part of the nineteenth century, denied that any of the Gospels were eyewitness accounts. The effect of this denial was to intimate that the Gospels themselves were not repositories of pure history. There then began that Protestant quest to separate the so-called historical materials from the nonhistorical. The effort was exhaustively surveyed about 1906 by the great medical missionary Albert Schweitzer as the "quest for the historical Jesus." And Schweitzer considered this quest a failure.

Perhaps these few words are sufficient now to enable us to summarize: on three fronts, biblical scholarship, free philosophical inquiry, and the growth and development of sciences such as biology, astronomy, and geology, the premises of traditional Christianity were acutely questioned.

Charles Darwin's theory of evolution was only one facet of a broad and encompassing intellectual challenge to the premises of traditional religion. Moreover, and rather pathetically, traditional religion at historical moments has taken stands, such as in the case of Galileo, in which it threw its support behind Church tradition, and in virtually every case, the spirit of modernism emerged from such contests triumphant.

Religious conservatism chose, as the way to meet these basic challenges from modernism, either to ignore everything modern in the scholarship, or else to scorn Western intellectual thought and Western political developments. In the Roman Catholic Church, Pius IX issued a "Syllabus of Errors" in 1864. A good friend of mine, a Catholic priest, has told me that it is the finest summary of Western culture that was ever made. What does Pius describe as errors? If you disbelieve in the divine right of kings, that is an error. If you believe in democracy, that is an error. If you believe in the separation of church and state, that is an error. The Church felt challenged; as a result, it tried to build a wall of separatism around itself. Had there not been this "Syllabus of Errors" by Pius IX, there would have been no need for John XXIII.

One more fact we must add to these brief hints. After the Protestant Reformation, when Protestantism itself became fragmentized and went through periods of intra-Protestant persecution and forced migrations and the like, there were great social problems. Moreover, religious wars were inhospitable to the developing commercialism of the age of colonialism, and the age of the Industrial Revolution and the developing urbanism.

As a consequence, there arose the theory of "toleration" (it had nothing to do with Jews), namely, that the individual ought to have the right to his choice of religion, among the many, and be free from persecution as a consequence of that choice. Not only did the idea of toleration win the day, for it promoted international commerce, especially in Protestant lands, but it resulted in many countries either in the actual separation of church and state, or else in limiting the power of the church, where the church remained linked to the state, as in Britain.

But then, again, something happened. In the eighteenth century, Western man had had two separate struggles for freedom. One struggle was for freedom from foreign conquest. When the French conquered Alsace-Lorraine from the Germans and the Germans wanted to be free, they wanted to be free of the alien conqueror. That is one type of freedom. The other type is the freedom of the individual from the power of his own government. The high spot of English history is the transition whereby, first in the Magna Carta, the noblemen were able to achieve some measure of freedom from the king, and progressively the rights of citizenship were granted to peasants, to serfs, and then ultimately, a House of Commons established. It is significant that in France and in the United States in the eighteenth century, as the result of revolution, the first act in each case was the setting forth of what the French call the "Rights of Man" and what Americans call the "Bill of Rights." These documents were designed to protect the individual not from an alien conqueror, but from his own government.

But in the nineteenth century, within the framework of protection from the government, developments arose significant to religion in two areas of concern. Antecedently, education had been the privilege or responsibility of the church, and social welfare too was its prerogative. But about 1840, there began slowly, but steadily, that development wherein the state undertook the responsibility for education and for social welfare, and thereby reduced the ambit in which a church, a local church or a national church, could operate.

Along with the reduction in the ambit of the church, and the decline of such traditional views as the divine right of kings and the special prerogatives of the church, there came to the fore what we might call modern secular culture. Within this culture, religion, by and large, has been held to be the prerogative of the private choice of the individual.

Accordingly, when my father, or your fathers or your grandfathers or great-grandfathers, came to this country in the nineteenth and early twentieth centuries, they came from a situation of isolation and religious fervor into one in which the religious scene was not only one of great chaos as between Catholics and Protestants, or Protestants and Protestants, or between Protestant modernists and Protestant fundamentalists but, moreover, one in which the tone of the country was officially indifferent to religion. Indeed, in many great universities religion was held in amused contempt. The only true place for religion was in the privacy of individual conviction; corporate religion became a trespass against man's freedom.

Jews came to the United States in numbers, often settling together and recapitulating facsimiles of European institutions, but sending their children to the public schools and universities, where they began to imbibe the atmosphere of the land with its broad indifference to religion, its relegation of religion to the private conscience, and even to the slight contempt in which religion was held in university circles.

The intellectual challenge to the truths of Christianity, by then already well established, came now to be transferred to Judaism. Our youngsters attend university courses in which the unhistorical character of the Gospels is taught, and in which the Mosaic authorship and the supernatural origin of the Pentateuch are no longer accepted. I think the fact must be faced squarely that religious challenges to American Jews would have been more tremendous than they have been were it not for the circumstance that enduring social lags kept us together as a community. I have in mind, for example, that abomination—the college fraternity. I belonged to one, so I know what I am talking about. The Jewish college fraternity, at least until about twenty-five years ago, epitomized a campus divided into Christians and Jews, at the same time that the intellectual aspects of the university denied the validity of both Christianity and Judaism. The Jewish youngster went to college looking for the great universals, and was forced into a Jewish college fraternity. And the Jewish college fraternity that I belonged to distinguished itself on the affirmative side by having Christmas and Easter parties and, on the negative side, by a regulation that no more than two Jewish girls could be invited to the local chapter's dances.

Moreover, the paradox of the supposition of intellectual and religious freedom, on the one hand, and the emergence of racial anti-Semitism in nineteenth- and twentieth-century Europe, on the other hand, besides being clearly tragic, is also one of the most ironic outcomes in all history. The universities had shattered the theological claims of Christians and Jews and, at the same time, society created its enforced congregations, if not segregation, which in Europe led to the most extreme persecution we have ever been subjected to in all of history.

But let us try, for our purposes, to set aside the sociological factor. If you ask how we can do so, how we can set it aside, the only answer I can give you is that in the generation after Hitler's time, our youngsters are often even more extreme theoretical universalists than we were before Hitler's time, as witness the rapid growth of intermarriage. If we set aside the sociological factor, our religious problem has been something of this kind: How can we create a persuasive synthesis between the values and the practices that we inherit from our traditional Judaism and the naturalistic, secular culture of our age? Though the sociological factors affecting Jews are different from those affecting Christians, by and large, the purely religious problems are similar to the point of being identical. The problem can be put as the tension between the assertions of a revealed religion as over against the contentions of a secularized intellectual tradition. This is our inner religious problem.

As to our external questions, our problem with Christians is both historical and theological. The historical problem in most of our minds looms as the reality of the persecutions of the past, which persecutions came from Christians and was justified on a Christian basis. But in nineteenth-century Europe persecution took the turn of being "racial" rather than religious. In the Western world, for all intents and purposes, religious persecution by Christians has disappeared. Persecution has been carried on by Gentiles, non-Jews, no longer by Christians as Christians. The abiding question between Jews and Christians can be put in this way: What can the relation of the traditions be to each other today, in view of the fact that one was born within the other, but ceased to be a part of it and, indeed, became an independent entity and an even larger entity?

Can we Jews and Christians, in trying to understand each other, and putting persecution off of the agenda as now it should be, come to some terms with this matter of history—that Christianity was originally a Judaism and then ceased to be?

It is this issue, of the Jewish birth of Christianity, that is the most formidable problem in our understanding each other. Indeed, the problem of understanding each other is so acute just because we share so much in common. The question of Jesus is one we do not share in common, and I think that this is the matter in which we have the greatest clarity, for, by and large, we Jews and Christians, if we know anything, know where we respectively stand. But it is in other areas, for example, in the common possession of what we call Bible and Christians call Old Testament, that we have difficulty in comprehending each other. Moreover, for most of us Jews, it is virtually impossible to understand certain facets of the teachings of Paul, whose teachings have come to dominate and to shape various facets of Protestantism. I have in mind here the circumstance that by and large our Judaism is based on what we Jews call *mitzvot*—obligations of things to do and things to abstain from.

The term that Paul uses for these religious precepts is "works," and it is his contention that the "works" that a man does are irrelevant to a man's righteousness. For him, righteousness is a matter of complete submission to God, for which Paul uses the term "faith." You will recall that Paul and subsequent Christianity abolished the Mosaic laws; we see the effect of this today in the circumstance that a Christian religious calendar does not conform with the calendar in the Pentateuch to which we Jews still adhere. Moreover, we Jews, in principle though often not in practice, still observe the dietary laws, or our own revision of them, whereas in principle the dietary laws as part of the Mosaic laws have disappeared from Christianity.

The point is that our Judaism is premised on the constant refinement of the meaning of the *mitzvot,* whereas the Pauline aspect of Christianity was premised on the irrelevancy of the totality of the *mitzvot,* and the contention that the Laws are no less than an impediment to righteousness.

Still another factor respecting understanding is that our inherited Judaism matured in Palestine and in Babylon to the east, whereas Christianity matured in the Greco-Roman world. Our two traditions inherit many common terms, but understand these terms in quite different ways. Jews and Christians do not mean precisely the same thing by sin or righteousness or salvation. On the very lowest level, understanding is very difficult. Appreciation, which can only come after understanding, is blocked by the formidable difficulty of mere understanding. In still a different dimension, Christians have normally assumed that Christianity represents a kind of reformation of Judaism, which reformation refined it and improved it, with the result that Christianity is, in substance, superior to Judaism. And this note of triumphalism is countered from our side by our contention that our Judaism is quite superior to Christianity and much "purer."

From still an additional standpoint, there are the aspects of the tone and character of religions to consider. For example, Christianity historically has been marked by a strong internal organization as is evidenced still today by the Roman Catholic Church, by officials with universal authority, and by bishops who in convened assemblies called "church councils" can make decisions on divisive religious matters, and distinguish between orthodoxy and heresy, and formulate the meaning of these distinctions by the discipline known as theology.

We Jews have lacked such an internal organization. We have lacked such officials. We have had no obligatory creeds as such, and no universal theories of orthodoxy or heresy, and we have had no bent for dogmatic theology until the last fifteen or twenty years.

You can understand best what I am saying along this line if you and I could suppose what is not true, namely, that there was absolutely no tension between Christian communities and Jewish communities, or between Christian individuals and Jewish individuals. Even if this were the case, as it is not, there would still be tremendous obstacles in the way of our understanding each other, and of our appreciating each other. It is paradoxical that religiously we face common problems, and we should be aware that religiously we are stirred by the same waves, or threatened with extinction by the same high winds that raise waves the size of mountains.

But even so, understanding is difficult. I would guess, for example, that Christians can understand Zionism and the State of Israel only in terms of persecution and a place of refuge, and almost never in the affirmative aspects that are repeated in so much of our sacred Jewish literature. The reason for their inability to understand is that it is normal for people to view other aspects of society from their own standpoints. Since Christians have no such thing as a religious tie to an ancestral land, they assume that our religion, like theirs, should be without such ties.

I would imagine that there are, in this community, dozens of instances in which individual Jews and individual Christians have come to a point of deep and responsible personal friendship. I do not think it overstates the case to say that profound personal understanding between individuals has taken place, even though the Jewish and the Christian factor in that friendship remains mysterious and unexplored, or else intuitive, and basically incorrect with respect to the facts, the doctrines, and the respective traditions.

Indeed how can religious understanding take place in view of the complexity in our day of the labels in which a Christian may be a Roman Catholic, Eastern Orthodox, Southern Baptist, or a modernist Congregationalist, and a Jew may be strictly Orthodox, nominally Orthodox, right-wing Conservative, left-wing Conservative, right-wing Reform, or left-wing Reform?

There are those who raise the question: Why try at all to understand each other? There are those who assert that we may have common social responsibilities with Christians, as in the matter of integration, or the Vietnam war, but they assert that there is no possibility of any theological common ground.

I recognize, and respectfully, those who see in the search for theological understanding a threat to the integrity of the Jewish community and who feel that the search will lead to an increased erosion from the Jewish community. I do not know of any adequate philosophical or ideological response to such reservations. I know only this, that in the United States the day-to-day contacts in varying measure bring about associations and relations, and a private but widespread search is taking place, and to say that it should not take place is to deny what is taking place.

To my mind, there is greater danger in sweeping the issue under the carpet than there is in recognizing the existence of the issue. There still exists, on both the Christian and the Jewish sides, great measures of suspicion and of triumphal arrogance and contempt. Both sides feel themselves participants in something that is superior to what the other has, and, by implication, that the person born into the one tradition is inherently superior to the person born into the other tradition. I also know that our youngsters on both sides challenge these assertions of superiority, and I get the impression that when they encounter them, their mood comes to be this: a plague on both your houses.

In my own thinking, when I ponder the Jewish religion and modern thought, I find myself driven more to the question of values, and to abiding values and or relevant values, much more than to the usual recurrent questions of theology, or theological uniqueness, or theological correctness. I find myself oppressed by the question: What are the verities by which one lives? And, what are the verities that one transmits to his children? And what are the standards by which we ourselves should live and rear our children? To my mind, it is quite possible for us American Jews to maintain our American Jewish community with its efficient organizations and its effectiveness in the mechanics of fund raising, and still fail to discover or fail to perpetuate values that inhere in life and in living.

The fact is, I am appalled by the rise in our time of the assertion that there are no values, and that the self-preservation of the individual is the only legitimate criterion. And that the only interest one should have is self-interest, and that institutions are phony, schools are phony, governments are phony, universities are phony, parents are phony, and everything is phony.

In my own thinking, I take this doctrine of phoniness to be Gentile (pagan). I cannot take it to be Jewish. I cannot take it to be Christian. I see in each tradition, in the struggle for theological certainty and the quest for definition or redefinition of religion, in the tenacity in which the religions have tried to hold onto the past, an aggregate of values, or rather, two aggregates of values, often identical, often similar, often dissimilar, but at least some aggregates of values.

I am aware of all the trespasses of organized religion in the past. At the same time, I see very little future for mankind except in the abiding verities that are resident in religious tradition.

Perhaps this is the point at which Jews and Christians share the most. Perhaps this is the point at which our collaboration and our cooperation is the most viable. Perhaps this is the point which is the most significant and important. When we think of a world in upheaval, wherein there has been a transition from the freedom of man from his government to the contention that the government must now provide for man, and provide economically, then we can understand that we incline to a social-welfare state which returns to the government certain prerogatives which in the eighteenth century we tried to take away from the government. In our day we are beset by vertical currents and lateral currents, so that we need to intensify freedom within the state, and yet we face in the twentieth century the need to be free from alien domination, from conquest.

And add to this upheaval the computer age and all that the phrase implies, then the question of living is this, what are the values you live with? And how do you make these values living reality?

I have written a half-dozen times (because I believe it so earnestly) that I believe whole-heartedly in cooperation with and collaboration with Christians, but always with a proviso, namely, that we Jews do not go more than 50 percent of the way. I am opposed to going 51 percent of the way. I am opposed to Christian-Jewish cooperation if it means that Jews for its sake must become obsequious or curry Christian favor. The dignity of equality seems to me a necessary prerequisite in Christian-Jewish collaboration. We and the Christians are in the same boat religiously; religiously, we will steer either a common boat to some haven together or else our boat will capsize and we will drown in each other's company.

But I do not want to end on this note. I want to end on a totally different note because I believe circumstances require it. A hundred years ago you would never have had Jews and Christians trying to understand each other. Let me attest publicly to the earnestness I see among Roman Catholics to try to understand Jews and to try to understand themselves. A hundred years ago this would not have happened.

Let me comment that the upheavals that we are going through with respect to the race problem in the United States, the upheavals that go on within Africa, the social forces which tend to plunge us deeper into tremendous difficulties—these are products of the long shadow that the vision of freedom in the eighteenth century conveyed to man.

We are now trying to work out these freedoms as human beings are wont to do. Any one of us could, on paper, draw up a plan whereby in the next five to fifteen years every black is going to have two chickens in the basket and two cars in the garage, and every colonial state in Africa is going to settle its internal difficulties, and we are going to come to an understanding of the Western world with the East, across the Iron Curtain. Oh, you can do this on paper easily.

But men do not work that way. Men work through trial and error, through mistake and retrogression. But do you know what happens? They do progress. They do move forward. Not easily, not readily. But they do move.

If you think that ours is an age of upheaval, it is an upheaval because we are now confronted with implementing an eighteenth-century vision, a vision that then delusively seemed to be near to reality. Now we will not settle for anything less than the reality itself.

Our unsettling problems come from our progress, and our progress has not ended.

7

The Husk and the Kernel *

IT SHOULD NOT be forgotten about Isaac Mayer Wise and Stephen S. Wise that each was primarily the rabbi of a congregation. The lasting contribution of these respective founders of the Cincinnati and New York Schools of the Hebrew Union College—Jewish Institute of Religion is to be discerned as clearly in their influence on people in their congregations as in the great educational institutions that they founded. Indeed, they founded the educational institutions primarily in order that men could be trained to serve as congregational rabbis.

The earlier Wise, by circumstance more of a pioneer than the later one, dominated a conviction of his which made his founding of a rabbinic school of importance quite beyond the mere founding itself. It was his conviction that Judaism in its essence was of tremendous and continuing validity—and that it had to be transmitted—and that the Jews of America needed it transmitted to them. The only way it could be transmitted, from his standpoint, was to create on these shores a school to train native-born scholars, trained in this country to be rabbis, who would minister to the needs of American Jews. As reformers went in his time, he was relatively moderate. His loyalty to the Jewish past could not have been greater. His concern for

* This paper is adapted from an address given on March 25, 1966, Founders' Day, as part of the participation of the Hebrew Union College in the 100th Anniversary of the Plum Street Temple in Cincinnati. Rabbi Isaac Mayer Wise, when Rabbi of the Plum Street Temple, had become the leading figure in the founding of the Hebrew Union College, in 1875. Rabbi Stephen S. Wise had founded the Jewish Institute of Religion in 1922. They were merged into a single institution in 1950. The address was mimeographed; it has not previously been published.

his age, for the Jews of his time, could not have been greater. His solicitude for Jews in subsequent ages could not have been more acute.

In the immediate years after Isaac Mayer Wise's death, around the turn of the century, there was a period of time in which his disciples revered him and spoke of him in such terms of adulation that there was bound to ensue a period in which he would be reassessed; this reassessment, if we may call it that, came in the late 1910s and in the early 1920s. At that time, it was "discovered" by some that Isaac Mayer Wise had been preeminently no more than a great organizer. That he was a great organizer is true; that he was preeminently an organizer is false. The several institutions that he founded were all motivated by one purpose, to strip away those accretions to Judaism which he regarded as not worthy of perpetuation or not capable of it, in order that the core of a pure Judaism would be the more readily discernible. He saw things in terms of the husk which needed cutting away so that the kernel could be better seen. He had the conviction that American Jews would readily recognize this kernel, this core, and would regard it with the same preciousness that he did and would readily acquiesce in his program to perpetuate it. So certain was he of what was precious in his inherited Judaism that he made the prediction around 1875—it seems fantastic to us today —that within twenty-five years, all of the United States would become converted to Reform Judaism. He wanted this to come about because he loved Judaism. He wanted it because he wanted Jews of his time to love it.

Isaac Mayer Wise was, indeed, a moderate reformer, yet there were times when he could go to extremes. Sometimes those of us who have occasion to read his writings wince a little when we read what he wrote about the Talmud in preposterous disparagement of that book. Nevertheless, as a reformer, he was still a moderate. He wanted the synagogue service to be free of any barrier between the worshipper and the service. He wanted the service to be so pure that nothing would mar it, nothing blemish it. Behind him, in his native Bohemia, lay his recollection of the traditional synagogue.

A key word in Reform-Orthodox debates a hundred years ago was the word "decorum"; in the traditional synagogue in those days there was no decorum as we today understand it. Each person prayed his prayers in his own singsong, at his own tempo, and in as loud or soft a voice as he wished. People visited around the synagogue—they felt at home there!—while the service went on, and it was not unusual for one man to walk across the synagogue to converse with another. From the standpoint of Isaac

Mayer Wise and the reformers of his time this represented a complete lack of decorum. Moreover, Wise felt that the sanctity of the service was being destroyed by the practice of selling the privileges of the synagogue by auction. Let me say in explanation that in the traditional synagogue, seven men are called upon to recite blessings during the Torah reading and the seven usually gained the right by outbidding fellow-worshippers; first, however, the synagogue service had to be interrupted for the auction to be held. When the persons who had bought the right (to be paid after the Sabbath was over) would come to the *bimah,* then a prayer acknowledging the "contribution" would be recited; East European Jews called this prayer the *misheberach,* from its first word; German Jews called it, after a word in the middle of it, the *shenodar* meaning "pledged," that is, the successful bidder pledged to pay the amount stipulated in the auction. Reformers like Isaac M. Wise thought it was necessary to get rid of the auction sale of synagogue privileges.

But as Reform came to develop, congregational participation diminished or disappeared as the sale of the privileges diminished or ended. One of the direct by-products of the diminution of the role of the congregants was what we might call the centralization of the rabbi in the synagogue. This was a change of tremendous significance from what the synagogue had been antecedently, and from what the rabbi had been antecedently. It comes as a shock to many American Jews to learn that the medieval synagogue seldom had a rabbi, and that when it had a rabbi, he was not a synagogue official. The rabbi was a layman, a businessman or a merchant, and he was rabbi only by virtue of his learning; the procedures in the synagogue, the "working" as it were, of the synagogue, was carried on by Tom, Dick, and Harry. Indeed, there are some documents that have come down from the Polish ghetto that allege that certain rabbis so scorned the common people that they stayed away from services, preferring private devotions to the public ones. In our day, so central has the rabbi become that it is he who reads the service, who preaches the sermon, who officiates at the wedding, who officiates at the funeral.

This extreme centrality of the rabbi represents something relatively new, relatively young in Jewish life. In part, it has been a great blessing; in part it has had some untoward effects which require our looking into.

It has not been good for congregational life for the rabbi to be the center of congregational life. The rabbi ought to be the resource person, the man of education, of learning and of wisdom. He was always that. He must continue to be that. When the rabbi becomes diverted, as is happening in a growing number of congregations in our day, into being not only the center of the congregational life, but also the executive director of the congregation, then things have gone in an improper direction.

Synagogues have now become places of activities, and the rabbi tends to become the entrepreneur who plans and executes these activities. These activities are worthwhile; their execution is necessary. Moreover, the work of people in the synagogue needs guidance. But for these particular responsibilities to replace the traditional responsibility of the rabbi to be the student, to be the scholar, to be the man of learning who conveys to the present the insights of the past, is something which we need to lament.

If we did not need to lament it, merely on its own basis, then we need to be honest and discern a derived and untoward effect, which is discernible again in the example of the *shenodar*. It was admirable to eliminate the unseemly *shenodar*. There was needed in its place some substitute form of income by which the synagogue would be maintained. Here American Reform Jews made a unique contribution to synagogue life: the annual dues, with bills submitted either annually, or quarterly, or monthly. Whereas antecedently, in the synagogue where there was no decorum, people made their financial contributions by purchasing the right to participate, the way now became open for a membership which could be primarily fiscal, and largely not participatory. Nobody planned it this way, and we must not cast scorn on those who brought about this arrangement, for it had its worthy purpose and was motivated by an objective that we can applaud. Yet out of this financial alteration some things have gone very much astray. Thus, in some parts of our country the relationship between rabbi and congregation has ceased to be a spiritual bond, but has become a contractual relationship, as in business, with terms and conditions and salary specified on paper and duly signed. With the ascendancy of the business spirit, from time to time an assessment is made of a rabbi, not on the basis of his learning or his piety or his dedication to Judaism, but rather on his effectiveness as an entrepreneur in congregational activities.

We are a generation who responded to Arthur Miller's *Death of a Salesman* and lamented the condition of Willie Loman, whose highest ideal was to be liked. Yet we rabbis have partially acquiesced in an arrangement in which the criterion for us too, is, Are we liked? The criterion is not, Do we stand for an educated Judaism, for a noble Judaism, for an exalted though risky Judaism?—but, Are we liked?

Our Reform forebears devoted themselves to planning and they created great institutions. Yet, if we are true to them, then we must ask in our day, in the same way that Isaac Mayer Wise asked in his day, whether our inherited Reform institutions have not again become the husk that conceals the kernel. Nobody sat down to plan that congregations in our time should number as many as 3,000 members, or 2,000 members, or 1,500 members. But what rabbi can serve this many people as a *rabbi*? In Isaac Mayer Wise's day the congregation was small, the people were homogeneous, they lived near each other, the rabbi knew everyone in the congregation. Today, not only does the rabbi not know many people in the congregation, but I have been present at homes when there has been present both a rabbi and his congregant, and previously the two have not known each other.

Where now, in an array of activities and organizations within the congregation administered by a variegated staff, is the essence, where is this purified Judaism that was so precious that it was necessary to form a seminary to preserve it, to form a union of congregations to foster the seminary? What happens to the essence, what happens to the learning? Is the rabbi, on graduating from our school, where he gets only a limited introduction to Judaism, to content himself with that introduction, or is he to go on and study? Is he to be so busy with Rotary or Red Cross, or the library, or the symphony society—all worthwhile things—that he ceases to be the representative of this noble tradition to which he has dedicated himself? Are we not, in our time, if we do not begin to examine our values, in danger of creating or hardening still another shell, still another exterior?

The exterior can seem to flourish. The synagogue can be busy and the rabbi can be busy, and rabbis in our time can work morning, noon, and night, tirelessly. But in what context and in what direction? Activity for the sake of activity? Program for the sake of program? Does the congregation get the full heft of the rabbi's learning and do the congregants receive from the rabbi that which he is able to give, eager to give, when we grow so large that our worship services come to be attended by a pathetically small number of those who fiscally maintain our institutions?

We got into this situation in good faith. We did not mean to; we did not plan to. It is a fact, though, that we have gotten into it. I fear that unless we revert in our thinking to what the rabbinate used to be, and move back in that direction, we shall find ourselves some day perilously close to spiritual bankruptcy.

The ancient rabbi did not struggle for time to study; it was his obligation to study. He was a rabbi by virtue of what he knew, not what he did. He was a rabbi by virtue of his expertness, not by virtue of having spent a certain obligatory number of years in a seminary. He was a man of piety because he took the leisure to cultivate piety, and he was a man of influence because his life was so unmistakably sacred, his identity so specific, his dedication so manifest, that he was someone to whom a person could turn, aware that the rabbi represented both learning and wisdom.

We must restore these as ideals. Indeed, at some time we will need the courage to reorganize our congregations so that a rabbi can be a rabbi to the number of people a man can be a rabbi to, so that our pepole can be taught by rabbis, and influenced by rabbis, and catch from rabbis some reflection of what it is that we see in Judaism which prompts us to become and remain rabbis. Here is the most urgent change that is needed in our American Jewish life. I trust it is clear that I am not speaking about mere pedantic scholarship, dry-as-dust book learning. I am not. I am speaking of rabbinic learning in the sense that learning must be humanistic, susceptible of relevancy to people. It must be exact, it must be profound, but it must be related.

We lose our calling when we become diverted into areas other than the spiritual life. I am not here deploring our concern with material life. We need this concern. Certainly rabbis have always been concerned with it. But rabbis were concerned with poverty, and with *tzedoko* (charity), because they recognized that the absence of a means of subsistence impeded the spiritual life. But only as we are able to recapture the vision of Isaac Mayer Wise of an educated rabbinate, of a rabbinate ever deepened in its spiritual dedication, and to refashion our congregational life to make it a living reality of the relationship of rabbi and congregant, is there any true hope for a creative Judaism in the future.

As Americans, we have an abundance of know-how. But know-how for what? From time to time the proposal is made that the curriculum of the Hebrew Union College reduce its academic aspect and increase its courses in "know-how." I can think of nothing that would be more to be lamented or a greater misdirection. No, what our age is going to need is better educated rabbis, congregations that understand better what a rabbi is, and congregations which support him in rabbinic functions of study and teaching, in the rabbinic concern with the essence of our religion and not with the external mechanics.

I am one of those who has read every book that Isaac Mayer Wise wrote that appeared in separate publication. Some of his books appeared only in *The American Israelite,* and while I have not read every past issue of *The American Israelite,* I have read most of them. I have written about Issac Mayer Wise (see Chapter 18, this volume); in his own way, he was a predecessor of mine in that he was the first American Jew to take early Christianity seriously. He began a book that he never finished entitled "Jesus Himself," a biography. I believe I correctly reflect Issac Mayer Wise in saying that it is necessary to restore congregational participation, to restore a living, throbbing Judaism, and to let the rabbi revert again to being essentially the man of learning and the man of wisdom. Organizer as Isaac Mayer Wise was, traveller as he had to be, he never lost sight of the rabbi in terms of the spiritual life of the congregation. This is the rabbinic image that it seems to me our people are yearning for. We rabbis, in the preachments we make, by the elections we make, in the decisions we make, need to be aware of what hangs in the balance: whether we in the present and in the future can recreate a thriving, vibrant, religious Judaism, or whether we will be content with a new shell, a new external. Can we muster within ourselves the resources to renew, to rededicate, to restore the rabbinate?

8

Jewish and Catholic Biblical Scholarship *

I T SEEMS TO ME that an assessment of Jewish and Catholic biblical scholarship can possibly be approached by dividing it into four parts and then adding a conclusion. Any such division implies a neatness of separation which cannot be completely justified; yet unless our material is arranged so that its great bulk does not dismay us, I know of no way in which we can focus our attention on the topic. In addition, I shall need to consider Protestant biblical scholarship indicating a motif there which is relatively absent from both Catholic and Jewish scholarship. I should want to make it clear that I shall be describing Protestant scholarship and not de-valuating it, for my attitude toward Protestant biblical scholarship is one of high admiration, even though I believe its initial impulse differentiates it from the Jewish and the Catholic.

My task would be easier and somewhat fresher if I thought I could as-sume the common possession of most of the facts, and could thereby limit myself strictly to interpretation. I do not think that I can do that. Let me assume that my task involves the wish to try to interpret Jewish biblical scholarship to Catholics and Catholic biblical scholarship to Jews.

Let me begin with the first part, which I shall label "Understanding" and the "Body of Interpretation," for herein is a chief clue to an approach among Jews and Catholics which is somewhat analogous. With this double rubric in mind, let us look first at the Jewish aspect.

* This paper was read at a symposium at St. Vincent's Archabbey, Latrobe, Pennsyl-vania. It appeared in *Torah and Gospel*, Philip Scharper, ed. (New York, 1966), pp. 63–79.

What shall we say is the difference, if any, between understanding and interpretation? On the first level, there is this distinction, that when an ancient text is found in one language and the vernacular used by a student is in a different language, translation is first needed for simple and bare comprehension. Let us then reserve "understanding" to connote "bare comprehension," such as is implied by translation. Thus, when Jews in Palestine ceased to use Hebrew as their spoken language and the language of mundane affairs, they had to deal with the translation of Scripture before they could arrive at an interpretation. By "interpretation," on the other hand, I would allude to that stage which comes after understanding, that stage which raises the question of the implication of that which is understood, or which causes the inferences to be drawn from that which is understood, or which transfers the understanding of the ancient by application to the contemporaneous situation.

There is an inherent, but demonstrable process in respect to a literature which is deemed sacred, whereby when understanding has developed into interpretation, then the reverse process can take place, with the consequence that interpretation thereafter comes to be the understanding. To illustrate this by an example, the half-verse Genesis 4:26b reads in the Hebrew, in respect to Enos whom Jews call Enosh, "then there began the calling upon the name of the Lord." Involved in the matter of the understanding of that passage is the Hebrew word which yields the root "to begin." Identical with this root, "to begin," is another Hebrew root which means "to profane." Related to these two roots is still another Hebrew root, *yahal,* which means "to await" or "to hope." Involved in understanding the passage is the need to determine which of these three root meanings is the appropriate one for the passage, and thereafter to supply a grammatical explanation of the particular form, *huhal,* so as to buttress the understanding by the aid of the grammar. Since one cannot have a word-for-word correspondence in a translation, allow me to translate this passage into idiomatic English: "Then man began to call upon the name of the Lord." This rendering is to be found in most translations. The question then arises: Why is it that in the ancient versions the text is translated in a variety of different ways? The Aramaic translation, called the Targum, renders it, "Then man *profaned* the name of God." The Greek rendering is, "This one *hoped* to call on the name of God." When the rendering is "profane" or "hope," are we in the area of understanding or in the area of interpretation? It is my opinion that we are in the area of interpretation. For, although the Hebrew verse contains no difficulty in itself, its implication does contain a difficulty, since the developing, interpretive tradition, even in very early times, attributed to Father Abraham the momentous discovery of the existence of God. Our half-verse, in seeming to ascribe the discovery to Enos, stands in apparent conflict with that broadly accepted theme, and each of the two ancient translations which I have cited contains an interpretation designed to divert the sense from the natural, and to make it conform with the broad and almost universal motif of Abraham's priority. Among the traditional Jewish interpreters and commentators on this half-verse, there is to be found an agreement that the verse meant literally that man profaned God's name. What I am contending is that when this conclusion arises, understanding has given way to interpretation, and interpretation in turn has come to affect understanding. That is, the Jewish understanding of the verse was the direct result of the interpretation of it.

A body of interpretive material is a conflation of the multiple instances in which a text, either uncertain or having a specific implication, comes to acquire a widely agreed upon meaning. Somewhat analogously, to cite two more well-known instances, an "eye for an eye and a tooth for a tooth" means, in the body of Jewish interpretive material, monetary punishment, not the literal, physical eye for an eye. The passage "Thou shalt not seethe the kid in its mother's milk" came to imply to Jews that they should make a dietary separation between meat dishes and milk dishes.

Once there arises a body of interpretive material which is transmitted from generation to generation, and which carries over into preaching and into the schools, then the interpretation becomes interchangeable with the understanding. In this sense the growth of a body of interpretive material becomes the clue to how a tradition understands its sacred text. But the next question must then be asked respecting this process whereby understanding becomes interpretation and interpretation becomes understanding: Wherein can there lie certain controls against caprice and against the farfetched? The answer would appear to lie in the observation that that process of making the ancient relevant to the contemporaneous carries in itself the inherent danger that the contemporaneous may distort, rather than elucidate and amplify. Accordingly, the ancient Jewish literature tells us about rules of interpretation formulated successively by Hillel and Ishmael, and then by others. These formulations not only give legitimacy to particular hermeneutic principles, but also, by giving legitimacy to particular ones, imply illegitimacy in others. We are somewhat in the dark about those which are implicitly illegitimate, but there are some stray clues to certain types of extreme interpretations in the form of allusions in rabbinic literature to "interpreters of difficult things and interpreters of 'closed-up things.' " It is conventional to explain these allusions as involving extreme allegorists and their unrestrained allegorical interpretation.

The ancient Jewish rabbinic writings contain a few allegories, and Josephus, who reflects a good bit of the rabbinic interpretive material, provides us with still others; but to know the full weight of the allegorical, we must turn to Philo of Alexandria. In Philo, a very apt student of Plato and the Stoics, allegory is the interpretive device whereby Plato and the Stoics intrude into the context of Scripture. Thus, Adam is mind, Eve is sense perception, and the Serpent is pleasure, so that when mind and sense perception become bent on pleasure, they lose the virtue of the Garden of Eden, from which four rivers flow—those four rivers being the four Stoic cardinal virtues. To cite another example, Cain is the man with poor arguments and fluent speech, and Abel the man with excellent arguments but halting speech; in this contest, the fluent always kills the halting.

So completely alien is Philo's body of allegoric interpretation to rabbinic interpretation that scarcely one reflection of this content is to be found in rabbinic literature. One might, from the standpoint of rabbinic interpretation, rule Philo to be illegitimate and classify him with the disqualified interpreters. Yet Philo himself speaks in a number of passages of "canons of allegory" as if to imply that even in his environment certain controls were needed. Philo, however, never directly states what these canons were. The only regulation that seems to me to operate in his case is this—that the allegorical quantity which he ascribes to a biblical character seems to be derived from the supposed etymology of the Hebrew name of that character. Thus "Abram," prior to the change of his name, means "lofty father" and implies that the patriarch, at that stage in his career, was a meteorologist— that is to say, an astrologer. When Abraham's name is changed (in the Greek the change of Abraham's name involves only the addition of an *alpha*), the name *Avraham,* Abraham, means "elect father of sound." In

Philo's interpretation, "elect" has to do with the circumstantial fact that Abraham had done nothing prior to God's call of him to justify God's call, which is to say that Abraham was either predestined or simply chosen. As for "sound," speech is the fallible brother of thought, and this whole allusion in Abraham's name is to Abraham's embarkation on introspective dialectics by means of which he moved from faulty thought to proper reason and arrived at the discovery of the existence of God. "Father" alludes to his capacity to order his mind and his reason. We have the paradox in Philo, on the one hand, that apparently his allegorical ascription of quantities comes from the Hebrew meanings of the names, and, on the other hand, he can be so elastic about the Hebrew meanings that one wonders just what limitation he might have seen in them!

The ancient rabbinic tradition was itself aware of modes of interpretation, as distinct from rules, and these modes included those in which the literal was, as it were, departed from. The four Hebrew consonants which make up the word *Pardes,* "garden," allude to four types of exegesis. The *P* stands for *pshat,* which means literal; the *R* for *remez,* which means that which is hinted at in the text, that is to say, an interpretation which is not devoid of some bond to the text. The *D* yields *drush,* which means that which is sought into, or possibly sought for, namely, an interpretation which would not arise immediately but which on inquiry might emerge; and the *S* stands for *sod,* which means secret, esoteric, and possibly alludes to a mystic type of interpretation. By and large, this mystic bent, insofar as it occurs in the Jewish tradition, is an embellishment of the three preceding ones and not a substitute for them; it exists side by side, but does not supplant the textually bound interpretation.

The implication of interpretation, and of controls on interpretation, and of the transmission of the interpretations controlled in this sense, means that from its scriptural side the rabbinic literature is a vast repository of scriptural exegesis. That early body of Jewish lore, called the Mishnah, consists of inferences drawn from Scripture, these stated laconically; in almost all cases, the succinct statement abstains from supplying the scriptural basis. The clarifying commentary on the Mishnah, called the Gemara, necessarily raises in its discussion the question of the Scriptural basis for the mishnaic statement; it therefore portrays this sage or that sage in the act of suggesting what the scriptural basis could be. Sometimes these sages, agreeing on the mishnaic utterance, disagreed on what might be the scriptural verse that justified it, for each could suggest what seemed to him a more likely source. So voluminous is the Gemara and so thoroughly quoted is Scripture that I would rather doubt that there are many Pentateuchal passages which do not appear in some form in the rabbinic literature. If one abstained from studying Scripture but studied only the rabbinic literature, he would coincidentally absorb a great deal of Scripture. But the Scripture that he would absorb would be the Scripture as this growing literature interpreted it and thereby understood it.

A definition which I might, therefore, give of the Jewish Bible is that the Jewish Bible is the Bible as understood and interpreted by Jews throughout the ages. Although I teach a course in Philo, I try to make it clear that Philo represents a unique instance of a body of Jewish interpretation of a tangential nature which had no permanent sequel in the unfolding Jewish tradition. The Jewish Bible is the Bible, the understanding of which has sequels down to our own time.

The Jewish Bible is, therefore, not Scripture in its pristine meaning, but Scripture as expounded in the Jewish tradition. It is true that in the Spanish-Jewish period there arose philologians who made inquiries into the plain and simple meaning of Scripture; their academic achievements, perpetuated through humanism and the Christian Hebraists, make their way into the commentaries of our day that are the most complete and the most incisive. Yet these excursions into the literal, as exemplified by Abraham Ibn Ezra or David Kimchi, did not lead to the discarding of the traditional interpretation. We see this most clearly in the case of the French rabbi, Rashi, who composed a commentary for virtually all of the thirty-nine books of the Hebrew Bible (or twenty-four if you want to use the traditional Jewish count). What is distinctive about Rashi's commentary is his ability to give for each verse, phrase, or word in the text the quintessence of the interpretation which lies in the voluminous rabbinic literature. Rashi is seldom original; his greatness lies in his ability to compress the content of a tremendous range of information which was at his fingertips to compress. In many passages Rashi simply quotes a few biblical words and then suggests that the literal meaning is the plain and simple meaning; but then he goes on to give the traditional Jewish understanding of that phrase.

Neither the Ibn Ezras nor the Kimchis nor the Rashis saw any direct tension between the literal and the interpretive, for the living Scripture to them was a combination of both, and especially of the latter. Side by side with the ancient rabbinic writings called the Mishnah and Gemara, which together comprise the Talmud, there was a body of writings called the

Midrash. The Midrash alludes to that body of traditional Jewish interpretation arranged according to the sequence of the verses. The content of this interpretation parallels and is often exactly identical with talmudic interpretation, for the distinction is preeminently that of arrangement, and not of content. In the Talmud, the citation of the verse depends upon context; the Midrash, however, is a verse by verse commentary, somewhat as if the talmudic interpretations were culled from it and arranged in the verse by verse order, or else the talmudic cited from the Midrash. When we speak of the Midrash Rabbah, we ordinarily have in mind the five exhortatory and edifying commentaries to the Pentateuch, as distinct from older midrashic commentaries called halakic, which were primarily legalistic. The Talmud and the Midrash, then, are in a real sense the body of interpretive Jewish material about Scripture, and they constitute the eyes through which Jews looked at Scripture. They are the body of what I might call "overmeanings."

Overmeaning supplants plain meaning; overmeaning implies contemporaneity, namely, a living and growing body of interpretation. Contemporaneity might be understood as the opposite of the pristine meaning.

Quite analogously, the Christian tradition developed its own body of interpretive material. The analogues with the rabbinic material are more those of form, naturally, than they are of content. They are also the product of the circumstance that, by and large, Christianity ceased to use the Hebrew and instead relied upon the Greek. The Letter of Aristeas, or as some prefer to call it, Pseudo-Aristeas, which deals with the supposed origin of the Septuagint, is significant in making the point that so accurate and responsible a translation was the Greek version that it is the equal of the Hebrew in its inspiration and in its reliability. There are, of course, an Origen and a Jerome who, as great scholars and academicians, make detailed inquiry into the writings to be reassured that the translation was equally eminent with the Hebrew original, but there are also Clement and Origen handling New Testament materials allegorically whenever the inner problems seem acute enough. To a later generation, the allegorical interpretation always seems outmoded, and hence it is normal for the allegorists of one generation to recede in significance as the generations go on. The Christian overmeanings include elements as diverse as the conviction about the original sense of the Hebrew of Isaiah 7:14, about which Jews and Christians quarreled, and in more recent times Christians among themselves have quarreled; also included are those passages in the Gospels in which the sisters and brothers of Jesus are interpreted to be cousins, this latter in the interest of the perpetual virginity of Mary. If I do not misunderstand the Christian tradition, which henceforth for purposes of distinction I shall call Catholic, these overmeanings take on the word "tradition," namely, the body of continuing "revelation inherent in the Church," a "tradition" which is broader than mere scriptural interpretation, yet also includes scriptural interpretation. As it applies to scriptural interpretation, tradition in this Catholic sense might be described as that body of continuing revelation of the implications of Scripture. To the Jewish analogue of this unfolding material the Jews gave the name of the Oral Torah, limiting Scripture to the Written Torah; in the Jewish conception, the Oral Torah is not only just as valid as the Written, but the tradition holds that it was revealed either in essence or in actuality to Moses at Sinai simultaneously with the revelation of the Written. What these two terms, the "Oral Torah" and the Christian "tradition," assert is that bodies of interpretation are not simply human concoctions, but are products of the divine.

I do not believe that in Judaism the question is ever raised that was raised in the sixteenth century after the Protestant Reformation, namely, the relative authority of Scripture and the relative authority of the Church. When the question was raised, Catholics gave the answer that it was the Church which was the teacher and guardian of Scripture, and, while the Church was not in any sense superior to Scripture, it was the Church which was responsible for the interpretation of Scripture. This was, by and large, as I understand it, a response to those Protestants who were saying that the Church was nothing and that Scripture alone was the authority. I do not know of anything comparable in any Jewish writings, for since Jews lacked authority of persons, there was no Jewish analogue to what is involved in Catholicism as the authority of the Church. For Jews, authority lay in Scripture, and it lay in the tradition which interpreted Scripture. But there was no authority of persons; there was only the authority in the tradition. Among Catholics, authority has lain in the Church as well as in Scripture, but never only in Scripture.

101

When Protestants contended that authority lay in Scripture, and Scripture alone, they began to develop those men who made contentions out of their own learning and out of their own conscience about what Scripture meant. These contentions contradicted the body of Catholic overmeaning, and the response of the Church was to designate commissions which could yield authoritative answers which would be binding on Catholics. Such took place in connection with the Council of Trent, and such took place in subsequent papal commissions, and one can say that by and large, until the past half-century, Catholic biblical scholarship was able to operate with profundity only in those areas allowed to it in the framework of the decisions of the authorized commissions. When the higher criticism first arose, Catholics participated in it, but were gradually impelled to withdraw from it, with the consequence that, by and large, the higher criticism was, until very recent times, an almost exclusively Protestant preoccupation. This was the case not only because Protestants were interested theologically in discovering what the pristine sense of Scripture was, but also because the march of scholarship was bringing into the forefront conclusions which were completely at variance with what is found both in the Jewish Oral Torah and in the Catholic tradition. The iconoclastic nature of much of Protestant scholarship is best discerned in the upheavals within Protestantism between modernists and fundamentalists; while they argue with each other from the standpoint of basically different assumptions, in neither case are these assumptions based directly on some body of tradition but emerge from preconceptions about the nature of Scripture. Thus, the fundamentalists argue on the basis of the supposed inerrancy of Scripture, and the modernists argue that a scriptural document should be approached just as any other ancient document. But fundamentalists and modernists hold in common that it was the individual learning or the individual conscience which was the decisive factor, and not some body of material intermediary between the nineteenth-century researcher and ancient Scripture.

To revert now to our words "understanding" and "interpretation,"

Protestant scholarship must be credited with a tremendous achievement toward the understanding of Scripture, in the form of the dictionaries, encyclopedias, handbooks, grammars of Hebrew, the cultivation of comparative linguistics, anthropology, and the like, with the result that even the fundamentalists who want to differ with the iconoclasm of the modernist interpreter feel called upon to utilize the grammars, dictionaries, and other tools created by these people. The fundamentalist could be shocked by and ignore the Graf-Wellhausen hypothesis, but he could not ignore the wealth of learning called into being to support that hypothesis. He had to deal with the cumulative learning, no matter how sharply he wanted to reject its bent. All too often the fundamentalist was caught in the vise of seeming to reject understanding as well as interpretation, and many a fundamentalist tradition chose to ignore understanding, simply because the interpretation was distasteful.

Roman Catholics, since they had tradition, have never been fundamentalists in the sense of Protestant fundamentalists, and they have had no need to defend a fundamentalist preconception. They could be disposed to disregard, really to ignore, the Protestant interpretation as wrongheaded, but when the time was to come that they felt ready to encounter it, they could often feel free to accept it or reject it on the basis of the inherent value or lack of value that they saw in it. That is to say, there was enough freedom in Catholic biblical scholarship for Catholics to confront the iconoclastic scholarship on its merits, and not have to shy away from it, as fundamentalists did, simply because it was iconoclastic.

Respecting Jews, the fact needs to be stated openly that, by and large, Jews were represented in the modern scholarship of the nineteenth century by remarkably few people. A few, such as Heinrich Graetz (1817–1891), can be cited as having worked within some of the framework of the higher criticism, but the fact is that Jews as yet were not truly to be found in the stream of Western intellectual thought, and certainly not in Western biblical scholarship. The German, David Hoffman (1843–1921), did write a book, the translation of whose title is *The Most Significant Errors of the Graf-Well-hausen Hypothesis;* his book was a rejection of the higher criticism not only because it was out of consonance with Jewish tradition, but also because Hoffman was among the succession of Jews who saw, in the higher criticism, an animosity toward Judaism. The fact is that this animosity can be documented, especially in the case of the great Septuagint scholar, Paul de Lagarde (1827–1891), but in the broader perspective, the German, Protestant higher criticism was just as much anti-Christian as it was anti-Jewish, for it was just as iconoclastic toward the Gospels as it was toward the Law of Moses.

If that succession of iconoclastic scholars can be convicted of anything, it is that they seldom challenged their own presuppositions, and they fitted neatly either into Hegelianism or into adaptations of Darwinism which prompted them to speak of the evolution of this or that; and they often made the documents fit into a Procrustean bed. We must beware, however, in our wish to point out the inadequacies of that scholarship, not to fall into the pit of distorting it or of failing to do justice to its tremendous achievements. The time was to come when the interpretation by the nineteenth-century German Protestants was challenged by, among others, Protestants themselves, but the contribution made to the understanding is not to be underestimated. This was particularly the case as more and more Semitic languages came to be understood, the knowledge of Hebrew enriched, and as archaeology both fed the knowledge of languages and increased the understanding of the biblical milieu. I think it can be said truthfully that in the nineteenth century Jews, like Catholics, largely held themselves aloof from the truly scientific study of Scripture, and only at the turn of the century did they begin to enter into its domain.

I suppose the most significant developments in the twentieth century have been the tremendous increase in the knowledge of the Hebrew language and of its Semitic relatives, the tremendous increase of archaeological data, and the progressive decline of the prevalence of the Graf-Wellhausen hypothesis. The limitations of time and space prevent recapitulating the whole story here. Catholics and Protestants in the twentieth century began to read each other's books, and Catholic and Protestant archaeologists began to become acquainted not only with each other's work, but with each other; Jews began to enter into the field of scientific Bible study and to read the Christian writings as well as to compose their own. The barriers here too began to fall, especially in the United States. In Palestine, in the days before it was Israel, the qualifying adjectives, Protestant, Catholic, or Jewish biblical scholarships were beginning to disappear, their place taken by simply "biblical scholarship." More and more individual Jews began to participate in this scholarship, sometimes with all the radicalism of the Protestant iconoclasts, and sometimes contending with the Wellhausenites on their own ground. When Palestine became Israel, Jewish biblical scholarship, especially the archaeological, came to be enriched. While the modernist crisis, principally connected with Alfred Loisy in 1910, slowed down Catholic biblical scholarship, its insights nevertheless proceeded to proliferate and to deepen.

The fact needs to be faced that this new and significant development represents a joining by Catholics and by Jews in the Protestant search for the pristine meaning of Scripture. At last we are united in common academic quests, reading each other's books, and agreeing and disagreeing with each other, not on denominational lines, but in the way that scholars differ in weighing the material they deal with.

Lastly, we must ask the question: What, in this light, is the status of the Oral Torah and the Catholic "tradition"? There are, I believe, two answers that can be suggested, though I am not sure that everyone would suggest both of the answers. The first of these would be quasi-theological, namely, that the body of scholars, whether Jewish or Catholic, carrying on the work of biblical interpretation, represent a continuity with the antecedent past, and that continuity would imply the continuity of biblical revelation through the biblical interpreter. If I understand the Catholic attitude correctly, the work of Catholic biblical interpretation would represent one aspect of the continuing revelation embodied in the Catholic concept of the Church as the vehicle for revelation. Certainly from the Jewish standpoint there has been the conception that the Oral Torah is unending and hence continuous.

The second answer is nontheological and represents quite a secular approach, derivative from the discipline called the history of religions. Here I feel on much safer ground if I make the assertion respecting Judaism, and

105

then leave it to our Catholic friends to comment on whether or not it applies to Catholicism. The assertion is this, that the rabbinic interpretation of Scripture comprises insights and doctrines and convictions which in themselves represent matters of significance and matters of value. I can best illustrate this, perhaps, by alluding again to Philo. His biblical interpretation is farfetched, and there was no sequel in Judaism to what he did; nevertheless, the body of Philonic material is not only itself worthy and of value, but also contains in itself material to edify and to instruct. If this is true of the Philonic material, which had no sequel, then how much more is it true of the rabbinic material which has had a sequel, and the effect of which has been of tremendous influence on unfolding Judaism. The visible aspects of Judaism in our day, namely, synagogue and rabbi, are not scriptural; the visible aspects of Catholicism are comparably not directly scriptural, for the papacy, the hierarchy, the totality of sacraments, and the religious orders are all developments of the ages after Scripture, however deeply rooted in Scripture they may ultimately be. I suppose the chief difference between Judaism and Catholicism, on the one hand, and Protestantism on the other—this is meant again to be descriptive and not comparative—is that neither tradition embraced the view of *sola Scriptura,* whereas Protestantism did, at least in principle.

However much scholars, transcending denominational lines, may unite in the common search for the correct understanding of Scripture and for the consistent, restrained, and profound interpretation of it, I for one am prepared to recognize, at least respecting Jews, that the pristine meaning of Scripture is quite distinct from the meaning which Jews came to find in it. I believe it is possible to distinguish between the pristine sense of Scripture and the developed sense. The pedant in me often rebels against attributing to the pristine sense of Scripture the tremendous insights which the rabbinic tradition derived from Scripture; I like to keep these separate so as to appreciate each more. They constitute a double heritage, or perhaps it might be phrased that they constitute double aspects of a larger heritage. It is wrong in methodology and it is wrong in understanding to play them off against each other, just as it is wrong to fail to make the distinctions between them. Both are worthy. But there is no Scripture without understanding and there is no Scripture without interpretation, however valiant the efforts have been by Karaites among Jews, and Protestants among Christians, to "return" to Scripture.

When we read each other's books on Scripture, when we read each other's books on the interpretation in our traditions of Scripture, we engage in a common, religious task, and insofar as we are able to enlighten ourselves and each other, inevitably our understanding is deepened, our horizons broadened, and that which in Scripture can be of benign influence radiates the more effectively among men.

9

Understanding and Misunderstanding:
Prepossession Versus Malice *

T HERE IS A sense in which Christian-Jewish relations in the realm
of the social confrontations is quite different from the religious
and the theological; such seems to me to be the case in these days in which
specifically Christian (as distinct from Nazi) persecution of Jews has ceased,
at least in the Western world. In this new context, it may be possible now to
comment on some of the scholarly efforts which Christians and Jews have
made to understand that age in Judaism into which Christianity was born.
In theory, scholarship is the detached, disinterested, objective search for the
truth. It would seem to follow, then, that the facts, the data, respecting first
century Judaism and Christianity could and would be ascertainable, and that
this scholarship, free of all conscious partisan bias, would be able to assemble
these data, and describe them, and make tolerably objective inferences in the
realm of interpretation and significance. To what extent has the scholarship
been successful?

The uncomfortable fact is this, that much of Christian and Jewish scholarship about the first Christian century still possesses large measures of what

* This article was originally published in *Dialog: A Journal of Theology,* 6 (Autumn,
1967): 284–89.

must be called justification, namely, the tendency to imply or to state that Jews in the first century were right in not joining in the new movement, or that Christians were right in abandoning Judaism and in fashioning the new movement. Such justifying tendencies are readily buttressed by a partisan assessment of the data found in the surviving literature. Such partisanship is susceptible of reduction, but scarcely of full dissolution, for the partisanship is bound up with at least the surface meaning of writings which to Christians are ultrasacred and to Jews not, or of writings quasi-canonical to Jews (such as the rabbinic literature), and to Christians not. Moreover, the rabbinic literature is either dimly known by or totally unknown to most Christians. Very, very few Jews are competent in the New Testament, and even fewer in the secondary scholarship on it; very few Christians have had any firsthand competency in the rabbinic literature. In general, even the most generous of Christian scholars are persuaded that Pharisaism was in at least some way either an evil or else a somewhat wrongheaded movement, to which Christianity was the antidote; Jewish scholars have evaluated it most highly as that flexible and elastic version of Judaism which facilitated the transition from the biblical religion of temple, priest, and animal sacrifice into the rabbinic religion of the synagogue, rabbi, and prayer. Even when it is granted, as much of Protestant scholarship has done, that the portrait of the Pharisees in the New Testament is neither complete nor totally fair, the noticeable revision by Christian scholars of earlier views on the Pharisees still falls short of the Jewish adulation of them.

On the other hand, those Jewish scholars who have written affirmatively and appreciatively about Jesus have done so by consciously or unconsciously detaching Jesus from Christianity, and it has been Jesus the man, Jesus the Jew, and not the divine Christ toward whom the newer, laudatory judgment has been directed.

I deliberately state the above in the way that I do as a prologue to a fuller consideration of a number of factors which impede Jewish and Christian understanding of each other. These factors rotate around what I would describe as an inadvertent misunderstanding, not a malicious one. One need spend no words in the context of this essay on those Christian books which arrogantly and condescendingly, and ignorantly, distort the nature of first-century Judaism in the interest of pleasing Christian vanity; so, too, with the smaller quantity of books which reverse the trend. Such Christian books, usually the older ones, but some often appearing even in our day, are quite unworthy of consideration. Similarly, one need not take into account some

Jewish books which have been written with a bitterness which I personally deplore even as I believe I understand the existential situation which produced them.

The significant theme of my paper is this: I am quite willing to believe that to a large extent that which strikes Jews as malicious in these Christian books is in reality not so intended, but is rather a blend of insensitivity and limited horizons, devoid of any awareness at all of inherent offensiveness.

What has created this situation of diverse and antagonistic scholarship arises from the fact that Christianity was originally a Judaism, and thereafter ceased to be. In a sense, Christianity declared its independence of its parent in a manner somewhat analogous to the independence which the thirteen colonies declared from Britain. Once it reached the point of independence, however, Christianity has tended to presume that its Britain had somehow ceased truly to exist, except as anachronistic vestiges, and that in some way the colonies were the true Britain, and in sole possession of the throne and the crown jewels, and that the royal line was transferred from that Britain to itself.

Yet whereas we Americans are able, even with our satisfaction in being independent of Britain, to regard the surviving Britain with some esteem, admiration, and affection, Christians have often found it difficult, even to the point of impossibility, until very recent times, of looking at Judaism in a comparable way. I believe that it is highly significant, as I point out in *We Jews and You Christians,* that the various quite noble Christian repudiations of anti-Semitism, such as the Declaration of Vatican Council II, confine themselves to urging a spirit of generosity to Jews, but do not say a word about Judaism.

The nub of the question of Jewish-Christian relations in the religious sense, as distinct from the social sense, is whether the tradition from which Christianity declared itself independent is susceptible of balanced and judicious appraisal by Christians, and whether the tradition which separated itself is susceptible of balanced and judicious appraisal by Jews. This fact of the birth of Christianity within Judaism and the separation of Christianity from it is the clue to the various consequent and subsequent misunderstandings, even by scholars.

Where I personally differ from most Jewish historians is that I do not see the great watershed between Judaism and Christianity in the career of Jesus, but rather in the career of Paul. I do not mean by this to deny the obvious truth that most first-century Jews abstained from regarding Jesus as the long-awaited Messiah, and that only a handful, his Jewish disciples for example, did so regard him. What I mean is this, that Pharisaic-Rabbinic Judaism worked on an assumption of the unbroken validity, indeed the eternity, of the Laws of Moses, whereas one of the contributions of Paul to Christianity was the contention that the Laws were of only temporary validity and once the Christ came, they were null and void, being replaced by faith.

Christians have, in general, accepted this view, though not always in Pauline terms. Pauline Christianity and Pharisaic-Rabbinic Judaism are, in regard to the Laws of Moses, antithetical to each other. I have tried to point out in my *The Genius of Paul* that the issue about the Laws was not in the realm of ethics, but rather on the question of the appropriateness of the Laws as a vehicle for attaining salvation, and I have repeated endlessly that Paul did not abandon the Jewish Scripture, but only the Laws which begin in Exodus 20. It has not seemed to me that the issue of whether or not Jesus was the long-awaited Messiah was in itself as disruptive of the relative unity of Jews as was Paul's attitude toward the Laws.

I am quite aware that Paul's attitude toward the Laws was only part of a larger complex, involving both a Christology which is significantly different from the usual Jewish messianism, and also eschatological expectations permeating all of Paul's writings, except for Philemon. From the Pauline attitude came the consequences of the abolition of the Laws, for example, an ultimately divergent Christian religious calendar, for Christianity maintained only those Jewish occasions which are mentioned in the New Testament (Passover in the form of Easter, and Pentecost, reinterpreted in a Christian way in Acts 2). Simultaneously a new type of officialdom developed, and a new type of liturgy arose, and contentions over who was God's elect became accentuated. Nineteen hundred years later, Christians and Jews have directly or indirectly debated the issue of the relative value of a religion based on "Faith" versus a religion based on Law, as if these two types of religion are susceptible of comprehension in such oversimplified rubrics, and as if value judgments are readily derivable from the oversim-

111

plification. The historic animosities of Christians and Jews to each other are, of course, an impediment to the weighing of the factors. But let us imagine that mutual hostilities and recriminations of the second and third century did not exist at all, and did not need to be banished from our recollection: How can commentators, respectively faithful to their traditions, find a common ground for assessing so direct an antithesis as that between Paul and the rabbis? The second- and third-century Christian polemics against Jews and Judaism did not create this basic divergency, but only accentuated it.

This kind of debate, Law versus Faith, is in a sense theological and quite distinct from the question of history, at least in part. The argument as to whether or not Jesus was indeed the long-awaited Jewish Messiah is primarily an historical question; however much the abolition of the Laws ensued from the conviction that Jesus was the Christ, the argument about the value of Law versus Faith can take place quite apart from that historical question. You cannot, of course, have a total separation, any more than you can divorce the Pauline view of faith from the Old Testament assumption of divine revelation. But an assumption by a scholar that value inheres either in Faith but not in Law, or in Law but not in Faith, arises as an obstacle to understanding the inherent issues, and to understanding the first Christian century.

Respecting the first Christian century, it may be relevant for me to make some highly personal comments as something of a specialist in the literature of early Christianity, not so much to speak about myself, but so as to highlight certain areas of scholarly procedures and judgments. First, my training in Old Testament, prior to my turning to New Testament, was scientific and modernist; I was a believer in the Graf-Wellhausen hypothesis, and still believe in my own radical revision of it. To the extent that I was, and am, a modern scientific scholar, my interest in the New Testament was scholarly and academic. I was taught by Protestants, liberal Protestants, and therefore my studies in New Testament have always been buttressed by an acquaintance with, indeed a relatively broad grounding in, the Protestant scholarship on the New Testament. If, antecedent to trespassing into that scholarship, I had a bare handful of problems about the Gospels, once I entered into that scholarship, these problems proliferated in number and in depth. I was required in my Ph.D. program to master that scholarship just as a Protestant minister seeking a Ph.D. needed to master it. I became familiar with the so-called Synoptic Problem, the priority of Mark, the two-source hypothesis about Mark and Q, and Streeter's extension of it into the four-source theories; I have read unlimitedly about the possible relationships, affirmative or negative, between the Synoptics and John. I would claim some good competency in the history of Protestant Gospel scholarship. I have written in profound admiration of its scope and its intellectual honesty.

But I must state as tactfully as I can that for me, personally, the results of this scholarship have largely been negative in the sense that certainty about the history reflected in the Gospels is quite as elusive for me as it is for more gifted and more specialized Protestant scholars. Let me cite two single examples. I worked through with rather good diligence two books on the parables of Jesus, one by Jülicher and one by B. D. T. Smith. Both books deal with the question of how much, if at all, the parables have been shaped by the developing Christian tradition, as by allegorizing, and whether or not it is possible to recover the pristine forms of the parables as Jesus might have spoken them. From Jülicher I believe I received more enlightenment on the matter of the growth of tradition than directly on the parables; as for Smith, it seemed to me that in removing the supposed secondary additions from the parables, the only authentic message of Jesus, so Smith seems to me to imply, was the negative one of criticizing his contemporaries, and Smith left nothing of an affirmative message. Next, in example, form criticism. I studied K. L. Schmidt, Rudolf Bultmann, Martin Dibelius and others, and for a time I was fascinated by the supposition that an inquiry into the *Sitz im Leben* would disclose the unimpeachable history behind the Gospels in a truly objective way; I have come, however, to regard form criticism as so thoroughly saturated with subjectivity and with challengeable assumptions as to find little tenable objectivity in the method.

That is to say, it had been my tacit assumption that by immersing myself in the scholarship, I could resolve the handful of antecedent problems. I have ended up with an abundance of problems, and am quite ready to abandon any supposition that scholarship will solve the historical problems about earliest Christianity. It was not any Jewish teacher or influence that has pushed me in this direction, but rather the Protestant scholarship itself.

113

I have recently studied S. G. F. Brandon, *Jesus and the Zealots*. One theme from this book may vividly illustrate this matter of historical uncertainties. Central to Brandon's thesis, which intimately links Jesus with the Zealots, is his need to comment on Mark and on the history in Mark. The chapter, "The Markan Gospel," is dominated by the view that Mark is a thoroughly apologetic writing, designed to commend a peaceful Christianity to the Romans, this by deliberately suppressing the sympathy which Jesus felt for the Zealots and by substituting a Jesus unrelated to the Zealots for a Jesus historically related to them. "The story is incredible both on historical grounds and because of its intrinsic impossibility" (*Jesus and the Zealots*, p. 262). If it is objected that Brandon's view represents an extreme position, then I would reply that it is only extreme, and not at all out of keeping with the general tone of the main lines of Protestant scholarship (except, of course, for religious conservatives and those who disdain careful exegetical study in favor of "spiritual" exegesis). The various reviews of Gospel study, by Schweitzer, McCown, Salvatorelli and others, even when the extremes are avoided, lead to an agnosticism about the figure of Jesus. (Sometimes I, trained in New Testament, encounter Christians who are not, and while the difference in judgments can seem to be distorted into a Jew versus Christian, the reality is that the difference arises from scholar versus layman).

Much ink has been spent on the moot question of the figure of Paul as reflected in his Epistles and as reflected in Acts of the Apostles. These issues will never be settled; there will never be an end to the writing of articles either affirming the congruency of Galatians 2 with Acts 15, or denying it. I have my own opinion, set forth in my *The Genius of Paul*. But here again, scholarship does not succeed in providing a universal solution of the problem, but again leads into a kind of cul-de-sac.

Yet in a dimension even deeper than the alleged irreconcilable data as between Acts and the Epistles lies the issue of whether or not Christianity accepted in toto Paul's attitude toward the Law, whether in Paul's time or after. The places of the Epistle of James and of the Sermon on the Mount in

Christian tradition are related to this question historically, and the answers given by scholars mutually contradictory. An historian, whether a Christian or a Jew, needs to try to understand in what way a Pauline impulse which declared the Laws abrogated might have been followed by a view which seems to have tempered that conclusion, and thereafter followed by the development in much later times of a canon law quite as casuistic as Pharisaic-Rabbinic law. Can we truly see the course of these intra-Christian developments? The facts of the case are not readily ascertainable, certainly not in a way to satisfy all researchers and to produce a broad concensus. My book *The First Christian Century* tries to set forth the areas of knowledge and also of either our uncertainty or of our ignorance.

Yet, respecting Christian-Jewish relations, there are on record value judgments which the elusive data can scarcely support. Let me cite only two of these. By atomizing Matthew, it has been possible for Jews to cite Matthew 5:17, "Think not that I am come to destroy the law, or the prophets: I am not come to destroy but to fulfill," and declare that this is an authentic statement of the Jesus of history—and then to ignore Matthew 28:20, as if it did not occur in the same Gospel; or else arbitrarily to ascribe that latter verse to the developing church, but 5:17 to Jesus himself. Is this not capricious procedure?

Secondly, the nineteenth- and twentieth-century assessments of Paul and his abrogation of the Law are accompanied by fantastic portrayals of Jewish life under the Law which are borne out neither by rabbinic literature nor by Paul's Epistles nor even in Acts of the Apostles. This rather new view envisages Jews as groaning under an uncongenial and despised yoke, which was fraught with the kinds of inconvenience that modern suburban life imposes on traditional Jews who must travel a great distance to find a kosher butcher shop. On the one hand, Jews never found the Law a burden in this sense, but rather a welcome obligation and privilege; on the other hand, Paul's abrogation of the Laws seems to me to have rested, as he saw things, on a matter of principle and not on such trivia as the distance to a kosher butcher shop. A chain of Protestant scholars has constructed a Judaism which never existed against which to vaunt a misdirected appraisal of Paul. The casuistry of Jewish Law has been travestied and burlesqued, always from the outside, as if there were no history of Christian casuistry, both in canon law and in theological refinements. In the case of such Christian scholars as Bruno Bauer and Paul de Lagarde, the only explanation viable is that of pathology. Elsewhere in the nineteenth century, it was inadvertently malicious, the product of prepossession, aggravated by scholars abstaining from examining their own presuppositions. The best case against this chain of Protestant scholars was made by a Protestant, George Foot Moore, in "Christian Writers on Judaism," *Harvard Theological Review,* 1921.

Basic in these distortions is the factor of modern justification of the occurrences in the first Christian century. Paul must have been totally right, and the rabbis totally wrong; or the rabbis must have been totally right and Paul totally wrong. Let a scholar simply pick his vantage point, and he can readily make an ego-satisfying contrast, whether a factual basis is available or not. So Paul had a fine religion, and the rabbis an abominable one, or vice versa.

I suspect that only a man from Mars can objectively approach Christianity and Judaism in relationship to each other. Those of us who are Christians or Jews can go different distances, and often very far, but scarcely the whole way. I am still a modernist, no observer of rabbinic laws, a left-wing higher critic of Scripture. On the conscious level, I feel that I owe a greater debt to the truth than to redeeming the tarnished reputation of the Pharisees. I believe that it is true that my attitudes in the controversial issues are matters of reaction, rather than of initiation, but let me confess that I do respond emotionally, and most negatively, to the disparagements of the ancient rabbinic Judaism to which I do not personally adhere as would a pious Orthodox Jew adhere.

When I read nasty passages in William Barclay, in Reginald Fuller, and in Matthew Black, it is emotionally that I respond, and to that extent the scholar in me is overcome by what is Jewish in me. I have never met any of these gentlemen personally. I would imagine that I would discover each to be an engaging, warm, and even tolerant person. I would doubt that they are in any way at all marked by conscious malice. But, why do these Christians write in the way they do, and what is there in me, detached scholar that I am, that does not deter me from reacting?

especting the future of Jewish-Christian relations, and deliberately over-
l king here the areas of tension, such as the Christian missionary impulse
d the Jewish resentment of it, what can the future hold affirmatively?

Perhaps religious understanding can be promoted if value judgments are
estrained, and tightly restricted to the area of the demonstrable. In such a
context, the following might be a tolerably prudent statement: In the age
of Jesus, there were many versions of Judaism, such as Sadduceeism,
Pharisaism, Essenism, Therapeutae, and Christians. Of this plurality, two
versions have survived to our day, Pharisaism-Rabbinism and Christianity.
These two traditions have each undergone many transformations as the
traditions have moved in time and in geography. Having much basic in
common, parallel motifs are necessarily present, and identity marks some
of these motifs. Since they went their separate ways, they have also developed each its own idiosyncrasies. Possessing the Old Testament in
common, the two traditions understand it in quite divergent ways, almost
as if it were not the same book.

Religious understanding supposes that these materials, the overlapping
and the divergent, lend themselves to calm and possibly to sympathetic
study. Such study can possibly produce dimensions of reciprocal comprehension which can replace both the clearly erroneous, and also the merely
intuitive.

What is the goal? Is it to refute? Is it to understand? If the latter, can
loyalty to one's own be accompanied by a responsible and fair assessment of

another tradition? Especially when they stand in relationship to each other of an historical, acute separation?

I often believe that religious understanding is in inverse proportion to proximity. The nearer traditions are, or have been, to each other, the more difficult it is for them to understand each other; the easiest comprehensions exist among traditions quite distinct in origin and free from a centuries-long history of contacts.

Again, what is the goal? For myself, it is to understand, so far as that is possible, with accuracy and fair-mindedness. I have made certain efforts, through writing, to convey to others the results of my studies. Sometimes I think I have succeeded a little. But I read reviews which pain me, not because of the substance of the criticism, but because of the imputation to me of ___ tive which I know is as unfair as it is uncharitable. Jews have written ___ ld me for trespassing at all into a field which is declared to be ___ alien to Jews; one Christian writer was not content with assert-___ 'd not understand Christianity, but he doubted that I had an ade___ rstanding of Judaism—though he, of course, possessed both. There ___ when I feel impelled to abandon the enterprise altogether, as a tha___ d impossible task, for I find myself on the verge of concluding tha___ is desired is not accuracy, and, in that sense, some approximation t___ truth, but rather that which nurtures partisan egos. Some Jews have ___ offended by my assertion that Christianity is a monotheism; some Chri___ have been offended by my agnosticism about the Jesus of history. One Christian correspondent, on the basis of a totally irresponsible review of a book of mine, and not through reading the book, wrote to inform me, in an unsigned letter, that he recognized my name despite its alteration (it has not been altered, except that probably in some remote generation it was Sandmehl, not Sandmel) as that of a Nazi well known to him.

I am normally readily able to dismiss this kind of thing as representing marginal, pathetic personalities. But even in moments of some encouragement, I find myself saying to myself that the goal of religious understanding is, even in favorable circumstances, most formidable, and possibly even insuperable.

Then, on the other hand, I encounter recurrently those Christian scholars who are men of integrity and as devoted as I believe I am to the quest for accuracy, and I find myself able to move on. I have in mind the project

118

which some Dutch scholars have sparked, a compendium of Jewish materials relating to the New Testament, recently inaugurated.

Yet what a mountain of wrong data, wrong premises, excessively strong prepossessions needs clearing away—and how inclusive and indistinct is so much of the relevant literature! The first chore for real dialogue, so it seems to me, is still far from complete, namely, the work that genuine scholars need to do, scholars with competency not in just one of the two traditions, but in both.

Judaism, Jesus, and Paul:
Some Problems of
Method in Scholarly Research *

W HEN ONE WRITES a paper on methodology, it is usually to
express reservations about previous procedures, and to rec-
ommend new, and supposedly better, techniques. But this is only part of the
present purpose.

Rather, it is proposed here to set forth an array of concerns, each of which
impinges on studies in either Judaism or Christianity of the first Christian
century. Much of the inherited scholarship has dealt with less than the full
array, and the difference in measure between parts and the whole is by and
large the index to faulty method. I propose to discuss the relationships of
Apocrypha, New Testatment, rabbinics, Graeco-Jewish writings, and Hellenistic literature.

Of all fields of study, none is so difficult of objectivity as the period of
the birth of Christianity. Different from the scholar, the pietist is less interested in precision and accuracy than in expressing his religious devotion. In
recent times novels, such as *The Robe* by Lloyd Douglas, or *The Nazarene*
by Sholem Asch, have utilized materials of first-century Christianity for
fictional purposes; this fiction is of course not to be regarded as interchangeable with scholarship. Again, other writers have looked to the New Testament (and to the Old) for the answer to specific modern problems. The
procedure, invariably, is for such writers to ascribe a given solution to
Scripture, and having put it there, exultantly proclaim that they found it
there. Such studies, many of which are motivated by lofty purposes and

* This article first appeared in *Vanderbilt Studies in the Humanities,* Volume 1 (Nashville, 1951): 220–248.

characterized by noble content, are not in reality studies in first-century Christianity, but rather the search for an ancient authority for a modern program. Within this group can be listed efforts as diverse as the demonstration that liquor ought not be drunk (or might be drunk); that socialism is good (or bad); that pacifism is commendable (or reprehensible); or that the Rennaissance view of the dignity of man rests on a fallacy. Such studies really use the Christian Scriptures only to begin with. A not unusual procedure is to lift some statement out of context: Jesus taught "turn the other cheek"; hence pacifism—overlooking the driving of money-changers out of the Temple area. Or, to generalize about the New Testament view of something such as sin, righteousness, body or the like—generalizations which overlook both a variety of New Testament views and the presence of conflicting views. Or, to search for (and even find!) a single predominating view or motif which, it is averred, is not alone primary to be exclusive in the New Testament, for example, "love." [1]

Such procedures have been followed with great frequency to the annoyance of specialists in New Testament, and even to the point that a rift seems to have arisen in Protestant circles between the specialists in Bible and the specialists in modern theology; for New Testament scholars have often failed to find in the New Testament what such theologians have asserted was there.

For our purposes, however, neither the fiction nor the overtly tendentious essay is relevant for any more than a quick buttressing of the contention that objectivity is hard to obtain. It is not proposed to deal with either of these groups of modern writings, but rather only with the work of specialists, with the scholarship which aims at accuracy and precision, and whose purpose is not aborted in advance by a conscious or demonstrable special pleading. It is rather with the genuine scholarly studies, designed not to solve modern problems, but to elucidate the ancient that we are here concerned. It is not, indeed, the problem of the objectivity of the scholar (though I shall say some things about that) but rather with his horizons.

The fact that any literature arises at a given time and place presupposes that some understanding of background is significant. When literature, or segments of literature, are related to each other, it is all the more important for their relationships to be understood. The historical setting needs constantly to be borne in mind. Historically, Christianity arose as a quasisect within Judaism, conceived some sense of its individual identity, proceeded to assert its difference and independence of Judaism, and then created the beginnings of a sacred literature of its own. Within Palestine revolt against Roman sovereignty led to reprisals, the chief of which was the destruction of the Temple at Jerusalem in 70 A.D., and as a result the character of Judaism shifted from a religion presided over by priests to a lay type of religion. Outside Palestine, Jews lived in such abundance as to be self-sustaining. The larger context against which these developments occurred was the Hellenistic-Roman world, with its abundance of philosophical schools, religious sects, and literary figures.

Obviously, to understand either Christianity or lay Judaism in its own terms requires a knowledge of both the specific and the general literatures, and an embarrassment of riches rises to plague the scholar. Prior to the New Testament there appeared in Jewish circles a class of writings called "Apocrypha," the term meaning "stored away," that is, books not admitted into the collections deemed sacred.[2] In addition to the Apocrypha there is a group of quite similar writings from roughly the same period of time whose superscriptions make the claim that they are the composition of very ancient worthies; to these scholars have given the name "Pseudepigrapha."

Apparently the initial stages of the assembly by Jews of books deemed sacred were the canonization of Five Books of Moses and of the Prophets; this was accomplished by about 150 B.C. It was not until toward the end of the first Christian century that the Jewish canon was fixed for the Hagiographa.

That is to say, down into the first century there was an abundance of literature, the ultimate subordinate status of which was as yet not fully decided; and whether this literature is in truth subordinate, or perhaps equal in religious content to what was canonized, it is at all events a repository of doctrines, attitudes, sentiments, and narratives illustrative of times and movements and personalities.

When one recalls that there is an interval of at least two hundred years between the youngest book of the Old Testament and the oldest writing of the New, one can quickly discern that a knowledge of the intervening literature can help to trace the process of the extension of Old Testament ideas into the New, or elucidate doctrines which arose between the latest Old Testament writings and the earliest Christian. For an example of the latter the word "Messiah" does appear, several times, in the Old Testament, but never in the sense in which it is used in the later writings; but Apocrypha and Pseudepigrapha present frequent appearances of the term.

As scholarship essayed to put the study of the New Testament on the high plane of the study of other ancient literatures it was natural that this extra-canonical literature was studied in some minuteness. Essays on the religious ideas contained in them are often labeled "intertestamental studies." Their significance for understanding the New Testament cannot be over-estimated. But the manner of using them can be the source of different scholarly opinions, and on fundamental issues. We shall see more of this in just a moment.

The Western world, with Christianity as the dominating religion, so focuses on the time of Jesus as crucial in the history of mankind that it is startling to some people to know that within Judaism the Christian movement made very little impression until well into the second or third century, and that neither Jesus nor Paul figure in their own lifetime in the abundant literature which Jews preserved subsequent to the "intertestamental literature." A convenient term for this Jewish literature is "rabbinics."

Rabbinic literature is a group of compilations of material originally transmitted orally, comprising the legal and ethical opinions of rabbis from a period beginning about 250 B.C. until about 500 A.D. It is in Aramaic and Neo-Hebrew. As indicated, where the rabbinic literature deals with Christianity, it deals with that which has already become a rival and antagonistic church, not just a sectarian movement within Judaism. Though rabbis contemporary with Jesus and Paul are quoted, and abundantly, neither Jesus nor Paul is ever cited. Jesus is mentioned, tendentiously, but these mentions are from periods long after the first century.[3]

And here an important observation is to be made. The rabbinic compilations are the results of assembly and redaction. The redaction of the most famous collection, the Talmud, was in two stages. First, a collection was made about the year 200 A.D. of terse, laconic legal statements; this is called the Mishnah, a kind of commentary on, and expansion of, the laws in the Bible. Next, the Mishnah itself was commented on, not laconically, but extensively; this commentary is known as the Gemara.[4] Two recensions of the Gemara exist, one made in Palestine about 450 A.D., and the other in Babylon about 500 A.D. Mishnah and Gemara comprise the Talmud. Thereafter the Babylonian recension became authoritative for Jews, who, when they speak of the Talmud, mean the collection with the Babylonian Gemara, and they specify "Palestinian" when they mean the less authoritative Talmud.

The Mishnah is a redaction of 200 A.D., and the Talmud of 450 A.D. or 500 A.D. The rabbis quoted, however, lived as early as 250 B.C. The oldest strata of rabbinics are contemporaneous with the intertestamental literature. The question can be asked legitimately, how accurately can the Judaism of a given, early century, such as the first Christian century, be reconstructed from redactions which might possibly be selective, or incomplete, or tendentious? We know, from a variety of sources, that before the destruction of the Temple there were a number of sects, Pharisees, Sadducees, Essenes, and the like, vying with each other for supremacy. Rabbinic literature is the creation of the Pharisees; in view of the sharp rivalries between the Sadducees and the Pharisees, can we expect an impartial and even full picture of Sadduceeism from the later, selective literature of their opponents?

Obviously, some caution must be employed in using rabbinic literature for the reconstruction of the earliest periods. The need for such caution is the more understandable when one notices that the rabbinic literature reveals very little knowledge of the Apocrypha and Pseudepigrapha, ignores much of their contents, and was created by people who did not themselves preserve this extra-canonical literature. From the rabbinic literature alone we should know nothing substantial about Apocrypha, Pseudepigrapha, New Testament, and the writings of a good many Jews who wrote in Greek, including Philo and Josephus.

There are points at which modern scholarship discerns the meeting of the "intertestamental" literature and the rabbinic. But the biggest single impression is that of diversity rather than congruency. As this appertains to New Testament study, is one to interpret Jesus and his teachings on the basis of the "intertestamental" literature or on the basis of the rabbinic literature?

Scholars have differed about the nature of Judaism at the time of Jesus. One elaborate construction, by Wilhelm Bousset,[5] was made almost exclusively on the basis of the intertestamental literature; and while the work was ostensibly scholarly, it was not without some condescending and superior attitudes toward Judaism which Jews with propriety resented. Perles,[6] a Jewish scholar, demonstrated that Bousset had not only set a convenient pattern for indicating the superiority of Christianity over Judaism, but had abused the small measure of rabbinic passages which he had cited. As the issue sharpened between Bousset and Perles, the scholarly world was to learn of an effort to distinguish in the Judaism of that time between the "folk," and their intertestamental literature, and the erudite and their rabbinic literature.[7]

Going a step further, a Christian scholar, George Foot Moore,[8] coined a new term which he used in great abundance in a book which was designed partly in reply to Bousset. Moore spoke of "normative" Judaism, implying, of course, that there was a type, or were types, which were not normative. Moore's book reconstructs Judaism primarily from the rabbinic literature.

When one begins with the assumption that there was a normative Judaism and that there was a non-normative, then such an assumption is fatal to the notion that a large collection, whether it is "intertestamental" or whether it is "rabbinic," will yield uniform points of view. The most significant fact about the Apocrypha and the Pseudepigrapha is their heterogeneous nature. Within the convenient laconic label there lies the greatest possible diversity of literary type, religious assumption, language of original composition, place and time of origin, and general purpose. It should therefore be obvious that a study of a doctrine in apocryphal literature which assumes that one and the same view will abide in each book in that literature starts with a faulty premise. It is a commonplace that I Maccabees comes from the hands of a writer sympathetic to the viewpoint of the Sadducees, but II Maccabees is a version of the same historic incident from the hands of a pro-Pharisee. Ecclesiasticus was composed originally in Hebrew, probably in the second Christian century; IV Maccabees was written in

Greek in the first pre-Christian or the first Christian century. Fourth Maccabees represents a quasi-philosophical approach strongly influenced by Greek attitudes; Jubilees, composed probably in Palestine, is a proto-rabbinic expansion of material found primarily in Genesis.

In the light of such diversity it is only with great reservation that one can accept a frequently encountered type of exposition which speaks of a particular doctrine as it is found in the Apocrypha and the Pseudepigrapha especially when some generalization about this doctrine is to be made. The infinite variety of possible variations, which on scrutiny actually emerge, are obstacles too great for the glib generalizer. It is not sound to speak of a particular view in a particular book as the total view; it is always necessary to concede the presence of divergent and even antagonistic views.

Against such a background, it is quite obviously improper to assume that there were only two modes of Jewish interpretation in the period under consideration, the normative and the marginal. The marginal, if that term is to mean anything, must include a plurality of views, and it should not be assumed that each type of marginal Judaism was interchangeable with each other type of marginal Judaism. Moreover, it is to be recognized that normative Judaism itself presents a diversity of viewpoints; and, indeed, rabbinic literature offers the student many differences of opinion, ofttimes sharp, within normative Judaism itself. Within normative Judaism one must, at a minimum, distinguish between what might be said to be the prevailing view and what can be spoken of as a minority view, or views. In a welter of types of Judaism, it is most infelicitous to speak of first-century Judaism without some specification or some qualification. To omit the qualifying adjective, such as "normative," "apocalyptic," or "Hellenistic" is in effect to fashion a meaningless sentence.[9]

The sense in which one may properly speak of the intertestamental doctrines or rabbinic doctrines in terms which have meaning is in terms of relative, prevailing trends, which are always accompanied by a receptivity to reservation. To give a dangerous example, one might say that apocryphal literature represents a Judaism in which legalistic conformity is as yet not dominant while rabbinic literature represents attitudes in which legalism is dominant. In apocryphal literature we can expect to read quasi-prophetic works, such as apocalypses, to make another dangerous simplification. Within the diversity of normative Judaism there is a relatively greater measure of uniformity and inner consistency; in apocryphal literature there is no such inner consistency and uniformity. One might go even further and say that the apocryphal literature comes from a period before the Jewish synagogue was consolidated into a rather stable and crystallized form, and therefore the apocryphal literature represents a "freer" type of speculation than would the opinions emerging from a settled and relatively serene type of objective religious experience.

Now having made these contrasts, I should be the first to proclaim that these are glib generalizations. That is to say, they are mostly true and are mostly applicable. But also, they are in part very much untrue, and in specific matters of research where specific ideas and terms are crucial, the generalizations which I have given would be inimical to the attainment of any well-rounded and sound scholarly understanding of a given doctrine.

This is relevant to the study of Christianity and Judaism in the first century, in that Apocrypha and rabbinic literature present too many variables for it to be possible for one to make nimble summaries of Judaism. The rabbinic literature, as indicated, comprises collections made centuries after the first century; there was no quasi-Christian interest specifically in the first century and hence no tacit or avowed purpose of demonstrating just what first-century Judaism was; the literature was created by the descendants of Pharisees, only one of the various groups that flourished in Palestine in the first century, and it tends to overlook, or even to disparage, the groups in rivalry of the direct ancestors in the first century.

Moreover, the most pronounced shift within Judaism occurred in the first century; the destruction of the Temple, and the triumph of the synagogue. There are innumerable questions, the answers to which are elusive; had the synagogue already tended to supplant the Temple before the year 70? Had the Pharisees already emerged as the dominant party in Judaism before the year 70? Was apocalypticism as unknown in Palestine before 70 as the rabbinic literature would lead us to conclude? Do these relatively late collections read back into the past the conditions of their own time, or are the historical data which they occasionally include partly if not completely reliable? [10]

With rabbinic literature representing the opinion of individuals separated in time as far as the second pre-Christian century is from the fifth Christian century and separated in place as far as Palestine is from Babylon, can we expect an unbroken uniformity throughout such long periods? Were there no significant differences evoked by the reason of the ingress of or exposure to Hellenism, Parthian religion, gnosticism, and trinitarian Christianity?

127

Was legalistic, objective Judaism the sole type of religious expression or do the laconic allusions in rabbinic literature to types of mysticism,[11] both theoretical and practical, represent movements wider in extent than the mere allusions in opposition indicate?

All these rhetorical questions point unmistakably to the conclusion: the precise status of Judaism in the first Christian century before the year 70 is well nigh not to be recovered. It is definitely not to be recovered in terms of convenient pigeonholes, simple categories, and unqualified assertions.

In the Synoptic Gospels there is considerable material which fits with much congruency into the milieu of the rabbinic literature. This material has to do with the life and teaching of Jesus. Can we elucidate obscure passages or amplify laconic ones in the Synoptic Gospels by a knowledge of rabbinic literature?

It is well to remind ourselves of some questions of chronology. Jesus belonged to first-century Judaism. It is the Judaism of Palestine, if we include Galilee in Palestine. We shall have to assume, accordingly, that Galilee was in no way distinct from other parts of Palestine. Within such a framework it is to be conceded that much light can be thrown on matters discussed in the Gospels by a knowledge of rabbinic literature.

But a number of scholars have tended to follow methods about which searching questions need to be asked. For well over a century rabbinic parallels to materials in the Synoptic Gospels have been gathered and published. In the last thirty years there has been made available a German work of staggering immensity in scholarship, Strack-Billerbeck, *Commentary on the New Testament*.[12] This work is a verse by verse, indeed a word by word commentary, illustrating from rabbinic literature the text of the Christian Bible.

Strack-Billerbeck can hardly be overpraised. But unhappily it lends itself to frequent misuse by scholars. In the first place, some scholars who have themselves never read connected passages in the rabbinic literature, either in the original or in translation, utilize the excerpts in Strack-Billerbeck as the basis for judgments that are not always sound. The excerpts cited may have only a tangential connection with the New Testament, contained in the accident of a similar word or phrase, but its major tenor may be quite at variance. Nevertheless, the coincidence in part between a rabbinic and New Testament passage is taken to be total coincidence and congruency. Strack-Billerbeck tried in several places to define the use to which their *Commentary* can be put, but the method of piling up excerpts of doubtful relevance becomes a dangerous invitation to the imprudent. Frequently these focus their attention only on phases which coincide with rabbinic literature and fail to notice more abundant phases where coincidence gives way to incongruency. The convenient arrangement in Strack-Billerbeck has spurred many scholars, not to compare and contrast rabbinic literature and New Testament material, but to try to blend them together without thought or care as to meaning, context, date and place of provenance, and the like. It is assumed, not that Strack-Billerbeck provide interesting parallels or quasi parallels to New Testament, but that Strack-Billerbeck provide the full means of explaining the New Testament.

Here a caution of a chronological nature has to be stressed. The earliest rabbinic activity precedes the composition of the Synoptic Gospels by a considerable length of time. This is attested to us by the presence in Jubilees and in the first-century writer Josephus of proto-rabbinic expositions which reappear, either modified or unchanged in the later rabbinic collections. But that some rabbinic material is earlier is not to say that all rabbinic material is earlier. Even the later rabbinic material, in addressing itself to a problem touched on in the New Testament, may be an interesting parallel. In this sense, it may be described as background material. But background material of such time is illustrative material and without any necessary chronological precedent. That is to say, Jesus did not in the first century speak against a chronological background of opinions of rabbis of the fourth century in Babylon. A good many scholars, using Strack-Billerbeck, proceed from literary background to an assumption of chronological background, and thereafter assume that this or that attitude of Jesus is shaped by the supposedly antecedent rabbinic discussion.

When questions are raised about the legitimacy of such dubious procedure, a common retort is to say that the rabbinic material is after all relatively homogeneous. The retort would be interesting if it were universal and applicable in every situation, but for each scholar who asserts this kind of homogeneity in rabbinic literature, there is another who in a different context will prove his point by demonstrating the relative heterogeneity of the literature. To cite names, and to introduce still another facet, the writings of Philo, it is asserted by Bamberger [13] that rabbinic literature is all of a piece, and that Philo is dependent even on the later rabbinic writings; while Marmorstein,[14] addressing himself to a striking difference between Philo and the rabbis explains the difference on the basis that in the second Christian century the rabbis underwent a change of heart and change of attitude. In the first case, dependency is proved by an assertion of homogeniety; in the second case differences are explained on the basis of heterogeneity.

Reverting to Strack-Billerbeck, the obvious difficulty in a set of excerpts is the likelihood of the rupture of context. It is not going too far to assert that a good many scholars who utilize Strack-Billerbeck do so even against the context of the rabbinic literature out of which the excerpts are made.[15]

But still another difficulty has to be encountered. If it has successfully been contended that the rabbinic literature, with its heterogeneity, provides us with one or more variables, then we must add that from the other side the New Testament provides a good many variables.

For well over a hundred years the chief impetus in the study of the Synoptic Gospels was the so-called recovery of the historical Jesus. This search rested on the quasi-theological notion, that the New Testament had undergone an incrustation of mythology and legend which hid fine ethical insights and guides for present-day conduct. All that was necessary was to remove the overgrowth and to find the historical Jesus, and thereby modern man would have a sufficient guide for himself.

In line with this assertion the Gospels were studied minutely. The results of the study have indicated the impossibility of recovering the historical Jesus. The reason for this is that in the Gospels legend and church interest of later times are so thoroughly interwoven with narratives about and words supposedly uttered by Jesus that it is quite impossible to disentangle the authentic from the inauthentic. While many conservative or fundamentalist Christians object to this scholarly conclusion, it is nevertheless a rather standard conclusion of the Protestant study of the New Testament.

Modern scholarship would assess the Gospels as throwing light not on the life and teachings of Jesus, but on the views of Jesus as they had crystallized at different stages throughout the developing Church. More concretely, the Gospels reflect the time and place of their composition, rather than the events which they describe. While some oral tradition goes back to Jesus, this oral tradition has been so worked over by the Church, that its pristine form is quite beyond isolation.

When one wishes to explain a New Testament passage by the rabbinic literature, he must remember from the New Testament side that the Gospels are products of the Christian community, coming after its self-conscious distinction from Judaism, and that they were written in Greek and in the Diaspora. Within any single Gospel there are heterogeneous views; the three Synoptic Gospels (Mark, Matthew, and Luke) provide an even greater measure of heterogeneity.

The Gospels, then, are themselves in the nature of a variable. For example, did Jesus teach that divorce under any conditions was inadmissable, as Mark and Luke state, or did he permit it in the case of adultery, as Matthew states? Shall we look in Strack-Billerbeck for examples of both the total prohibition of divorce and for permission of divorce in the given type or situation?

The recognition that Luke and Matthew utilize Mark, expand him, alter him, and rewrite him should lead to the recognition that the changes and expansions in Luke and Matthew stem not from Palestinian Jewish soil, but from Diaspora soil. They are Diaspora reformulations of what is itself a Diaspora product. Accordingly, there is often little point to looking in rabbinic literature for the exposition of matters coming from a background and a set of interests completely alien to the rabbis.

The measure in which Strack-Billerbeck can be helpful in understanding the New Testament would seem by and large to be restricted to those passages in the New Testament where there is really a meeting of Judaism and early Christianity within a Palestinian Jewish setting. For such passages a considerably smaller number of total pages is needed than the five large volumes of Strack-Billerbeck.

The mention that the Gospels are products of the Greek world can be a good point of departure for asking the question: how Greek was the Jewish world of Palestine? Most scholarship is in some way or other influenced by Matthew Arnold's famous distinction between the Hebrew spirit and the Greek spirit, and usually the question of Greek influence is approached with either one or more sets of mind. The standard assumption is that the rabbinic world and the Greek world were diverse in content as they were in form, and that at each point they represent divergency rather than congruency. The Hebrew world is intuitive, the Greek world philosophic; the Hebrew world is poetic, the Greek world speculative.

131

For our purposes it has to be borne in mind that the Greeks conquered Palestine at the end of the fourth pre-Christian century. Greek institutions were established in Palestine. The Greek language is represented in considerable abundance in the rabbinic literature. But essentially, how Greek did Jewish Palestine become? Was Diaspora Judaism, in the Greek regions, more intensively and extensively Greek than Palestinian Judaism?

It is known that about 175 B.C. the issue of Greek influence in Palestine became a crucial one. Difficulties arising from political events, coupled with heavy-handedness on the part of the overlord, the Syrian Greeks, led Jewish Palestine to a revolt, successively accomplished under Maccabean leadership. Within the Jewish population there were anti-hellenizers as well as hellenizers. After the Maccabean Revolt, by and large any previous hospitality to Greek notions diminished, possibly nearly to the point of total exclusion.

Scholars differ as to the measure of Greek influence in Jewish Palestine, but the usual assumption is that the influence was surface or formal, but never penetrating or substantial. Accordingly, an intertestamental literary work is allocated for its place of origin largely by this assumption. For example, a work in Aramaic or Hebrew would come exclusively from Palestine and a Jewish work in Greek would come exclusively from outside Palestine.

In this light, one can allude to passages in the rabbinic literature (from the period considerably after Jesus) which speak with hostility toward the Greek language and Greek works such as Homer. Most scholars are inclined to agree that the rabbis forebade the reading of Homer. More recently a study has tried to show that it was the study of Homer as distinct from the cursory reading of him which the rabbis prohibited.[16] This latter study, an excellent one, represents a protest against the usual reconstruction of events, for it contends that Hellenism was far less than unknown in Jewish Palestine.

The single and most dramatic distinction between Palestinian Judaism and Greek Judaism focuses on the translation of the Bible into Greek. The place of translation was probably Egypt, and more specifically Alexandria; traditions of some credibility allocate the translation there. Certainly by the time of Philo (20 B.C.–40 A.D.) the Greek Bible, called the Septuagint, was so pervasively the Scripture of Greek-speaking Jews in Egypt that the anniversary of its translation was celebrated as a holiday. Greek Jews (and Christians) considered it to have the fullest measure of inspiration. Considerably later in Palestine a rabbi was to declare that no misfortune was as great for Jews as the translation of the Bible into Greek. This attitude stemmed undoubtedly from difficulty with Christians who were utilizing the proof-texts based on divergences of the Greek from the Hebrew for the substantiation of Christian contentions. But forgetting the fact that the festive observance and deep deploring are not attitudes of the same period, we still see a wide variance in the attitude of Jews, Palestinian or Diaspora, toward the Greek translation.

We know from passages in rabbinic literature that the rabbis were aware of certain places where the Greek diverges from the Hebrew. These divergencies, the rabbis explained, were the result of efforts of the translators to avoid incurring the wrath or suspicion of Gentiles. For example the passage in Leviticus 11:6, which lists the rabbit as prohibited food was altered to avoid the "rabbit," since the Greek word for rabbit was the same as the surname of the reigning Ptolemy.[17]

The issue of how much hellenization was implicit in the translation of the Bible has been fought out in the scholarly circles. From time to time it has been alleged that Greek philosophical conceptions are woven into the translation. By and large such efforts have been shown to be ill-founded, and most of the hellenizations in the Greek Bible can properly be called surface. These include the Grecianizing of names and the equipping of these names with Greek case endings, and also the occasional use of Greek metrical forms where the original Hebrew metrical form was inappropriate.[18]

Yet even with the concession that the hellenizations are surface, it is obvious that there cannot be what Marcus has described as a word-to-word correspondence between the original and the translation, since the idiom of two different languages is not going to be identical. Accordingly, the Greek Bible is full of paraphrases and circumlocutions and the turning of a Hebrew phrase into an idiosyncratic Greek phrase. When the Greek Bible came to be studied by Greek Jews they searched Scripture as diligently as any other generation at any other time, and operating on the assumption that the Greek Bible was itself endowed with all the necessary qualifications of inspiration, they were ready to infer whatever they wished from the accidental wording of the Greek. In the same way that the study of Homer was accompanied by deducing elaborate lessons from the accident of the wording of a verse of the Iliad, so elaborate lessons were deduced from the Bible. And as rationalists among the Gentiles interpreted Homer allegorically so as to find in Homer the precursor and indeed the origin of their own philosophical systems, so Greek Jews began to interpret the Scriptures allegorically.

However little hellenization there might have been in the Bible itself in its Greek version, certainly the growth of allegorical interpretation increased rather than decreased the amount. Furthermore, as the allegorical interpretation took the form of deducing from the accidental readings of Scripture philosophical and religious notions from the Greek world, the hellenization had grown apace.

But it is quite a difficult question to decide in some cases where the Jewish aspect leaves off and the Greek aspect begins. For example, the Jewish notion that God is invisible to the eye and the Greek view that *to on* was discernible only to the intellect but not to the senses, are not dissimilar. When one finds in the allegorical explanation of the Greek Bible the statement that God is not to be discerned by the senses, that view can stem either from the Jewish background or from the Greek background.

There are some areas that are congruous; there are some areas that are incongruous. For example, every harmonization which has been made of Greek philosophy and Jewish revelation has had to assert the primacy of certain biblical notions. Accordingly, medieval philosophers who were Aristotelian in outlook could not square Aristotelianism with the creation story in Genesis; creation *ex nihilo* and the eternity of matter do not coincide.

Between the extremes of matters which are completely incongruent and matters which are congruent, there is quite a range where the issues are not as sharply drawn. By and large it can be said that the Jewish anthropology distinguished between man's body and man's soul, but not to the point of finding them antitheses to each other. By and large the Greek view was the view known as pessimism, which ascribed positive virtues to the soul and negative qualities to the body. Yet there is implicit in the Palestinian Jewish distinction between body and soul, some of the contrast in a restrained form which becomes extreme in the Greek world and the Graeco-Jewish world. Accordingly, in passages in which Philo contrasts body and soul, we can sometimes find ourselves within the framework of the Jewish view of the congruency of body and soul but elsewhere we move into the Greek notion of the incongruency. The line of demarcation between the congruent and incongruent is not always easily discernible. This is particularly true where the Jewish and Greek notions are in their original form so parallel to each other that they can become merged in the same way that parallel lines seem to meet, as astronomers put it, in infinity.

To resume, it is not always possible to say of a given doctrine or view that it is either Jewish or Greek. Sometimes it is one or the other, but sometimes it is a mixture of both. Indeed space must be allowed in modern scholarly divisions for a broad area of a Graeco-Jewish world, of several centuries duration, sufficiently remote from Palestinian Judaism, but loyally Jewish in its own terms, so that its own peculiar character can be rather well defined.

Contrasts, indeed, can be noted between Graeco-Jewish thinking and rabbinic thinking, both in form and in substance. This is not to rule out the bare possibility that in Palestinian Judaism there was judaization of Hellenism so advanced that the Hellenistic background tends to be lost to view; and, conversely, that outside Palestine a hellenization of Judaism was so complete that the Palestinian origins in the Old Testament or of the early post-Old Testament period are well concealed. Hellenization, in the far-flung Jewish settlements, took place in varying measures and in varying degrees of penetration. Rabbinic Judaism, in its native Palestinian form, was not unmindful of Hellenism. It did not embrace superficial forms or welcome philosophically involved aspects of Hellenism. Its essential Hebraic quality was never overshadowed. But as an organism living in the Hellenistic world it could not help but be affected if only in minor aspects by the prevailing world intellectual and cultural streams.

It is possible to speak roughly of three degrees of hellenization. The rabbinic literature gives us only overtones of Hellenistic influence. In the second degree, the writings of Josephus show us the hellenization of a Palestinian Jew who knows the Greek world rather well, but from the outside. He is hellenized, but only in limited measure, and he falls short of profundity in hellenization. Not only did he require Greek secretaries to assist him in writing his book, but also his efforts at reflecting Greek philosophy show that he had heard about it but not studied it. A third degree of hellenization is that of Philo, who wrote theosophical works. Here hellenization is at its maximum. But let one not forget, it is a hellenization of Judaism. That is to say, Philo is not a witness simply to Hellenism, but to a specific kind of Hellenism.

It may be well to pause and consider some concerns focusing on Philo. His writings, which are in the process of incorporation in the Loeb classics, have already reached nine volumes, of a planned eleven. Philo wrote in Greek; he wrote both sermonic tracts, based on a sequence of verses in the Bible (known as the Allegory of the Law) and a freer type of composition (known as the Exposition). Philo quotes extensively from Greek writers, whom he mentions by name—philosophers, poets, and playwrights. It is uniformly agreed that he is trying to demonstrate the congruency of Greek philosophy with Judaism, on the contention that Scripture, properly assessed by the allegorical method, yields an anticipation in time to the Greeks, and a profundity and truth beyond what the Greeks achieved. Later generations of the Church said about him, either Plato philonizes, or Philo platonizes.

Despite a long history of Philonic research, an outstanding scholar declared only twenty-five years ago that the fundamental problem about Philo was still unsolved: Was he a Greek philosopher with a Jewish background and loyalties, or was he a Jewish thinker who merely couched his Judaism in philosophic terms? [19] In our day, two extremes of interpretation exist, the one asserting that complete hellenization is to be discerned in Philo, and the other asserting that there is hellenization only in the language and other external matters.[20]

Prepossession can control or even determine the judgment in such a matter. Some scholars, principally Jewish scholars, have started with the premise that loyalty to Judaism demanded a total rejection of Hellenism, and hence it is to be assumed that Philo rejected all Hellenism, utilizing only a philosophical shell. The prepossession consists of an unwillingness to admit of alien influences on a Jew so loyally Jewish.

A similar prepossession is to be found among Christian writers concerning Paul. Like Philo, Paul also wrote in Greek, and also utilizes Greek philosophical trappings and even terms from the Greek mystery religions. It is asserted by some scholars that Paul is thoroughly Greek; the assertion is buttressed by recourse to the more recent researches in the United States and Germany in the Acts of the Apostles; it is from Acts that we get a picture of Paul as a student of Gamaliel, a speaker of Hebrew, and observant of the Jewish Law. Those scholars who contend that among the motives of the author of Luke-Acts was the delineation of both Jesus and Paul as undeviatingly faithful to Judaism; motive dictates the presentation of Paul in a portrait at great variance with that which Paul writes in his Epistles. Such scholars would not tend to use Acts as a source of knowledge of Paul; [21] and for them the Paul of the Epistles emerges as a hellenized Jew.

If this is so, then much of Paul's doctrine has a "Greek" background, rather than a "Jewish" one. But, again, prepossession enters in at several points. First, a passage in the Fourth Gospel (4:22) contends that salvation is of the Jews; to argue for a Greek origin of a New Testament doctrine is, for some, to reduce the stature of its salvationary power. Moreover, researches of some forty years ago in Hellenistic religion led scholars to identify a good many of Paul's teachings with similar or parallel ideas found in the Greek mysteries; the view was expressed with some frequency that Pauline Christianity was in essence a mystery religion.

This judgment was often made not in a descriptive sense but in an evaluative sense. It was at the culmination of over a century of effort to regain the historical Jesus—which, in other terms, meant the removal of Pauline "aberrations." In general, secular historians tended to emphasize Paul's hellenization, some even to the point of denying that a historical Jesus ever lived.[22] In the interest of such secularism, the label of "mystery" for Pauline Christianity was in effect a negative judgment on Paulinism.

Christian historians, affronted by the oblique attacks on Paul, tried originally to defend Paul on the basis of the reliability of Acts; it is, however, only in England that Acts continues to be regarded as historical—British scholarship is often blissfully unaware of American or German scholarship. A more prudent method was embarked on, by other scholars in a whole series of books, of conceding Paul's hellenization, but in demonstrating that Paulinism was not a mystery.[23]

Such judgments rested on the basic premise that the mysteries were not only error, but also evil; Plato's praise of the mysteries as symbolic of fundamental truth was unknown or disregarded.[24] The mysteries were assessed solely on the basis of the licentiousness, of sexual excesses, and orgiastic frenzies. To demonstrate the lack of connection between Paul and the mysteries was to fend off a derogation of Paul. These defenses have been interesting in the tortuous effort to find not only significant distinctions between Paulinism and mysteries, but also in efforts to find everywhere distinctions without weighty differences.

The assertion of the absence of mystery elements from Paul cannot be accompanied by an assertion of the absence of mystery terms from his writings. But a harmonizing explanation would argue that Paul uses mystery terms but not in a mystery sense; such an explanation, too, is given in the case of Philo.

The difficulty with removing the mystery connotations from Philo and Paul is that as a result both of them would seem to be speaking from a vacuum rather than from a vibrant period of human self-search. It is only as scholars overcome the Judeo-Christian bias not only against the externals of the mysteries but also against the spiritual strivings within the mysteries, that a more balanced appraisal of the relations of both Philo and Paul to the mysteries can result. When the term "mystery" ceases to be a term of insult or opprobrium, but is no more than a description of historic religious approaches by means of which people have tried to penetrate to ultimate reality, then these relationships can be objectively assessed. In such a context, the goal of scholarship is not to assert superciliously or deny indignantly the relationships to mysteries, but to note the specific differences in a framework of large similarities between Philo and his Greek environment, and Paul and his.

Another aberration which needs constant correction is the failure of scholars to distinguish between the origin or genesis of a religious doctrine or ceremonial and the understanding of that doctrine or ceremonial in the mind of the adapter. People in our day who shake hands are not uniformly aware that the practice is said to have developed from the days of knights in armor who showed they were unarmed by baring their hands and clasping each other's. It is not at all inconceivable that people in our day who shake hands have no more in mind than to follow a current practice of the amenities.

There have been those scholars whose preoccupation with the background of Christian and Jewish practice has led them to equate their antiquarian discoveries with the practice of a later generation. For example, it is not to be denied that the Jewish Passover is the result of a merger of a pastoral sacrifice held at full moon and an agricultural festival of disposing of last year's grain and the consumption of some of the new crop of grain. But when Jews, after several centuries, saw in the Passover the anniversary of their release from slavery in Egypt, then what Passover meant to them was the ancient release from slavery in Egypt, and it did not mean to them the holiday merged out of two distinct primitive folk festivals.

Those who trace the origins of doctrines and customs as they are found in the rabbinic literature and Christianity often tend to confuse the origin with the view of a later day. Some scholars do not stop to consider that the authors of books of the New Testament and those statements in the rabbinic literature did not possess the recondite scholarship available in modern days, so that the person observing either the Eucharist or the Festival of Tabernacles really did not know the folklore history of these observances.

138

Moreover, the ancient writers expressed their ideas and their convictions not in a vacuum but in a living world. While it is true that in the background of Paul's thought there are discernible reflections of the myth of dying and rising savior-god of the mystery religions, it is still another thing to say that Paul in speaking of a crucified and resurrected Christ was simply repeating a folk motif that he knew. Paul's mode of expression of his belief grew, indeed, out of his environment. But what distinguishes Paul from his environment is the singularity of the combination of background currents which he channels into one stream, and in this feat of intellectual (or, if one prefers, religious) engineering, he leaves clear traces of his own highly individual artisanship.

It is absurd to suppose that Christians of later days who accepted Paulinism were aware that the pagan myth of the dying and rising god was latent in their belief. Some scholars, on the one hand, ascribe naïveté and ingenuousness to ancient writers, and in the same breath ascribe an amazing wealth of historical learning to them. There are those who interpret the passage in II Kings 19:35, of the Assyrian hordes who went to bed and woke up in the morning to find they were dead, as an example of a slip of the pen of a naïve author—these scholars not being aware that even the ancient writers might have had a sense of humor or of the ridiculous. At the same time they will credit a supposedly naïve writer with the possession of relatively recondite data. Sometimes scholarship forgets that the authors of ancient books varied in individual character and in disposition. It is quite inconsistent, however, to credit the same author with naïveté and at the same time with erudition.

The aberration in the study of the origins, or in the study of the background, of either the study of the rabbinic literature or the New Testament, is that scholars tend to confuse the origin with the facets which developed out of these origins. Relating specifically to works in the Hellenistic-Jewish Dispersion, whether by a Jew like Philo or by a proto-Christian like Paul, the study of the origin of doctrines may cast light on the author, but the proper question is not this: What is the background of such-and-such a passage? but, rather: In the light of such-and-such a background, what does this passage mean in its context?

The school of the Christ myth thought it was sufficient to show the folklore origin of certain doctrines and thereby to demolish them. They seemed to have given no thought to this, that somebody like Paul or Philo could hardly express himself except in a language used by people and from a background in which people lived. Can we reasonably expect Paul in giving his exposition of Christ to speak like a Chinese Confucian? Shall we expect Philo to speak like a French Deist?

The issue, I repeat, is not to deny the validity of the study of origins; it is to assert that the study of origins is a supplement to the primary study, the meaning of a passage in its own context and in the light of its own purpose.

Where varying degrees of hellenization exist, and where elaborate studies in background have been made, it is not surprising that excellent lexical work has been done. One cannot overpraise the lexicographers. But scholars have occasionally carried such refinement to the point that they have attributed to a given author refinement and subtleties which are not always appropriate. Specifically, neither Paul nor Philo always utilizes precisely the same word to express precisely the same idea. Neither ever dreamt that he would be the subject of lexical studies; neither ever felt the necessity of distinguishing, let us say, between "door" and "portal," or between "soul" and "higher mind." Paul's letters are a random collection, the remnant of a larger group of letters. Philo wrote tracts. Our modern interest is to analyze, assemble, and classify the notions in these writings. Neither Paul nor Philo ever wrote analytical, systematic treatises on subjects such as God, the logos, or the nature of man. We know their views as we bring together related passages in our own system. But ofttimes we see too much, and too many distinctions in the accidental words that the author chanced to use in given passages. We commit him to a verbal precision which none of us ever attempts in his random correspondence or in his daily oral lectures. Scholarship has often been overperspicacious in analyzing both Paul and Philo.

But still another danger inheres in such word studies. It is true that scholarship has been aware that a word such as "righteousness" means something different to the rabbis from what it means to Paul and from what it means to Philo. But what is especially true of the rabbis is also true in large measure of both Paul and Philo. Their métier was not to establish definitions or to fashion unassailable semantic fortresses. Since basically they were either expounding the Old Testament or else were rooted in the Old Testament, they conceived their views not in abstract terms but in more personal and concrete ways. For example, the rabbis tell us what a holy man is, or what a good man is, but never what are holi*ness,* good*ness,* and righteous*ness.* They illustrate these traits by pointing to Old Testament characters, Abraham, Isaac, Jacob, or others. If we are to understand their thought, then we must follow their method of thinking. The danger in lexical studies, or in analyses made on subject headings, is that they fail to do justice to the intent and conviction of the ancients. Thus, some scholars speak of rabbinic doctrines of free will or predestination. But to interpret their views as concepts or as fully developed doctrines is to be untrue to rabbinic method. Along the same lines of reading modern analytical trends into the ancients, Professor Wolfson has given us a two-volume work on Philo which can be said virtually to ignore Philo's treatment of the patriarchs and Moses; yet these characters are the medium of Philo's exposition of his views.[25] Certain German scholars have given us elaborate, and even ingenuous, analyses of rabbinic theology, always in terms of subjects and abstractions, and seldom with appreciation for the rabbinic method.[26] In dealing with Paul, many scholars have been so preoccupied with classifying the different subjects they believe Paul discussed that they pay no attention to such things as Paul's use of Scripture, Paul's deviation from the usual allegorical method, and Paul's basically unphilosophical cast of mind.[27]

It is often a little startling to read the contrasts that are said to exist between Paul's profundity and Philo's shallowness. This contrast is made not on the basis of the emotional involvement which each finds himself in where it might be said that Paul is highly emotional and Philo rather serene; it is assumed by some Christian scholars that Paul's intellectual equipment not only matched Philo's, it even exceeded it.

Such subjective judgments stem not only from a sectarian bias, from which no one is completely immune, but also from an inability to see either Paul or Philo in proper dimension and against a living background. The tendency toward a neat categorization is often as great a peril to objectivity as is antecedent evaluation.

A by-product of the effort to rescue Paulinism from the rationalist attacks of the nineteenth century has been an interesting segment of scholarly literature. Since the time of Renan, to whom is usually traced the neat phrase that Paul substituted for the religion of Jesus a religion about Jesus, there has emerged quite a spate of essays and even volumes which, in refutation, have essayed to show the congruency of the teachings of Jesus and those of Paul, and, indeed, the direct dependence of Paul on Jesus. While few scholars have gone as far as Klausner,[28] who, despite the absence of any testimony in any literature, believes that Paul knew the historical Jesus, other scholars have written to show that Paul was well acquainted with the details of the life of Jesus.[29] In part, such demonstrations rest on Paul's knowledge of the traditions of the death and resurrection; but there is in all the Pauline corpus but a single passage in which Paul reveals any unmistakably clear

141

and sharpened knowledge of Jesus, the passage in which he quotes Jesus in discountenancing divorce (I Cor. 7:10–11). Beyond this, we have only a random and scattered series of overtones.

The traditional approach toward these overtones has been to look in the Pauline corpus for congruency with or reflection of Gospel materials, and then to assume that, as Jesus preceded Paul in time, so the overtones are later than Jesus and dependent on him. But modern scholarship, through the application of *Sitz-im-Leben* principles, and from the analyses made by form critics, is uniformly persuaded that the Gospels reflect the interest and beliefs of the later Church.[30] Traditional material going back to Jesus was shaped and altered by the later Church; and material, reflecting constantly changing issues in or crises from the Church, was created and read back into the career of Jesus. For example, the point of controversy recorded between Jesus and the Pharisees on the matter of the washing of the hands is that Jesus nullified the Jewish food laws; such implicitly is the purpose of Mark 7:1–15 and Matthew 15:11, while Luke 11:41, has Jesus explicitly saying, "Behold all things are clean to you." If the question of foods had been settled in the time of Jesus, it is surprising for it to arise as though *de novo,* as it does in Galatians, or for it to be the subject of a Jerusalem council decision, as Acts 15 shows. The question of foods is but a single instance of more such problems, where modern scholarship would ascribe the priority in time of an issue and its solution to the Apostle Paul, and whatever dependency is indicated to the evangelist; in the present instance Luke is ascribing to Jesus the settlement of an issue that arose in the time of Paul.

To generalize from such a particular, where the older scholarship looked for traces of influence of Jesus on Paul, the modern turn of scholarship would be to find the reflections of Pauline doctrine in the Gospels. While some decades ago scholarship looked for Pauline doctrines in the *obiter dicta* in the Gospels, the search for such influence can legitimately be extended even to the words which the evangelists put into the mouth of Jesus. The older scholarship looked for "the mind of Christ in Paul"; an advantageous direction of modern scholarship is to look for the mind of Paul (among other early influences) in the words and events centering around Jesus.

The significant contribution of Paul was that he provided the justification for the early Christian church to make a significant departure from Judaism, namely, the abrogation of the Law of Moses; Paul emphasized faith, rather than works of the Law. Christian scholarship in general assumes not alone that Paul urged something different from his non-Christian Jewish contemporaries, but that he urged something deeper and finer. Traditional

142

Jewish scholarship following Renan, sees Paul as a *bête noire*. In either case, evaluation has often obscured a clear understanding of just what motivated Paul, and just what his intentions were.

To regard Paul as superior is inevitably to regard legal Judaism as inferior. The Epistle to the Hebrews, in addition, allocates to Judaism the role of the imperfect foreshadowing of the perfect realization, Christianity. The conviction that these evaluatory attitudes are objective judgments colors many an antecedent state of mind among the scholarly researchers. A by-product has been a series of unhappily polemical studies. A German Christian scholar, Fiebig,[31] declared that the superiority of the parables of Jesus over the parallel parables of the rabbis lay in the fact that Jesus drew on an abundance of references to nature which the rabbis totally ignored; in response, a Jewish scholar, Feldman, produced a long volume of rabbinic parables limited to references to nature.[32]

Moreover, the denunciation put into the mouth of Jesus of the Pharisees in Matthew 23[33] has led to the inadvertent but natural equation of Judaism and the externals of religion, these to be contrasted with the sincere internals of Christianity. While modern Christian scholarship has largely freed itself from the prepossession that rabbinic Judaism was an arid religion of externals,[34] the residuum of the Epistle to the Hebrews attitude still abides.

An antecedent conviction that legalism is *per se* a mark of a poverty of religious expression is hardly conducive to a sober evaluation of the rabbinic literature. Many scholars forget that the genius of rabbinic literature is that it is legalistic literature, and they remain perpetually capable of being startled at finding legalism in it. What does one expect to find in the library of a law school but collections of typical cases, acute hair-splitting for the purpose of distinguishing between the factors in one case and the factors in another case, or examples of the arguments of opponents about the relevance of a mutually congenial general law as it applies to a specific point in dispute? In its good sense, casuistry is the process of applying a given principle to a succession of actual or suppositious cases, each slightly different from the other, so that the law in each of the derived specific cases can be known. The rabbinic literature is legalistic and casuistic; this is neither an accident nor fortuitous, but the natural effect of the underlying assumption basic to the rabbis, that God had revealed a Law, which needed to be known and applied in every possible human circumstance.

When one throws rabbinic literature into contrast with the New Testament one should be aware that he is comparing and contrasting two literatures, one of which is avowedly legalistic and the other of which is predominantly basically anti-legalistic. The scholarly Procrustean bed by means of which a New Testament statement is made to lie comfortably in a rabbinic bed, or a rabbinic statement in a New Testament bed, is less than infrequently to be encountered. Some Jewish scholars, eminent rabbinists, seem to feel that since the milieu of Jesus was Jewish and Palestinian, one can proceed directly from the Talmud into expounding the Gospels; and some Christian scholars, personally committed to anti-legalism, utter astonishing judgments on the contents of rabbinic literature.[35]

The New Testament has come down to us in Greek. Jesus spoke Aramaic, the language of Palestine of his day, as the preservation of Aramaic terms in the New Testament demonstrates.[36] Translation of something, either of oral tradition or of written materials, took place somewhere along the line. J. Wellhausen, Burney, and C. Torrey have made convincing cases for the presence in the Gospels of instances of faulty translation.[37] Though some Semitists follow Torrey, almost no scholar whose approach is from the New Testament goes along with him in his view that the Gospels as we now have them were originally composed in Aramaic and that translation took place after the Gospels were written. It is only in the case of Revelation that a substantial number of scholars would concede the possibility of a whole document's having been translated.

Except for Revelation, then, the rest of the New Testament, in its recorded form, is a product of the Greek world, not the Aramaic-speaking world. While Matthew may have been composed in relative proximity to Palestine,[38] the rest of the New Testament comes from the more distant Dispersion, as far west as Rome.

It is curious, accordingly, that New Testament scholarship pays relatively little attention to the Graeco-Roman world. In seminaries, the usual historical courses pick up with Alexander the Great, go through the Maccabean revolt, the Hasmonean Dynasty, and get down to the time of Jesus. The Greek Dispersion of Jews is usually mentioned, but often even the mention is absent. The seminarian gets his introduction to the New Testament literature without any comparable effort to portray the conditions economic, political, social, and religious which existed in the Roman Empire out of which the New Testament books were written.

Only in studies of the later period, in which Greek philosophy and Christianity become blended, is the Greek world examined, and then almost exclusively for philosophy, and within philosophy primarily for Plato. The living religions and religious philosophies of the Hellenistic period are almost totally ignored. Indeed, the Graeco-Jewish writings become the property not of the New Testament scholar but of the specialist on the periphery of the New Testament.

The greatest neglect is the religious writings of the pagans. Not that there have not been studies by eminent scholars like Reitzenstein, Cumont, Wilfred L. Knox, Wendland, A. D. Nock, and Goodenough [39] who have collected and interpreted the materials of the Hellenistic world. The state of mind which rejects Hellenism as unworthy of Christianity I have spoken of above; in the present context, the issue is that the basic materials for understanding the environment out of which the New Testament books were composed are ignored, even though they are available. This is much more true of American scholarship than of German, yet it applies to the Germans, too.

The testimony of the non-literary papyri, and the inscriptions on gravestones, are important sources for our knowing the people whose religious inclinations led to the creation of the books of the New Testament. Not alone Plato himself, but Plato as intermediated in his successors is highly significant for New Testament study.

It is my conviction that the center of gravity of New Testament studies needs some drastic shifting. To understand, as far as it can be recovered, the Palestinian background of Jesus, Apocrypha and rabbinic literature are focal. But to understand the Gospels (as distinct from Jesus) and the rest of the New Testament, it is the Graeco-Jewish writers who are focal, and these writers, Philo, Aristeas, and Aristobulus, can be most clearly understood only against the wider background of Gentile Hellenism.

That the mastery of all these disciplines by a single individual is a staggering task is to be conceded. It is at the same time an unavoidable necessity. A single person cannot be a pin-point specialist in each of these pursuits. The lament made here is that the work of the specialists is by our day relatively readily available, but is nevertheless not utilized. It needs to be used, if what is desired is well-rounded scholarship, rather than fractional scholarship.

The Graeco-Roman world did not know the arbitrary boundaries that modern departmentalizing in most universities occasions. Hillel, a celebrated rabbi shortly before the time of Jesus, devised a legalistic formula by means of which a direct requirement of the Pentateuch was set aside, this not capriciously but out of a social need; the formula was known not by a Hebrew or Aramaic term, but by the Greek word *prosboule*. An assembly of elders, which functioned both before and after his time, is known by the Greek term *synhedrion*.

Can the dimensions of this man, a great sage, a great teacher, a religious personality whose impression on his contemporaries was vivid in the extreme, be known without our knowing the Greek factor in his life? How extensive were the Greek influences to which he was exposed, and was there any measure in which he responded to these, to accept or repel them? Did his *prosboule* rest on a native, Jewish dialectic method, or was he in some way influenced by Greek rhetoric? The fullness of the man can be recovered only as we fill in as much as the sources permit us the range of environmental factors. Out of these Hillel will speak not as a disembodied voice, but as a living and breathing human being.

So, too, the writers of the New Testament can cease to be the impersonal voices of unspecified times and places, but rather warm and yearning people whose confrontation of the problems of life and its meaning are always of significance to other human beings.

However elusive the final bits of data may be, and however we may, by the absence of complete information, have to look at things darkly, surely a more rounded scholarship, sensitive to a full array of considerations, and mindful of inevitable variables, can be able to see that crucial period more clearly, and to meet its people face to face.

11

Prolegomena to a Commentary on Mark *

I N MY *Genius of Paul: A Study in History* I set forth some opinions and tentative suggestions about the Gospel According to
Mark.[1] These opinions derive in greatest part from whatever academic and
strictly scholarly inclinations I have, yet also from my experience as a teacher. I
teach "an introduction to the New Testament," a course prescribed in our curriculum for rabbinic students. The course has several purposes, and among
them that of leading the students to a beginning appreciation of the religion
and the Scripture of our Christian neighbors and friends. The friendly interpreter and the pedant are often blended harmoniously in one single person, but
at times they are not. For me to try to portray affirmatively what seem to me
to be Christian attitudes toward the Gospels cannot always preclude the
assessment which the pedant in me must make of the Gospels. Accordingly,
there are junctures at which I am impelled to say something of this kind,
that while the Gospels have come over the centuries to mean "X" to Christians, in my judgment, when they were written they meant "Y."

About a year ago I was with a close and warm friend whom I had not seen
for several years. As the talk veered to his future writing and mine, I men-

* This article first appeared in *The Journal of Bible and Religion*, 31 (1963): 294–300.

tioned my intention to write a commentary on Mark. In the friendliest possible indignation, he said, "What the devil do you have to say that hasn't been said a hundred times already?" There is, of course, a large sense in which he is right, for much that appears in a commentary simply repeats, out of requirements of completeness, what is the common property of commentaries. The area in which to say something new is hence limited. This is as true for me, a Jew, as for any other scholar.

That commentary on Mark ought to reflect solid learning and not simply the curiosity that its author is Jewish. I was taught New Testament not by Jewish teachers but by Protestants. A book I wrote, *A Jewish Understanding of the New Testament,* evoked a frequent comment that it could have been written by a Protestant; this was sometimes said in praise, and sometimes in lament. My commentary on Mark, then, will reflect not as much my being Jewish as my being whatever I chance to be. A Reform Jew, I suppose my relationship to the long Jewish past is kindred to that of an extreme Christian modernist to the Christian past. Hence, there is a sense in which my approach to Tanak (Old Testament) or rabbinic literature is kindred to my approach to the New Testament; these ancient writings call for answering the questions, when was this written, where, by whom, and for what purpose. In externals the method would be the same.

But beyond the externals of method, there is the subtle yet real question of one's relationship, of one's feeling toward the document he is studying. I feel, for example, a sense of deep and direct relationship to such books as Job, Amos, and Jeremiah. Toward Chronicles I feel a much lesser kinship. This difference is the result of how I chance to respond to some particular context. Toward rabbinic literature my relationship involves ambivalences, for there is much I respect and admire, and some that I do not; basically my attitude is, or I think it is, that this literature represents, worthily, an age and a genre now happily past. Yet I would be untruthful if I did not say that along with my personal rejection of the ancient rabbinic Judaism as authoritative, or even normative, for me, there still abides in me some affirmative sense of relationship to it.

Respecting my relationship to the New Testament, this question of relatedness or unrelatedness often baffles me. This is probably the case because of fluctuations that are the product of changing moods. Thus, when I read an old-fashioned liberal like Frederick C. Grant, I have a feeling of affirmative relationship both to his scholarship and to what he studies, but when I read the newer scholars, especially the neo-orthodox, I sense in myself a negative relationship to both. Any approach I would have to Mark, or some other New Testament book, would consciously or unconsciously derive some part of its substance from this matter of relatedness.

I think I am aware of my tending, mostly but not entirely, to some scale of values. Thus, I have a much, much higher regard for Paul than for any of the canonical evangelists (*the evangelists, not Jesus*). Yet my feeling for Paul is close to my feeling for Philo; they were both men of great gifts, and they evoke my ungrudging admiration, but never my assent. On the other hand, there is much in the Gospels which evokes both admiration and assent, with the end result that I feel a relatedness to portions of the Gospels which I chance to admire less than Paul, and less relatedness to Paul, even though I admire him more.

Mark fascinates me in the same way that a first class enigma can fascinate. I feel no affirmative kinship with its author, nor with his presentation of Jesus. It is Matthew's Jesus somewhat, and Luke's much more, to whom my relatedness exists. But the contents and the form of Mark intrigue as a puzzle might, and as an essay might not. I think that I have seen, or at least glimpsed, in Mark things which others seem to me not to have seen. Perhaps I have seen correctly, perhaps I have not. But if there is something which I have seen and others have not, this is due not to better eyesight on my part, but to the accident of the angle of vision. And it is to express as clearly as I can this matter of the angle of vision that I have felt the need of the fore-going.

Those readers acquainted with my book *The Hebrew Scriptures* will know that in one important matter I swim against what seems to be the current today; namely, I am not an affirmer of the history encased in scriptural writings. I am not the thoroughgoing skeptic that many nineteenth-century German scholars were, nor, like certain present-day journalists who popularize archaeology, the thoroughgoing affirmer. Rather, my conscious assumption is that ancient writers were not modern historians. They were not trained in research, and were not habitués of archives, and, moreover, history in Ranke's definition was never their intention. Hence, to try to meet scriptural authors on our modern plane of historical reliability is to be inevitably working on the wrong level, and must result in our minds never truly meeting theirs. If the historical statements they make chance to be reliable, this is only coincidental.

These quasi-historical writings are, of course, theological. This statement, correct as it is, tends also to become a cliché and to sanction an avoidance of clarification. If it were to be stated more precisely, the judgment would run along these lines, that the ancient writer had a theological viewpoint, itself a composite of multiple items, and when he wrote, it was in reflection of, or in exposition of, or in advocacy of this complex of multiple items. The ancient writer may have been a poor or an expert craftsman; but his possession of craftsmanship or his lack of it is far less significant than that he had a viewpoint, and that his viewpoint affected what he wrote.

I stress this because it is in opposition to the opinions, implicit or explicit, of what needs to be denominated as the "tape recorder" theory of ancient writers. In such a theory, the writer's heart and mind are supposedly of no import whatsoever, for the writer only recorded, and without change, what he heard or read. This theory is implicit in some versions of the "folk-memory" hypothesis, and is explicit in an important work in form criticism, Dibelius, *From Tradition to Gospel:* "A community of unliterary people, who await the end of the world today or tomorrow, has neither the capacity nor the inclination to produce books, so that we ought not expect from the Christian community of the first two or three decades the production of real literature." [2]

My own opinion is exactly the reverse. No man ever picked up a pen without having some purpose in writing.

Indeed, there have been to my mind three deficits in form criticism. First, the method is unreliable, for it builds up a suppositious case about the universals in the growth of folk literature (and hence the classifications into types) and then proceeds to try to make Gospel materials fit the preconceived paterns—and subjectivity has nowhere been more rampant in scholarship than in New Testament form criticism. Second, the inference of form criticism is that the content of a Gospel under study is the *altered* form of inherited material, so that back of a pericope used by a Mark or a Luke there must always, *always* lie a source or sources. Ergo, an evangelist never created material, he only copied it. The key word here is my word "always"; this is not to deny that writers used sources, but only that when scholarship spends its energy in ferreting out sources virtually to the exclusion from study of how these sources were used, or whether any source at all underlay a pericope, the Gospel under study comes to be distorted. To many workers in the field, form criticism is distasteful because in attributing this or that to the faith of the early church, it left very little to Jesus himself. Though Henry Cadbury in "Between Jesus and the Gospels" [3] thought Bultmann's *History of the Synoptic Tradition* (*Geschichte der synoptischen Tradition*), excessively skeptical, I must comment that form criticism strikes me as a desperate effort to find a basis and a method for salvaging historical reliability in the Gospels. Cadbury stresses this point. The "negative" results of form criticism seem to be adjudged too harshly by those who fail to discern that it was actually intended to come up, impregnably, with some items which would be positive, this in an era when Gospel study revolving about historicity was largely negative. The bent of form criticism was to suggest that one could strip off layers of the onion and get back to the pristine vegetable; instead, when once the theory was applied, one stripped and stripped and there was practically no onion left. Form criticism, then, was a valiant effort to find a basis to affirm history; the conviction that the "history" is at best coincidental leads me to believe that form criticism is a wrong method the results of which, whether they are negative or positive, are inevitably wrong. Such a view does not, of course, deny that accurate bits of history are in the Gospels; it denies that form criticism or any other method hitherto devised can enable the modern scholar to separate the historical from the unhistorical, if the scholar once concedes that unhistorical materials are to be found in the Gospels. The greatest distortion in form criticism is that it unduly elevated the problem of historicity. The theory of the priority of Mark predisposed this Gospel in particular to the distortion; and while scholars from time to time have stressed that Mark is as theological as the others, even John, I suspect that a poll-taker would find a considerable number of votes for Mark, theological as it is, as yet the *most* historical.

The third deficit in form criticism is that it directed scholarship to the study of pericopes, to the Harmony or Synopsis, and as a consequence the appraisal of Gospels, each as a totality, virtually ceased. If there was still lip service to the mathematical theorem that the whole is the sum of its parts, form criticism acted as an obstacle to the adding up of the parts so as to assess the whole. We have had in recent decades few essays or books that treat the total Mark in its own terms; essays, many good and some bad, have dealt with special theories (e. g., Mark and liturgy), but apart from Enslin's "Twixt the Dusk and The Daylight," [4] I can recall little recent writing that deals searchingly with Mark in Mark's own terms.

The question of historicity in Mark, like that of historicity in Genesis, is at most a subtopic in any full treatment of the writing. The question must not arise too early and thereby obstruct an understanding and appraisal of Mark. Indeed, historicity should be placed as the final subtopic; it must not be allowed to elbow its way to the head of the topics.

It is a truism that first there were writings and only after that was there a canon. There exist a good many books, Jewish as well as Christian, which assess the ancient writings exclusively through the spectacles of canonicity. Some pious works even attribute to the unknown canonizers measures of inspiration exceeding that allotted to the writers. New Testament scholarship, possibly under an influence such as that of Irenaeus, who wrote eloquently in the second century (*Against Heresies,* 3.11.8) as to why there were four and only four Gospels, seems to me to treat Mark without regard to its having had some precanonical existence.

The assumption seems almost universal today that each Gospel, on being written, promptly gained assent from those who then read it. The theory of the priority of Mark would imply, so it is to be inferred, that Matthew approved of Mark, as did Luke, but each had some more to tell. The possibility that Matthew and Luke disapproved of Mark, and had good reasons for doing so, remains largely unexplored. Ernest Colwell, in *John Defends the Gospel,*[5] proposes that John wanted to supplant the Synoptics, but his seems to me a somewhat lone voice. I myself went beyond Colwell in a paper, "Myths, Genealogies, and Jewish Myths and the Writing of Gospels" (see Chapter 12, this volume). It is suggested there that Matthew wrote because he disapproved of Mark; and Luke, because he disapproved of Mark and Matthew; and the judgment is expressed that all four were disapproved of in a work designed as an appropriate and approvable form of Gospel composition, namely the Epistle to the Hebrews. In that paper, I tried to raise the question, in the light of Hellenistic conventions, of what were the factors involved in the writing of a Gospel, and how did a Gospel sound to different levels of readers, especially in its precanonical days. When the Pastorals denounced genealogies and Jewish myths—recall that the Pastorals are regarded as among the latest of New Testament writings—is the allusion to material now found in Talmud and Midrash? Or is it, in the supposedly latest of New Testament writings, to intra-Christian concerns, such as the discordant genealogies in Matthew and Luke? And why does Hebrews use (about Melchizedek, though the author means the Christ) the phrase "without father, without mother, and without genealogy"?

In short, modern interpreters do not raise the question, what is Mark like that Matthew and Luke reject him, but handle the so-called "synoptic problem" as though Matthew and Luke were benign supplementers who had more data than Mark. Those who study pericopes necessarily note tiny items involving rejection; hence the convenient summaries in the commentaries of *Abweichungen* ("deviations"). But the really insistent question is, what is Mark as a totality? Indeed, the process of comprehending a Gospel, since we have multiple Gospels, seems to me to require the following: The first step is the reading of the totality, with no attention to the pericope parallels; next, one studies the pericopes, for the differences in a pericope common to two or more Gospels will disclose for us, as dye does for the microscope, things we might otherwise miss; thereafter, however, one must return to the Gospel as a totality.

Having myself done this with tolerable thoroughness, I find, at least to my own satisfaction, that Mark in many treatments is explained incorrectly because Matthew and Luke (and John) are read with him.

I will here confine myself, in illustration, to three topics.

The first is the role of the disciples. I allege that Mark regards them as villains. (Pious interpreters sometimes phrase this in the form that Mark is "rather hard" on the disciples.) The disciples do not understand who and what Jesus is, do not understand what he says, cannot follow through on his wishes and instructions, and at the crucial moment abandon him. Chief among the villainous disciples, as Mark would have it, is Peter. Not only does Mark portray Jesus as saying to him, "Get thee behind me, Satan," but at the climax Peter three times denies him. Pharisees and Sadducees and chief priests (how much ink has been spilled on the plural priests!) are hostile and opaque; they are the enemies. But the disciples are worse, for they are an epitome of disloyalty. The only man who really comes out well (the women do) is the *goy*, the Roman centurion who can see what the Jews, disciples as well as opponents, have missed, that Jesus was truly the "Son of God."

Mark's treatment of the disciples is not some minor thread. Indeed, it is a major motif which almost vies for attention wish Jesus himself. It is a large part of the warp and woof of Mark. Not only do Matthew and Luke omit or soften in details Mark's black portrayal of the disciples (and Luke introduces a theory of an unlimited number of disciples, but only twelve "apostles"), but the villainy of the disciples recedes in Matthew and Luke to mere stray bits. (Luke 22:32 portrays Jesus as saying to Peter, "When you have turned, shepherd my flock.")

Is this unsavory role of the disciples historical? If so, did Paul know nothing of it? Is it conceivable that he would have abstained in Galatians from throwing into the teeth of Peter-Cephas some recollection of Peter's triple denial? I do not think it is historical; by chance I also do not think that Peter-Cephas-Simon are historically one person; they are at least two.

Mark is not correctly interpreted unless the interpreter is prepared to receive what Mark is saying in Mark's terms. When the interpreter introduces into Mark the favorable attitude to the disciples characteristic of Matthew and Luke, he is distorting Mark.

The second item is the phrase "Son of Man." Here is a locution which has claimed the attention of countless writers, both the strictly academic and also the pious. The greatest barrier to its comprehension probably lies in the circumstance that Mark employs it as Jesus' term for himself. Yet the student must press on and inquire what the term meant to Mark, or to put it differently, what Mark meant by the term. I have published a paper called "Son of Man in Mark," (Chapter 13, this volume) in which I use the previous researches, principally Lietzmann,[6] as the point of departure, namely, that the phrase is borrowed from Daniel and that only with Mark does it become a title. In proceeding, however, I diverged—to an extent, unprecedented even for me!—from antecedent scholarship and declared that "Son of Man" is a *literary device* in Mark. I reviewed the other titles ("Messiah," "Lord," "King," "Son of God") for Jesus, and concluded that none of these was consistent with Mark's needs and purposes. I defined these latter as requiring a sufficiently mystifying effect so as to make it possible for the reader of Mark to understand Mark's Jesus, while simultaneously Mark's characters, principally the disciples, can fail to understand him. None of the other possible titles can serve this double and contradictory purpose of clarity and mystification, for so specific are these titles that the disciples could scarcely credibly misunderstand and misconceive who and what Jesus is. But "Son of Man" does serve in this way. I went on to suggest that as a literary work Mark has a kinship with "disguise" dramas in which the writer and the audience share information which key characters lack.

This treatment of "Son of Man" moves considerably beyond the implication of Mark's portrayal of the disciples, for the Gospel, to my mind, is not simply a partisan tendentious writing, as the "anti-disciples" motif would imply, but is, actually, a studied and artful creation. The simplicity of Mark's style, as a consequence, is misleading; interpreters who have stressed the unornate character of his writing have failed to grasp that involved sentences and orotundity result not from skill so much as from pretentiousness, and that in Greek, as in English, it is more difficult to write simply than to write complicatedly. While I would not attribute to Mark the great felicity which I think characterizes Luke, I regard Mark as an inordinately skillful writer.

I fail to grasp the bases on which some have characterized Mark as a Gospel of little profundity, as if it had only one dimension, that of surface. To my mind Mark is replete with nuances and overtones carefully put there by the author. Whoever wrote Mark was neither a simple writer, nor a simpleton, but an artful writer usually in full control of his pen. He slipped a few times. With the Syro-Phoenician woman, it is infelicitous that Mark has her, rather than Jesus, say the tolerant thing. He should have credited Malachi as well as Isaiah for his opening quotation. And he should have given more care to the passage "It was two days before the festival. . . ."

I say "more care," for to my mind, and this is my third item, Mark is a rewritten Gospel, not a brand-new creation. Some form of the theory of an earlier version, an Ur-Mark seems to me a necessity, even though I cannot pretend to be able to reconstruct it. The oft-cited words of Papias that Mark was Peter's interpreter writing down Peter's reminiscences cannot be applied to the canonical Mark. They might conceivably apply to an Ur-Mark, if only we could find that hypothetical document.

If there was indeed an Ur-Mark, and if the canonical Mark is an artfully rewritten tract against Jewish Christianity, then Mark has a long and complicated literary history. It does not seem to me reasonable that Ur-Mark was a polemic against Jewish Christianity. If the Passion narrative was the first portion to have been set down in writing, it could conceivably have been anti-Jewish, or, more precisely, anti-Pharisaic, not so much out of animus as out of an effort to increase the pathos of the writing, for Hellenistic writers tended to use pathos. But the point of this guesswork about the literary history of Mark is to underline a conviction: the conviction that the canonical Mark bristles with problems many of which are beyond solution, but many of which, hitherto unsolved, tend toward solution when they are looked at from a completely new angle of vision. For example, the ending, *ephobounto gar* ("for they feared"), previously viewed as abrupt and possibly truncated, can now emerge as the exactly needed last sentence, for it brilliantly passes a scornful judgment on the scorned disciples. That Mark closes without a Resurrection appearance would no longer be a surprise, for how could an artful author depict Jesus as appearing to the disloyal and the deniers? The words "Tell his disciples and Peter that he is going before you to Galileee" (16:7), now take on a new sense, for they are not so much the promise they are usually thought to be, but are instead a prime rebuke, meant to be understood as conveying contempt. (Luke and John allocate the Resurrection appearance to Jerusalem.) The date of the crucifixion in Ur-Mark was what John gives (neither Ur-Mark nor John knew the exact date, for the association with Passover is theological, not historical), and the shift into Passover night is tendentious, and reflective of the author's slip. The Quarto-Deciman controversy in the early church gains a little illumination from such a recognition, for we see the more clearly that the historic controversies were not just abstract viewpoints, but reflect vibrant people earnestly and forcefully in conflict. Not impossibly Mark's dating of the crucifixion is an end result, a literary creation emerging from Christians who, still in some proximity to Jews, felt that the occasion must have been on Passover, and not the night before—an end result, rather than the source for the dating.

Moreover, if interpretation is able to get over the hurdle of questions of historicity, then the inutility of certain historical questions is manifest. Sober scholarship need not agitate itself with inquiries into the birth, growth, and development of Jesus' messianic consciousness. A Gospel, in my view, is a tract dealing with the human career of a being conceived of as divine; it is not a tract dealing with a human. The questions about whether or not Jesus in his lifetime claimed to be the Messiah—and related questions deriving from Wrede's brilliant but wrong assessment of the "secret" [7]—need not detain serious scholarship.

Lastly, at least here, we can view in perspective the contours of the new quest for the historical Jesus, and perhaps discern how empty of real significance is much of the writing which seems to me to have turned the respectable word "kerygma" into a mere slogan. It is as easy, and methodo-logically as sound, to recover the historical Abraham the patriarch from the fancies of Philo, Josephus, and the rabbis as to recover the historical Jesus from the kerygma. The Jesus of the nineteenth-century scholarship which Schweitzer surveyed never existed. The new quest can at best turn up a twentieth-century Jesus who never existed.

What is it that is being sought? A man, superbly gifted, but still only a man? Or is it a man who was more than a man? The new questers ought to try to understand that the most they can come up with, through historical research, is only a man. My judgment is that the quest cannot succeed. But if it by chance should succeed, will it be the desired success, or will it be, paradoxically, that success that is indistinguishable from failure?

No one who takes Mark seriously can make the claim that he has learned to know the Jesus of history. That there was such a Jesus I firmly believe. We cannot get to know him, unless new documents should turn up.

We cannot get to know Jesus the man. It is Gospels we can know, not Jesus. Mark can be known, and a better knowledge of Mark can in turn lead to a better knowledge of Matthew, Luke, and John. The first step is to know Mark.

12

Myths, Genealogies, and Jewish Myths and the Writing of Gospels *

T HIS PAPER IS frankly speculative, for the allusion to myths and genealogies and Jewish myths in the Pastoral Epistles is, on the testimony of distinguished commentators, quite uncertain.

Two usual explanations, separate or blended, are quite hoary. I Tim. 1:4, which speaks of myths and genealogies, is usually explained as reflecting a gnostic practice,[1] involving aeons and their successions, such as Irenaeus describes.[2] This is a plausible explanation for I Timothy.

The second explanation, however, couples the Timothy passage with Titus 1:10–14, where the indulgers are described as "Jewish" and the fables as "Jewish." Commentators at his point turn away from the gnostic explanation and speak, sometimes most omnisciently, of the Talmud and its frivolous exegesis of Scripture.[3] Though no one would deny that the Talmud contains some frivolities, it chances that these particular ones needed here are not to be found in it. Strack and Billerbeck, with their remarkable gift for assembling parallels, quasi parallels, pseudoparallels, and irrelevancies, abstain here from quoting even one little stray passage.[4] There is such a quotation, however, reproduced in Dibelius' commentary,[5] from Baba Batra 91a,[6] we should not conclude that Strack and Billerbeck overlooked it, but rather that they properly recognized its ineptness. This second explanation of talmudic myths is most implausible.

It would seem that the disposition to regard the allusion either as talmudic or as gnostic is conditioned by one's accepting or rejecting the Pauline authorship of the Pastorals. That is, if Paul wrote these words, then they

* This article first appeared in *Hebrew Union College Annual*, 27 (1956): 201–211.

would seem to be reflecting Paul's quasi-rabbinic experience intimated in Acts, and represent an early problem faced by the church. On the other hand, if they are from a later hand, then they are concerned with orthodoxy and heresy, that is, internal problems of a later day, and consequently more likely to fit some gnostic source than a rabbinic one.

Now in the judgment of most of the commentators, gnostic tendencies and rabbinic frivolities are mutually exclusive. How, then, could they understand the blend of gnosticism and Judaism in the Pastorals? A way out was suggested by F. J. A. Hort in 1894.[7] The Judaism represented in the allusion, we are told, is not to Pharisaism but some "speculative form of Judaism out of which some forms of 'Gnosticism' may later have been developed . . . So far as it is extant still it is to be found comparatively little in the Talmud, much more in the Midrash, partly also in Philo and Josephus. But we can perhaps form a still better conception of it from the book of Jubilees . . . It might with good reason be condemned by St. Paul as trashy and unwholesome stuff."[8] Hort makes no further effort to identify this form of Judaism.

F. H. Colson, writing in 1918, makes the telling point that the expression "genealogies and myths" was in use by literary critics of the time.[9] It was a frequent phrase of disparagement of a mode of writing history. Such Hellenistic critics held that to use genealogies and myths was to be preoccupied with the inane and the trivial. Since such criticism in the Hellenistic world would scarcely have touched on rabbinic haggada, Colson goes on to describe the Judaism under allusion as a "somewhat conceited pseudo-hellenized form."[10] Perhaps this is correct. But one has the suspicion that this Judaism represents some group whose existence is needed to lend some substance to the thread of wavering explanation, and it would appear that having been created because of the text, it can, at the next turn of the circle, be directly elicited from it.

Easton, who accepts the explanation of gnosticism, said, in 1947, about the passage in Titus: "Strictly speaking there was no such thing as Jewish gnosticism . . . If a Jew became a gnostic he renounced his religion. A renegade Jew, however, might have become a gnostic; of these Simon Magus is the most familiar."[11] We move, accordingly, from Colson's pseudo-hellenized Judaism into apostate Judaism, and what is consistent about the motion is that it carries us away from talmudic Judaism.

Now Colson, in his article,[12] has made the point that interpretation had coupled the I Timothy passage with that in Titus because they are so similar, but that if one had not had Titus, nothing in I Timothy would have suggested some Jewish group. This seems to me to be exactly right. The line of thought which I have been pursuing in my own study has been to try to understand the passage in Titus in the light of Timothy, rather than Timothy in the light of Titus. My initial query to myself went along these lines, why in the midst of pseudonymous epistles devoted to internal matters do we suddenly encounter this allusion to something from the outside? Easton, renders, *malista hoi de ek tes peritomes* by the phrase "Jews, especially." Notice, though, how different the nuance is when we turn to Moffatt who rendered it, "those who came over out of Judaism." The Revised Standard Version reads "especially the circumcision party." Easton's rendering is an unhappy one.

The conclusion seems right to me that the issue raised by the Pastor is indeed an internal one and that "Jews" involved are Christians. When once this is recognized, one can diminish his efforts to find either a frivolous talmudic Judaism or a conceited hellenized Judaism.

Then why search in Judaism and its literature for relevant genealogies and myths? Is this not an issue of inner Christian partisanship? Why not do the simple and obvious thing of searching in the New Testament? No commentator to my knowledge has suggested this.

Perhaps the issue of terming certain teachings "myths and genealogies" is a clue to what may have been a broad subject of warm discussion and debate in Christendom between 100 and 125 A.D. That subject might have been phrased in this way: "How shall an acceptable Gospel be written?" The answer would suppose requirements, as for example, that a Gospel should promote faith rather than, by infelicities, engender resistance or skepticism. Its appeal should be broad: to old and young, to poor and rich, to the lowly and the lofty, to the dull and the quick-witted, to the unlettered and the erudite. Moreover, and here would be the most important facet, a proper Gospel should depict the humanity of Jesus without impugning his divinity, and his divinity without repudiating his humanity.

A Gospel able to satisfy all possible readers—*at a time previous to its canonization*—may well have been too formidable a challenge for successful accomplishment by any one single effort.

Both Matthew and Luke set forth genealogies. These have been quite a problem to centuries of interpreters. They have a different scope and order, and where they overlap they do not accord, nor do they conform to data in the Old Testament. Moreover, the Matthean genealogy in 1:16 reaches its natural high point in Joseph, whose son, according to the Greek text, Jesus was not, though the Syriac contains a well-known different reading. Mark, on the other hand, both lacks a genealogy and rejects (12:35-37) the Davidic descent: "David himself calls him Lord; so how is he his son?" One recalls John 8:58, "Before Abraham was, I am." Why is there no genealogy in Mark? Or was there a time when Mark also began with a genealogy? Does the first verse, which lacks a verb and also an article for *arche*,[13] replace a genealogy which was present and later excised?

John likewise has no genealogy, but instead the oft-debated "logos" prologue. It has been said over and over again that the logos disappears from John, except by implication, once we pass the prologue. Is the "logos" prologue a replacement for a genealogy once there—something I doubt—or is it an affirmative prefix designed to divert an expectation of a genealogy?

John, moreover, as is well known, gives us only a scattering of incidents about Jesus. Such Synoptic material as the birth in Bethlehem, the baptism, the temptation, the transfiguration, the agony in the garden, the ascension—all these are ignored. Not one parable or pithy saying appears; the many miracles, healings and exorcisms of the Synoptics are reduced in John to what Peter Schmiedel[14] has called one example of each class of miracle, and what miracles John does use in common become enhanced and appear in a context in which the narration is clearly secondary to the significance of the miracles. Did John regard the abundance of Synoptic material as myths?

Could it not seem that John in writing his Gospel, was making an effort to avoid genealogies and myths? If Ernest Colwell is right,[15] and I believe he is, that John is trying to supplant the Synoptic Gospels, does the procedure not seem to reflect some repudiation of genealogies and myths? And if such materials were uncongenial to John, is it too much to suppose that they were uncongenial also to the Pastor?

It is a commonplace that the Fourth Gospel and Paul have some doctrinal similarities or affinities. What shall we make of Paul's aside, found in II Corinthians 5:16, that he once regarded Christ *kata sarka* but does so no longer? Is it a reference to the earthly life and deeds of Jesus? [16] Some commentators reject the suggestion, but what they offer in its place is hardly persuasive or illuminating. Let us go beyond the direct evidence and suppose that it is indeed a reference to a practice which Paul had once followed but had abandoned, namely, that in his preaching he had formerly appealed to this or that incident in the human career of the Christ Jesus, but now he did so no more.

Why?

It is because for all the attractiveness of this or that incident, they pale into insignificance compared with the majesty of the conception which Paul has of the total import of the Christ Jesus. Is it then conceivable that, even before John, Paul came to the conclusion that this or that detail, such as the Synoptics furnish, when weighed against the totality, was little better than a "myth"? [17] If this seems unlikely, then how shall we explain the tendency in the ante-Nicean fathers [18] to allegorize the materials in the Gospels which by their time had become canonical? One does not allegorize a text which is not, in some way, troubling; allegory, as every student of Philo knows, is the device by which one binds himself to a text which he both holds to be sacred and also feels to be disquieting. Would Paul have liked the Synoptics, or would he have preferred John? Do not the Pastoral Epistles and John come from the same general period, 100–125 A.D.? Is John a Gospel which the Pastor may have found more congenial than he found the Synoptics?

In the time since Irenaeus, [19] the fourfold Gospel has evoked from Christendom exactly those attitudes which canonization calls forth. From the vantage point of accumulating centuries it may be difficult to envisage the possibility that individual Gospels, now uniformly adulated, were at times regarded with suspicion and antagonism in portions of the early church. Yet anyone who accepts the priority of Mark and who uses colored pencils on a Synopsis of the Gospels, comes away with a sense that bits and pieces in Mark dissatisfied Matthew or Luke or both. That such dissatisfaction could extend to the totality of a Gospel, because of its tone and method, may seem unlikely and unreasonable. Yet the Gospels existed before they were canonized; and canonization in general did not preclude opposition both before and after. Witness the rabbinic perplexities about Ezekiel, Canticles, Ecclesiastes, and Esther.[20] Canonization does not mean that there was not some passing or abiding opposition.

Indeed, when one sees how Jubilees, or Philo, or Josephus [21] exercise selectivity, recasting, and *eisegesis* in working over a canonical book, Genesis, then even canonization does not prevent a commentator from having some marked reaction and response to what he reads.[22] To object to what is in a canonical book is markedly more drastic than to object to a book as yet uncanonized.

Reverting to John, my suspicion is that his objection to the Synoptics was not so much to details, though he has such objection, but rather to the manner and method of them. An equation can be set up which runs like this: The rabbinic haggada is to Philo as the Synoptics are to John. The rabbis regale us with haggadic anecdotes about Abraham; Philo has not one. For Philo is trying to express what to him is the higher significance of Abraham (or Isaac or Moses) and folksy materials are scarcely on the austere level which his humorlessness demands. John, it seems to me, has no admiration for the method of the Synoptists, out of a comparable preoccupation with what is to him the abiding significance of Jesus the Christ.

In short, it seems to me possible that our passages in the Pastorals are directed toward such Gospels as the Synoptics in particular. As for the phrase "those out of the circumcision," to regard the Pastorals as coming from Paul was not impeded by an effort to bring the tone of Titus near to that of the Galatians,[23] and to label the indulgers in genealogies and myths "Jewish" was to indulge in an ancient anticipation of a modern tendency to damn by epithets. The Pastor seems to be saying that genealogies and anecdotes are trivial and a waste of time, and moreover, they are something that "Christian" Christians will have no truck with—they are a "Jewish" predilection.

The merited attention which form criticism has focused on pericopes seems to me to have had this debit, that here has been little attention paid in recent New Testament scholarship to the Gospels as totalities. Granted that Mark or Matthew is each the sum of its parts, there is need to proceed beyond the abundance of details and into an assessment of each of the Gospels as an entity. Plural Gospels should alert us to the probable existence of

163

plural views; plural views ran the gamut from mild divergency through direct antithesis.

If this is reasonable, then there are in it implications for understanding early Christianity. Thus, Matthew wrote *because* he objected to the tone and content of Mark, and he had some deficiencies to supply. Luke wrote *because* he objected to both Matthew and Mark. John wrote out of objection to all three.[24]

And did John fail to elicit objection? Epiphanius tells us, punningly, of the shadowy Alogi who objected to it.[25] Were there others? Was there an attitude such as this, that John did well in eliminating the genealogy and in reducing the number of incidents, but he still has some. Is there not a different and better way?

Does not Hebrews avoid more successfully the pitfalls inherent in all four Gospels? What shall we make of Hebrews 7:3, with its sequence of "without father, without mother, without genealogy"? Do these words mean no more than Davidson's comment, in his commentary (p. 131): "The words do not mean that Melchisedec came into existence having no father and no mother, but that in the picture presented of him in Scripture, he stands unconnected with any family, and yet a priest"? [26] While it is true that the verse is about Melchizedek, and not about Jesus, what the verse is trying to show is the similarity between the two. Is not Hebrews, despite its quasi-epistolary form, a kind of Fifth Gospel, devoid of genealogies and free of that kind of narrated incident which a captious critic might have called a myth?

The author, or authors, of the Pastoral Epistles would seem to stand somewhere in between the canonical evangelists and the "docetic" heretics. They do not, as did the latter, deny the humanity of Jesus; they seem, however, to be uncomfortable about some ways of describing the historical Jesus. Whether it is only what they regard as infelicitous in the Synoptic tradition which elicits their disapproval of genealogies and myths, or whether they went on to virtually total disinterest in the historical Jesus, is beyond precise identification. Indeed, it might have been a combination of both.

Though the above is admittedly speculative, it is hardly mere conjecture to conclude that the allusion to "Jewish" myths is meaningful only on the basis of its being a problem internal in Christendom.

13

"Son of Man" in Mark *

THE TERM "Son of Man" may be said to constitute something of a problem in early Christian writings; it is not a problem in the same way in Jewish writings. Ezekiel's use of the term (and he uses it frequently) is readily discernible as connoting simply "man"; it is in Daniel 7:13 that the reading, "someone in the likeness of a son of man," brought to the phrase "Son of Man" the special connotation of a messianic role. IV Ezra and Enoch use the phrase, but in the light of Daniel, as is the case in at least two passages in Mark. In rabbinic literature, however, the term seems unknown as a name for the Messiah. When Hans Lietzmann studied the term in his fine monograph *Der Menschensohn* in 1896, he came to the conclusions herein summarized.

Lietzmann makes the valid point that previous to the Gospels "Son of Man" was merely a phrase; in the Gospels, however, it is transformed, as it were, into a title. I see no reason to disagree with this conclusion of Lietzmann's.[1] Yet there is reason to inquire into the nature of the phrase as a title, particularly in Mark, the earliest of the Gospels. Applied as it is by Jesus to himself, it is one of several titles found in the New Testament: "Messiah" (*Christos*), "Lord" (*kyrios*), "Son of David," "Son of God," "King of the Jews," and the like. Other terms are "logos" and "servant." Virtually all commentators see a certain synonymity in the terms, though, of course, they have seen specific differentiation: a frequent view, for example, is that the title "Son of Man" was utilized by Galilean Jewish Christianity, whereas *kyrios* was utilized by Dispersion Gentile Christianity.

* This article first appeared in *In The Time of Harvest*, Daniel Jeremy Silver, ed., (New York, 1963), pp. 355–67.

166

In Lietzmann's procedure, he lumps together all occurrences of the phrase in the four Gospels, but gives us not one single word in characterization of any one of the Gospels in which the term occurs. So too his successors. Is it valid that the problem of the phrase is unchanged from Mark through Matthew, Luke, and John? That it could remain unchanged, could well be the conclusion of a scholar; in Lietzmann, and in virtually all other scholars, however, this is a tacit a priori assumption.

It does not seem to me that New Testament scholarship has adequately assessed the phrase "Son of Man" in what I regard as the prime requisite, namely, its contextual use within the Gospels. In this essay I confine myself to the phrase in Mark.

Any study of the context of the phrase "Son of Man" in Mark is dependent on an antecedent question, namely, a judgment on the purpose, method, and *Tendenz* of Mark. A consensus exists among scholars, although, of course, there are deviations within that consensus. Mark was composed, perhaps 68–72, at Rome; the church tradition, with which the name Papias is associated, and according to which Mark recorded the recollections of Peter about Jesus, can hardly be taken fully at face value, yet there might well be a reflection in Mark of primitive oral tradition. Indeed, it is possible that there existed an Ur-Mark,[2] an ancient version, much more faithful to the reminiscences of Peter than the canonical, and later, Mark turned out to be. This canonical Mark contains the repeated motif of a "secrecy" which seems to obscure Jesus' messiahship even from his disciples; a somewhat standard explanation of the motif avers that the belief in Jesus' messiahship arose only after a belief in his resurrection emerged, and that in his lifetime Jesus never made the claim to messiahship.[3]

My own approach to Mark is quite different and would appear to those who are middle-of-the-roaders quite extreme. It seems to me that the consensus judgment views Mark partly through its derivatives, Matthew and Luke, and partly by clothing Mark with that understandable veneration bestowed on canonical books. I have suggested that Mark was precanonical before it became canonical, and that it ought to be viewed by scholars in its own light, without respect to its derivatives and without respect to that special status which canonicity confers, for that status can obscure the true import of a document.

When Mark is viewed in its own light,[4] it is an unmistakable polemic against Palestinian Jewish Christianity. Mark alleges that Pharisees, Sadducees, and "chief priests" were vicious enemies of Jesus. The disciples, also Palestinian Jews, neither understand Jesus nor were able to follow his example or fulfill his mandate; at his arrest, they abandoned him. The chief culprit among the disciples was Peter, who crowned his opaqueness by three times denying Jesus. The demons and the Roman centurion alone knew who and what Jesus was. I have concluded that the motif of "secrecy," upon which the theory that Jesus never claimed to be the Messiah was built, is in reality quite different; it is, rather, the motif of the opaqueness of the disciples. I have felt it necessary to diverge from the corollaries found in much scholarly writing about the theorem of the "messianic secret."

When I first conceived and even published the view of Mark as a polemic against Jewish Christianity, I had not explored in any depth the "Son of Man" passages. On turning to them, I have found, at least to my own satisfaction, that the passages fit congruently with the view of Mark as a polemic.

Lietzmann's valid distinction between "Son of Man" as a phrase, and its use in the Gospels as a title, implies that before the term became a title, it had some good currency as merely a phrase. We should be prepared to find in Mark echoes of "Son of Man" in its more pristine usage as merely a phrase, as in Daniel, as well as in its special usage as a title. Our inquiry is this, why does Mark bend toward this particular title, and why does he use it in the way that he does? Is Mark's singular use of the term in this way to be regarded as deliberate selection, and not mere coincidence?

The first passage we advert to is Mark 13:26, a chapter often called the "little apocalypse." The verse occurs in a sequence of quotations from the Tanak; with 13:26 being largely a citation or paraphrase of Daniel 7:13. We need not here enter into the problems of Mark 13; it is sufficient for our purposes to make two comments. First, nothing in the passage makes it out of accord with the general tone of Daniel 7 or of related passages in Enoch; second, the passage only indirectly identifies Jesus as the Son of Man. To restate this last more clearly, the necessary inference from Mark 13 is that Jesus is the Son of Man, but this connection is not specifically stated. The usage of "Son of Man" in Mark 13:26 is momentarily to be classed with the pristine, rather than with the new usage we will see elsewhere in Mark.

In a second passage, 14:62, the high priest, so it is related, asked Jesus, "Have you no answer to make?" . . . But he was silent and made no answer. Again the high priest asked him. "Are you the Christ, the Son of the Blessed?" Jesus said, "I am, and you will see the Son of Man. . . ."

The closing words, indicated by my ellipsis, are a second paraphrase of Daniel 7:13. The response of the high priest to the reply of Jesus is to tear his mantle and to accuse Jesus of blasphemy. In what the alleged blasphemy consists is not told to us. Inferentially, it would seem that Jesus' identification of himself as the Son of Man is either the basis or else the point of departure for the charge. This passage is a second demonstration that Mark was quite well acquainted with Daniel 7:13. The usage here, while it has nuances of the singular, echoes the pristine use.

We turn next to 8:31. The context is the "confession" at Caesarea Philippi. We read that Jesus "began to teach them that the Son of Man must suffer many things, and be rejected by the elders, and the chief priests and the scribes and be killed, and after three days rise again." In Mark, Jesus is depicted as predicting his "passion" three times; the present passage is the first of the three. In the first prediction, Mark, as he continues the narration, adds that Jesus said these things plainly (Greek, *parresia*). The narrative continues that Peter began to "rebuke him. . . . He rebuked Peter, and said, 'Get behind me, Satan! for you are not on the side of God, but of men.'" The passage would seem to be saying that though Jesus spoke clearly, Peter at least objected to the import of what Jesus said. Whether Peter objected because he failed to understand despite Jesus' clarity, or whether Peter understood and consequently objected, is here left uncertain. That Mark implies that Peter misunderstood, or failed to understand is a possibility.

In the continuation, however, in 9:9, a fourth use, Peter, James and John are charged not to tell anyone of the "transfiguration" which they have just witnessed "until the Son of Man would have risen from the dead." In the next verse, 9:10, we read that "they kept the matter to themselves, questioning what the rising from the dead meant." Here the explicit statement averts the uncertainty of the previous use alluded to above; the disciples, we are told, do not understand.

A fifth use is in 9:31, in the context of another prediction of his passion. Jesus says, "The Son of Man will be delivered into the hands of men, and they will kill him; and when he is killed, after three days he will rise." Here again Mark appends an unmistakable comment about the disciples: "They did not understand the saying, and they were afraid to ask him."

As a title, "Son of Man" conceals rather than reveals.

The next uses at which we look, 9:12 and 14:21, add to the puzzle of understanding the phrase. I italicize what to us are the key words in 9:12:

"It is written of the Son of Man, that he should suffer many things." There is, of course, no Tanak passage about the Son of Man suffering; the introductory formula can be taken to allude to Isaiah 53 or Psalms 22 and 69 (the two Psalms are paraphrased in the passion narrative). It is only by equating "Son of Man" with other views of Jesus, such as the "Suffering Servant," that the introductory formula of a citation or allusion to the Tanak is intelligible. In 14:21 the phrase occurs twice; again I italicize the key words: "The Son of Man goes, *as it is written of him,* but woe to that man by whom the Son of Man is betrayed." We are in these passages, in view of the italicized phrase, no longer in the pristine use of "Son of Man" as in Daniel, but well into the boundaries of advanced Christian interpretation, well into Mark's singular use of the term.

A ninth use of the term is in 14:41. At Gethsemane, the disciples fall asleep during Jesus' prayers. Three times he prays, and then comes to them: "He came the third time and said to them, Are you still sleeping and taking your rest? It is enough, the hour has come; the Son of Man is betrayed into the hands of sinners." While commentators have found various ways of exculpating the disciples (as did later Gospels), the implication in Mark is quite clear that at the height of Jesus' preparatory agony, the disciples merely slept. When Jesus is promptly betrayed and arrested "they all forsook him and fled" (14:50). And the chief of the disciples, Peter, three times denies Jesus, even to the point of taking an oath (14:66-72). The progression from opaqueness through denial is completed.

The tenth use is again in a prediction by Jesus of his fate; there the sequel is different from what ensues at the other predictions. It retains the motif of opaqueness, but examines it from a different viewpoint. Jesus makes a prediction of the Son of Man's sufferings (10:33-34). The sons of Zebedee make the request [5] to sit "one at your right, and one at your left, in your glory." Jesus rejects the request, at which the other ten disciples had been indignant. He says "The Son of Man . . . came not to be served but to serve" (10:45). In this passage opaqueness is still the motif; this time it is not opaqueness as to who or what Jesus is, but opaqueness about authority among the disciples.

Three passages remain. In 2:10, Jesus states that the Son of Man has authority on earth to forgive sins; in 2:28, the Son of Man is "Lord even of the Sabbath"; in 8:38, the Son of Man will be ashamed of those ashamed of him "when he comes in the glory of his father and with the holy angels." It has been proposed, and I have myself written, that in certain passages, such as the last three, "Son of Man" is equivalent to "I." This opinion now seems to me wrong, for I hold now that the personal pronoun would necessarily lack those overtones which are necessary to Mark.

"Son of Man" is Mark's principal title for Jesus. Though he is addressed as "Son of David" and as "Rabbi" (10:47-51) these titles are sporadic. Notably infrequent is the term "Christ"; it is used seven times; perhaps though, we should number the uses as six, for Mark 1:1, "The beginning of the Gospel of Jesus Christ, the Son of God," may be a title to the document supplied by a hand later than Mark. If 1:1 is a title added later, the first use occurs at 8:29. Jesus is at Caesarea Philippi; he asks his disciples who men said he was; they answer, John the Baptist, Elijah, or one of the prophets. To his question, what do you say, Peter answers, "the Christ." He charges them to tell no one about him (8:27-30).[6]

In 9:41 a reward is promised to "whoever gives you a cup of water to drink because you bear the name of Christ." In 12:35 Jesus, in the Temple, is denying that the Christ is a "son of David." [7] In 13:21 a warning is sounded against believing anyone who says, "Look here is the Christ"; the next verse speaks of "false Christs and Messiahs," and still in the same context.

The high priest (14:61) asks Jesus, "Are you the Christ, the Son of the Blessed?" The chief priests mock Jesus, on the cross: "Let the Christ, the King of Israel, come down now from the cross" (15:32).[8]

So infrequently does the word "Christ" appear in Mark that were it not for 1:1 we should ordinarily make little association between Jesus and "Christ" in Mark. "Christ" is a coincidental title in Mark; the title focused on is "Son of Man."

There is a device used frequently in literature wherein author and reader share information not shared by a character within the narration. Indeed the device has become so conventional in the theater as to constitute a cliché. In Noel Coward's play, *Cavalcade*, a honeymoon couple stand on the deck of a ship planning their future. The scene ends with the wife removing her wrap from the nearby life preserver, so that we read the word *Titanic*. The dramatic impact comes out of the audience's knowing something which the characters do not. The movie biographies of Edison and Pasteur have used the same kind of device; the audience knows that Edison's inventions and Pasteur's researches come to succeed, and therefore, they respond, as it were, to the beginning efforts of the two and to the obstacles the two encounter with increased sympathy. This same device is present in very many of the Greek tragedies. In *Oedipus Rex*, for example, the plot line was thoroughly familiar to the audience; the drama consisted in their sharing in the emotional vicissitudes of the characters who do not know what the audience does know; and the foreknowledge of the outcome by the audience not only does not decrease the interest but through heightened empathy increases it.

All "disguise" plays and stories use this same device, whether it is Shakespeare, as in *Twelfth Night*, or whether it is a farce such as *Charley's Aunt*. Perhaps preeminently in the drama is Rostand's use in *Cyrano de Bergerac*, wherein Cyrano, unseen to Roxane but visible to the audience, provides Christian with the words with which to woo Roxane, and later, and most pathetically, Roxane relates to Cyrano the great ardor which she ascribes to Christian.

Preeminently among the Gospels, John employs the device unsparingly, even to the point of making sure that it is not missed. In John 2:19 Jesus says, "Destroy this temple and in three days I will raise it up"; 2:21 tells us that "he spoke of the temple of his body." Nicodemus, in 3:4 asks how a man can enter his mother's womb for rebirth; 3:5 ff. explains that the "rebirth" is of "water and of the spirit." In 4:11–15, the Samaritan woman has "living water" explained to her; in 4:34 Jesus says that his food is to do the will of him who sent him. In these and in innumerable other passages, John's procedure is to have Jesus encounter someone who appears to misunderstand something which the reader clearly understands; the character's misunderstanding becomes the point of departure for Jesus to clarify to the character what is already perfectly clear to the reader. Such evocation of the knowledge, superior on the part of the reader to that of the character, increases the empathy in the Gospel.

Mark too employs the device. Indeed, Mark's aim is not to inform his readers of what they do not know, but rather to employ the knowledge that they already have to heighten the emotional impact. They know that Jesus was crucified; they believe that he was resurrected. They hold him to be more than a man, the Son of God. They know that Jews did not share in this belief. They already believe that the crucifixion was neither a surprise nor a defeat, for they believe that the divine Jesus knew in advance what was to happen to him; that is, Jesus is depicted as knowing in advance of the events what the readers of Mark knew after the events from Christian preaching on Jesus. Mark hence portrays Jesus as going through a preordained schedule of events; accordingly, Jesus three times predicts his crucifixion. He informs his disciples that one of them will betray him; he informs them that they will fall away; he tells Peter that Peter will three times deny him. At Gethsemane, Jesus says "The hour has come."

The thesis in Mark's Gospel, the "plot" of which was known to the reader, is that Jesus was abused by Jewish opponents, misunderstood, betrayed, denied, and abandoned by his disciples, but recognized only by the demons and the Roman centurion (and the blind beggar Bartimaeus who "sees" who Jesus is). Mark had need of a title which could simultaneously mystify his characters and still be fully clear to his readers. Had Mark focused on a title such as "Christ" or "King," he could not have portrayed his characters as mystified. But "Son of Man" served admirably for this purpose in that the characters in the Gospel fail to comprehend the title, but Mark's readers understand it immediately. A brief résumé of Mark's Gospel from this special viewpoint will support the contention.

Mark's first use of the phrase, 2:10, occurs after the exorcism of the demon in the synagogue at Capernaum, the healing of Simon's mother-in-law, and the cleansing of the leper. At Capernaum again Jesus heals a paralytic, through forgiving his sins. The words, especially in context, "the Son of Man has authority on earth to forgive sins," alert the reader both to Jesus' description of himself and also to the title he uses himself.

This latter is confirmed and strengthened in the controversy over the Sabbath (2:23–28), with the conclusion, "The Son of Man is Lord even of the Sabbath." Now the reader knows clearly that "Son of Man" is Jesus' way of referring to himself and that the title connotes his divine role.

It is men who do not understand Jesus' role; demons, though, do. In 3:11 the unclean spirits fall down and address Jesus as "Son of God"; his friends, however, believe him insane, while the scribes say he is possessed by Beelzebub (3:21–22). In Chapter 4 Jesus tells his disciples the parable of the sower; the reader understands the parable, but the disciples do not, so Jesus has to explain it (4:10–20, 33–34). He quiets the wind; his disciples still do not know who or what he is, so (4:41) they say to one another, "Who is this that even wind and sea obey him?" Promptly, in what ensues, the Gerasene demoniac (5:1–20) addresses him as "Jesus, Son of the Most High God." Jesus performs more healings (5:21–43); when he teaches in the synagogue, the Jews are astonished at him, thinking him to be only "the carpenter, the son of Mary" (6:1–6). His fame reaches even King

Herod; the character of Jesus (so clear to the demons and to the reader) is unclear to Herod, for Jesus is variously identified (6:14–16) as the resurrected John the Baptist, as Elijah, or a prophet.

Jesus feeds five thousand with five loaves and two fish (6:30–44); he and his disciples embark on a boat for Bethsaida (6:45–52). Jesus walks on the water. The disciples "were utterly astounded, for they did not understand about the loaves . . ." (6:49–51). He feeds four thousand people with seven loaves and a few small fish (8:1–10). He declines to give a sign to the Pharisees (8:11–13). In a boat with his disciples, he warns against the "leaven of the Pharisees, and of the leaven of Herod." The disciples, not understanding, say to one another that they have no bread; Jesus thereupon reminds them of the two miraculous feedings. To the reader it is clear that Jesus is commending himself as "spiritual" bread (see John 6:35). He says to his disciples (8:17), "Do you not understand?" The question is unmistakably intended as a sharp rebuke.

At Caesarea Philippi, Jesus asks his disciples who men say he is; they answer, John the Baptist, Elijah, or one of the prophets. He asks, "But who do you say I am." Peter answers, "You are the Christ." Jesus charges them to tell no one about him (8:27–29). One might suppose that now all is clear; but it is not. Jesus "began to teach them that the Son of Man must suffer many things. . . . And he said this plainly." Peter rebukes him, and he rebukes Peter (8:31–33). Jesus then proclaims what the responsibility of a disciple is to be—a responsibility which these disciples are destined not to meet. This proclamation is made to "the multitude . . . with his disciples." He says, "Whoever is ashamed of me and of my words . . . of him also shall the Son of Man be ashamed. . . ." Clearly the passage (8:34–9:1) is an admonition against infidelity, made to those whom Mark regards as unfaithful, and whom he will presently plainly portray as unfaithful.

Next comes the transfiguration, wherein Jesus is identified by a voice from a cloud as "My beloved Son"; he charges Peter, James, and John to tell no one about the transfiguration until after the Son of Man will have risen from the dead. Even so, they do not understand what rising from the dead means (9:2–10). They inquire about Elijah as the forerunner. Jesus replies that Elijah has already come, and (with the execution of John the Baptist in Mark's mind) Jesus says, that "they did to him whatever they pleased. So too The Son of Man will suffer many things, and be treated with contempt." In both cases, we are told, the incidents conform to what "is written" (9:9–13). Next, he exorcizes a demon from a boy, this after the disciples were unable to do so (14–29). Passing through Galilee, he teaches his disciples a third time that "The Son of Man will be delivered into the hands of men, and they will kill him; and when he is killed, after three days he will arise." The disciples do not understand the saying (though the reader does), and they are afraid to ask (30–32). The disciples discuss who among them is the greatest; Jesus disparages their talk and takes a child in his arms, this to emphasize his disparagement of their wish for greatness (33–37). The disciples complain to him of a man not among them who casts out demons in his name. Jesus says, "Do not forbid him . . ." (9:38–50).

The disciples want to obstruct children from coming to Jesus; he replies, ". . . to such belongs the kingdom of God" (10:13–16). A man, told to dispose of his wealth and thus to follow Jesus, was unwilling. "Peter began to say, We have left everything and followed you." Jesus gives the double answer, that the faithful will be rewarded—and Mark does not regard the disciples as faithful—and that "many that are first [i.e., the disciples] will be last; and the last [subsequent Gentile followers] will be first" (10:17–31).

On the road to Jerusalem, Jesus again tells them that "The Son of Man will be delivered to the chief priests . . . and after three days will rise." The passage tells that, before these words, "they were amazed; . . . and afraid." The response to Jesus' words is the request of the sons of Zebedee for preferred places. In his reply, Jesus says, "Whoever would be first among you, must be your slave to all . . . For the Son of Man also came not to be served but to serve" (10:35–45).

At the Temple, Jesus is questioned about his authority (11:27–33). He speaks a parable—this time a clear one, as though Mark has forgotten that he had ascribed to parables the function of concealing. The parable about the vineyard owner is not really a parable, that is, it is not a didactic anecdote, but a symbolic story; it alleges that Jews (the tenants) had killed the prophets (the vineyard owner's servants) and his son (Jesus). God (the vineyard owner) would come and destroy the tenants and give the vineyard to others (the Gentiles; 12:1–12). Jesus, questioned about taxes, replies that to Caesar must be rendered what is Caesar's, and to God what is God's (13–17). He debates resurrection with Sadducees (18–27). A scribe praises him for his answer on the commandments and he praises the scribe. Thereafter "none dared ask him any question" (28–34). He denies that he is descended from David (for he is a divine preexistent being; 35–

37); he denounces hypocrisy, extolling a poor widow for her mite (38–44).

In the "little apocalypse," he predicts the destruction of the Temple (readers knew that it had been destroyed in 70). The disciples ask when this will be, and what the sign will be (Mark 8:12 had stated that "no sign [shall] be given to this generation." Matthew 16:1–14 and 12:38–39 and Luke 11:29 amend the view; Jesus' three days in the tomb, equated with Jonah's three days in the whale, is a sign which is to be given). Jesus tells them only to "watch."

Next, we are told that it is two days before Passover. In Bethany a woman pours nard over Jesus' head. He says, "She has anointed me beforehand for burial" (14:1–9). Judas, who, as the reader knows, is to betray Jesus, goes to the high priest. In an upper room, while eating with disciples, Jesus says that one of them will betray him; "the Son of Man goes as it is written of him, but woe to that man by whom the Son of Man is betrayed." (Mark does not relate what happens to Judas; Matthew 27:5 tells that Judas hanged himself; Acts 1:18 tells that Judas, "falling headlong, he burst open in the middle, and all his bowels gushed out.")

At the Mount of Olives Jesus predicts that Peter will deny him three times before cockcrow (14:26–31). At Gethsemane, Peter, James, and John fall asleep. All, however, is working out as foreordained: "The hour has come; the Son of Man is betrayed into the hands of sinners (32–41). Judas betrays Jesus with a kiss: Jesus says, ". . . Let the scriptures be fulfilled" (43–52). Jesus is brought before the high priest; Peter is at a distance, "with the guards, and himself by the fire." The high priest asks, "Are you the Christ, the Son of the Blessed?" Jesus says, "I am; and you will see the Son of Man sitting at the right hand of Power. . . ." They condemn him as deserving death; the guards rain blows on him. A maid says to Peter, "You were with the Nazarene, Jesus." He denies it; "I neither know nor understand what you mean." She tells the bystanders "This man is one of them." Peter denies it. The bystanders say, "Certainly, you are one of them." Peter swears, "I do not know this man of whom you speak." Immediately the cock crows (14:53–72).

Jesus is led before Pilate, who asks, "Are you the King of the Jews?" Mark scarcely prepares us for this question, for the only thing that has come before that has in any way associated Jesus with kingship is in the shouts of the crowd at Jesus' entry into Jerusalem. "Blessed be the kingdom of our father David that is coming" (11:10). The reply of Jesus, "You have said so," has yielded an abundance of interpretations; some assert that Jesus is acquiescing, and some that he is ignoring the question.[9] From the sequel (The chief priests accused him of many things and Pilate again asked him, "Have you no answer to make? See how many charges they bring against you?"), I am led to suppose that Mark's intent here is to suggest that Jesus was silent, a motif borrowed from Isaiah 53:7. Pilate's wish to free "the King of the Jews" is frustrated by the shouts of the crowd, "Crucify him." Jesus is first mocked and then crucified. The inscription of the charge is "King of the Jews."

When Jesus has died, the Roman centurion says, "Truly this man was the Son of God." The Gentile has seen what the Jewish disciples and the Jewish opponents were unable to see.

His death was witnessed, Mark tells us, by three Galilean women (no Galilean men were present; they had fled). It was Joseph of Arimathea, not a disciple, who buried Jesus. The two Marys saw where Jesus was laid; Salome, the third woman, joins the two; the three buy spices and go to the tomb, but it is empty.

Had Mark chosen to put into the mouth of Jesus some phrase other than "Son of Man," he would have had an inordinate difficulty in carrying through his theme that Jesus was misunderstood by his disciples and by other Jews. Any other term—"Christ," or "King"—would have been too clear to permit misunderstanding, and unless Mark could convincingly portray opaqueness, misunderstanding, and infidelity, his thesis was gone. "Son of Man" served him in that it could be clear to his readers, but not understood by his characters.

"Son of Man" as a title is a literary device of Mark. While conceivably the Jesus of history in his lifetime may have been associated or identified either in his own mind or in that of his disciples with the "son of man" in Daniel, we are in the realm of conjecture. What we can be sure of is that Mark's use of the phrase as a title is a literary device, and not primarily an echo of the Jesus of history. In Mark "Son of Man" has only the dimmest echoes of the antecedent Jewish use. Mark is far from being a document faithful to the Jewish scene; it is a tendentious, highly theological document, coming from a Gentile Christian environment.

The phrase in Matthew, Luke, and John is a subject for another essay.

177

14

Jesus in World History *

CONSIDERATIONS WHETHER OF honesty or of mere communication require a prologue to my paper, a short statement to identify the point of departure from which it is written, and also its chosen scope. In the first place, the record will demonstrate that I qualify for the term "liberal" not only by virtue of my affiliation with that wing of Judaism called by different terms in different countries—Liberal, Reform, or Progressive—but also by a minor public record of publications. Secondly, we must face directly the circumstance that I am Jewish and that my topic is Jesus. Let me concede that although I have certain qualifications as an impartial historian, I am nevertheless Jewish, and therefore not immune from certain presuppositions. The issue here is not that of conscious partisan bias, for I know that I am relatively free of it; the issue, rather, lies in the realm of the unconscious, in the apperceptive mass, in the words one chances to choose, in the basic loyalties which are impinged on. If you could accept my assurances that as far as I can know I am able to approach the figure of Jesus without hostility but also without adulation, then perhaps the tone of my remarks will be all the clearer. But the third issue is the truly troubling one, for while theology is of course central in religions, religions also have texture and warp and woof, and when one studies a particular tradition strictly from within one's own, then automatically he is viewing the tradition he is studying from the outside, and not from the inside. Accordingly, let me suggest this, that certain religious attitudes ani-

* This article was adapted from a lecture given at the London Congress of The International Association for Liberal Christianity and Religious Freedom (IARF), August 5, 1966.

mate Christians which do not animate Jews, and vice versa. Chief among these I would list the matter of the theological point of departure, this as distinct from theological content; and in the light of the theological assumptions let me state that to Jews Christianity appears much more articulately theistic than Judaism, and to Christians Judaism appears much more humanistic than Christianity. I do not think that the difference here is between conservative and liberal Christians, but rather between Jews and Christians, without regard to conservatism or liberalism. As to the scope of this paper, it has gone through several stages of rewriting, so as to acquire, if possible, some reasonable focus. At some point, one simply runs the risk and says, I am going deliberately to limit myself to what can be said in the stipulated time. This paper is unusual for me, in that I am primarily a technical scholar who deals in a restricted period of past history. This morning, however, I shall do little more than touch on that scholarship, and instead I shall deal with what I conceive to be its significance.

The issues relating to the recovery of the Jesus of history seem so well known here, or at least the bulletin of the IARF gives that impression, that there is no need to linger over the details. Let it suffice that we know only so much about Jesus as the New Testament materials let us, and for over a century and a half scholars have been struggling to find an objective way to distinguish between the purely historical, on the one hand, and the legendary or theological on the other hand. To this I must return later in the paper. A typical distinction, which was highly accentuated around fifty years ago, was the effort to distinguish between the Christ, that is to say Jesus as theologically considered, and Jesus, the man viewed only historically. It is my opinion that the New Testament provides no adequate basis for this distinction, for it is logical, modernistic, and anachronistic, rather than being contained in the documents; yet I must at this point find a way in which to formulate some description of Jesus, at least for the purposes of this paper.

I am aware, as I assume you are also, of that abundance of scholarly endeavor which tries so desperately to find a source from which every author must have derived his content, as if the author barred from some tiny spark of creativity, and therefore I am tolerably well familiar with the laborious and often labored tracing of the teaching of Jesus to this or that predecessor, or, as is the case in some research, to this or that successor. In general, I would comment that when originality is attributed to, or conversely, denied to Jesus, this often turns out to be the pedestrian question of priority, and therefore equally important questions have been ignored: for example, that the possible originality of Jesus may have been in the combination of factors, and not in the novelty of single items, or else may have been in the profundity of insight and not in the newness. Except in those passages in the Gospels which speak of the role of Jesus, his religiosity conforms to the Judaism of his time.

Yet there is no violation of the canons of historical research in using as our point of departure the incontestable datum that Jesus the man came to be conceived of as the supernatural Christ. This is true to history, whether we believe in the supernatural Christ or not. Accordingly, the question which we may legitimately inquire into is the nature of the personality and of the religious impulse provided by Jesus which led to his being identified with the Christ. In my judgment, it is wrong to follow those scholars who assume that Jesus in his lifetime was virtually nothing, and that it was only the resurrection conviction which prompted his followers to read back into his career elements which, according to this scholarship, were then lacking. The thesis of Professor Wilhelm Wrede that the messiahship of Jesus was never thought of during Jesus' own lifetime seems to me to stem from a wrong assessment of materials truly present in the Gospels. Wrede's view has had an extensive influence, and also some preposterous sequels; but I do not hesitate to term it an infelicitous conclusion. Respecting Paul, I once wrote that in him Christianity underwent a second beginning, and I couched my opinion in that way to leave room for what to me is an inescapable historical necessity, that some kind of first beginning necessarily goes back to Jesus himself. I confess that I cannot specify precisely what that impulse was; I can describe it only in cautious and general terms.

To fill in that description, I invite your attention to a difference that all too often goes unnoticed between two eminent prophets of the eighth pre-Christian century, Amos and Hosea. By and large the message of Amos is almost exclusively concerned with social ethics, this in conformity with the Hebrew assumption that while the essence of religion is man's relation to God, the substance of that essence is man's obligation to his fellow man. Amos has little to say on the subject of the proper liturgical worship of God, and the little that he has to say amounts to an almost total denial of the efficacy of any or all ritual. Hosea, on the other hand, is preoccupied with the question of the proper relation to God, this to the point that he has almost nothing to say in the sphere of social ethics. Hosea is so emphatic in his denunciation of Ba'al worship, that is, of improper relationship, that he is a major source for our knowledge of the Ba'al cult. Hosea says little about man's obligation to his fellow man.

In the respective emphases of these two prophets we can perhaps see the epitome of the dual aspects of Judaism, man's relationship to God and man's relationship to his fellow man.

I would take it that the impulse supplied by Jesus was in some way concerned with these dual aspects. I would add that in the interval of time between the eighth pre-Christian century and the first, the march of thought proceeded from the strictly corporate, communal conception of religion, to add the factor of a heightened individualism, and the legacy which came to Jesus from the past included a typical Jewish concern for the single, solitary individual. Accordingly, we can think of Jesus as both echoing the corporate and personal Judaism of his time, and also as someone through whom an increased sensitivity and awareness were lived and taught. And we should consider the impulse to have been strong enough to have molded the thoughts and the lives of those whom he came into contact with.

We must not, however, neglect to comment on the identification of the man Jesus with the supernatural Christ. I have no answer to the disputed question of whether or not Jesus himself made this identification. In our present context, let me select one single item to pursue, of the many that could be studied, namely, a turn which individualism took after the time of Jesus, a turn which so emphasized the individual as to imply a nullification of society. The question of personal salvation came so to dominate the thought of a Paul that social responsibility as a religious requirement is virtually absent from his Epistles as from the chapters of Hosea. To Paul and not to Jesus is to be attributed the distinction—which was then and now still is alien to normative Jewish thought—between works and faith, and also the derogation of works as a viable religious enterprise, on the double basis that man is unable to work his own salvation and also whatever man tries to do on man's own ends up in failure.

This is not the proper place to renew certain inquiries I have made elsewhere into the sequence and significance of certain developments in the early church. Here it must suffice to notice that the contribution of the religious genius of Paul to Christianity makes us now summarize a usual and typical Christian stance as composed of the older Jewish aspects of man's relation to God and man's relation to his fellow man, and also an individualism heightened to the point that social responsibility could either be de-emphasized or else disappear. Parenthetically if, as I believe, it is incorrect to interpret Paul as disinterested in social ethics, it is nevertheless not incorrect to assert that he is used as an authority by certain Christians who want to shield their Christianity from social obligation.

The consequence of adding Pauline thought to the older matrix of developing Christianity was to put on Christianity an increased burden of some discomfiting inner contradictions. Antecedently, the preexilic prophets had denied the efficacy of ritual, but in the Old Testament the Pentateuch describes an obligatory sacrificial ritual in full detail; therein lies an inner contradiction visible to anyone who wishes to see it. More pronouncedly, the combined Old and New Testaments present the contradiction of beginning with Pentateuchal law, and proceed thereafter to Paul's Epistles which nullify the laws previously presented. After Paul's time, indeed long after it, Christianity became so multifaceted that it could contain both the strand of man's relationship to his fellow man, and also a denial that such a relationship was indigenous to Christianity.

To revert to our context of Jesus in world history, Jesus was not the entirety of developing Christianity, but only its centrality, and that centrality was often diversely understood and interpreted. With the passing of time, not only was there Jesus but there was also the New Testament, there was also the church, there was also the liturgy—and ultimately there were also the orthodoxies and the heresies, the sects and movements, and even the wars. If at times Christendom, in its unfolding, forgot the meaning of Jesus, it did not forget the name, and therefore from time to time there were to arise those who would call Christians back to a more vivid recollection of Jesus. Accordingly, it is inappropriate to play off, as it were, Jesus and unfolding Christianity as if they were always readily and permanently separable. Despite periods of Christian infidelity to Jesus, Christianity has retained —whether in actuality or only in potentiality—its central focus in Jesus. Therefore, where Christianity spread, so also the name and influence of Jesus spread as a teacher, as an exemplar, or as the divine Christ. For almost seven centuries, the expansion of Christianity proceeded to expand despite ebb and flow.

Christianity captured all of Europe; it spread eastward through Persia to India; it spread into Africa, both southward and westward. It spread despite great internal upheavals such as the Arian heresy or the Spanish "adoptionism"; it spread despite the rivalry, even at the time, of Eastern and Western Christianity. If here and there in the then Christian world, the Christian conviction was at most surface, there is no gainsaying its expansion in breadth.

But from the seventh until the fifteenth century Christianity ceased to expand in breadth, for it was contained by the Mohammedans, and even lost ground to them. The expansion of Christianity resumed in the fifteenth century through the explorations and colonialism of the Christian nations of Europe; its expansion into Mohammedan, or even Buddhist territories, was relatively negligible.

One can properly speak of the four or five centuries before the Reformation as the age in which Christian Europe intensified its Christianity. Simply to mention two widely different areas of human achievement may possibly epitomize this deepened Christianity: first, the building of cathedrals; second, the flowering of scholastic philosophy and the founding of the great universities.

Certainly, then, one must speak of a deepened Christianity. Yet when one reverts to the impulse which Jesus represents, then one must join in the large group of devout, traditional Christians who lament that all too little of Jesus was represented by medieval Christianity. Indeed, almost the only thing that one can salvage as affirmatively reflecting Jesus is the work of the church on the lowest levels of society, in matters of alms and hospitals. In the upper levels of society, paganism at its worst perpetuated in Christian Europe the intrigues with which we are familiar from the Hellenistic-Roman period. More than one Pope emulated or surpassed the most evil of the wicked Hellenistic rulers in matters of disreputable politics and even of personal immorality.

The varieties of abuses and iniquities in the medieval church which called forth the earnest but limited reforms prior to Luther, and then the Reformation itself, and thereafter renewed inner reforms, are perhaps sufficient testimony to the curious state of affairs in which the centrality of the figure of Jesus in Christianity was capable of being forgotten or, worse, ignored. To

183

an outsider to Christianity, and to one who admires cathedrals and respects medieval scholasticism, the wonder seems to be that the medieval church did not find a ready way to maintain a balance between its legacy of Jesus and its legacy of highly institutionalized achievements and austere intellectual attainments. Perhaps the historian is more prone to notice the latter, and to concentrate on them, and to distort the picture through an inadequacy of materials about the life of plain, common people and about their piety, and perhaps the records in the stones of the cathedrals and the books of the philosophers fail to give a full reflection of Jesus in medieval Christianity.

But, and here I tread onto uncertain ground (my knowledge is limited as I am no specialist in this period), it was inevitable that some reformation had to take place. This is the case whether one fixes his attention on the schism between England and Rome, in Henry VIII's marital difficulties, or notices the commanding but rather mild personality of Erasmus, or the mercurial figure of Luther. Reform was inevitable, not so much because of the acknowledged abuses alone, but because the centrality of the figure of Jesus was available, in actuality or potentiality, as a standard by which Christians could assess the highly developed church. With the inevitability of reform, the only issues were whether the political, social, and economic conditions would result in reform from within, or in revolution and reform which would move outside.

What puzzles me is that the two great reformers Luther and Calvin seem to have owed their largest debt to Paul. Perhaps each of them was so deeply involved in the confluence of scholasticism and renaissance humanism that their religious bent was theological rather than pietistic. But by and large the line of tradition to these reformers was from Paul through Augustine and then to their own profound application of Pauline doctrine to their time and to its extension. Except for the pietist movements, the key New Testament figure in the reform movement was Paul and not Jesus. I believe that today we can see the consequence, even if to the Reformers this vision was denied—namely, that a religious reformation focused on Paul and not on Jesus was destined to undergo further revision, for Christianity is centered in Jesus and not in Paul.

The logical outcome should have been further major inner upheavals as Christians pressed on from Paul to Jesus. But either in defiance of logic, or else in a deeper version of it, the Reformation led beyond such internal reforms, and bred a strange kind of quasi-external development; before Luther one can speak of Christian humanism, after Luther one encounters the factor of humanism without the qualifying epithet. And when humanism led to deism, the questions raised and the challenges hurled at the historical claims of Christianity, were not about Paul but about Jesus. The deists seemed, in a curious way, prepared to attack the Gospels but not the figure of Jesus. In the deist rejection of supernaturalism, the figure of Jesus, especially as he is portrayed in the first three Gospels, lent itself readily to an admiration for his profoundly admirable human traits and hence they charged the Gospels with a detestable supernaturalism and therefore with distorting the truth about the figure of Jesus. If the sixteenth-century reformers played off the New Testament against the church, then the eighteenth-century deists and rationalists played off a human Jesus against the New Testament.

It was at the close of the eighteenth and the beginning of the nineteenth centuries that the academic search for the Jesus of history began. This was a Christian response to the deist challenge that Christians must prove the case for Christianity on historical grounds, or, as the phrase went, historical evidences. Then, as now, history was perhaps overemphasized, especially regarding its potential for penetrating complicated matters and simplifying them. We need to remind ourselves not only of the religious atmosphere of the time, but also of the immediately antecedent movements. I have in mind the age of commercialism, the industrial revolution, and the rise of employer and of workingman classes, the political revolts in France and in the United States, and the emergence of democracy in much of Europe. I suppose that in a sense modern man begins to arise at the end of the eighteenth century, and the sense in which I speak of modern man is this: that philosophies or attitudes arose to govern the immediate and ultimate concerns of men in a context in which religion was no longer the major and decisive factor, but only a relatively minor facet within the array of the larger concerns. Moreover, the plurality of Protestant sects had moved through the stages of persecution and warfare into that neutrality called tolerance, and then in large measure to the supposition that religion was inherently a private and individual matter. While traditional churches in various countries managed to retain some measure of official standing, and to be manipulated by governments, or to try to manipulate them, by and large even in those countries where there was an established church, its power was more formal than direct and decisive, and in most countries the established church lost its pristine authority to coerce.

The quest for the Jesus of history was largely the effort of independent scholars to inquire with relatively complete freedom into historical questions, as if historical inquiry would settle all uncertainties. By our time we take this right of free inquiry so much for granted that we are often unaware of an important implication which usually remained tacit: When scholars in the realm of religion asserted their right to make free inquiry, then in a sense they were substituting the authority of their learning over both the authority of the traditional view of Scripture, and, in fact, over Scripture itself. We should not be misled by the nods of obeisance which the scholars made to tradition or to Scripture. The fact is that they were challenging the authority of Scripture, and they were doing so in the supposition of accurate, profound, and thorough learning. If the scholars themselves failed to notice their iconoclasm, the traditionally minded church people were quick to see the implication. While the higher criticism began within Catholic humanism, Catholics began to withhold themselves from the higher criticism and remained outside of it until very recent times. David Friedrich Strauss's *Life of Jesus,* in 1835, lost him his academic post; Bishop Pusey stood trial for heresy in England, and W. Robertson Smith in Scotland. American Protestantism underwent division, at different times, into modernist or fundamentalist sects within a common denomination.

The search for the Jesus of history was more than an academic quest. It was in all truth a search for an authoritative human figure to replace the challenged or abandoned authority of a supernatural Scripture. It can be put in this way, that the object of the search was for a Jesus whose example and whose teachings could still serve modern man, once the weeds of theology and legend and myth were cut away.

Anyone who has worked in the scholarship, especially that of the Germans, must admire it for its thoroughness, its breadth, and its honesty. If it was overconfident about its answers, then that overconfidence resulted more from limited horizons than from laziness, or incompleteness, or caprice. Theories of sources, namely, that Mark was utilized by Matthew and by Luke, and that Luke and Matthew each reflected a source, Q, unknown to or not utilized by Mark, were exhibited in the arena of public notice and won their way through their inner power of persuasion. No single word of the New Testament was left unresearched and unexplored. No theory, no matter how farfetched it might have seemed to be, failed to receive careful weighing and assessment. An F. C. Baur accounted for the supposed rapid hellenization of Christianity by denying the rapidity of it, and by asserting that most of the New Testament documents were second century pseudepigraphs; a Bruno Bauer attacked the premises of David Friedrich Strauss and the Frenchman Ernst Renan who had asserted that there had been a growth and development from Jesus the man into Jesus the divine Christ and then God; Bruno Bauer preferred to believe that first came an abstract view, the logos, and that the logos then became concretized into Jesus, and that Jesus had never existed. The handbooks to the New Testament, called Introductions, dutifully recorded each and every theory, both those destined to endure and those which are recalled only because the handbooks preserve laconic citations.

The history of the nineteenth-century scholarship of Jesus was written by Albert Schweitzer around 1906. Others, McCown and Salvatorelli, have since then written to round out some incompleteness in Schweitzer (who noted almost nothing but German scholarship), or else to bring the record up to more recent times.

We stand today almost where we stood in Schweitzer's time. He spoke of the effort to recover the Jesus of history as a brilliant failure. When he wrote, there were those who were either offended or unpersuaded by his conclusions.

Biographies of Jesus continue to be written despite the almost unanimous judgment of modern scholars that such biographies cannot be written. The direct consequence of an overemphasis by scholars on historical reliability and historical accuracy in all details has been an inescapable abundance of skepticism and uncertainty, and historical study, which was embarked on to produce certainty, has yielded such certainty primarily in its negations. Today we have come through a period of form criticism, dominated by the names of Martin Dibelius and, more eminently, Rudolf Bultmann. This discipline begins with a scrutiny of what is universal in folk tradition and literature, and notices what seem to be the inescapable tendencies. Knowing these rules, one can apply them to the Gospels, and thereby determine how the materials about Jesus grew and developed. In procedure, the Gospel materials were first set into categories according to form, whether a pithy aphorism, a brief anecdote terminating in a didactic statement, or else an extended episode. The developing tradition was conceived of as layers of tradition successively piled upon earlier layers, and as one peeled off layer after layer, he could finally arrive at what was authentically historical about Jesus. The difficulty, however, was that in the case of Bultmann, virtually no authentic layer remained over, for Bultmann saw authenticity primarily and almost solely in the eschatology. We are being assured today, however, that we now live in a post-Bultmann era. The Dead Sea Scrolls have led to the creation of an immense literature which tries to establish, sometimes desperately, a relationship between the Scrolls community and early Christianity; perhaps the fad aspect of the Scrolls has by now also passed away. Currently, at least in the United States, there is also a movement called the "new quest" for the historical Jesus. It appears to rest on the premise that the kerygma, the preaching about Jesus, can convey a tolerably good historical likeness, especially relating to Jesus' "existential self-realization," and that this procedure can replace the nineteenth-century preoccupation with the direct statements of the Gospels.

But we remain where we were when Schweitzer wrote his conclusion in the sense that mere historical research cannot solve the problems in the Gospels about the Jesus of history. The accumulated scholarship only emphasizes how earnestly scholars have tried but failed to find a way to disentangle the historical from the nonhistorical. Let us be clear on an important point: to deny that Jesus ever existed is quite different from the question of whether or not the details in the Gospels are reliable about Jesus. Those who, like me, would deny the historical reliability of the Gospels are saying this: that the Gospels give a mixture of reliable and unreliable history, but we do not know any responsible method to separate the strands from each other.

Yet to my mind the key question for religious men of our time is not the historical question. It is something quite different. Similarly, the problem for liberal Jews is no different in essence from the problem for liberal Christians. To make my meaning unmistakably clear, let us imagine two non-existent situations. The higher criticism has yielded mostly negations. But let us imagine that the higher criticism of the Old Testament gave us assured results about Moses at Mount Sinai in a most affirmative way; let us imagine that the higher criticism of the New Testament gave us assured results about Jesus in a most affirmative way.

If such were the case, then we would nevertheless stand in a position not significantly different from that of orthodox Christians or orthodox Jews. We would then, as liberals, have the reassuring answer to one of the two questions always of concern in the Jewish-Christian tradition, but we would still lack the answer to the second question. The first of these questions is: What shall I believe? Whether we accept the authority of Scripture, or of creeds, or of a church, or arrive at our answers through a kind of relativism, kindred to humanism, we should each be able privately to possess some answer to this first question. As in Hosea, we would know where we stand in relationship to God.

But the second question in the Judeo-Christian tradition is: What shall I do? What shall I do?

Here again we must remember our context. Fifty years ago there was not a single non-Christian state in Europe, and not a single Communist state. Today we speak of an iron curtain. If a generation has matured that does not remember Spain, or World War II, or Korea, certainly we all are aware of Vietnam. We are all aware of space exploration, and of earlybird satellites, and of the proliferation of independent nations in Africa.

Around the turn of the century there was a movement in Protestantism which took various forms, and which emerged from earlier patterns. In Europe there were formed political parties with names such as Christian Democratic, or Christian Socialist; in the United States a significant movement called itself the Social Gospel.

These blends of religious and political movements were actuated by unquestionably sensitive and high-minded concern, as in Amos, for the welfare of society. One can have only praise for the purposes and for the efforts. In their own time, they were criticized for espousing programs which went against the self-interest of industrialists who were members of Christian churches, and who denied that the proposals were inherently Christian; also, a viewpoint ordinarily termed "Calvinism" opposed the social concern in these movements as if that concern was in some way a contradiction of the predestined economic plight of the unfortunate. Some fifty years later two different criticisms were made of the tendencies. The one criticism, which we might label theological, spoke of the futility of these efforts and of their irrelevancy to the basic Christian message, for these movements supposed that man could do something about man's plight, whereas man's incapacity to do anything convicted these efforts of inordinate and improper pride, and of pursuing concerns outside the legitimate ambit of religion. It must be conceded that this type of criticism can be justified by recourse to appropriate scriptural and scholastic passages, for there is of course this strand, though in less extreme form, within Christian literature. If one were to say in rebuttal that the criticism supplanted the totality of Christian thought with but a single theme of that totality, one would still fail in persuading the earnest men who made the criticism. But the second criticism seems to me to contain even more aptness than the critics themselves understood. It has run along this line, that while it is very good to conceive of Jesus as a social reformer, and to seek the sanction for reform proposals in the Gospels, an analysis of the proposals of the religiously minded men a half century ago did not reveal anything substantially different from what was being advocated by the secularists. Granted that the basic motivation between the secularists and the religionists was different, if the programs advocated were similar or in part even identical, then how could one claim the authority of Jesus for one version, which in a second version invoked no such sanction or even rejected it? Were not such programs offered by religionists in reality secular programs attributed to Jesus only through strained and farfetched exegesis?

We have now reached what I conceive as the nub of my paper. The ancient documents, whether Old Testament, or rabbinic literature, or the Gospels, do not provide the modern age with the answers to the question, What shall I do? This question demands specific, precise answers, suitable to our complex age, but the most that the ancient documents can provide is vague guidelines and general ethical norms; the ancient documents do not and cannot provide us with concrete and specific guidance whereby we can turn to the abstruse problems of the modern world and feel assured that we know exactly what to do and how. Let me try to illustrate by example, and take the question of integration of Negroes to clarify my intention. It would not be too difficult to assemble evidence from Old and New Testament passages such as Amos or the incident of the Ethiopian eunuch in Acts (other passages would need to be overlooked) that integration has a religious sanction. As one person, I have full clarity in my mind as to the goals and conditions of full integration. As one person, I do not know how exactly to get there. I find myself confronted from time to time by dilemmas which involve tactics and strategy. Is a march as at Selma useful and yielding, and shall I support it? Or is it only a highly dramatic gesture, devoid of sequel and significance, and hence not the best strategy? Again, I have no doubts about supporting the legal justification for full rights for blacks; I do not know, however, how to remedy the economic plight of those Negroes who cannot find a means for making legal rights meaningful by translating them into the possibility of earning enough money to live comfortably and to gain the education so vital for economic welfare in our age. I do not know the way to provide that training, nor do I know any way in which to provide the skills in fullest immediacy, so that I find myself confronted by an inescapable gap between what I conceive to be the economic right of the black and the realistic prospect of his achieving and enjoying that economic right.

In similar fashion, I am as a religious person profoundly disturbed by Vietnam, by the impasse between the Arab countries and Israel, and by the matter of the population explosion; I find myself puzzled on the one hand by my tendency to support self-determination of peoples and hence the plurality of new governments, and on the other hand I tend to want less and less nationalism, a united humanity, and not simply a federation of nations. I do not know how to reconcile my favorable disposition to the formation of self-determined nations and my greater disposition to one world.

I think that I have no doubts about what I believe in terms of standards and of goals, and I have no difficulty relating these to ancient religious documents. I am aware that in making such relationship I will be guilty of partial judicious selection, but that does not greatly trouble me. My anxiety is that even after I am certain in my own mind what I want, I still do not know how to reach the point of my desire. Perhaps, though, my question can be put in this form: What can we reasonably expect from the past? Is it just and rational to expect specific guidance? Do I not possibly want too much, both in the sense of what the past can provide, and also in the sense that the more I expect from the past, the less I am prone to expect from myself in the present and in the future? Am I exempted from my own need to think, to envisage, to dream, and to plan?

To return now to our context, Jesus in world history, I am certain that no one would presume to suggest that any reflection of Jesus is discernible in the international affairs of the past two hundred years. The nations of the Christian world have acted as though he never existed, and never lived an exemplary life, and never taught. They have acted as if he was of no guidance and no concern. The recollection of him has been kept alive only in the segments of the population which still do honor to his name, but in neither national nor international affairs is there to be found any large echo of his life and words. I am aware of the efforts of Christians, as for example at Amsterdam some two decades ago, to speak on what they called "World Order," and of the brilliance and high-mindedness of the papers which were prepared for that conference. Ofttimes I, an outsider to Christianity, have thought that in our day there is ample dedicated Christian leadership, but how little of a followership there is. Especially in high places.

Modern nations are secular, even when their populations are predominantly Christian, at least nominally. Moreover, I find in my reading of history little substantial difference in the sins of modern secular states and the sins of the medieval Christian states. Then Jesus received lipservice, but little more; today nations pay him even no lipservice. I am one who does not wish for an ecclesiastical state; a reading of history should discourage us for all time from wanting any such thing. Yet I still cherish the sentimental hope that a nation as an entity could be as religiously virtuous as a person can be. How dim and distant that prospect seems.

But if one is to address himself to the issues of religious liberalism and the contemporaneous context, then one must try to draw some fair-minded distinction between the challenge of our respected brothers in the traditional religions and ourselves.

As liberals we contend that we have the freedom to inquire, the freedom to doubt, and the freedom to assert. The past for us is edifying, but the past is not necessarily normative. Conservative critics of liberal religion often chide us with having made religion easier; the allegation is made that what we have freed ourselves from is the discipline and the sense of obligation of traditional religion. Certainly this criticism has some aptness, for there are those who espouse liberal religion as a liquidation of all that was uncomfortable in traditional religion, and have used liberalism to discover and attain a cheap and superficial comfort.

Yet I would affirm that liberal religion in its profound aspects is a more difficult religion than traditional religion. Indeed, it is the traditional religion which is characterized by comfort, and liberalism which is uncomfortable, uneasy, and disturbing. To my mind there is no question but that religious liberalism is more difficult and makes more profound demands than does an easy orthodoxy.

Then what shall we expect from the past? What shall we expect from Old Testament or New Testament, from Moses, or Isaiah, or Jesus? Shall we await nimble solutions to the staggering problems of our time? Are we so naive as to suppose that the gifted minds in various governments which have struggled to try to find solutions to the problems of the age will suddenly discover them by recourse to ancient writ? We all know that this is not possible. We all know that the great figures of the past can provide us with inspiration, with general guidance, with standards, and with norms, but they cannot and will not solve our problems for us.

Will we solve our own problems? If so, we shall not do so easily, or readily. We shall all of us have to face the need to work out each for himself what his own individual understanding leads him to suppose is the right thing to do. In the words of a North Carolina folksong, you have got to cross that river alone. And each in his own way has to speak, or to write, or to labor for his objectives.

But how shall we set our sights? By expediency? By what is ready at hand? Or is it in the question of the standards we should espouse that the past can intrude to shake us, and to guide us, and to elevate us? Man must work, and man must travail—but he must know what he is working for, and why.

Let me emphasize, and herein the humanism that is Jewish comes back, that I cannot subscribe to the supposition that man can accomplish nothing and that man should therefore do nothing. We Jews formulate our obligations in somewhat the following way, that we pray for God's guidance to help us in what we endeavor to do. Man must always endeavor; an ancient rabbi formulated matters this way, "It is not incumbent on you to finish the task, but you are not free to withdraw yourself from it." Our sages liked to point to a passage in Exodus. When the children of Israel were at the Red Sea, with the Egyptians pursuing them from the rear, they sent up a shout to God. The divine answer came in these words to Moses: "Why do you shout to me? Speak to the children of Israel, and let them journey on." We too need to journey on. Through uncertainty, and doubt, and defeat and setback.

Yet we in our day can possibly do more justice to the great figures of the ancient world where our religion was born than was done in the recent past. Moses, Isaiah, and Jesus have almost disappeared from world history. Perhaps we can help to bring them back.

15

Paul Reconsidered *

THERE ARE TWO clear debts which I personally owe to Claude G. Montefiore. First let me say, possibly with some immodesty, that I have learned a great amount from his vast and precise scholarship. Second, his example, that is, of a liberal Jew willing to study the literature of Christianity in some depth, has served me in a variety of ways. I wrote in the introduction to my *A Jewish Understanding of the New Testament,* that Mr. Montefiore had commented on the loneliness of the task, and I commented that with his work before me the task was not as lonely as it had once been.

There is possibly a third debt which I would willingly admit if I thought it were so. Mr. Montefiore wrote always with calmness and detachment, and his writings are not tainted by a lack of civility. I cannot make the same claim for my own writings, but I think I can say that I too have tried to write with calmness and detachment. What I am not sure of is whether I have been influenced by him in this respect, as much as by my own personal disposition and by having learned elsewhere the virtues inherent in scholarly dispassion.

The circumstance that in some sense I am a disciple—unhappily not through personal contact, for I never met him, but through the written word —enhances for me the honor of having been invited to deliver this paper.

Mr. Montefiore's book, *Judaism and St. Paul,* published in London in 1914, is a somewhat curious one. It consists of two essays and an appendix.

* Previously unpublished, this paper was presented at the Liberal Jewish Synagogue in London, England, on June 5, 1969, as the Claude G. Montefiore Lecture for 1969.

The appendix is a long quotation in French from Alfred Loisy in support of certain statements in the book, and is irrelevant to the present discussion.

The shorter of the two essays is "The Relation of St. Paul to Liberal Judaism." To what Montefiore has written in this essay I have nothing to add; possibly, though, I would formulate some of his points a little differently. In essence, Mr. Montefiore states that the significance of Paul for liberal Jews is to be found in aspects of his personality, such as his steadfastness, his earnestness, and his poetic gifts, and not in his doctrines. Montefiore, however, finds some similarity in his own approach to traditional Judaism and that of Paul, in what he describes as Paul's cautions and compromises. Perhaps one single quotation may suffice. In discussing biblical Judaism and its relation to Jewish laws, Montefiore writes:

> If the liberal Jew chooses to observe the dietary laws—whether biblical or Rabbinic—let him do so. . . . To our principles, we [liberal] Jews must be true, and if we are speakers or writers, we must give expression to them. But it is not necessary to put them into practice on every possible occasion in season and out of season. . . . If I am seen to smoke on a Saturday, I may not only offend my traditional brother, but I may hurt the conscience of my brother to whom tradition and orthodox Judaism has become unreal and impossible of acceptance, but who cannot as yet carry out, without injury, the principles of Liberal Judaism in all their application. I must be careful not to injure [his conscience]. He lives to God without smoking on Saturday quite as much as, and perhaps better than, I who smoke.[1]

This statement is in essence a paraphrase of Paul. If this quotation is ample support of my statement that it is not so much Paul's doctrine as his personality which Montefiore sees as relevant, I have possibly discharged my obligation with respect to his shorter essay. I must, however, indicate a certain reservation, or at least a reflection of a disposition to phrase things differently. When Montefiore speaks of freedom from the law and equates infractions of Jewish law as comparable to Paul's putting the spirit above the letter,[2] I might possibly assent to what lies behind Montefiore's words, but I find more wrong in the words themselves than I find right, for "spirit" in Paul was scarcely a colorless term. This is scarcely crucial, though, for this essay of Montefiore is not of great consequence, whether from the standpoint of its content or of its subsequent influence.

The other essay, by far longer and far more important, has curiously stirred little notice in the scholarly literature. Whereas what Montefiore wrote on the Gospels or on Jesus continues still to be quoted, what he wrote about Paul has elicited very little attention. I shall presently turn to a notable exception, but it is necessary first to face the reality of this inattention, and then to raise the question, Why? Perhaps the answer may lie in this, that the title which Montefiore gives to his long essay is "The Genesis of the Religion of Paul" [3]—and the essay is true to the title. That is to say, the nub of the essay is not an exposition of Paul's doctrine or significance; these Montefiore takes as universally known. Montefiore abstains from offering any clarification of the doctrines of Paul. Rather, the word "genesis" in the title of his essay is very much determinative, for Montefiore is inquiring into the origin of Paul's doctrine, in the sense of asking: From what kind of Judaism did Paul appear? This is by no means a trivial question, but it is obviously quite different from an effort to describe and appraise Paul's religion.

Montefiore was not writing in a vacuum. He wrote against what I might describe as a three-faceted background. First, there are data about Paul in the Acts of the Apostles which delineate him, for want here of any better phrase, as a "typical" Jew of the first Christian century. Let us emphasize the word "typical"—before we raise the inevitable quibbles about the word— and notice the phrase "of the first century." In Acts, Paul is a student of the great Pharisee Gamaliel, he can speak Hebrew and he observes the Laws of Moses to the extent that he circumcises his traveling companion Timothy, and that his final difficulties with his fellow Jews ensue on his journey to Jerusalem to pay a vow at the Temple. We may put it in this way, that throughout Acts Paul appears as a traditional Jew, a usual Jew of the time, who merely chanced to become a participant in the new movement.

The second background item is that of the Protestant scholarship, especially as practiced in Germany. In this scholarship, Paul's becoming a participant in the new movement represents his stepping out of an inferior thing into a superior thing; moreover, since Paul was reared as a Jew, within the Jewish tradition, he knew it so responsibly that these scholars could accept at face value his denigration of his inherited Judaism, and could proceed even beyond Paul to denigrate it further. To put this into the plainest English: for such scholars Judaism was a miserable form of religion, as Paul knew from vivid personal experience, and moreover, Judaism continued to be an abominable form of religion.

The third background item is complicated, especially for the person who has not been deeply inducted into the issues on Paul, and I think that for clarity I should here provide a longer explanation than the importance of the item itself justifies. Let us begin at the point of supposing that the data about Paul supplied by the Acts of the Apostles is at the minimum unreliable, and at the maximum an amalgam of distortions. If this seems startling, it was precisely such a view that arose in Germany in the 1830s, in the so-called Tübingen school, the chief representative of which was F. C. Baur. Let it be crystal clear that neither Montefiore nor I, Jews, have initiated this assessment of the Acts of the Apostles; to the contrary, it is fully embedded within the ambit of free Protestant scholarship. Since the 1830s, scholarship (except among ultratraditionalists) has had to try to come to some terms with the alleged disparities and discrepancies between the data about Paul found in his Epistles and the data about him found in Acts of the Apostles. The direct difficulties may be stated in this way: that the Paul of Acts is characterized by his agreeable conforming, and the Paul of the Epistles by his cantankerous nonconformity; this nonconformity is as much characteristic of Paul's career as a participant within the new movement as of his career respecting his antecedent Jewishness. In Acts, then, Paul is depicted as subservient to the authorities of the early church in Jerusalem, but in Galatians he boasts of his full independence of them; in his Epistles, he asserts, as the proper text reads, that he sturdily refused to circumcise Titus. Paul's Jewish Scripture is a Greek translation, and nothing in his Epistles would lead one to suppose that he knew any Hebrew. Again, nothing in his Epistles alludes to any period as a student of the eminent Gamaliel. Accordingly, a notable portion of Protestant scholarship has declared that Acts and the Epistles simply cannot be reconciled, and one must choose between them, accepting one and rejecting the other. But if Paul was not a usual Jew of his time, then what was he, and into what different background does he fit?

Montefiore was personally fully persuaded of that case which he wanted to make in the essay on the genesis of Paul's thought, namely, that Paul could not be understood or explained on the basis of rabbinic Judaism. This was the case respecting both his preconversion Judaism and his postconversion Christianity.

In Montefiore's opinion, rabbinic Judaism, with its countless pages of Talmud and Midrash, is susceptible of being analyzed into tolerably clear major and minor motifs. If one were to proceed from that analysis into a genetically related synthesis, then rabbinic Judaism would emerge as a stable entity against which one could set the figure of Paul, and the acute differences would quickly emerge to Montefiore.

But an immediate objection would need to be raised in the realm of methodology. Granted that rabbinic literature provides the ready means for such analysis and synthesis, a chronological impediment arises. For those to whom this chronological issue is new, it can be stated in the following way: Let us assume that Paul's career was contained within the years 35 to 55 A.D.; the roots of rabbinic religion are admittedly earlier than Paul's time, but the date, about 200 A.D., of the written recording of rabbinic literature is long after Paul's time. Not only could one raise the general question of the reliability of the report in later sources about movements and attitudes which occurred in earlier times, but, moreover, there intervened between Paul's period, 35–55 A.D., and the time of the recording of the rabbinic literature, about 200 A.D., the most significant event in Jewish postbiblical history—the destruction of the Temple in the year 70 A.D. and the termination of the priestly cult. To put this in another way: the biblical (that is, Old Testament) religion of the Temple, the priests, and the animal sacrifices, came to a permanent end in 70 A.D., and Judaism would have perished had there not antecedently developed the elementary forms of a new version of Judaism. Prior to the year 70 A.D., the synagogue was, as it were, a supplement to the Temple, the rabbinate was then an inchoate and vague office, in no way in competition with the priesthood, and prayer was primarily a concomitant of animal sacrifice. But after 70 A.D., the synagogue, the rabbinate, and prayer fully replaced the Temple, the priesthood, and animal sacrifice.

The rabbinic literature, though preserving recollections of the period before 70 A.D., was shaped after 70 A.D., and saturated by the maturity of those factors which were only vague impulses before 70 A.D. Completely forgetting for the moment about Paul, the question can be asked: Is it possible to peer back from the year 200 when the Mishnah was recorded, or from the year 500 when the Gemara was recorded, and see what the state of Judaism was in the period between 35 and 55 A.D.?

To this question Montefiore gives the ready answer, No. If that answer should, perhaps logically, preclude all comparison of Paul and the Judaism of his age, Montefiore nevertheless asserts most cautiously that the Judaism of 200 or of 500 is a developed extension of the Judaism of the period before the year 70. As an extension, it contains motifs and attitudes which can be considered to be reliably characteristic even of the early period. I should stress again the words I used, "most cautiously," for Montefiore was never reckless in his scholarship; indeed, one sometimes wishes that he had been perhaps a little more venturous. Within the framework of his caution, however, he makes the contention as strongly as it could possibly be made that whatever was Paul's preconversion Judaism, it was not that version of Judaism which is known and knowable from rabbinic literature. As an example of his caution, I should comment that Montefiore makes only minimal use of the extensive Protestant scholarship which, through its challenge to the reliability of the Acts of the Apostles, thereby automatically removed the likelihood of Paul's being representative of rabbinic Judaism. Montefiore did not call on this scholarship; let us note that if one disbelieves that Paul was a student of Gamaliel, a circumciser of Timothy, competent in Hebrew, faithful to a need to pay a vow at the Temple, such denials would preclude there emerging the putative Paul whose relation to rabbinic Judaism would then come under question. If one discards Acts, then there is no rabbinic Paul to deal with. But Montefiore abstains from such a procedure.

Still another related facet of the broader scholarship which Montefiore largely avoids entering into is the question of the hellenization of Christianity. We can lead into this topic by noting that Paul wrote in Greek, and that modern scholarship holds that all the Gospels were written in Greek. The area, however, in which Jesus lived and worked was Judea, and the Greek Gospels, especially Mark, quote certain words of Jesus in Aramaic. By hellenization we would mean, at the first level, the transition from the Judean scene to the Diaspora, and the supplanting of the Aramaic and Hebrew languages by the Greek language. At a different level, we could ask to what extent Greek philosophical and religious terms and ideas intruded and were blended with the Christian tradition in its process of growth and transformation. No one has ever doubted Paul's fluency in Greek and no one has doubted the presence in Paul's Epistles of Greek philosophical and religious terms. What scholars have debated respecting these latter is the extent to which Paul is truly appropriating the *substance* of the Greek terms, for conceivably he is merely borrowing words which were part of the common coin. Yet even were we to say that Paul himself was only using a handy Greek vocabulary, nevertheless his conversion at around 35 A.D., a half decade after the death of Jesus in 29 or 30, means that the new movement underwent a rather rapid though possibly superficial hellenization. But if one ascribes to Paul's Epistles the second, and more profound, level of hellenization, then all the more must one wonder at the rapidity with which the movement became hellenized.

Long before Montefiore there were efforts to explain how this rapid hellenization, centering around Paul, came about. One chain of scholars,

Gfrörer, Dähne, and the infamous Bruno Bauer ("infamous," for he was a vicious anti-Semite), gave a more or less common explanation, however much they differed in detail. What is common in this view is that it was not in Judea where the vivid religious currents flowed most freely and vigorously, but rather in Alexandria in Egypt. There it was that the Pentateuch had been rendered into Greek almost three centuries earlier; there it was that scriptural exegesis was born and that postscriptural religious ideas were born. All that was necessary to understand the rapid hellenization of Christianity was to posit that an antecedent hellenization of Judaism paved the way for the easy hellenization of Christianity. Bruno Bauer went even further, alleging that Christianity too was Alexandrian, not Judean, and indeed, Jesus was to be understood as the humanization of abstract Alexandrian doctrines, and that the Jesus of Judea and of the Gospels, according to Bauer, never existed.

From Tübingen and F. C. Baur in the 1830s there had come a quite different explanation of the rapid hellenization of Christianity. In Baur's view the hellenization necessarily required a very long time, to be measured not in years, but in many decades. Accordingly, documents, such as those Epistles attributed to Paul which reflect some profound hellenization, cannot possibly come from the years 35–55 A.D., but must come from a century later. Therefore, those Epistles attributed to Paul which exhibit facets of profound hellenization cannot be by Paul himself, but must be instead second-century writings falsely bearing his name. In short, Baur handled the problem of the rapid hellenization of Christianity by denying that there ever was any rapid hellenization.

Montefiore, to repeat, does not enter to any extent into this kind of professorial discussion. One can say, without undue unfairness, that if we attribute to Montefiore some success in breaking down any relationship between Paul and rabbinic Judaism, then his case is almost entirely the negative one of telling us what Paul was not, not what Paul was. Strong as Montefiore's case may be judged to be on its destructive side, though couched always in genteel words, he does not try to make any case on the constructive side.

At the time that Montefiore wrote, there had come into a new ascendancy a discipline known in Germany as *Religionsgeschichte*. The translation of this term into English falls completely short of indicating the character of the discipline. In its method, *Religionsgeschichte* was a free, detached inquiry into the phenomenon of religions and how they developed; in substance,

Religionsgeschichte, disregarding the canon and the supposed sanctity of Scripture, sought to explain phenomena in Christianity by relating them to the general phenomena. In all ages there is some problem in differentiating between superstition and religion; by and large *Religionsgeschichte* assumed that such a difference is a figment of the imagination and a product of special pleading. The Paul who emerges from the studies in *Religionsgeschichte* is no longer the figure over whom some controversy could rage as to his being or not being a Pharisee, but rather someone in whom one can discern magic, demon possession, and a preoccupation with astrology, or at least with astral influences. Perhaps two concrete terms may suffice to illuminate what this changed form of study implies. When Paul speaks of subjection to the "principalities" of this world, the traditional explanation is that they were human monarchs, the new explanation that they were the demonic forces in the world; the *stocheia* were previously explained as the elements, possibly the four—earth, air, fire, and water—of Greek philosophy; and the new explanation was that these elements were the demonic powers in the world by which man is trapped.

This *religionsgeschichtliche* kind of explanation, as can be seen, required some kind of reconciliation with at least two unmistakable and incontrovertible facts. First, Paul was a Jew. How, then, could there be in him so resounding an echo of the sheerest paganism? Second, Paul asserts that he was educated in Judaism, that he surpassed his schoolmates in his prowess, and we can see how effortlessly he quoted Scripture. If it were to be granted that an ignorant, an unlettered Jew could be a prey to pagan influences, is it not wrong to associate this literate Paul with some dimly discerned syncretistic—half-pagan, half-Jewish—movement which we know about? A host of writings appeared both alleging and denying a relationship between Pauline thought, the pagan movements, and the pagan religions of his time.

In general, those who denied the allegations were unwilling to admit that any Jew or Christian could be brought into any affirmative relationship with the mysteries, for the ample reason that Paul and other Graeco-Jews of his time, particularly Philo of Alexandria, had no hesitation in denouncing the mysteries as false and deceptive. A convenient way out of the dilemma was to concede that while Paul and Philo do use the terminology of the mysteries, they thereby make absolutely no concessions; they use, as it were, the slang, not the substance, and certainly not the nuances of the mysteries.

But even if the grudging concession were to be made that more than the terminology of the mysteries is used by Paul and Philo, then an important residual problem remains. These men were but two people, and apparently isolated individuals, creators of literature that has survived. To what extent, if any, can they be conceived of as representative of groups, or, beyond mere groups, of masses of people?

Returning again to the scholars, Gfrörer, Dähne, F. C. Baur, and Bruno Bauer, especially F. C. Baur, we encounter the view that a Jewish Christianity once existed represented by the apostle Peter. Comparably, there was an entity, Hellenistic Judaism, which was in many ways in sharp contrast to the Palestinian, rabbinic Judaism, represented by Paul. Much of the discussion about Hellenistic Judaism rotates about Philo. Philo's dates are roughly 20 B.C. to 40 A.D. He wrote an enormous amount, and relatively little of what he wrote failed to survive. He wrote in Greek, he was erudite in his knowledge of Greek philosophy and the philosophers, and no one has ever challenged the thesis that at least on the level of language he represented a hellenization. Now, however, the proposal has been made that he represented and reflected a significant, advanced hellenization in substance. This allegation was promptly met by denials. When a pogrom against Jews in Alexandria occurred in 38–39 A.D., Philo was part of a three-man deputation to Rome to protest against what had happened. This incident, coupled with the Jewish fidelity in every paragraph he wrote, assures us of Philo's Jewish loyalty. Could so loyal a Jew, even if he wrote in Greek, be guilty of sullying his Judaism with any profound measure of hellenization?

In this context a scholar emerged to try to steer a way through the rocks and shoals. He was Erwin Goodenough of Yale. Respecting Philo's loyalty, Goodenough asserted that this was neither in question nor truly relevant,[4] for the hellenization was a substance to be measured and weighed, and not dismissed *a priori* simply because admittedly Philo was a loyal Jew. But, Goodenough went on, one must not be misled by Philo's recurrent denunciation of the Greek mysteries as frauds into failing to discern that Philo converts Judaism itself into a mystery, into the one true mystery. For Goodenough, Philo does more than borrow the style of the mysteries, he borrows and adapts the thought-patterns and the goals, and reads them into Judaism. To state it over-briefly, Philo's Judaism is a mystery in the sense that he, and those initiated into his thought, can utilize Judaism as a means of escape from the evils of this world and as a means of rising above death, that is, of avoiding it. Such "salvation" is possible through an approach to man and the universe which in a dualistic way separates body from soul or spirit, and the physical world from the immaterial world.

Philo's Judaism, according to Goodenough, is the prescription whereby man achieves salvation and immortality. The Greek mysteries are false in that they do not truly provide these boons: Judaism is true, and the only truth, in the sense that it alone does. Moreover, Goodenough saw in Philo what he considered was evidence of cultic units, *thiasoi*,[5] and if this were right, then Philo was not merely an individual but was representative of a mass movement of some undetermined proportions.

Goodenough wrote little about Paul, but just enough to put Paul into relationship, not with Philo himself, but with that Hellenistic Jewish trend which produced Philo. In Goodenough's *By Light, Light* there is an essay, a very difficult one, titled "Law in the Subjective Realm," that is relevant to our discussion.[6]

Montefiore had raised, as was natural, the question of Paul's attitude to the Law of Moses; namely, that Paul had declared the laws obsolete and cancelled, for Paul had seen in the laws obstacles to righteousness. But what was Paul's deep personal involvement with the laws that made them a problem to him?

In the interest of brevity, let me use my own language to paraphrase Goodenough's essay. In the objective realm of life, contrasted with the subjective realm, laws as such are enactments which are external to the individual. That is to say, as an individual I can encounter royal decrees which try to shape or coerce my conduct, but these are forces outside myself. On the one hand there is within me, as a decent individual, a mind which can learn and weigh and assess, and on the other hand I am partly body and I am susceptible of being driven by bodily needs and desires; that is, by my senses and passions. My body may covet more food than my mind advises me is beneficial, or a passion for a woman can destroy my discretion to the point that I may pursue her and lose position and wealth and loved ones and integrity. In the subjective realm, law is that balance inner to a man, a balance free from external force, whereby a maturing and matured mind can regulate his senses and passions and keep them usefully in check.

As related to Paul, this distinction between objective laws, external to a person, and subjective law, internal within a person, gives a possible explanation of the background of the annulment of the Laws of Moses on the part of Paul. A distinction between objective and subjective law is Hellenistic, not Jewish. Conceivably the Hellenistic background of Paul could explain also the broader facets of Paul's religion, and conceivably the assumption of a Hellenistic environment could solve the problem of the genesis of Paul's religion as Montefiore had raised it.

Thus, to continue, if that vague term, righteousness, is something internal, within a man, then so too is sin, and if sin is internal and, as it were, imbedded within a person, then neither righteousness nor sin is a matter of choice and selection by a person out of available alternatives. Rather, sin is a condition of man and thereby not susceptible to dissolution by repentance, and righteousness is not an attainment susceptible to being reached by fidelity to laws, but is, rather, a matter of internal equilibrium.

I am by no means sure that a statement so laconic does full justice to Goodenough. Nevertheless, I want to proceed to draw some inferences which Goodenough has abstained from drawing. Chief among these inferences, as related to our context, is that these ideas must be classified as Hellenistic rather than Jewish. At the minimum, one must say that when these particular ideas are made to blend with the Jewish tradition of the revealed Laws of Moses, the end result is a hellenized Judaism significantly different from the rabbinic Judaism depicted in Montefiore's long essay. That is to say, whereas Montefiore abstained from suggesting affirmatively where Paul belonged, and contented himself by saying only where Paul did not belong, Goodenough has provided, more through hints than clear articulation, a solution which Montefiore abstained from giving.

In the realm of scholarship, it is a phenomenon worthy of notice that even where the evidence is abundant, and relatively clear, scholarship normally turns up a no to every yes, and a yes to every no. The view that Paul was a hellenized Jew, as we have said, involved a rejection of the clear data supplied in Acts of the Apostles. But now an additional factor enters in. Quite beyond the data in Acts of the Apostles is a theme consistent in Luke-Acts to the effect that Christianity represents an unbroken continuity with Judaism, and indeed that Christianity is the truly legitimate continuation of the ancient Judaism. Such a view requires as a concomitant that Christianity be conceived of as emerging from the very center of Judaism, and not from the fringes. Consistent with the view of centrality, the Gospel According to Luke allocated the resurrection appearance of Jesus to Jerusalem rather than to Galilee. When Luke narrates the incident of the overturning of the seats of the money-changers, he follows it immediately with the statement that Jesus was daily in the Temple, teaching; that is to say, the incident is handled as if it were both relatively minor and also as if it elicited no reaction from the priests. Let it be recalled that Luke alone provides a childhood narrative about Jesus, specifically, the incident in which the parents of Jesus journey to the Temple in Jerusalem but depart without being aware at first that Jesus is not with them; they return to the Temple to find him discussing

205

with the people whom Luke calls doctors of the law. Again, after the death and ascension of Jesus, the community in Jerusalem lives in an affirmative relationship to the Temple; it is in Jerusalem that Christian matters center, and Jerusalem is still, shall we say, the headquarters. When certain of the apostles are arrested, so Acts 5 narrates, an angel releases them from prison, and these apostles then resume standing in the Temple and teaching there. They are brought before the Sanhedrin where the same Gamaliel who later in Acts is described as Paul's teacher, advocates that the members of the new movement be let alone, for if their undertaking is only of men, it will fail and need not be opposed; if it is of God, the Sanhedrin will be unable to overthrow them.

In sum, the view of Acts of the Apostles is that Christianity was no marginal movement in Judaism, and it did not arise in the peripheral areas of Judea, but rather in Jerusalem, in proximity to and in harmony with the Temple. But if Paul should be judged, against the data in Acts of the Apostles, to have been a hellenized Jew from the periphery of Judaism, it is not simply the matter of Paul which is at stake, but by implication the Jewish authenticity of his Christianity.

There is a considerable amount of scholarship dedicated to trying to solve the array of problems raised by this assertion of Jewish centrality to Christianity. For example, the Tübingen school of the 1830s held the view that the purpose of Luke-Acts was to commend in the second century a unity of the church by describing the wondrous unity which had presumably existed in the early period in the first century, indeed a unity which glossed over deep tensions and hostilities. The Tübingen school held that Luke-Acts was tendentious (we would say propagandistic) and not historical. From a different standpoint, a living American, John Knox, associates Luke-Acts with the second century figure, Marcion. This Marcion, it will be recalled, held the view that Christianity was neither born in Judaism nor was in any way related to it; Knox has set forth the opinion that Luke-Acts is designed against Marcion, and it therefore stresses the direct continuity and congruency of Christianity with, to borrow a modern term, the mainstream of Judaism.

As this issue presents itself in considerations larger than simply the figure of Paul, it is now the issue of whether or not Christianity emerged from the mainstream of Judaism. At stake in any projected answer is the implication for some people of the very authenticity of Christianity, for, in the views of some commentators, the opinion is implicit that the authenticity of Christianity is the greater as its origin in the center of Judaism can be maintained, and the more one would ascribe its origins to the periphery, the less would its authenticity be defensible. Against this background, sometimes explicit, sometimes tacit, there have been the endless disputes among the commentators respecting the Hellenistic elements supposedly to be found, or not found, in early Christian documents. There has been a noticeable amount of Christian scholarship which is determined to see a total absence of Hellenistic elements, and to insist on the essentially Jewish character even of the apparently Hellenistic. It is no accident, then, that a small number of scholars have wished to make the case that the Gospel According to John, admittedly the most Hellenistic of the Gospels, is in reality a Jewish Gospel, and that it was not written in Ephesus as Christian tradition has believed, but in Judea itself.

But back to our specific context. A British scholar, now resident in the United States, William Davies, addressed himself to the problem of Paul in his notable book, *Paul and Rabbinic Judaism.*[7] Not only does Davies's book assert that passages in the rabbinic literature are fully capable of explaining Paul, but his procedure involves him in first addressing himself both to Montefiore and to Goodenough. That is to say, he precedes his statement of his case by first trying to demonstrate the inadequacy of the opinions and views of these two allied though unrelated commentators. Respecting Goodenough, Davies's procedure is to challenge the entirety of Goodenough's view of a hellenized Judaism. Respecting Montefiore, his case is made along the following lines: Montefiore has constructed a view of the Judaism in the age of Paul on the supposition that the rabbinic Judaism of the year 500 A.D. was an extension of a hypothetical Judaism of the period before 70 A.D. He does so through generalization and a merely summary view, and without a scrutiny of individual texts and individual passages. Without denying Montefiore's generalization, Davies was able, to his own satisfaction, to show some large array of passages from rabbinic literature itself which seemed both to refute Montefiore's generalization and also to prove the case that Paul affirmatively echoes sentiments found in rabbinic Judaism.

Mr. Davies is something of a rarity among Christian scholars in that his knowledge of rabbinic literature is both vast and acute. Nevertheless, one can raise objections to details in his presentation concerning the tenability of the alleged similarities which he finds and the reliability of the parallelism in what he adduces as parallels. But, in my own view, Davies abstains from inquiring into the major matter itself, namely, how can one extract from a body of literature, whose premise is the validity and the eternity of the Law, sentiments which assert that the Law is abrogated and an invitation to sin? If one were to grant that all the alleged parallels adduced by Davies between Paul and the rabbis were true and convincing parallels, one can still wonder if the nub of the problem has been truly appraised.

Two other matters, broader than Paul, but related to him indirectly need now to be brought into our perspective. Until the turn of the century the word "gnostic" was reserved for certain second-century Christian figures whose views the rest of the church regarded as objectionable. Gnosticism was characterized by an extreme dualism, putting body and spirit in unrelieved opposition to each other, by the rejection of the view that God himself had created this miserable world. Moreover, the gnostic was sure that he knew the way to the God concealed from the ordinary mind and ordinary eyes. Three dangers in second-century gnosticism troubled its Christian opponents. The gnostics constituted themselves as a sort of elite, setting themselves over and against the remainder of the church. They made claims equivalent to prophetic knowledge and tended to regard the view that Christ had become incarnate as Jesus as a mere symbol and not historical fact. There was a tendency to belittle the Jewish antecedents of Christianity, for the first chapter of Genesis, with its repeated refrain that "God saw and behold it was good" was a palpable lie, for this world was an evil place and not Moses but demons had written the Pentateuch.

Around the turn of the century, the word "gnosticism" underwent a wider application among scholars, and was no longer strictly reserved for Christian heretics. It became a term to describe the religious approach adapted by these second-century heretics from an earlier and broader religious stance. The usual academic battles raged. There were those who asserted that there had existed a pre-Christian Jewish gnosticism, and those who denied it utterly. There were those who asserted that gnosticism was strictly a pagan or strictly a Hellenistic manifestation, and those who asserted that it was found in Judaism but scorned by the ancient rabbis and therefore not clearly reflected in the surviving rabbinic literature. If by these words I have adequately indicated a facet of research and its controversial nature, then we can proceed to apply it to Paul. There were those who were not content to make the statement, almost never challenged, that Paul was the authority on whom second century gnostics relied, and that Paul himself was a gnostic. Sometimes this assertion was made with "gnostic" in mind in its broader sense, but interpreted in its previous limited sense, and there took place that all too common scholarly procedure of one scholar refuting what another scholar has not said at all. Where there was a better meeting of minds, however, the older overtones came to be reechoed, namely, even that in the wider use of the term, "gnostic" was essentially Hellenistic, but Paul was a rabbinic Jew. Into the same context there entered echoes of the older issues of the Jewish authenticity of Christianity versus the implied inauthenticity if Hellenistic elements were conceded. A number of circumspect studies were made of the apprehension of God as found in Paul, and I have the impression that most such studies insisted that this apprehension was Jewish,[8] not Hellenistic. I do not recall any such studies in the last fifteen years; possibly the discovery of late gnostic Gospels in Egypt, now being studied and restudied, has put the emphasis back on the Christian character of gnosticism.

The sectarian documents of the Dead Sea Scrolls (as distinct from the Scrolls which are full or partial or fragmentary books of the Bible or the Apocrypha and Pseudepigrapha) have been brought into relationship with Christianity in general and with Paul in particular. Very, very few scholars have gone the length of Professor Jacob Teicher of Cambridge, who identifies the wicked teacher of the scrolls with Paul.[9] Most students have not accepted this identification, for among other reasons, that the Scrolls lack the pegs on which to hang such specific history. On the other hand, the Scrolls reflect a dualism which is surprising; this dualism may be said to be beyond any dualism reflected in rabbinic literature, but yet less than the full dualism found in the second-century Christian gnostics. Nevertheless, the antecedent assumption that dualism was Hellenistic and restricted to areas outside of Judea was controverted by a dualism that appeared to be both Jewish and also native in Judea. From this standpoint, it becomes possible for scholars previously reluctant to see dualism in Paul now to see it there, but to retain Paul's essential Jewish rather than Hellenistic character.

I am uncertain at just what point the scholarship on the Dead Sea Scrolls and Paul now stands. The reason for this uncertainty lies in the circumstance that immediately after the discovery of the scrolls incautious and even flamboyant statements were made, but since then there has been a steadily developing sobriety and reserve. I would say with some tentativeness that as of today the testimony of the Scrolls is regarded as general and as related to the variety of Judaisms within Judea, rather than specifically relevant to Christianity itself. To say this in another way, even those scholars who see some nexus between the community of the Scrolls and early Christianity see it not as a direct nexus, but as the indirect one of a broadened view of

209

first century Judaism, rather than the limited view, as the immediate context in which to set Christianity.

For myself, the problems of the genesis of Paul's thought in the form in which Montefiore raised the question is not greatly affected by these matters and developments. The key decision remains now what it has been, namely, whether or not the Paul of Acts is the same kind of figure as the Paul of his Epistles. Some twenty years ago a scholar asserted that there were two Pauls, the Paul of Tarsus and the Paul of Rome. Most scholars are completely unpersuaded by this theory, regarding it preferable to believe that there is an understandable, and excusable, discrepancy between Acts and the Epistles, rather than to believe that there were two different men. No truly objective conclusion is possible; subjectivity is inevitable. I am among those who see Paul not as a rabbinic Jew, but as a hellenized Jew. Indeed, in my view, a hellenized Judaism long antecedent to Paul paved the way for Paul to have inherited a Jewish Hellenism much older than he. To my mind, Paul is more readily understood as a Hellenistic Jew than as a rabbinic Jew.

Yet, having said this, I do not see that I am more able to explain the genesis of Paul's religion. I am still baffled by the question of how a person whose loyalty to Judaism as he saw it (not as I see it) is unchallenged, could have come to the point of negating the Laws of Moses. That is, I believe that I can with reasonable accuracy give an exposition of *what* Paul's views were, but I remain at a loss to understand how they came about, whether his background was rabbinic or Hellenistic. Indeed I now believe that this question is unimportant. I do not thereby lament that it has been raised, whether by Montefiore or by others, but I mean only this, that in my view Paul is so individualistic that conceivably he could have come from any kind of a background. While I find him less intelligible against the background of rabbinic Judaism than of Hellenistic Judaism, I do not think that this background is important either for those, like some nineteenth-century Protestants who aspersed Paul, or for those who adulate him. This question of his background is, in my view, of very restricted significance.

Much more to the point is the personality of Paul, his religious intuition, his sense of religious discovery and of religious certainty. I have written elsewhere [10] that from his own standpoint Paul regards himself as an exponent of the truest version of Judaism. I have written that he in no sense regarded himself as a convert from one religion to another, but as one steadfastly within the one true religion. He was profoundly puzzled, profoundly baffled that his fellow Jews did not share in his discovery, and did not accord with his intuition. From his standpoint it was they who had moved away from Judaism, not he. I should not want to be misunderstood. I am not saying that Paul was not a Christian; I am saying that he was, but that he would have denied it, asserting instead that he was a Jew. I have written that he was not a scholarly person like Philo, but possessed of an equally good, if undisciplined mind. He was brilliant, he was scintillating. He was abrasive, he was sharp, he was combative. Placid people like Philo preserve ongoing religious institutions. Personalities like Paul upset them, shake them, and found new forms or new aspects. I have, of course, not entered here at all into the question of Paul and Jesus, for that is a matter for some other occasion. Paul was inventive, resourceful, eloquent, restless—there is no end to the adjectives which could be mustered. For myself, not sharing in his religious discovery, I have no hesitation in repeating here what I have written elsewhere, that I find him an irresistibly fascinating individual.

16

Modern and Ancient Problems in Communication: Rabbinic Judaism, Hellenistic Judaism, and Early Christianity *

I KNOW OF nothing more difficult than accurate understanding, and nothing more elusive than the accurate understanding of the past. Try as we will, we are inevitably hemmed in by our own age and our environment, and while we can break out beyond our limitations through determined effort, we can scarcely do so completely, but remain always caught, at least to some extent, in the toils of the present. Even were we to succeed in breaking out of our present, we can have little assurance that thereby we succeed in breaking fully into the past, for such daring breaches are beyond man's capacity, and moreover, it is never the complete, the full array of the past that we break into. Yet even to the extent that we succeed in breaking from the present into the past, the moment we try to interpret the past to the present, we come up against tremendous, formidable problems of communication. Suppose that the past is clear to us, are we able so to describe it and to formulate its contours and its nuances so as to make it comprehensible in its own terms to the present? And can we succeed in the more difficult task of making relevant to the present that which we only imperfectly convey from the past?

Such comments could apply with cogency to research in any facet of history, and therefore apply also to research in religious documents of the past. Respecting the latter, however, there are additional difficulties, one of which especially requires our attention. In all historical study there are periods in which some single facet of interpretation gains a transient ascen-

* Previously unpublished, this paper was presented at the John XXIII Bible Symposium held at St. Xavier College, Chicago, March 20, 1965.

dancy, as illustrated by a primacy given, for example, to economics, or to sociology, or to psychology, and then, after a while, when the scholarly fad has run its course, it gives way to some other facet. This is the case, also, in the research in religious documents. Yet there is a difference, in degree if not in kind, respecting religious documents, and this difference is exemplified by the words "traditional" and "untraditional." I use the word "traditional" in the sense of the usual, customary interpretation normative in a continuing religious community. Thus, for example, the views of the second-century bishop Papias on the authorship of the Gospels, and those of the rabbis in the talmudic tractate Baba Batra 14b on the authorship of Old Testament books, are in this sense traditional. When modern scholarship presumes to inquire into authorship as if these questions are open, then the bare assumption that the questions are open represents an incipient untraditionalism. If the modern scholarship proceeds to a conclusion at variance with the ancient opinion, then it is markedly untraditional. Vertically, traditionalism versus untraditionalism in scholarly research is present in Protestantism, Catholicism, and Judaism today. Horizontally, Protestant and Catholic scholars occasionally, or often, part company in interpreting certain crucial passages, such as Matthew 16:18, "on this rock I will build my Church," in accordance with antecedently fashioned loyalties; while Christian and Jewish scholars occasionally, or often assess the surviving literature and its religious content in the light of disparate presuppositions, or else as if the mission of modern scholarship is to justify what the respective communions have perpetuated out of the ancient. Though all of us would agree in principle that assessment should follow description, the fact is that description seems inevitably to partake of assessment. If this is a blemish, it is a blemish in all scholars, and no scholar can make the claim for more than the earnest effort to transcend the blemish.

Let me try to illustrate with specific examples some of the ways in which antecedent loyalties or transient fads enter into the scholarly interpretations and become impediments to communication among scholars. I confine myself to more or less typical instances, and I make no effort to be complete. Example number one: Who are or what were the Pharisees? By and large Christian scholarship depicts them consistent with Gospel assessments, and by and large Jewish scholarship represents an effort to exonerate them of that assessment. Between these extremes there exist some worthy efforts to make the portrait of the Pharisees much fuller than the brief characterization in the Gospels. In some amplifications, the extremes of contempt or adulation give way to appraisals which are possibly more rounded, and here and there is an effort to inquire into the historical significance of Pharisaism, as for example, in contrast to Sadduceeism. But it is no exaggeration to say that 99.44 percent of even modern scholarly literature is designed either to blame or to praise the Pharisees.

A second example is the question of the relationship of Jesus to the Judaism of his age. Where Jesus was critical, was he loyally critical from within Judaism, or was he, to the contrary, ever and in all ways, over and against it? Did he address himself to that universal plague in all religions and hence present in his age—hypocrisy; or was he opposed even to the un-hypocritical? There are scholarly works which earnestly attempt to detach Jesus totally from Judaism, and, rather quaintly, some of this scholarship is Christian and some of it is Jewish.

A third example is the question of Paul and the Law of Moses. Herein, of course, there lies a complicated issue. Nineteenth-century Protestantism contained some themes which amount to this, that to first-century Jews the Law was a resented burden, a distasteful yoke, for its requirements were multiple, and to Jews scattered in the Graeco-Roman world, the Law occasioned what are described as great "difficulties." The precise issue which I raise here is this, was Paul's attitude toward the Law premised on its difficulties and inconveniences? Did he turn against laws, as it were, because kosher butcher shops were beyond walking distance, and diverse sets of dishes a bother, and the multiplicity of requirements a nuisance? Or did he turn against laws on an issue of principle, namely, that they were not, as he saw things, an effective instrumentality for attaining the goal of religion? I personally embrace this latter opinion respecting Paul, not only because my own understanding of him points in that direction, but because I have looked in vain for confirming evidence in Paul and in other Jews that the Law ever was assessed as an inconvenience or a nuisance. The scholars in the nineteenth century often constructed a nonexistent Judaism against which a first-century Paul rebelled on a nineteenth-century premise. And since most of these scholars were Protestants, and opposed to priestly religion, it is not surprising that this scholarship identifies Jesus as a prophet (for which the New Testament evidence is rather scanty) but abstains from identifying him with priesthood, despite the explicit passages in the Epistle to the Hebrews. There is, I must allege, a persistent, almost ineradicable theme in Christian scholarship denigrating and scorning Jewish legalism, and I would assert that this theme is at variance with both the testimony of the New

Testament and the testimony of the rabbinic sources. Since there exists this assault on the ancient Judaism, there exists a modern Jewish scholarship that retorts to the assault. Let me set it down as a rather general rule that on the subject of ancient Jewish legalism, Christian and Jewish scholars are most imperfectly in communication.

A fourth example may be described as a scholarly vagary. It is the typical academic pursuit of the well-known wedding of source and derivation. The issue here is the way in which a sense of balance disappears, and the way in which the illumination of broad backgrounds is distorted into theories of plagiaristic copying. If certain Babylonian laws are similar to certain Hebrew laws, then all Hebrew laws were borrowed from the Babylonians. If certain aspects of messianism are found in the pseudepigraphic Book of Enoch, then elaborate connections can be found between New Testament messianism and the Book of Enoch. If certain motifs are found in the Dead Sea Scrolls, then the evangelists, or Paul, or James, drew everything they said from the Dead Sea Scrolls. Let it be clear that I am not denying that source and derivation are realities, for I hold that they are. In my essay "Parallelomania" (Chapter 22, this volume), I described by the term "parallelomania" certain facets of the accumulated scholarship. By "parallelomania" I was alluding to exaggeration and to distortion, for I had, and have, the conviction that the quantity of parallels has been grossly overdone, and the quality of the genuine parallels capriciously handled. What I lament is the relative absence from consideration of what to me is a necessary ingredient, and, indeed, the principal element—creativity. Did Paul say nothing original? Did James have no insight of his own? Must we assume that a literary artist like Luke had no capacity for creating poems and hymns, and must we premise that everywhere there were sources he drew them from? Was John so without capacity to originate that he had to draw the "logos" prologue to his Gospel from some gnostic hymn? I allege that the theories about source and derivation are tremendously distended; moreover, the theories abuse even the sources that truly exist, by usually ignoring the use to which a derived source is put by a new writer.

Yet granting that there have been exaggeration and distortion, the fact remains that there are indeed parallels and quasi parallels, and there are themes which are analogous. It is about these that I make the present observation, that just as there are problems of communication today, so there were comparable problems of communication in the ancient world.

The three bodies of literature mentioned in my topic have certain common characteristics. First, they come from roughly the same time. Second, they reflect an advanced stage of development in the practice of applying exegesis to the Old Testament. Third, they are shot through with new insights, either developed from Old Testament hints, or else arrived at through the response of people to environment and to stimulation and to intuition. Fourth, the age which witnessed the growth of this literature was the Graeco-Roman age, and therefore Greek culture is reflected in them; the Roman is only secondarily so, for in the east the Roman political conquest was accompanied by a cultural surrender to Greece.

The issue immediately before us is no longer that of modern scholars, it is the issue of these bodies of ancient literature. The theme which I will here develop begins with a thesis: that when diverse civilizations encounter each other, and interpret each other, they never quite understand each other, for they understand each other not in the light of the authenticity of the encountered civilization, but in the light of the encountering one. The interpenetration never becomes total, but remains always partial, and that partial interpenetration involves accommodations which bend and thereby alter the content of both.

By the age of Jesus, the encounter between the Hellenistic and the Jewish civilization was already three centuries old. In that span of time the extent of their interpretation, though uneven in diverse parts of the Jewish world, was great enough to have had its own vicissitudes. On the one hand, Jews in Alexandria not only possessed their Scripture in Greek, especially the Five Books of Moses, but had developed a body of transmitted interpretation. On the other hand, hellenization in Palestine had penetrated enough to produce a vaguely outlined group of Jewish hellenizers and also a large body of those who deliberately rejected aspects of the hellenization. The Maccabean revolt was both political and religious, and while it succeeded in ending Hellenistic political control, it only slowed down the hellenization by extirpating the grossest and most manifest forms of it, while Hellenistic ideas still managed to penetrate. The distinction between the Jewish community in Alexandria swimming in a sea of Hellenism, and the community of Palestine into which trickles of Hellenism continued to flow, is plain on the surface. One might put it into an overneat phrase, that in Alexandria Jews plunged unto Hellenism, while in Palestine Hellenism sprayed its foam over the Jews. A Philo Judaeus in Alexandria who speaks and writes in Greek becomes an apt disciple of Pythagoras, Plato, and the Stoics; but in Palestine only overtones of these three become absorbed more into the Hebrew and Aramaic speech than into their thought. Philo manages through allegory to make the Five Books of Moses a huge repository of Greek philosophy; while in Palestine, echoes of that philosophy resound, but only dimly. Neither Philo nor the Palestinians abandon their Judaism, nor reduce their Jewish loyalty. Philo came to understand Judaism in the light of Hellenism, but also to understand Hellenism in the light of Judaism. That Philo has a clearer understanding of Hellenism than that found in rabbinic literature must not obscure the essential fact that his understanding of it is Jewish, not Greek.

The relevancy of these comments becomes the more apt if we will, for the purposes of analysis, make a partially tenable and partially untenable distinction. Let us suppose that there is a certain difference between the static on-going elements in a religion and those elements which come to the fore out of new historical circumstances and historical crises. Thus, we might speak of a usual, customary eschatology, and at the same time recognize that an event like Pompey's conquest of Palestine in 63 B.C., or Varus's partial burning of the Temple in 2 A.D., or Titus's destruction of it in 70 A.D., heighten, intensify, and even alter the eschatology. On the one hand, there are the calm, tranquil moments in which the eternal questions are raised, such as the relative merits of Jewish versus Greek laws, and then there are acute times of tension in which Jews undergo martyrdom at the hands of Greeks on behalf of the Laws. Theodicy in tranquil moments is a leisurely intellectual adventure, and a luxury; in crises and in disasters theodicy is an urgency.

In the first sense, that is, of the on-going, a Palestinian Jew could raise the question of whether or not the Laws of Moses were or were not preexistent; he could note that in Scripture they postdate Abraham, and he must therefore answer to himself the question of Abraham's relation to those Laws. Through a dim understanding of Plato, he could conceive of eternal and preexistent ideas, attribute preexistence to the Laws, and conclude that Abraham observed these preexistent laws long before Moses formulated his codes. Philo, on the other hand, can, and does, provide a well-rounded formulation of the "law of nature" and of particular laws. Accordingly, whereas the rabbis make Moses the norm, and bring Abraham up to that norm, Philo makes Abraham the norm, and brings Moses up to him. This difference is unimportant in the sense that it is a sort of prescholastic scholasticism, a theoretical debate to which no crucial issues inhere. Yet, in Paul, this same issue loses its theoretical character and becomes associated with program, and that program emerges out of a sense of great urgency. For Paul, Abraham was the norm, and he does not hesitate to declare Moses' law passé and inoperative.

There is all the difference in the world in first, the manner in which tranquil Palestinians toyed with the problem of evil and divine justice; second, the relative absence from Philo of any discussion of theodicy; and third, the profound and eloquent inquiry found in IV Ezra, written shortly after the events of 70 A.D. Again, Philo is content to ascribe evil to man's being a mixture of spirit and body, responsible for his inclination toward one or the other. Fourth Ezra asks *why* God permitted evil to be implanted in man; and Paul seeks divine help to be redeemed from the consequence of evil, sin. The Palestinians could speculate about the Messiah; or else they could rise against Rome as in 132 A.D. under Bar Kochba. Philo can write generalities about his remote and colorless conception; or the New Testament writings can proceed to draw inferences from the conviction of a real experience of the Messiah in a past so immediate that it extends into the present. As to evil in man, there is a range discernible from the monistic Palestinian view of man, through the dualism of Philo, and culminating in the extreme dualism of Christian gnostics.

That body of literature usually called "pseudepigraphic" (which is apocalyptic) invites some attention. Most of this literature failed to find reception into the canon, whether of the Hebrew Bible or the Greek Jewish Bible. Produced in great quantity, it necessarily represents a frequent impulse in Palestinian Jewry; yet the rabbinic literature scorns it and rejects it. No trace of the apocalyptic is to be found in Philo, for while as a mystic he is sure he has communed with God, whose logos has suffused his being, Philo is so rationalistic that he can explain even scriptural miracles as nonmiraculous. The Christian doctrine of the *parousia,* the Second Coming, inevitably abetted and spurred apocalypticism; perhaps there is some significance in the circumstance that one and only one Christian apocalypse, that of John, found its way into the New Testament, for like the rabbis, Christianity found that excessive apocalypticism needed some control and countering.

These diversities in the Judaism of the age of Jesus are customarily regarded as if they were self-contained products of isolated individuals. It is conceded, of course, that the Pharisees and the Sadducees had contact and quarreled, and the "conflict" passages in the Gospels also reflect contact and quarrel, and Jews and Christians had contact and quarrels, but I find almost no predecessor before me engaged in any effort to raise the question: What was the nature of the communication and what was the response to it? Thus, let me ask, was Philo totally unaware of the intellectual and religious streams of Palestine, and Palestine unaware of Alexandria? When the question is asked in this way, there have been some easy, and some wrong answers given. For example, around 1820 one of the scholarly fads was to assume that Alexandria was the source for all Jewish scriptural exegesis found in Palestine, just as there were those who believed that Christianity was born in Alexandria and then moved to Galilee, where the logos, as it were, became Jesus (who, it was declared, had never existed). Similarly, there have been, and are, views which hold that a creative Palestine radiated an influence over an inert Alexandria. Implicit in such theories is the notion that there was communication. Yet as I read these theories, they seem to imply that there was communication, but seldom encounter, communication but seldom reaction, and that communication resulted in prompt acceptance and compliance but never in resistance.

It does not seem to me, abstractly, that these latter opinions conform to my own observation of human beings. Granted that there are always those who rush to accept the new, it seems to me to be inherent in men that what is new stirs opposition and even rejection. Moreover, when one turns to these bodies of literature, I find, at least to my satisfaction, an abundance of reflection about the usual results of communication. I find reflections of acceptance, but even more those of rejection. And I find, moreover, that where rejection exists, it is all too often accompanied by a misunderstanding, a distortion of what is rejected. Within the New Testament, there must be some significance in the controversies reported, as in Galatia and at Corinth. But among these large bodies of literature, I believe that I see reflections of great intellectual turmoil, as if ideas, then as now, resulted in great struggles.

I do not suggest that this factor is easy to weigh. The relevancy of the distinction which I drew between the on-going and the crisis amounts to at least this, that the intellectual encounters were not always on the same plane or in the same mood. I have elsewhere commented on the comparisons and contrasts between the teachings of the rabbis and the teachings of Jesus, that issues of chronology tend to be overlooked, that the issue of multiple teachers versus one teacher is overlooked, that the issue of the nature of the respective literatures is overlooked, and that anachronistic questions of originality in the sense of priority are introduced. Accordingly, I am by no means saying that merely to say communication and response magically explains each and every utterance.

What I am suggesting is something quite modest and restricted, but important in its own right. I am not contending that responsiveness is immediate and specific, in the way in which a present-day author writes to the *Saturday Review* to protest against some assessment of his book in the previous issue; rather, the ideas were circulated slowly and slowly elicited responses. I am suggesting that much that is in the literature is not the self-initiated expression of ideas, or the facile parroting of them, but the reaction to ideas encountered.

The Hellenistic factor enters in, to my mind, in at least two ways. Since it was a civilization alien to Judaism, its content was not uniformly, accurately, or fairly understood; since it permeated the Jewish communities in uneven measure, the unevenness combined with inherent misunderstanding to compound the problems of communication. Just as today, one scholar successfully refutes what another scholar is sure he has not said, so in ancient times, clashing opinions resulted from misinterpretation as well as from accuracy of comprehension.

Let me mention an item which may possibly illustrate my thesis. It is the matter of "unwritten law," for which the Gospel phrase is "tradition of the elders." The preliminary definition of the term might be this, that it is a body of oral explanation of the written Scripture. The rabbinic phrase for it is *Torah she-be'al pe,* "the Torah transmitted orally." Let us first note a distinctive difference in the basic conception as between the ancient rabbis and passages in the Gospels. The rabbinic view is this, that along with the written revelation to Moses there took place an oral revelation which was equally as valid as the written. The consequence of this view is the rabbinic conviction that the contents of the Oral Torah, as products of divine revelation, are not human in their origin, but rather originate with God. In the Gospels, on the other hand, there is the contention that the vow of Corban, the developed details of which are part not of the written Scripture but of the "tradition of the elders," can bring it about that an item in the oral law can nullify an item in the written law. The Gospel account asserts: "You leave the commandment of God, and hold fast the tradition of men" (Mark 7:8). What is here to be noted is the basic cleavage, for in the one view the tradition of the elders is divine, and in the other it is human. These mutually exclusive basic assumptions cannot exist in isolation, but reflect a direct and focused exchange, and this exchange takes on a richness of background only as the divergent views are discerned to result in a deeper probing of the fundamental issue. When, in addition, Philo's approach enters in, a still greater breadth becomes discernible. On the one hand, Philo speaks eloquently in a number of passages of the high significance of ancient custom, and of the need for later generations to conform to tradition. On the other hand, he writes in many passages about the "unwritten law," which to him is the "law of nature." There is a distinct cleavage between the Philonic (really, Stoic) phrase, "the unwritten law," and the similar sounding rabbinic phrase, "the unwritten Torah." What Philo means is clarified to us by our knowledge of the use of that phrase in Greek philosophy; for Philo the unwritten law is the ideal pattern, and the Mosaic laws are an imitation, a reflection of the ideal. There is in Philo no clear indication of anything remotely resembling either the tradition of the elders of the Gospels or of the unwritten Torah of the rabbis. Yet his writings contain frequent expansions of the written Scripture which are analogous, though in their own way, to the rabbinic expansions. We face the situation, then, of what might be termed a three-pronged approach, in two of which (the rabbis and the Gospels) the difference of implied definition is no less than antithetical, and a third approach (Philo's) which in formulation turns everything topsy-turvy. I doubt very much that any Stoic who agreed with Philo's Stoic definition of the unwritten law would have gone on to agree that Moses' laws were the best possible specification of the unwritten law, or that these written laws were in fullest conformity with the unwritten, for Philo must resort to very tortuous allegory to demonstrate the conformity. Is it possible that when Philo turns these matters upside down, he is using the same elementary material but feels that that material must conform to some responsible and rational philosophy? To my mind that is distinctly possible; and if it is the case, then Philo is not so much innovating as he is responding to something in his environment. Respecting this particular item, I would judge that the Gospel passage about the "tradition of the elders" understands the rabbinic conception, but disagrees and rejects it, while Philo misinterprets the same passage through being constrained by his environment not to understand it.

There are, to repeat, many such items, for example, the origin of the written law. According to Paul, the Law was mediated by the angels, in the plural, and according to the rabbis unmediated, and according to Philo the Law was simply the beneficent result of the logos become specific; the Word does not become flesh, but becomes Moses' requirements. A further example is this, that the common monotheism takes on in the rabbis an unbreakable inherent unity, preventing it, in their view, from any exposition relating to its supposed componency. In Philo there is in one passage a trinity, which

221

shatters the inherent unity in monotheism by designating the way in which aspects of the one God are knowable to man, a knowledge consistent with the innate ability of individual men; only the best minds discern this trinity as a oneness, surpassing, as Philo puts it, all other oneness. There have been strained efforts to connect Philo's "logos" directly with that of John. Even if we reject the strained effort, can we not discern in the Christian approach to monotheism analogies to Philo in method if not in detail?

The point of my paper can come into full focus. An abundance of topics found in these three bodies of ancient literature are more than accidentally parallel items. They exist in a framework of communication, and they reflect differences of approach to common ideas. The formulations are often efforts to be distinct from other formulations, and they often exhibit that misunderstanding which imperfect communication entails. People can understand each other perfectly and still disagree. But very often disagreement reflects the hazards which lie in communication.

17

Bultmann on Judaism *

IT IS MY opinion that Rudolph Bultmann is not only the greatest New Testament scholar of our day, but also one of the truly great of all times. In details here and there I would exercise the prerogative of disagreement with him, but I believe that I have learned more from him than from any New Testament teacher and that he has shaped my judgments more than any other. The one personal contact, when he lectured at Vanderbilt where I taught, was a week of unbroken pleasure.

The fact is, however, that my opinion on Dr. Bultmann's portrayal of Judaism in his writings constitutes the most serious area of my disagreement with him. Presently I shall specify this in some detail. Yet certain words of prologue are necessary, for I should not want my disagreement to appear simply as a parochial Jewish protest, such as have had to be made about other scholars, and which are justified and with which I associate myself. The comments I make on Dr. Bultmann's scholarship are almost entirely in a different realm.

The typical Jewish protest against New Testament scholarship is this— that in the various lives of Jesus in the nineteenth century, scholars, albeit unconsciously, tended to write the "biographies" of Jesus as if they had no belief in his divinity. Consequently they seem to have sought, even desperately, to discover some human achievement for him. Since Apocrypha,

* This article first appeared in *The Theology of Rudolf Bultmann,* Charles W. Kegley, ed. (New York, 1966), pp. 211–20. Professor Bultmann's reply to my essay appears on pp. 282–84 of the same volume.

Pseudepigrapha, and translations of rabbinical literature have, for at least the past three centuries, established a general congruency of the teachings of Jesus with the Judaism of his times, it was impossible to separate Jesus from that Judaism on the basis of substance; instead, a separation was made on quite another basis, by depicting the Judaism of the age of Jesus as cold, arid legalism, indeed, as mechanical and devoid of heart. Prophecy, so we were reminded, was by then a thing of the past, and the trivia of legalism, with cut-and-dried doctrines of reward and punishment, had supplanted the warm charismatic religion of the preexilic luminaries. Accordingly, Jesus arose in the midst of this religious sterility, so the scholarship asserted, to restore to Judaism the religious heart which it had lost. (One needs to note the margin of difference between Jesus as the incarnate logos as in the Fourth Gospel, and a Jesus as, one must say, a somewhat lofty enthusiast.) The net effect of the contrast drawn between an arid Judaism and, as it were, a fervent Judaism preached by Jesus was to set Jesus over against Judaism rather than within it. A Jesus at variance with Judaism was a repeated motif in the nineteenth century. This is a startling reversal of the judgment of all but the Marcionites in the early Church, for the early Church held that Jesus, and the Church also, was the continuation of Judaism. This nineteenth-century trend in New Testament scholarship was brilliantly described by George Foot Moore in "Christian Writers on Judaism," in the *Harvard Theological Review* in 1921.[1]

Three late-nineteenth-century writers, Weber, Bousset, and Schürer, were the principal objects of Moore's devastating strictures. Here we can confine ourselves to Schürer's chapter, "Life under the Law," in his *A History of the Jewish People in the Time of Jesus Christ*,[2] as an epitome of the procedure of nineteenth-century scholars. In Schürer's one-sided and unsympathetic portrayal, the Law was a burden under which Jews groaned, for it stifled both creativity and religious spontaneity. As a burden, the Law represented to Jews something simultaneously repelling and compelling; any Jew with any sense, we might infer, would have been pleased to get out from under. So much for Schürer.

The God of the Jews was not so much transcendent (a favorable word) as remote (an unfavorable one). He was no factor in the lives of people, for He never entered in as a favorable force in the day-to-day existence. He was the fierce and fearful disciplinarian, and never the loving, solicitous, tolerant, and forgiving father.

It was such portrayals, travestying rather than depicting Judaism, which called forth a series of Jewish protests. Whenever I reread these, I am compelled to agree with the bill of particulars in them; when I find in these protests a sporadic bitterness, such as in the just contention that most Christian scholars have known rabbinical literature only from compendia and through translations, I lament that the tone of nineteenth-century Christian scholarship called forth from Jews a tone equally lamentable. Some of the infelicitous, indeed ugly tone of nineteenth-century Christian scholarship abides into our day, as, for example, in the International Critical Commentaries on the New Testament. The contrast in tone between the *ICC* and the *Moffatt* series as regards Judaism is notable; so too, the *Interpreter's Bible* has very largely, but not quite completely, avoided the distortions, and has, indeed, brought matters to a better balance. Where imbalance persists, the explanation seems to be in the persistence of aspects of the heritage from nineteenth-century scholarship, or in the misdirection caused by Strack and Billerbeck's *Kommentar zum Neuen Testament aus Talmud und Midrash.* This compendium is staggering in its size, and more than one scholar who has never read a full page in a rabbinical text has been grossly misled. (Note how I too become condescending and superior at this point.) I have elsewhere discussed Strack and Billerbeck at some length,[3] and I see no purpose in beating the same dog over and over again. Let me simply summarize by saying that Strack and Billerbeck do not approach rabbinical Judaism properly, and hence the scholar who relies upon them is misled.

The works of Bultmann to which I here allude are *Jesus and the Word* [4] and *Primitive Christianity.*[5] I have used these in my personal study much less than three others, *The Theology of the New Testament,*[6] *Das Johannesevangelium,*[7] and *Geschichte der synoptischen Tradition.*[8] But my wish here is to discuss a certain main line in Dr. Bultmann and not to produce a plethora of details.

I have found not one ugly sentence about Jews or Judaism in the writings of Bultmann which I have read. I do not see him in the same way as Israel Abrahams [9] necessarily looked at Schürer. My differences with Bultmann are academic and not personal; they are the differences which emerge from two individuals' understanding and interpretation, and are not denominational in the sense of Jew versus Christian. It is my belief that at some crucial points his viewpoint turns incorrect; at no point have I found even the incorrect viewpoint vicious.

In *Jesus and the Word,* Bultmann has a chapter entitled "The Historical Background for the Ministry of Jesus." In it, he speaks of the Law "which properly has only this meaning: to release man from the world, to separate him from any interest in an independent cultural development, and to humble him in obedience to the transcendent power of God" (p. 17). I must comment that the first phrase says too much; the Law did not mean release from the world but guidance and direction *within it.* The second phrase strikes me as very inappropriate, for it raises as an issue something which seems to me scarcely to have entered into the ken of Jews; it is a modern construction, not an ancient Jewish one. The third phrase elicits my disagreement only in its formulation; I should put it, rather, in this way: that the meaning of the Law was to *raise* the Jew in obedience to the living immanence of the transcendent God.

Bultmann sees in that Judaism a balance between the Law and hope. He says, "In rabbinical Judaism after the beginning of the Christian era the hope retreats more and more into the background. . . . The rabbinical Judaism finally rejected the apocalyptic, leaving it to Christianity, and concentrated on the Law." I comment that Christianity, too, eventually so retreated from the apocalyptic as virtually to abandon it, and that it is most inappropriate to limit hope exclusively to the apocalyptic. I would insist that it was the apocalyptic that Judaism abandoned, not hope, and that Judaism abandoned it and Christianity retreated [10] from it for the same reasons, namely the sad experiences arising out of the apocalyptic. Predictions made too clearly and too specifically led to frustration or to disaster rather than to well-being; and this same thing is attested in Christendom as well as in Judaism.

But this summary of Judaism as comprising law and promise, obedience and hope, seems to me to be much too nimble. Perhaps this arises from an understandable need on the part of Bultmann to compress, or even from a use of terms in some special way. Yet the suspicion arises that it derives from an unconscious setting of the stage, from a preparation as by a playwright to explain Jesus, rather than from an endeavor to depict Judaism without regard to Jesus.

I am by no means certain that the movements of John the Baptist and of Jesus were "essentially unpolitical" (p. 25). There is not sufficient evidence either to affirm or deny. A stronger case can be made for a political aspect to Jesus' movement than for John's (see the Gospel of Mark and the Book of Acts). Certainly whatever political aspect there was to Jesus' movement was almost completely winnowed out in developing Christian thought.

Bultmann's contrast between the eschatology of the prayer in the "Eighteen Benedictions" and a passage from the Lord's Prayer (pp. 41–42) is hardly apt, for here Bultmann has succumbed in both cases to arbitrary selection. And I must not refrain from expressing my opinion that, on pages 44–45, in discussing the coming of Gentiles into the kingdom of God, the scholar has given way to the homiletician, for here it seems to me that Bultmann has faltered. So, too, his contrast (pp. 91–92) between the "demand of the law" and "the demand of God" is either homiletics or else a confusion of Jesus with Paul; in Judaism the Law was deemed God's demand, and to divide these as Bultmann does into two differing demands is quite untrue to Judaism. The Jewish formula for a "benediction" declares that God is blessed for He "has *sanctified us by his commandments* and commanded us to . . ."

A clue, however, to Bultmann's procedure is to be found (p. 155) in his statement: ". . . Jesus stands within the limits of strict Judaism, and differs from it not because he presents especially original ideas about God and the world, but because he apprehends the Jewish conception of God in its purity and consistency." Whether this conclusion is tenable or not (and I think it is not) is scarcely the point in this essay. The true point is that, unlike Schürer, Bultmann has not conjured up some reprehensible Judaism against which to contrast Jesus. Rather he seeks to find in an admirable Judaism a Jesus whom he finds even more admirable.

So much for *Jesus and the Word*. Turning to *Primitive Christianity*, we may advert to his statement (p. 60): "By binding herself to her past history, Israel loosened her ties with the present, and her responsibility for it. . . ." Two comments are in order. First, if what Bultmann is saying is correct, it would be as applicable to Christianity as to Judaism; and, in fact, in view of the dualism present in so much of even "orthodox" Christianity, it would be even more applicable to Christianity than to Judaism. Second, Bultmann is incorrect. Granted there is some sense in which loyalty to a past dilutes the confrontation of the present, in normative Judaism present and future were deemed to be intimately and inseparably connected with, not isolated from, the past. The passage in the Passover haggada says this clearly: "In each

generation a man must regard himself as though he himself has been redeemed from Egypt." Furthermore, the statement (again p. 60) that there
was no possibility of science and art among Jews, is only partially correct,
and the partial correctness rests on a basis different from the one Bultmann
gives. In respect to the plastic arts, it was the accrued objection to depicting
the human form which tended to stifle sculpture and painting; decoration,
though, did take place. As for science, enough evidence is available about the
understanding of astronomy to suggest that lawyer's literature—which is
what the rabbinical literature is—is scarcely evidence for or against the existence of science. I do not dispute Bultmann's description here, but his explanation of what he has described.

Again, in the area of what Bultmann seems to see as history, one reads his
statement that since "proselytes actually had to join the Jewish community,"
this is "another instance of the way Israel was cutting itself adrift from
history." Not at all! The proselyte was simply admitted into the community
and *into its history*. The documents would not sustain Bultmann at this
point, nor would logic; the would-be proselyte was invited to become part of
the historically centered community.

Bultmann's statement on page 62 reveals his most serious misunderstanding, and, in fact, some continuing partial bondage to Schürer and Bousset.
According to Bultmann, the Bible in synagogue worship "was no longer
primarily a historical record of God's dealing with his people, but a book of
divine Law." To conserve space I must here condense my objections. First,
Law and Bible never were as identical as Bultmann supposes; in the Jewish
view the Bible *contained* laws, but was not interchangeable with them, as
witness the Psalms and the Prophets. Bultmann forgets that haggada was as
important to the rabbis as halaka; he truly misses the point about Jewish
legalism. In his view, apparently, the legalism was virtually the entirety of
Judaism; in point of fact, the legalism was directed toward clarifying the
ambiguities and uncertainties of scriptural legalism; it is methodologically
unsound to use a people's clarifying legalisms as if they exhaust the total dimensions of a people. When Bultmann goes on to say that "life was alienated
from history," he is saying something which every pericope in rabbinical
literature would refute. And he completely distorts Judaism in saying that
the holiness sought for was designed to be "above all worldly interests and
ideals." Quite the contrary; in so far as such modern terminology conforms
to ancient documents, the Jewish quest was to have holiness permeate
worldly interests and ideals, not rise above them. No, there was no effort to
separate sanctity from life, but rather to sanctify life.

My purpose in picking on these details in Bultmann is not for their own sake, for there is truly very little involved in them in themselves, and it would be a very minor consideration whether or not Bultmann has phrased his analysis felicitously. These details, however, serve him as a sort of prologue to the contrast toward which he is heading, namely, the *obedience* in Judaism and the *radical obedience* which he conceives of as characterizing Jesus.

He defines radical obedience as involving "a personal assent to the divine command"; he ascribes to Judaism what he calls a "formal obedience." I doubt whether the ancient rabbis, or Jesus, or his disciples would have understood the distinction. Would not obedience *to all the forms* exemplify and demonstrate radical obedience? Or does "personal assent" imply an exemption from the formal? I find no reality in Bultmann's words here, and absolutely no applicability in them either to rabbinical Judaism or to Jesus.

In these pages in his book (pp. 50–71) Bultmann is setting the stage for his consideration of Jesus; to put it clearly, he is stacking the cards—this by describing a Judaism that never existed so that he can set a special view of Jesus over against it.

True, he insists that "the proclamation of Jesus must be considered within the framework of Judaism" (p. 71). But at this point we again encounter the strange paradox that the scholar who more than anyone has taught us how little of Jesus is authentic in the Gospels, now finds him there abundantly. It is outside the realm of this essay to deal with that topic. Yet I must go on to say that in dealing with the Sermon on the Mount (p. 72) Bultmann abstains from reflecting a common view that Matthew, not Jesus, was its author; and he is dead wrong in asserting that the Sermon contrasts the Law and the will of God, for the Sermon is *a new law, more rigid than Moses'*; and it is certainly not to be summarized nimbly as the will of God. Moreover, Bultmann's special pleading leads him to say that "without contesting the authority of the Old Testament Jesus discriminates between its various aspects." This statement is quite irresponsible, and does violence to the Sermon, with its formula, seven times repeated, "You have heard it said, but I say to you," and six of the seven quotations are Old Testament quotations.[11]

Bultmann seems to me at his best in interpreting Judaism when it is Hellenistic rather than rabbinical Judaism to which he addresses himself. I have some competency in Philo;[12] I regard Bultmann's essay in *Primitive Christianity* (pp. 94 ff.) as a truly brilliant achievement.

229

Having conceded, it seems to me, what the facts require, that Bultmann is never guilty of an offending attitude toward Judaism, I must go on to comment further on what seems to me the major infelicity. It derives from manner and disposition, not from basic assessment. It is Bultmann's tendency to create his own categories and to superimpose these on Judaism, or else to make Judaism fit into them. All too often these categories can be applied only by forcing Judaism into them. It seems to me that they do not arise from what a study of Judaism yields, but rather represent Bultmann's special subjective conception. It is not to Judaism alone that he applies this procedure, but he does so to Christianity too.

To my mind this procedure involves mostly a debit, for even when distortion is free from malice, it is nevertheless distortion. But it would be grossly unfair to a magnificent scholar to leave this allegation unmodified. I am not charging Bultmann with a capricious, that is, thoughtless, creation of categories, but with an arbitrary creation of them—this in the etymological sense of the word "arbitrary." He has studied the material thoroughly; he has pondered it carefully. It is thereafter that he has not resisted the tendency to supply categories which are simultaneously true and untrue to the material. He has devised terms and labels for utterances which are intuitive, unrestrained, and devoid of inner consistence. He has made quasi-systematic a body of ancient thought which is notably unsystematic. It is not that he has betrayed material by putting it into the wrong categories; it is that he has put into categories of today thought which defies putting even into ancient categories.

The Judaism which emerges from his pages is too sharply defined; it is too crystal-clear; it is too highly focused.

Yet, paradoxically, I must state that his procedure, much as I have reservations about it, contains its own admirable illumination. He has devised categories (such as "promise" and "hope") that I think I would never have dreamed of, certainly not in his way; but in my scrutiny of the material, in the light even of those of his categories which I feel I must reject, I find myself gaining some new insights and responding to nuances which I have previously failed to notice. So penetrating is Bultmann's weighing of the material that he who studies Bultmann, and disagrees here and there, has the sense (so at least I do) of having penetrated further and better because of him.

Certain scholars, especially very young ones, seem to me to put an undue premium on whether another scholar is right or wrong. We discern this especially in the book reviews which younger scholars write. For them certainty is ready at hand, and a minor error (such as a wrong reference not caught in proofreading) is as heinous a sin as mayhem or murder. Most scholars outgrow such juvenility. In the highest rungs of scholorship, especially in the humanities, there is no such thing as right or wrong; we are all acquainted with that class of scholar "who never gets a footnote wrong or an idea right." Scholarly differences are often matters of individual mood and temperament; there is no book on Paul which I admire quite as much as that by Machen, a fundamentalist, with whom I almost completely disagree.

Respecting Professor Bultmann, I repeat that I count myself as one of his disciples. What I have written in my first paragraph in assessment, I have often and repeatedly expressed in the spoken word. The area wherein I, as it were, agree, is enormously large; the area wherein I differ is small, restricted. It is to me a source of continuing gratification that I regard his views on Judaism as sometimes incorrect, but never improper; sometimes out of balance, but never unbalanced; sometimes too neat, too pat, too apt, but never hateful and hating.

18

Isaac Mayer Wise's "Jesus Himself" *

I SAAC MAYER WISE, the founder of the Hebrew Union College, is quoted only rarely in the scholarly books which deal with the question of Christian origins. The occasional quotations are almost exclusively from a book, published by Wise in 1868 in Cincinnati and called *The Origins of Christianity and a Commentary to the Acts of the Apostles.* In Gösta Lindeskog's *Die Jesusfrage im neuzeitlichen Judentum* (Uppsala, 1938), this largest of Wise's writings passes unlisted, although three minor items of Wise are mentioned. While Lindeskog paraphrases many of the Jewish writers on Jesus, he limits his treatment of Wise to the mere listing of the titles.

In addition to *The Origins,* Isaac Mayer Wise penned other works relating to Christianity. *The Martyrdom of Jesus of Nazareth: a Historic-Critical Treatise on the Last Chapters of the Gospel* appeared in 1874. Two works appeared in 1883—*Three Lectures on the Origin of Christianity* and *Judaism and Christianity, Their Agreements and Disagreements.* A fourth appeared in 1889—*A Defense of Judaism versus Proselytizing Christianity.*[1] To my mind, however, the most interesting and noteworthy of his writings relating to Christianity never appeared in book form. It is a series of chapters entitled "Jesus Himself." The first of these chapters appeared in Wise's weekly newspaper, *The Israelite,* on July 9, 1869. The tenth chapter, which appeared on April 1, 1870, carries at its end the legend: "To be continued."

It was never continued. That the work was never finished is likely the reason why "Jesus Himself" never appeared in book form.

* This article first appeared in *Essays in American Jewish History* (Cincinnati, 1958), pp. 325–58.

Equally as interesting as "Jesus Himself" is a series of chapters, translated from the German by Wise and published in *The Israelite*. Written by Gustav Adolf Wislicenus, this German work has a title which in English would be *The Bible Considered for Thinking Readers*. The Old Testament part appeared in 1863; the New Testament section, in the following year. There seems to be a dearth of information on Wislicenus, for he was a man of no great importance. We know, however, that he was born in Germany in 1805 and that he studied for the ministry. He participated in some revolutionary movements, for which he was jailed (possibly around 1848). Thereafter, he fled to America, but later returned to Europe and settled in Switzerland.

Wislicenus was a popularizer of the scholarship of his time, especially of the iconoclastic and shocking variety. His preface tells us:

> Though earlier the Bible was considered exceptional compared with other books, it is now aligned with others as something which appeared in history, as an attestation of the human spirit, and as an organ in the development of the species. Great and wondrous toil has been brought to bear in the field of Bible study, so that now a clear light has been shed over it, despite efforts to becloud clear sight and to revert to earlier presentations.

The portion of Wislicenus which Wise translated and published in his newspaper was only a segment of the New Testament section, that dealing with the Gospels and the Epistles of Paul. Wise did not translate, or at least did not publish, the Old Testament portion. I doubt that this was an accident, for although Wislicenus was quite as radical in his approach to the Old as to the New, Wise was not similarly inclined.

In his survey of the life and teachings of Jesus, Wislicenus expresses doubts about the reliability of the supposition that everything which the Gospels attribute to Jesus is really from him or about him. Indeed, Wislicenus is a fairly good reflection of the skepticism which in radical form was expressed by David Friedrich Strauss and in a more moderate (I cannot withhold the modern word "schmaltzy") way by Ernest Renan.

Wise not only translates Wislicenus, but also annotates him. The author and his annotator, however, are separated by a notable gap: while in a good many places Wislicenus doubts that such and such a statement was really made by Jesus, Wise goes beyond him to doubt that Jesus ever lived.[2] For example, Wislicenus makes the statement that the four Gospels were

233

"written in Greek, because Christianity, although originating among the Hebrews, soon stepped beyond those limits, and Greek was then the universal language of the East." To this Wise comments in a footnote: "It is by no means certain that Christianity originated among the Hebrews. Its Alexandrian origin has been maintained by many. See *Diegeses* [sic] by R. Taylor, p. 136."

Who was Taylor, and what was this business of Alexandrian origin? Robert Taylor (1784–1844) was a former Anglican priest who, after a checkered career, embraced deism and wrote a number of books attacking Christianity from the deist point of view. *Diegesis, A Discovery of the Origin of Christianity,* was published in Boston in 1832. Since I have not been able to procure a copy of the book, I can judge its tone only on the basis of the illuminating chapter on the deists' attitude to the problems of the New Testament which F. C. Conybeare summarizes in Chapter 3 of his *History of New Testament Criticism* (London, 1910).[3] On the negative side, the deists either emphasized the discrepancies or what seemed to them incredibilities in the text; on the other hand, they offered explanations supposedly more reasonable and cogent. It is to be presumed—for the matter is scarcely important enough to justify research—that among the explanations offered about the "real" origins was the theory that Christianity really emerged somewhere in the Greek world. What place was better for this suppositious origin than Alexandria? In a deistic-like book, *Christian Theology and Modern Skepticism* (London, 1872), the Duke of Somerset writes: "Some ingenious writers have endeavored to trace the source of Christianity to the schools and synagogues of Alexandria. They would even interpret the prophecy, Out of Egypt have I called my son (Mt. 2.15), in a mystic sense" (page 70).

The deistic explanations of various and sundry items in the New Testament exhibit what I would call a notable lack of self-criticism and restraint. Indeed, just as the pious imagination of the faithful managed to expand the sense of the passage in Matthew into a stipulation of how long Jesus sojourned in Egypt, and exactly where, so the imagination of the skeptical opponents soared far above texts and above sobriety. We shall come to see, I believe, that Wise himself absorbed from the deists both their attitude and their manner.

We must conclude, therefore, that the deists did not offer their theories in any direct and vivid relationship to the text or its meaning. Or, to put the matter in a way which risks the charge of condescension, the deists were dabblers. The source of the Alexandrian emphasis is probably August Friedrich Gfrörer (1803-1861), a responsible scholar who could scarcely foresee how the irresponsible would abuse his erudition. A long series of books under the general title *Geschichte des Urchristentums* appeared from 1831 to 1838. The first part, in two volumes, was on Philo (20 B.C.—40 A.D.) and Alexandrian theosophy. Gfrörer believed that Alexandrian theosophy was very old and that it came to be transplanted in Palestine. That Gfrörer was not on solid ground is not to be taken as indicative of limited or poor scholarship, but rather as the consequence of his having created and defended an idiosyncratic theory.

It chances that another German, Bruno Bauer, a vicious anti-Semite, also came to a judgment about Alexandria and its significance in Christian origins. To Bauer, a thoroughly trained and competent scholar, Schweitzer devotes Chapter XI of *The Quest of the Historical Jesus*.[4] Bauer began as a skeptical critic, but he had no great doubts initially as to the historicity of Jesus; later, in a three-volume work published in 1841-1842, he arrived at the conclusion that Jesus had never lived.[5] Not until 1874 did Bauer publish a succinct account of his view. This he set forth in a little book—I found it caustic and entertaining—which he called *Philo, Strauss, Renan und das Urchristentum*. Bauer contended that the efforts of Jesus' two "biographers" to separate the legendary and mythical from actual history were misguided. They had supposed that the Gospels exhibited the growth of a man through legend into divinity. To the contrary, Bauer held that the concept of Jesus as a human being was the result of a humanization of certain metaphysical concepts found in the writings of Philo.

Bauer and Gfrörer were, in every technical sense of the word, thoroughgoing scholars. The deists were rather dilettantes. I have found in Wise no indication of his having read Bauer. I rather imagine that he obtained his material from writers like Robert Taylor.

One observes that, in summoning the support of Taylor to refute Wislicenus, Wise was smiting a broken reed with an equally broken reed. One wonders if he was as critical in his reading of Taylor as he was in his examination of Wislicenus. We do not know. What we can be sure about is that in 1865 Wise was confident that there had never been a Jesus.[6]

Four years later Wise began the task of writing a biography of Jesus. I do not know what brought about the change of heart. Perhaps it was due to his reading Abraham Geiger. This great German Jewish scholar had published a book of lectures in 1864; the book was translated into English as

Judaism and its History (New York, 1866).[7] Three of the lectures (IX–XI) were on Christianity. Geiger contended that Jesus "was a Jew, a Pharisean Jew with Galilean coloring." Perhaps this affirmation by a great Jewish scholar, following as it did the affirmation (1856) by Heinrich Graetz,[8] exercised some influence on Wise. Yet my reading of Wise keeps persuading me of the relative independence of his mind, both where independence was a virtue and where it was not necessarily so.

If it was not the reading of Geiger which changed Wise's mind, then I confess to not knowing what it was.

It is reckless to make too great an inference from a small matter. In 1866 Wise commented on Wislicenus' account of Jesus' activities in Jerusalem. Wislicenus had remarked that the "cursing of the fig-tree" (Mark 11:12–14) is the sole miracle attributed to the Jerusalem period. Concerning this Wise comments: "It is not at all wonderful that Jesus wrought no miracles in Jerusalem . . . it is only remarkable that the evangelists invented none for him" (*The Israelite,* March 12, 1866, p. 293). It is to be noted that here we no longer deal with an outright denial of the existence of Jesus, but with the beginning of the separation in Wise's mind of Jesus from those who wrote about him. Here the dichotomy is only hinted at: three years later the distinction blossomed. We move from denial in 1865, to a grudging and vague acceptance of historicity in 1866, to an effort at biography in 1869.

Though I cannot explain what made Wise change his mind, to speculate about it is harmless. Indeed, from something which Wise says in his very first chapter, I suspect that Wise, on mulling over Wislicenus and others, noted what so many modern Jews have been quick to see: that items in the Gospels impinge on materials found in the rabbis, and what is rare, or rather, was rare, is that this impingement was either not noticed or else not handled with accuracy and authority. Wise wrote:

> Besides Lightfoot's and Isidor Kalisch's fragmentary essays, no book or essay in the English language has become known to us which treats on the Ancient Rabbinical Literature in connection with, and in comparison to, the New Testament, to illustrate the circumstances which must be fully understood in order to form a correct conception of the person, events, and lessons described by the authors of that collection. (*The Israelite,* July 9, 1869).

Wise undoubtedly thought that through the use of rabbinic literature he could do a much better job than his predecessors had done. It is my conjecture that through his sense of competency in rabbinics he became confident of his ability to surpass these others. This newly found understanding, I believe, led him out of his skepticism about Jesus and into an avowal that Jesus had really lived.

Isidor Kalisch, referred to by Wise, was born in Krotoschin in 1816; he came to the United States in 1849, and died in Newark in 1886. So numerous are his essays—unhappily, never gathered into a book, but scattered throughout *The Israelite, The Occident,* and the *London Jewish Chronicle*— that I have not been able to determine exactly which essay Wise had in mind. As to Lightfoot, there is this quandary. There was a British bishop, Joseph Barber Lightfoot, who was born in 1828 and who was a great New Testament scholar. Wise might possibly be referring to him, but I think that this is unlikely, for his literary activity seems to have begun just about the time that Wise himself was writing.

What is more reasonable is to understand the reference as being to John Lightfoot (1602–1675), who became quite a notable Talmudist. His *Horae Hebraicae et Talmudicae,* composed in Latin between 1658 and 1674, gave talmudic parallels to much (though not all) of the New Testament. The *Horae* was published in an English translation in 1859. Lightfoot wrote a good many essays, one edition of which was published in 1822–1825. It is likely, then, that it is John Lightfoot whom Wise means; but I am unable to say which is the particular essay to which he refers.

In his first chapter, Wise outlines for his readers what his procedure will be:

> The authors of the New Testament maintain that they have described the words and actions of Jesus. Their books must be considered the primary source to this work. This standpoint suggests a number of inquiries. By what means did those authors obtain possession of the matter they communicate? Were they eye-witnesses of the events which they describe; did they borrow them from written records, or from traditions; or, did they invent them? Were they able to write the full truth, and was it their intention to do so, or merely to write in defense of preconceived doctrines? Which is fact and which embellishment? Have we the means of distinguishing the fact from the embellishment? Are we, at this distance of time, able to understand those authors correctly? Can we tell with certainty when, where, by whom, and in what language those books were written? (*The Israelite,* April 9, 1869)

Wise proceeds to discuss the Jewish backgrounds, making the usual mention of the Essenes (Wise takes his stand with others who believe that the

237

word is corrupted from the word *Hasidim*), the Sadducees (the aristocrats), and the Pharisees (the democrats).

As to the Gospels themselves (which he discusses in *The Israelite* of July 23, 1869), Wise makes a number of statements which are both interesting and also regrettably less than completely clear. One of his first is a tiny misstatement of no great significance, except possibly to alert us to the frequency with which unimportant misstatements appear in these chapters. The four Gospels, he says, are called canonical, "in contradistinction of the Apocryphal Gospels which were rejected by the Council of Nicea [9] (325 A. C.) as fraudulent productions." He goes on to explain what is meant by the italicized words "according to" in such titles as the Gospel *according to* Mark or *according to* Luke: the names are not the names of the authors of the Gospels, but these men "taught Christianity to these respective congregations out of which the ultimate authors of the written Gospels arose." This explanation is quite ingenious; thus far I have not met it anywhere else. It is the reverse of a frequent and familiar explanation of the phenomenon. Most scholars who see growth in the process of Gospel formation would regard "Matthew" or "Luke" as the final step in the procedure by which oral materials or rudimentary written sources become transmuted into Gospels; with Wise, however, "Matthew" and "Luke" supply the original impetus, and only thereafter does a Gospel ultimately achieve its present form.

Wise was certain that none of the Gospels in existence today "existed in the first century" (*The Israelite,* July 23, 1869, p. 9). While most scholars of today would undoubtedly differ with Wise, he was in his own time not too far removed from the dates which some Protestant scholars were assigning to the Gospels.[10]

That the Gospels were relatively late literary products meant to him that their reliability was thereby impugned; "Their statements rest upon no known authority. Nobody can tell who made those statements, when or where they were made. Therefore nobody can reasonably vouch for the veracity of those authors . . ." (*The Israelite,* July 23, 1896).

Yet the nature of the content of the Gospels prompts Wise to make a distinction which for him (and for our understanding of him) is of great significance.

> The pages . . . are adorned with accounts of miracles, exorcism, thaumaturgy, the words and deeds of angels, demons and Satan himself. . . . In vain are all the attempts of rationalistic expounders to

allegorize, or explain away otherwise, the extraordinary performances and preternatural phenomena. . . . Those superstitions weaken the authority of the Gospels. . . . There is no connection between the doctrine or fact and the miracle wrought to prove the former. The written miracle is perfectly useless. We have before us a doctrine and a miracle. If the understanding declared the doctrine true, the miracle is superfluous, as the doctrine can be no better or more true. If the understanding doubts, the miracle can not improve the case. For we must first believe the miracle on the authority of the witness or of the writer, which has no affinity with the understanding, in order to believe also the doctrine which anyhow must offer some affinity with the understanding. . . . Doctrines surpassing the universal understanding of man are absurdities which no miracle can change into legitimate propositions. . . . All the miracles can not improve a fact, or make it one, if it is not . . . (*The Israelite,* July 23, 1869).

The distinction which Wise draws is that only that material in the Gospels which is totally devoid of the miraculous is worthy of being regarded as historically reliable. The initial test for historical reliability, then, will be the "naturalistic" content of the Gospels. One by-product was Wise's ability, after this decision, to bypass almost all the chapters in the Gospels which deal with the career of Jesus prior to his entry into Jerusalem.

But even before he can proceed to matters of substance, Wise has more words of introduction. Not only do the Gospels contain the "preternatural," but as literary documents their relationships with each other need to be defined, for they cover the same material about Jesus, often with divergencies, but often, too, with similarities and near-identities. While by Wise's time the so-called "two-source theory" (that Luke and Matthew independently used Mark and a body of "teachings" known as Q, *Quelle,* "source," as sources) had been articulated and was on the way to becoming a cornerstone of Gospel study, Wise cites no scholars as authority, but instead offers his own judgment:

Mark may have seen Matthew's book, or vice versa. Luke must have seen Matthew's and Mark's Gospels, and John knew the three Synoptic Gospels and the Acts of the Apostles. Nevertheless they disregarded and contradicted one another, not only in the particulars of the story, but also in the speeches and the parables ascribed to Jesus. . . . The evangelists did not consider one another reliable authorities, and each of them took the liberty to change, amend, omit, and add . . . (*The Israelite,* July 30, 1860).

239

This statement addresses itself, of course, to the divergencies in the Gospels. But Wise was equally under obligation to account for the similarities:

> They could not have copied from one another the passages which they have, literally alike, unless they were in possession of a fixed standard, by which they judged that certain passages were genuine, and others were not. This consideration naturally leads to the hypothesis, the passages, literally alike in the Gospels, must have been copies from an old work of this kind. (*ibid.*)

Wise was neither the first nor the last to suppose that some primitive Gospel underlay the four which came to be canonical; scholarship today still deals, though passingly, with a by now old theory concerning an Ur-Mark, a primitive version of Mark out of which the present Mark was composed. For my own understanding, I find the theory of an Ur-Mark an inescapable necessity; but I should not dream of supposing that this Ur-Mark was a standard to which all the evangelists adhered. Yet this is Wise's supposition, at least at this point in his writings; elsewhere he seems to me at times to hold related but slightly different views.

Having supposed that there was at one time a primitive Gospel, Wise goes on to identify it for us. He finds it in a Gospel known in quotation from the Church Fathers as the Gospel of the Hebrews. Wise is aware, of course, that modern scholars [11] consider the fragmentary Gospel of the Hebrews to have been derived from the canonical Gospels, especially from Matthew; yet Wise believes, to the contrary, that the true source of the acknowledgedly spurious Gospel of the Hebrews was an earlier Gospel. Wise implies that others have considered a primitive Gospel in Hebrew or in Aramaic to be merely a hypothesis. "With us, this is no hypothesis. We can produce positive evidence that a Gospel existed in the apostolic age, and that Gospel was either in Hebrew or in Aramaic" (*ibid.*).

Wise's proof leads him through what he himself calls a "chain of rabbinic reasoning." He uses oft-cited passages in Tosefta Yadaim II, 5 (and in Shabbat 116a, restored from the excisions by medieval Christian censors) which state that certain "scrolls" (*gilyonim*) were not worthy of being rescued from a conflagration on the Sabbath. Two rabbis, Meier and Johanan, punned on the word *gilyonim*, yielding the equivalent of *evangelyonim*, that is, "Gospels." A huge literature exists on these passages.

Wise has an ingenious, although improbable, interpretation of his own to add to the rabbinic passages. He is not content for them to be second-century statements alluding to a Hebrew or Aramaic Gospel, but he finds some need (which eludes me) to derive the word *evangelion* from the Hebrew root *GLH*, "to reveal," rather than, as *gilyon* would be derived, from the root meaning "to roll" (as in a scroll). The Greek, of course, is a compound of *eu* and *angelion*, "good" and "tiding." But were Wise to have conceded that the rabbinic pun rested on a Greek word, his case for a primitive Gospel in Hebrew or Aramaic would have been weakened, or even shattered. By means of the Hebraic etymology, Wise was able to persuade himself that Jewish Christians had a Hebrew or Aramaic sacred book, for "the primitive Christians . . . when still included in the community of Israel, had sacred books which they considered equally holy with the Bible. Those books must have been Hebrew or Aramaic, as translations of the Bible itself were not included in the Sabbath statute" (*ibid.*).

But Wise has not yet finished his proof. In this additional item, he goes lamentably astray. The Palestinian Talmud records that one Ben Stada brought necromancy from Egypt (and now note the key words) "in this same kind of writing." The context of this passage in the Talmud did not excite Wise's attention; it is likely that he knew it from memory and desisted from checking on it. Let us suppose, for a moment, that the Talmud does relate that one Ben Stada brought some kind of writing from Egypt. It is a hoary matter that Ben Stada and Jesus were identified with each other in Jewish tradition.[12] At first glance, following Wise, it would appear that Ben-Stada-Jesus brought some kind of writing from Egypt, and this would give us an Alexandrian origin. The fact is, however, that in its own context in the Talmud the kind of writing under discussion does not refer to the scroll form, or the papyrus form, but to writing on one's own skin! The correct rendering of the passage would omit the words "in this same kind of writing," and read instead: "Did not Ben Stada bring necromancy out of Egypt in the same kind of way [on his own skin]?"

As noted above, Wise went astray as an autodidact often goes astray, through lack of some measure of self-restraint. I have reproduced this item, not out of the wish to disparage a man whom I truly admire and whose memory I truly reverence, but only out of honesty and out of the conviction that the minor error is too petty to require forgiveness. Men, trained more rigorously than Wise ever had the opportunity to be, have in the last decade written things about the Dead Sea Scrolls infinitely more startling than this divagation of Wise.

Let us now return to Wise's main line of argument. One may cast aside the miraculous in the Gospels. But the Gospels, especially the Synoptics (Mark, Matthew, and Luke), do have a large measure of agreement with each other, and this agreement, Wise states, results from the common use of the original Aramaic or Hebrew Gospel. In such agreement in the Synoptic Gospels, Wise says, there are historically reliable elements.[13]

This preface over, Wise is now ready for the substance of his study. His first problem is the date of the birth of Jesus. Wise, like Protestant scholars, tries his hand at reconciling the material in Matthew, Luke, and Josephus. Stated briefly, Matthew 2:1 offers the datum that Jesus was born in the time of Herod, who died in 4 B.C. Luke identifies the time of the birth with a census which is either now totally unknown, or is possibly to be identified with a census, not the worldwide one of Luke, but one known to us from Josephus as a strictly local one which took place in 6 A.D.[14] Luke 3:23 relates that Jesus, at the height of his career, was thirty years old; John 8:57 seems to suggest that Jesus was then "nearly" fifty. According to Wise, one needs then to determine Jesus' age as between John and Luke, and the year of his birth as between Matthew (4 B.C.) and Luke (6 A.D.). Wise notes that some manuscripts of John read "nearly forty" and he adopts the latter reading as correct. (Modern scholars consider it a deliberate change so as to avoid the sharp conflict between Luke and John, for thirty and "nearly forty" are not quite so far apart as thirty and nearly fifty.) As to choosing between Matthew and Luke, for Wise this is easy.

> The infant stories of Matthew are manifest inventions. No critic will attempt to save them. The massacre of the babes at Bethlehem is an imitation of the passage in Exodus narrating the birth of Moses and the babes drowned in the Nile by command of Pharaoh. Also the astrologers and the star are taken from rabbinical legends on the birth of Moses.[15] Like Luke, so nobody now, outside of the church, believes Matthew's infant stories. . . . In the following book we treat of the year 36, A. C., which is the year of the national career and death of Jesus of Nazareth (*The Israelite,* August 6, 1869).

Wise moves promptly, as I have intimated above, from the establishment of this chronology of the birth of Jesus to the end of his career in Jerusalem. The Galilean period, the journey to Jerusalem, with all the various and sundry details, seem brushed aside, for they contain miracles, but the period in Jerusalem does not, and Wise without delay brings Jesus to the Holy City.

Prior to recounting the entry of Jesus into Jerusalem, Wise presents a character analysis. The Herodians were wicked persecutors.

> Persecution invariably contributes to the elevation of the victim. . . .
> The persecution of Herod attracted the masses to Jesus of Nazareth, the meek and unpretending teacher of a small circle of disciples from the humble and neglected class of society. The keen eye of public inquisitiveness discovered the hiding places of Jesus upon the shores of the Sea of Galilee. . . . Friends and opponents congregated around him, to listen to his lessons, or to oppose his doctrines. . . .
> Resistance and success . . . developed in Jesus the desire to become the savior of his people, whose misery then must have touched the heart of every patriot. His name, Jesus, which signifies savior, undoubtedly contributed to the birth of this idea in him, which the combination of circumstances ripened to solid resolution.
> A great design, once conceived and embraced, changes the entire character of the man. . . . The same was the case with Jesus. Having resolved upon becoming the savior of his people, the simple enthusiast under the very eye of his disciples, as it were, was transformed into a being of higher powers. This is the sense of the transfiguration legend which is copied almost literally from Plato's Phaedon.[16]

In the account, as Wise rewrites it, there is a culprit—but it is not Jesus. True, Jesus had the intention of becoming the savior of his people. But

> Peter suggested the idea, how to rouse and captivate popular enthusiasm in favor of the master and his designs. The messianic mania had taken hold of the Hebrews, in a most deplorable manner. . . . Peter suggested the idea—"Thou art Christ," the Messiah. Jesus, fully aware of the dangers connected with that position, was startled by the novel idea, and prohibited his disciples to publish it. But the word was spoken, the spark had fallen on combustibles. The mission of the master had assumed shape and form in that popular word. . . .
> Jesus expostulated with Peter, pointing out clearly the perilous condition in which the Son of Man was placed. Peter attempted to overcome the master's apprehensions, and succeeded in obtaining the tacit consent of Jesus to this hazardous enterprise. Jesus never claimed the messianic dignity. His disciples, on the suggestion of Peter, claimed it for him (*The Israelite,* August 13, 1869, p. 9).

It is worthwhile here to interrupt Wise's account in order to notice how close he came, in different though overlapping terms, to a somewhat related theory in *Das Messiasgeheimnis in den Evangelien* (1901), by William

243

Wrede. Both Wise and Wrede notice the phenomenon in Mark that Jesus never makes a clear claim to messiahship; for both, some secrecy seems to shroud it. Wrede explains the motif by asserting that the affirmation of Jesus' messiahship arose only after the belief in the resurrection from death had gripped his followers, and that Jesus in his lifetime never claimed to be the Messiah. The German title of the book by Albert Schweitzer known as *The Quest of the Historical Jesus* is *Von Reimarus zu Wrede*—the same Wrede. Since the turn of the century there has been under Wrede's influence a host of writings which echo the assertion that Jesus did not claim the messiahship; many writers seem bent on protecting Jesus from the supposed arrogance implicit in such a messianic claim. I might add that neither Wrede, with all his subsequent influence, nor Wise, with all his obscurity in this area, appears to me to have recognized what the Gospel of Mark is really saying; namely, that despite all the miracles which Jesus accomplished, his foes, the Pharisees and the Sadducees, did not believe him, and his own followers did not understand him.[17] Mark, in short, is not stressing Jesus' silence, but rather the opaqueness of the disciples who see but do not understand Jesus' miracles.

To move on, Wise notices that for the journey to Jerusalem from Galilee Mark and Matthew set a route that leads eastward across the Jordan, southward to Jericho, and then a recrossing of the Jordan and a westward trip to Jerusalem, while Luke has Jesus remain always west of the Jordan, thereby obligating Jesus, in his account, to pass through Samaria. The difference Wise suggests, "is somewhat obscure."

As to the entry into Jerusalem, Wise notices that Mark and Luke suggest that Jesus entered on one ass, while Matthew suggests two animals (for Matthew misunderstood the proof-text from Zechariah 9:9 which he quoted). Wise, however, gives his atention primarily to explaining why an ass was needed: without it

the Messiah could not possibly have come to the satisfaction of the masses. . . . Popular superstition would have the Messiah to come riding on an ass, and Jesus had to submit to it. . . . Although the story of the ass, as before us in the Synoptics, bears the stamp of fiction, nevertheless, from the concurrence of the Evangelists, it appears certain that Jesus was persuaded to enter Jerusalem riding on an ass, in order to comply with a popular superstition (*The Israelite,* August 13, 1869).

As to the journey, the entry, and the reception of Jesus, it is irrelevant here to reproduce Wise's struggle with the Gospel accounts. We can turn directly to his summary:

The facts in the case appear to have been these: Jesus at Caesarea Philippi having consented to play the messianic role, he went with his disciples on by-ways, always evading the authority of Herod, down to the line [Wise means the boundary] of Judea, crossing and recross-ing the Jordan until he reached Jericho, from whence they traveled fast to reach Jerusalem unmolested. Here the brilliant feat was to be rapidly carried out, Jesus proclaimed the Messiah, to rouse the popular enthusiasm, the people thus won and amazed, to be relied upon in case of an interference by the government, and the whole affair to be ac-complished by one brilliant and rapid movement. . . .

That Jesus found many and ardent friends and admirers among the multitudes in Jerusalem, can hardly be doubted. But they were not as numerous nor as enthusiastic as the disciples expected from the messianic appeal to the masses. Little regard was paid to the Messiah, although considerable attention was bestowed on the words and lessons of Jesus, who had laid aside altogether the messianic character, and appeared as the young sage of Nazareth, expounding his scheme of salvation. This gained him friends and admirers, while the messianic pretensions of his disciples made him ridiculous with the learned, ob-noxious to the Roman authorities, and drove thousands of peaceable citizens from him; because they knew from sad experience that almost any pretext sufficed Pilate for massacre and pillage. So Jesus, who had been a persecuted fugitive in Galilee, entered now upon his na-tional career under the worst auspices. He stood upon a threatening volcano, and he knew it well (*The Israelite,* August 20, 1869).

The incident of the "cleansing of the Temple" provides Wise with an op-portunity to distinguish between a historical item and a legend. The texts of the Synoptics (Mark 11:17; Matthew 21:13; and Luke 19:46) accompany the cleansing with a quotation by Jesus from Isaiah 56:7 and Jeremiah 7:11, "My house shall be called a house of prayer for all people but you have made it a den of robbers." The "turning over the tables of the money changers," Wise asserts, is not historical, but rather the application to Jesus of a biblical passage, such application of Scripture being frequent in the Gospels. The verse in question is the very last verse in Zechariah which, translated vari-ously (for one word in it means both "Canaanite" and "trader"), runs as follows: "There will be no trader [Canaanite] in the house of the Lord of

Hosts on that day." The cleansing, derived as it is from a biblical passage, is pure legend in Wise's eyes.

But the citation from Isaiah is, according to Wise, "a memorandum of the first part of the speech which Jesus made in Jerusalem, a memorandum written exactly in the style of that age—*rāshē peraqīm.*" [18]

Wise believes that this speech of Jesus was a full and unrelenting attack on the system of priests with their sacrifices. He would have Jesus emphasize that it is prayer which the Temple should foster, not sacrifice.

> With Jesus striking at the very root of their existence, the chief priests must naturally have felt alarmed. The larger the number of his admirers was, the more cause of apprehension existed. The brief memorandum of that speech gave rise to the unskillful expulsion story which is incompatible to the general character and behavior of Jesus, and bears in itself characteristics of improbability (*The Israelite,* August 27, 1869, p. 9).

Wise then proceeds to give a full account of the priestly system, both in extent and in history. A part of this is truly amazing.

In the first place, Wise asserts, the laws relating to sacrifices in the Pentateuch are inconsistent and replete with conflict. How to account for this? Wise finds the answer in Exodus 20:24, which prescribes an altar of stone where one, to paraphrase Wise with my italics, *"might, if he wanted to,"* offer sacrifices. That is, Moses initially wanted sacrifices to be voluntary, but after the incident of the golden calf,

> Moses realized that many of his people were not sufficiently free of Egyptian superstition to adhere to the pure worship of the one and invisible God, without the aid of external means to which they had been used.

Therefore Levitical institutions were added, the purpose of which was

> to prevent the relapse into idolatry, and to educate the people gradually to the pure knowledge and worship of God. Had Moses intended the Levitical system *for all eternity* [my italics] . . . the first passage . . . [would] have been entirely omitted in the Bible as being of no force and no value. . . . Psalmists and Prophets, Essenes and Pharisees, at times when idolatry had been effectively overcome, opposed the Levitical laws and institutions. . . .
>
> It appears . . . to have been an acknowledged fact among the an-

cient Hebrews, as it is among modern critics, that Ezra was the final compiler of the Pentateuch. In the holy archives, rescued out of the destroyed Temple, he must have found two kinds of ancient documents, the Prophetical and the Levitical. . . . Among the Prophetical scriptures, Ezra found the laws and speeches of Moses. Among the Levitical scriptures he found the Levitical laws, also ascribed to Moses. He compiled and harmonized both as best he could.

Against the Levitical institutions, we have on record an almost uninterrupted line of opposition throughout the Bible, and down to the Essenes and Pharisees, without any evidence that they, or a large portion of them, originated with Moses. . . . Jesus coincided with that party in Israel, which opposed the Levitical institutions. . . .

. . . The Essenes and Pharisees offered theoretical opposition only, which did not directly interfere with the priestly immunities and prerogatives. But Jesus had come with the avowed intention to do it. . . . Therefore the chief priests must have hated and opposed him with all the power at their command (*The Israelite,* September 10, 1869, pp. 8–9).

Behind the story of the cursing of the fig tree in Mark 11, Wise finds the second part of Jesus' sermon. The story itself is, Wise assures us, absurd:

No figs on any tree are edible in Palestine about Passover time. . . . It involves a wickedness to destroy a tree which God has intended to grow, when the Law prohibits the wanton destruction of fruit trees even in the time of war. It involves a rashness on the part of Jesus . . . which . . . cannot be harmonized with his general character. But the purpose of the incident is to let Jesus speak on the power of prayer (for so the incident concludes in both Mark and in Matthew).

Wise digresses momentarily to assert that Jesus never taught the Lord's prayer, for it was common knowledge among Jews, and then he returns to his point. In the first part of his sermon, Jesus had argued in favor of abolishing the sacrificial system; "he dwells in the second part of his speech on the power of prayer in general and the forgiveness of sins in particular, as the mode of worship to supercede [sic] the sacrificial polity."

These sentiments of Jesus were not, Wise assures us, new. But his sentiments "alarmed the chief priests." They knew "how popular and deepseated the anti-Levitical theories were, and felt the magnitude of the threatened danger."

Jesus' demand that the form of worship be changed from sacrifice to prayer was, Wise tells us, "a main feature in the messianic scheme of redemption and which Jesus attempted at Jerusalem. This explains . . . the charges against Jesus . . . that he could destroy and rebuild the Temple in three days, which refers only and exclusively to the radical change in the form of worship" (*The Israelite,* September 17, 1869).

Wise proceeds to the next point in the Gospel narrative, the conflict over the question of authority. Jesus, it will be recalled, is asked (Mark 11:27 ff. and parallels) by what authority he is acting. He is reported to counter with the offer to answer the question if first his questioners will tell him whether the baptism of John was from heaven or from man. When the questioners evaded responding, Jesus in turn refused to answer them. What did Wise make of all this?

Wise contends that in Hebrew history the issue of authority had never been fully resolved. It lay partly in priests, partly in prophets. In Jesus' time the Pharisees inherited the prophetic mantle, but authority had at that juncture been usurped by the priests. Now, if Jesus had claimed prophetic authority in the controversy, he would have been asked for credentials which could not be forthcoming and consequently he would have been ridiculed; we recall that, according to Wise, Jesus did not work a miracle in Jerusalem.

And even if Jesus were truly the Messiah, Wise argues, he could scarcely maintain that the Messiah had the power to abrogate laws which had been in existence for 1,500 years! Could Jesus confront the guardians of the sacrificial system with a contention that he had been granted the authority to abrogate that which they were dedicated to maintain? (*The Israelite,* September 24, 1869, pp. 8–9).

The nature of Jesus' reply—that of a simple Galilean now confronted by brilliant and educated minds and thereby choosing a counterquestion—must not be misconstrued as an unseemly dodging of the issue. Unable to point to a prophetic or messianic authority, Jesus

> pointed to the authority of John who had baptized and appointed him as one of the anti-Levitical and theocratic teachers in Israel, as a representative man of those who demanded the abrogation of the Levitical institutions and priesthood. . . . He spoke in the name and the authority of the laws and the people from the standpoint of a Pharisean associate, which he considered better than the authority of the king and the prophet . . . (*The Israelite,* September 24, October 1 and 8, 1869).

Jesus' view of "Pharisean" authority is discernible, according to Wise, in the parable (Mark 12:1–12 and parallels) of the vineyard owner who sends a series of servants to obtain fruit from his tenants; the tenants not only beat the servants, but finally they kill the owner's son and heir. Wise requires three issues of *The Israelite* to arrive at his explanation of the parable, for he digresses to discuss both John the Baptist and Jewish baptism.

The "parable" is not a parable, modern scholars tell us, but a loosely-knit group of symbolic events. The tenants are Israel; the owner is God. The "collectors" are the prophets; the son is Jesus. In the view of virtually all modern scholars, the "parable" arose long after Jesus' time. But, after asserting that Jesus would not skip about from subject to subject, Wise tells us what the parable means.

In Wise's explanation, it is John the Baptist who is the son, the temple is the vineyard, and the tenants are the priests.

> If our suggestions are correct, the parable is genuine, and the reply of Jesus is complete. . . . God . . . entrusted this national sanctuary to the priests [tenants], who for centuries have been rebuked by the prophets [the servants], whom they have abused and scorned. Now the lord of the vineyard sent his son, John, who preached repentence [sic] and remission of sin; but he was killed [by Herod].

Wise, as though not quite sure that his interpretation is correct, spends several paragraphs defending its tenability. And having thereby protected Jesus from the possible charge of being evasive, he speaks warmly on "how Jesus confronted his powerful opponents. He did it nobly, boldly, and admirably, worthy of a great cause and a good man."

Wise interrupts his eulogistic summary:

> We hope to defend Jesus of Nazareth against his adversaries and to save him from his friends. If the reader will patiently follow us through the labyrinth of researches which we must pass on account of the entirely new path we have to level, he shall finally have a full and correct image of Jesus himself, the historical man as he lived, taught, acted and suffered (*The Israelite,* October 15, 1869, pp. 8–9).

Wise turns now to what he terms in his chapter heading "The Positive Element in the System of Jesus." Wise contends that Jesus espoused Jewish theocracy to the point of being unwilling to handle or even look at a Roman coin bearing an effigy of Caesar.

Therefore, in strict conformity with the law of the land, he decided that every coin bearing the effigy of Caesar should not be turned to any earthly use, but returned to Caesar. This decision was not only satisfactory to Pharisean law, and the Pharisean contempt of wealth and luxury; it was a capital hit on those who loved the Roman coins too well, better even than their laws and their country (*The Israelite,* October 29 and November 5, 1869).

A long essay (in the issue of November 12, 1869) sets forth the view that "there is, indeed, ample material on record, to prove that Jesus respected the law, and considered salvation an obedience to it." A week later, Wise gives first a definition of the Kingdom of God, and then his opinion of Jesus' view. The definition which Wise gives he labels in very many places in his writings as "theocracy." The kingdom of God signifies "the unlimited dominion of God on earth as in heaven, and the connection of all men with him by the holy ties of supreme love. . . . The kingdom of heaven is in time and eternity, above and below, in this and every other world, in life and in death, unlimited, immutable, eternal and universal. . . ." The commentators, however, says Wise, make of the kingdom of heaven "a mystic phantom beyond the stars for some ascetic, weeping and praying misanthropes." Jesus wanted to abolish Levitical laws and to usher in the kingdom of heaven; he was opposed to human kings, whether a Jewish Herodian or a Roman Caesar. Jesus

> had come . . . to deface the Levitical priests, to make an end of corruption in high places, to return the Roman money to Rome, to restore the dominion of justice and love, to reconstruct the kingdom of heaven. . . .
> Did Jesus preach this gospel to Jews alone, or was it intended for the whole world? Like the prophets of old, he must have believed in the final triumph of truth, the redemption and fraternization of the human family in justice, freedom and peace. . . . All pious Israelites believed it, and repeated it thrice every day in their prayers. But Jesus knew this was not the mission of one man or any one age. . . . Our age is not ripe for the consummation of that divine purpose, how much less was the age of Jesus; and he must have known it. He considered it his mission to restore the kingdom of heaven in Israel. "I am not sent but to the lost sheep of Israel," if not his words, expressed certainly his sentiment (*The Israelite,* November 19, 1869, pp. 8–9).

In several succeeding issues of *The Israelite,* Wise discusses the relationship of Jesus to Jewish law. As before, he again asserts that Jesus advocated "theocracy." Wise then states that, when Jesus' teaching of the law of love evoked the observation that "no man thereafter durst ask him any question" (Mark 12:34), it meant that there was satisfaction among most of the Jews with his viewpoint and that "the triumph of Jesus with that class of Pharisees was complete" (*The Israelite,* November 26, 1869). Wise goes on to concede that this latter conclusion is discernible only in Mark and in Luke.

The proof which Wise offers is the passage in which Jesus is asked, "What is the greatest commandment?" In Mark, Jesus replies: " 'The first is, "Hear, O Israel: The Lord our God, the Lord is one." The second is this, "You shall love your neighbor as yourself." There is no other commandment greater than these.' " Matthew and Luke, however, lack the citation of the "Hear, O Israel." Wise goes astray here, attributing the lack only to Matthew, and mistakenly asserting that Luke, like Mark, contains it. He would have been on sounder ground to have contrasted Mark with both Luke and Matthew, rather than Mark and Luke with Matthew. Having made the error, Wise goes on to state that Jesus' triumph with the Pharisees was complete, but "Matthew, whose anti-Pharisean [sic] tendencies we will discuss in another chapter, turns the statement of the two other Evangelists, to convey the direct contrary (XXII, 46)." It is nevertheless clear, says Wise, that "had Jesus entertained the remotest idea of abrogating the law, this question and the subsequent reply [which we find in Mark] would appear simply absurd. . . ." But why the different reply in Matthew, where the "Hear, O Israel" is omitted? Rather laconically, Wise gives an answer, and we must supply some words which Wise lacks. Mark (and in his mistaken view, Luke) is a strict unitarian; "it appears that 'God is One' was [an obstacle] in Matthew's way, who was acquainted with Paul's Son of God."

Yet, despite the differences in the Gospel accounts, there is a basic agreement in the matter of the question and the answer, says Wise, to show that the love of God "is an integral part of Jesus' scheme of salvation."

Wise now proceeds to set forth at some length a distinction between "Love" and "Gnosis." Love was for Jesus, as for Moses, the "Postulate of Ethics." To hold such a view was "in strict compliance with one class of Pharisees." The "gnostics" (not to be confused, says Wise, with the heretics of Christian history) were those who emphasized study and contemplation. They included the Essenes and the Therapeutae of Egypt, as well as those rabbis who expressed scorn for the *'Am Ha'aretz* (the untutored). The principal exponent of such gnosticism was Rabbi Eliezer ben Hyrcanus, upon whom the anti-gnostic Pharisees imposed a ban shortly after the fall of Jerusalem. From this latter incident it is clear, says Wise, that Pharisees "as a class were not responsible for this peculiar gnosticism. They held views entirely contrary. . . ." Passages in *Aboth,* such as "knowledge (research) is not the main thing, deeds are," represent the Pharisean school of love. The Levitical laws gave rise to Gnosis; the Mosaic, to Love. "Jesus advanced the law of love as the criterion by which to recognize the eternal and unalterable laws, the only infallible guides to happiness. . . ." [19]

The agreement of Jesus with the Pharisees was not only in the "Postulate of Ethics"; it was also in what Wise terms "the Postulate of Hermeneutics." This latter, according to Wise, is expressed in the following passage: " 'Thou shalt love thy neighbor like thyself,' says Rabbi Akiba, 'is the cardinal principle of the law.' Ben Azai [sic] said, ' "This is the book of the genealogy of man" is a principle superior to the above.' " In a footnote Wise supplies the Hebrew and his source, "Yalkut 613 from Saphira." A few paragraphs later, Wise cites Hillel's formulation of the Golden Rule as still another example of the Law of Love.

We need not linger on Wise's extended remarks on tangential issues. After several such pages, he proceeds to what he calls "A Review":

> Jesus expected to save the people of Israel, to restore the kingdom of heaven. It was wise, sublime, thoroughly Jewish and worthy of a pious, enlightened and enthusiastic patriot. . . . The scheme was eminently religious and eminently impractical. Rome would not favor any policy or tolerate any popular movement which might have rescued Israel from the doom of destruction . . . great souls feel common disappointments much deeper than vulgar ones do. . . . Jesus standing upon the ruins of his hope of hopes . . . must indeed have exclaimed, "My God, my God, why hast thou forsaken me?"

What office, asks Wise, did Jesus fill?

> Peter's Messiah, a Jewish phantomism; Paul's Son of God, a Pagan vision from Olympus; and John's Logos, a purely Alexandrian product of speculation, are ideas as widely different from one another, as all of them are from the Godhead Jesus of trinitarian orthodoxy. They were three distinct epochs in the origin of Christianity. None of these titles does Jesus use or claim in the Gospels (*The Israelite,* December 31, 1869).

Jesus himself never made the claim to Davidic descent (*The Israelite,* January 7, 1870). Rather, there is evidence "from fragments in the Gospels on the dissensions among the disciples about rank and precedence in the kingdom of heaven" that some of the disciples "must have speculated for Jesus on some kind of spiritual governorship in the reconstructed Theocracy" (*The Israelite,* January 14, 1870). The office of Jesus, in his own eyes, was "Son of Man." This "was the title of the prophets in and after the Babylonian exile." Indeed,

> the prophet was to be the chief man in the Theocracy. This is the position which Jesus expected in the reconstructed kingdom of heaven. It was not an office with emoluments. . . . It was simply and exclusively a moral position. . . .
>
> Had Jesus actually restored and maintained the Theocracy he would have been its prophet. . . . Had his disciples not committed the unpardonable blunder of proclaiming him the Messiah, he might have escaped crucifixion. . . . But yielding to the ambition and false calculation of his disciples, he sealed his death warrant (*The Israelite,* January 28, 1870).

Next Wise turns to a problem: "Jesus of Nazareth was a Pharisean doctor. He coincided with that party in every point of Theocracy." Then why, asks Wise, do New Testament writings attack the Pharisees and distort what they were? In answer, Wise combs rabbinic literature so as to be able to assess the Pharisees justly; and such quotations he balances by the assertion that "The anti-Pharisean passages of the gospels were written long after the death of Jesus . . . when the Jewish sects besides the Pharisees and Christians almost disappeared, and Pharisaism and Judaism had become synonymous; and still later, in the second century, when Judaism and Christianity had become two distinct religions" (*The Israelite,* March 4, 1870).

In the next issue (March 11, 1870) Wise studies the anti-Pharisaic elements common to all three Gospels (and thus, in his view, part of the aboriginal Gospel), sifting them so that they emerge no longer as anti-Pharisaic, but only as a denunciation of "hypocrisy, avarice and morbid ambition." The same pursuit occupies him in the following issue (March 18, 1870). He prolongs the study still one more issue; therein he aligns Hillel with exponents of the Law of Love, and Shammai with the gnostics. On this basis he is ready (April 1, 1870) to conclude that Jesus "clung most tenaciously to the genuine Hillelites."

Wise proceeds in the same issue to try to distinguish between the genuine aphorisms of Jesus and the spurious. Those aphorisms which agree with the rabbis, and especially with the Hillelites, are genuine; the others are not.

For perhaps the twentieth time Wise repeats that Jesus was a "Pharisean doctor of the Hillel school." He ends the segment of his essay with these words: "He spoke of his people with respect. He said to the Samaritan woman, 'Ye worship ye know not what; we know what we worship, for salvation is of the Jew' (John 4:22)."

In capital letters there appear the words, "to be continued." Nevertheless, this was the end.

Why did Wise not continue? Why did he not finish? We do not know. Perhaps his reason was profound; perhaps he simply ran out of time. Indeed, it may have been that he had said all that he wanted to say.

If it should be suggested that he abstained from finishing because he had little confidence in the reliability of what he had written, then it can be reported that, in those instances where his subsequent writings touch on the contents of "Jesus Himself," the basic viewpoint and even specific details remain virtually unaltered. While I have not encountered a second mention of an aboriginal Gospel which served all three or four, or a clear repetition of his division of Pentateuchal religion into the Mosaic and the Levitic, yet overtones of both reappear, for example, in the material on Jesus in *History of the Hebrews' Second Commonwealth*.[20] Moreover, his portrait of Jesus recurs without change in a work, originally published in 1874, which enjoyed three printings, the last in 1888; I refer to *The Martyrdom of Jesus of Nazareth*.[21] The Jesus who walked in the pages of "Jesus Himself" walks these pages, too. Indeed, *The Martyrdom* is in a sense the conclusion to the unfinished "Jesus Himself," for in *The Martyrdom* Wise takes up the account virtually where it left off.

Wise is not to be classified as a scholar in the same sense in which we rank David Friedrich Strauss, or Ferdinand Christian Baur, or Oskar Holtzmann, or others of his time. Scholarly, perhaps, but a scholar of New Testament he is assuredly not. His writings in this area are devoid of any lasting scientific value; he was essentially a shrewd, self-taught homiletician who wrote farfetched things. But here is a matter always to be remembered: Bible, whether Old or New Testament, has always attracted the mind that is capricious and cavalier. Wise was doing the same kind of thing that many second-rate Protestant scholars were doing. He is more farfetched only when we isolate single instances; in the totality of the effect, one need only peruse those who have summarized the overabundant books called "The Life of Jesus" to see that Wise was in the main stream of the imaginative Protestant dilettantes.

But when one assesses the total man—a very busy rabbi, the editor of both an English and a German weekly, a traveler, a novelist (sometimes he had two novels running serially at the same time), and the compiler of a prayer book—and when one remembers that he fathered the Union of American Hebrew Congregations, the Hebrew Union College, and the Central Conference of American Rabbis, then one wonders how he had the time to devise and record his ingenious theories, and the tenacity to stick to them. He had neither the training nor the discipline for exact and lasting scholarship.

Yet his writings on Jesus in general, and the incomplete book which we have surveyed in particular, have an importance which transcends by far their lack of permanent academic merit. Wise began by doubting that Jesus ever lived; then, as we saw, he began to write his biography.

Nineteenth-century New Testament scholarship among Protestants was aimed, both consciously and unconsciously, at recovering the Jesus of history and at placing him in his Jewish setting. To accomplish this meant to Wise's Gentile contemporaries exactly what it meant to Wise: to peel off layers of legend and theology and to restore the man. Except among those Christians and Jews who made a Gentile out of Jesus, such a reconstituted man was plainly and simply a Jew. It seems to me justified to suggest that, at the time Wise was denying that Jesus ever lived, he was negating a "Christian" Jesus. Once the thought came to him that Jesus was a Jew, Wise not only affirmed his existence, but made him the protagonist, indeed the hero, of his account.

Truly, for Wise, Jesus was a noble Jew whose only misdemeanor was his mistake in yielding to the importunings of Peter and the other disciples. It is they who are the villains to Wise——except that he finds an even greater archvillain when he deals with the apostolic age and directs his attention to Paul.

Wise, however, falls short of something which later Jewish writers, both scholars and dilettantes alike, endeavor to do. In Wise there is an effort merely to *restore* the Jewishness of Jesus; in later writers the quest extends to *reclaiming* Jesus for Judaism. Joseph Klausner, in *Jesus of Nazareth,* does some reclaiming:

> . . . Jesus is, for the Jewish nation, *a great teacher of morality and an artist in parable.* . . . If . . . this ethical code be stripped of its wrappings of miracles and mysticism, the Book of the Ethics of Jesus will be one of the choicest treasures in the literature of Israel for all time.[22]

If the distinction which I intend between restoring and reclaiming Jesus is clear—the distinction is one of degree and thereby almost one of kind—then the significance of Wise's writings begins to emerge. The age-old antipathy, as reflected in the travesties on Jesus, as in *Toledot Yeshu,* was inconsistent with an age of enlightenment and broad horizons. Moreover, there was no spiritual or physical ghetto in the United States, and Jews and Christians lived side by side in a relatively high state of harmony and good will. Christianity inevitably intruded into the consciousness of Jews, and so did Jesus.

Wise wrote as he did because he was Wise; he was moved so to write because no Jew breathing the free air of America could refrain from coming to grips in some way with Christianity and with Jesus. Indifference and total lack of contact were possible only in ghettos where medievalism had survived. Wise wrote because he had to write; he could not be the leader of an American Jewish community and not do so. In 1876, Max Schlesinger, a rabbi in Albany, published *The Historical Jesus of Nazareth;* in the same year, Frederic de Sola Mendes published *Defence, not Defiance: A Hebrew's Reply to the Missionaries.*

I have spoken above of a distinguished work by the Swedish scholar Gösta Lindeskog, *Die Jesusfrage im neuzeitlichen Judentum* ("The Question of Jesus in Recent Judaism"). It is an excellent summary of books by Jews on Jesus, as well as of articles appearing in scientific journals. If there is any weakness in the book, it is the understandable failure to include the sermons and the small tracts which American rabbis produced in some number. When Klausner's book first appeared in its English translation, another Wise, Stephen S. Wise, reviewed the book from his pulpit (December, 1925). The press accounts disclose that the sermon was a "reclamation" of Jesus, and a historic storm broke over the head of Stephen Wise.[23] It is this kind of incident and writing which is lacking in Lindeskog.

Joseph Bonsirven, a French priest whose book *Les Juifs et Jésus* was published in Paris in 1937, addresses himself in quite good measure to the sermons and tracts of American rabbis; in fact, he asks whimsically if it is the usual practice among American rabbis to publish their sermons. He mentions the Stephen Wise matter several times. Bonsirven records with acknowledged pleasure that the Jewish attitude toward Jesus has undergone the notable change from disparagement to reclamation. He says somewhat plaintively (p. 213): "Jésus, ils entendent de tirer chez eux, ils ne veulent pas venir chez lui" ("The Jews mean to draw Jesus to themselves, they do not want to come to him"). The impression which one gets from Bonsirven is that the reclamation of Jesus is, or has been, a matter of the twenties and thirties of this century. The rabbis whom he cites include Hyman G. Enelow, Abraham J. Feldman, G. George Fox, Solomon B. Freehof, Ephraim Frisch, Emil G. Hirsch, Ferdinand M. Isserman, Joseph Krauskopf, Louis I. Newman, Abram Simon, Ernest Trattner, and Stephen Wise. The book, then, is weighted toward Bonsirven's own day and ours.

The fact is, however, that restoration, or even reclamation, began a full half-century before the period which Bonsirven discusses. No one has yet studied in detail the Jewish "reclamation" of Jesus. It could well make a fascinating subject, especially if one went away from the highroads which Lindeskog maps out and into the earlier bypaths of the American congregational rabbis and their minor publications.

Such a study would give us a fuller perspective on Isaac Mayer Wise and his approach to Jesus. He marks a significant chapter, if not in the reclamation of Jesus, at least in his restoration.

19

The Parting of the Ways *

T HE DIFFICULTIES INHERENT in any inquiry into the parting of the ways between Judaism and Christianity are complex. They are compounded by the proximity, indeed the overlap between Judaism and Christianity, with the consequence that at recurrent stages in the continuing history, a clear line of demarcation is somewhat elusive. This latter consideration must constantly be borne in mind, and the possibility always left open that what amounted in one decade to an implication of a full separation was often blurred in subsequent decades, and this makes us aware of some ebb and flow in the parting of the ways. In a short essay, it is not possible to enter into all the details and to protect oneself with all of the desirable scholarly reservations. Though there are other conceivable ways to approach the material, I have chosen to divide the topic into four sections.

Around the figure of Jesus there exists in the documents a progressively divisive development that may be described as follows: His claims, or the claims made about him, to messiahship are to be allocated to the earliest

* This article was published in Holland, in *Phoenix Bijbel Pockets, Het Evangelie in Jeruzalem en Antiochie*, 25 (1967): 137 ff.

period as something inner to Judaism; that is, they were a matter about which Jews disputed with other Jews. Ultimately these inner disputes were destined to give way to disputes between the inner and the external. Respecting the inner disputes, nascent Christianity grew out of that segment of the Jewish population which accepted the messiahship of Jesus in a context in which other portions of the population denied that messiahship, though far more Jews knew nothing whatever about Jesus and his activities. Indeed, we cannot know to what extent the totality of Jews had an opinion one way or the other; but it is conceivable that, within the lifetime of Jesus, less than one percent of the Jewish population was involved in either the affirmation or the denial. In the Synoptic Gospels, Jesus is portrayed as in conflict with Sadducees, Pharisees, and priests, that is to say, with fellow Jews. If it had chanced to come about in the history of the world that Christianity had not developed into a separate entity but had been reabsorbed into Judaism and had thus disappeared, and we in our day were to discover the Gospels in caves in the same way that we have discovered the Dead Sea Scrolls, we would have the general impression that we were dealing primarily with an inner Jewish problem.

Consistent with this primacy of the difference as inner, one notices in the Synoptic Gospels, especially in the conflict narratives, two categories of disputes which, still internal, can well be separated from each other, at least analytically. In one category Jesus and his Jewish opponents are separated in the diversity of their ways of interpreting a commonly held tradition. Thus, in the conflict over the Sabbath, the common premise is held by Jesus and other Jews that the Sabbath ought to be observed, but there is a difference between what Jesus would consider consistent with Sabbath observance and what his opponents would deem consistent (Mark 3:1-6 and parallels). In still other conflict stories the issue is not the diverse interpretation of a commonly held tradition, but a denial by Jesus of the entire validity of an aspect of the tradition. This is the case with the controversy over the washing of the hands, and the radical conclusion: "Thus Jesus said making all foods clean" (Mark 7:19). If this last statement indeed goes back to Jesus, it amounts to a rejection of Mosaic dietary laws.

If the question is asked: How many of these recorded conflicts are truly historical, in that they actually took place within the lifetime of Jesus, and how many of them took place after the age of Jesus but were read back into his career, then no objective answer is possible, for scholars will make their election on the basis of their prepossessions. To the extent that the conflicts may historically have been entirely inner, namely, only a difference in interpreting a commonly held tradition, to that extent Christianity is a sectarian movement within Judaism, and it is improper to speak of a genuine parting of the ways. It is only if and when the issues deal with Jesus as over and against not only Jews, but the inherited Judaism, that it is appropriate to begin to speak of the parting of the ways.

In a number of passages in the Gospels, moreover, there is unmistakable intimation, and even clear statement, that Christianity is a replacement of Judaism, or, more precisely, that Christians have replaced Jews in God's favor. This is the meaning of the passage that God can create sons of Abraham out of stones (Luke 3:8). It is also the meaning of parables such as Mark 12:1-9 and parallels; Matthew 22:1-10 and parallels. To add to our perplexity about what is historical and what is not, there is the motif in the Gospels that the death of Jesus (which was believed to have brought salvation to mankind) was the result of malevolent hatred on the part of Jews. Are the motifs of replacement and of dual hatred historical respecting the age and career of Jesus or are they, instead, a product of the time after the parting of the ways and then read back into the career of Jesus?

Again, all of the Gospels, but especially Matthew, present us with interpretations of Scripture (Old Testament) in which it is asserted that certain passages are predictive of Jesus. Such scriptural interpretation, consistent in manner with the way in which Christians, rabbis, Essenes, and Philo all approached Scripture, must become for us a clue to our understanding that a development took place whereby the common Scripture came to be interpreted in the two communities in divergent, mutually exclusive, and contradictory ways. Again, we are on uncertain ground as to how much of this scriptural exegesis is properly to be assigned to the age of Jesus, or to Jesus himself, and how much of it is a reflection of the later Church.

Despite these uncertainties, it may be a prudent conclusion respecting the career of Jesus that, for the most part, the issues were internal in Judaism and fell short of any advanced parting of the ways.

We are on firmer ground in history concerning the parting of the ways when we deal with the figure of Paul. It is recorded in his Epistles that he advocated the abolition of the Laws of Moses. Inasmuch as in the Gospels there are passages which portray Jesus as critical of the inherited Judaism, we are not able to say whether Paul derived the impulse to abrogate the Laws of Moses from Jesus or whether this was something of his own creation. It is possible that there was something in the tradition about Jesus and his rejection of some aspects of Judaism which moved Paul to go further than Jesus. It is manifest that Paul went that additional distance.

Indeed, there are two distinct problems in any effort to understand Paul and his contribution. One is the problem that has plagued scholars for almost a century and a half, namely, whether or not the portrait of Paul in his Epistles can be squared with that in Acts of the Apostles. This much seems to be clear, at the minimum, that the position Paul takes in his Epistles respecting the Mosaic Laws is much more extreme than the quite restrained position attributed to Paul in Acts of the Apostles.

It is also clear that what Paul in his Epistles is challenging, this on a matter of principle, is the abiding validity of the Laws of Moses; and in challenging that abiding validity, Paul is setting himself against that which is central in every version of Judaism that we know about. Even when it is granted that Paul's intention was not antinomian, but that he saw faith as a vehicle better suited to effect the intent of the Law than the Laws themselves could, the conclusion is inescapable that in Paul the ways part respecting Judaism. Moreover, on the level of people encountering people, Paul was repudiating what other Jews considered central in the religion, and therefore Paul and the Jews of his time were in direct conflict. I have written elsewhere that from Paul's standpoint he did not feel that he was deviating from his inherited Judaism, but, rather, that he was preaching the surest and truest version of it. Yet even while holding this opinion, I would have to say that there is a genuine parting of the ways on the matter of Paul and the Laws of Moses.

Secondly, Paul was an apostle to the Gentiles, this by his own declaration. He was an apostle within the framework of his abiding Jewish loyalties and of his consternation that his fellow Jews did not go along with him, either in his beliefs or in his deductions from these beliefs. He is careful, especially in Romans 9–11, to continue to assign some sort of priority to Jews in God's favor, and to regard God's turning to Gentiles as a temporary state of affairs, and, indeed, to speak of Christians as shoots that have been grafted on the tree of Judaism. But all of this takes place in the framework that God had sent him to people who are to replace or supplant the Jews. The comment can be made that what Paul envisaged as something possibly temporary, later Christians took to be something permanent and fixed. I am persuaded that Paul of the Epistles would not have consented to the view that Jews as such were permanently replaced in God's priority and favor, but it is a fact that this view came to be dominant in other Christian writings.

If one were to distinguish between the Gospels, the Epistles of Paul, and Acts of the Apostles on the one hand, and the other New Testament writings (the Catholic, Pastoral, and Johannine Epistles) on the other hand, then I believe it would be a valid distinction that the first group of writings deal with or touch on matters related to Christians and to Jews, but that the later writings deal almost entirely with inner Christian concerns. The Epistle to the Hebrews is possibly the sole exception, but this unique writing seems to be primarily of inner Christian concern too, though much of its substance is a contrast between the imperfect foreshadowing that Judaism is conceived to be, and the perfect realization of that foreshadowing which Christianity is conceived to be. The Epistle of James deals with the inner Christian concern of whether faith completely without works is effective or whether faith must be blended with works. The Pastoral Epistles deal largely with inner organization and the shattering effects of heterodox Christian teachers and teachings. So, too, the Johannine Epistles deal almost exclusively with inner Christian problems, especially the problem of proper doctrine. By and large, Jews and Judaism are noticeably absent from attention or consideration in this second group of material. There is a sense, then, in which one might say that these writings deal no longer with the parting of the ways but with the ways that have already been parted.

But that conclusion too may be premature and hazardous, for even if the main themes of the writings are as I have indicated, there is still the possibility that in the day-to-day life of the Christians the issue of the relationship and the separation was still moot; the documents abstain from informing us. I would hold that the Epistle of Barnabas and Justin's Dialogue with Trypho the Jew, both of which come from the second century, give us clear indications that the ways have not been parted as completely as the second group of New Testament writings seem to imply.

Scholars still dispute whether or not the Pastoral Epistles are by Paul. Those who hold that they are not, and I am among them, note that in I Corinthians 12–14—that is, in Paul's time—there is as yet no clearly defined Christian officialdom; while in the Pastoral Epistles, we have the more-or-less well-defined offices of the Episcopos, the Presbyter, and the Deacon. When we come to this stage then, the new entity is sufficiently separate from the old that it has had to develop an officialdom of its own. At least institutionally, the ways have been completely parted.

The sense of parting is strengthened by the development in the middle or toward the end of the second Christian century whereby Christian writings came to be regarded as Scripture, with the end result that to the older collection, namely the Old Testament, there was added a newer collection, the New Testament. To the older disputes over the valid way of interpreting commonly held Scripture, there is now added a body of material which one community holds sacred and which the other community does not. For all intents and purposes, with the canonization of the New Testament, the parting of the ways was complete.

Yet here too one needs to enter some reservations. If the parting of the ways was so complete at the end of the second century, then why does St. John Chrysostom (347–407) face the need to advise and urge the Christians of Antioch not to attend Jewish worship? Moreover, if the parting of the ways was so complete, why is it that it was not until Nicea in the fourth century that Christians developed the uniquely Christian way of dating Easter, this on the first Sunday after the first full moon after the Spring equinox, in place of observing it on the Sunday within Passover week? Again, why is it that some of the Church Fathers divided the world of human beings among barbarians, Jews, and Christians, instead of into two groups, non-Christians and Christians, unless it was that Christians felt a sense of some continuing threads still holding Christians and Jews together?

The new movement, according to Acts, did not have a name for itself beyond "the way," until the term Christianity which appears to have arisen in Antioch (Acts 11:26). Suppose that the name "Christians" had not arisen? Suppose that the new movement had continued to use the terminology of Paul, who never discusses who is the true Christian or the untrue Christian, but rather who is the true Jew. While first- and second-century gnostics were eager to see Christianity as completely separated from Judaism, and while some nineteenth-century German scholars, such as Delitzsch, also argued for the lack of relationship, the prevailing Christian view was, and continues to be, as John 4:12 puts it, that salvation is of the Jews.

In our age it is not too difficult to enumerate some of the significant differences between Judaism and Christianity, in realms such as theology, their diverse histories, and the sacred calendars. Perhaps for the long history of the two traditions, the phrase I used above for the early period, namely, that there was an ebb and flow rather than a final clear line of demarcation, applies also to our time. Had the parting of the ways come to be as total as a Marcion would have had it, then our age would not have been able to witness the possibility of communities coming to some sort of rapprochement. To what extent and in what direction this rapprochement may develop lies in the obscurity of the future. In my reading of history, I am persuaded that one-hundred years ago no Jew and no Christian would have dreamed that the limited rapprochement of our day could ever have come about.

It is possible to see, however much the details are hidden from us, how the communities became separated from each other, and how the separation increased. One of the great achievements of the last fifty years has been the beginning of a recognition by Christians that Judaism did not come to an end with the age of Jesus, but has had a continuing history down to our time, and that despite the great difference in numbers, the Jewish people and the Christian people represent two on-going and continuous communities. There is a sense in which Christianity is the logical development from the premises of Paul, and rabbinic Judaism the logical development from a premise concerning the Law which is exactly the opposite of Paul. To zealous partisans of our day the separations of the past are not only complete, but also must be rigidly maintained.

Yet perhaps the historian, whose perspective is that of centuries, can be impelled to say, as I would myself say, that the threads were not all of them cut; rather, some threads have defied all the vicissitudes of history, and these hold the two communities to each other in our day, however tenuously.

Philo and his Pupils:
An Imaginary Dialogue *

S IMPLY TO MENTION Philo's dates—he was born about 20 B.C. and died about 40 A.D.—will remind us of the time in which he lived: Long after the acceptance of the five books of Moses as canonical, and shortly before the fixing of the canon of the entire Jewish Bible took place. That Philo was an Alexandrian Jew, well versed in Greek philosophy, greatly influenced by certain "wisdom" doctrines, makes it the more readily apparent that when we deal with Philo we encounter someone in whom there is blended the "Jewish" idea of revelation and the Greek rationalistic explanation of the nature and reliability of that revelation.

An initial problem which we encounter is that Philo has been studied so abundantly for almost every other purpose but that of understanding Philo, that scholarship has often read Philo not for what he himself has to say but for what light he tends to throw on other and apparently more weighty writings. Or else, some special approach can govern a scholar. A characteristic example is the approach of Wolfson,[1] in the first of his two volumes on Philo in which he discusses Philo's doctrine of revelation. Wolfson's approach is that of the medieval Jewish philosopher who divided his topics into logical headings in a well-defined system. Wolfson imagines that Philo can be similarly systematized. In sum, what he tells us is this, that before Philo's time the acceptance of the Bible as revelation combined with certain Greek ideas of the wisdom of God as being intellectually knowable, resulted in Philo's rationalistic interpretation of the revelation which he antecedently accepted.

* This article first appeared in *Judaism: A Quarterly Journal of Jewish Life and Thought* 4 (1955): 47–57.

Now all this is not entirely wrong. In fact, its difficulty is that it is partly, and even mostly, right. But it falls so short of indicating the depth into which Philo plunged in trying to assert the divine nature of the Bible that Wolfson's presentation is little less than inadvertent distortion.

For our present purposes we shall understand Philo the better if we forget that he does throw some light on Paul, and on the Epistle to the Hebrews; forget that he does throw some light on the canon and the original text of either the Septuagint or some such early Greek translation; and forget that Philo in some respects anticipates the medieval Jewish philosophers. We might, for momentary advantage, forget also that Philo is alleged to be the exponent of a Jewish "mystery," [2] but by others he is regarded as no more than a great repository for the variegated obscure religious ideas which floated around in the Hellenistic Roman Empire. Our task is really a modest one, to find out just what Philo said. The antiquarian interest in the source of this or that doctrine of Philo need not concern us; nor need we bother with the thousands of minutia that have so allured the pedants in their approach to Philo that they seem to have found almost everything but Philo himself.

A second prefatory word. We need to distinguish between the form in which Philo couches what he has to say and that which Philo is saying. Philo is adept in allegory. Nothing seems more artificial to the modern age than the form of exegesis which this Alexandrian adopted. It can be conceded that allegory is cumbersome, capricious and even fantastic, but if we are to really get into Philo's thought we have to overlook the unfortunate nature of the medium which was at the height of its fad in his day, and look rather to what he is saying than how he is saying it.

We are now ready for the substance of Philo's thought. Let us note in passing that he is preoccupied almost entirely with the Pentateuch. He does quote occasionally from the Psalms and from some of the Prophets but there are no less than five books of our Old Testament which remain uncited in his works. While there have been those who have contended that Philo quotes from the Apocrypha, and there are some passages which echo dimly certain passages in the noncanonical literature, most scholarship concludes correctly that Philo either does not know the Apocrypha or that he knows it so poorly that it does not in reality come to his mind. His preoccupation is with the Five Books of Moses, and it is his understanding of these Five Books which is the clue to our approach to his view of the Bible as revelation and as an authoritative word of God.

266

Whatever the word "Torah" may mean in Hebrew (there are many quarrels as to its exact connotation) it is an unfortunate fact that it became rendered by the Greek word *nomos*. This word means "law." There is no doubt that the Hebrew word "Torah" has a very much wider connotation. The word *nomos* of itself attributes a character to the Pentateuch for Graeco-Jewish eyes which in the eyes of rabbinic Jews the Torah has never seemed to have. Similarly the predisposition of some, or even many Protestants to see in Judaism a religion which was purely "legalistic" constitutes so strong a mental block on their part that I despair of anyone ever completely circumventing it. The appraisal of normative Judaism as "purely" legalistic stems largely from the circumstance that the Greeks translated the inclusive word "Torah" by the limiting word "law." Out of this circumstance there has arisen the view among many Protestants—not unaccompanied by condescension—that rabbinic Judaism was a religion of arid legalism, devoid of mysticism and devoid of warmth so that one could properly wonder how in the world Judaism was able to bring any kind of religious solace to its bearers in two thousand years of wandering and of bitter persecution.

While Philo himself under the influence of the word *nomos* conceives of Judaism as legalistic, it should not surprise us that this legalism impresses him quite differently than it did the nineteenth- and twentieth-century Protestants. In the world in which Philo lived the problem which he faced intellectually respecting the Bible was that *nomos* as such was not limited to Jews. He could not defend the Bible on the basis that *nomos* was something unique, especially in the light of the fact that in Greek history there were the famous law codes of the Greek cities and by his time Roman law had become operative in his native Alexandria. He could not say to some imaginary auditors that the difference between Judaism and the rest of the religious systems of the world is that we Jews inherit "law," for they could readily reply, Who does not have "law"? What Philo had to contend was that the law of Judaism was superior to every other law, and that its superiority lay in the unique circumstance that it was revealed by God. It was not simply better law, it was also Divine Law.

This contention on the part of Philo would have been easier for him to make were it not that the Greek world by this time had inherited an abundance of speculation on the nature of law. In lecturing on the supposed superiority of the Jewish law, Philo was not the antiquarian specialist operating with a technical vocabulary, but instead Philo spoke to those who knew intimately his highly specialized language. From Aristotle's time the question of the nature of law had become a commonplace in the Greek philosophical schools. And even before Aristotle's time, as in Plato's case, the attention to the nature of law had been considerable. But after Aristotle's time every petty school of philosophers had to devise some explanation of what law was. Moreover, those who, on one basis or another, wanted to justify the political organization which turned into kingship, had to demonstrate in what sense the law which a king promulgated was in reality law. Implicit in such distinctions was the notion that law was the intermediate stage, the golden mean, between tyranny and anarchy. The promulgator of true law could be no ordinary man, but the doctrine, which has abided until almost modern times, that the king ruled by divine right and that the king himself was the law, was by Philo's time a commonplace. There was an immense body of theoretic literature, either written or oral, about the nature of kingship and the nature of law. Almost everything that Philo has to say about the nature of *nomos* is to be understood against this background. Philo is defending the *nomos* of Moses not in a vacuum but in a period of intense intellectual activity.

Moreover, there is ample reason to believe that the nature of the defense which Philo makes for the Law of Moses is in part shaped by the character of those who attack it. It has often been assumed that much of Philo's writing was intended for Gentiles. Since anti-Semitism seems to have had its initial historic appearance in Philo's lifetime about 38 A.D., it has usually been thought that the defense by Philo of the Law served an apologetic purpose in commending the Law to non-Jews. While some of Philo's writings may have this purpose, it is a growing belief that Philo's audience is not the Gentile anti-Semite, but rather the "intellectual" Jew of his time who has been so entranced by pagan civilization that he unconsciously makes comparisons between it and Judaism. Judaism did not come out well in such comparisons. It seems to me that I have encountered exactly such Jews in American universities as those for whom Philo is usually writing. It is a group of Jews who inherit some knowledge of Judaism, but mostly inexact, and who are so allured by the prospects of social contacts with Gentiles that these take on not a normal relationship but appear to be the reward for an attained social status. Consequently the manner of these Jewish critics is different from what that of the Gentile philosopher would be. We could expect the Gentile philosopher to be reasonably curious and reasonably courteous about Jewish antiquities. The passion of some of Philo's replies indicates that he is dealing with those with whom familiarity operated in the normal manner, and his curt dismissal of some of the questioners as people with vile tongues who ought to shut their mouths, indicates that Philo is not giving simply a philosophical reply, but is also exhibiting unphilosophical vexation.

Accordingly, Philo is defending Scripture, not only from the hypothetical onslaughts of nameless Greek philosophers, but from the even more bitter cant which comes out of the Jewish community. The character of Simone Weil is unhappily not an isolated instance in Jewish history, and it is for the Simone Weil type of enemy of Judaism to whom Philo feels constrained to address most of his arguments.

A challenge which an auditor might make to Philo might take the following form: "You, Philo, tell us that the Five Books of Moses are a revelation of God and that the Bible is a book of Divine Law. How can that be? In the first place, we know from our Greek tradition that law operates on two levels. On its lowest level there is a law of the city or the law of the state, promulgated either by a king or by some council. This law is written down in some law code or else it is put on stone. If it happens that a certain law has been promulgated by king No. 1, it remains in force only as long as king No. 1 reigns. When he is succeeded by another king this law may be abrogated and a new law instituted. It is in the nature of recorded laws that they are not permanent. They are altered either by the wisdom of the new king or even by his caprice.

"Moreover, Philo, if you examine the nature of written laws, you will find that the law at Sparta is different from the law at Athens, and that the law at Alexandria is different from the law at Ephesus. This is bound to be so, for it is the nature of the written law to be temporary and superseded. By your own concession the Law of Moses is a written law. Therefore, it is no whit different from the law which is written down at Athens or Sparta. As they are temporary and supersedable, so is your law temporary and supersedable.

"Moreover, Philo, look how much in your law is sheer rubbish and nonsense. There are laws about such things as circumcision, abstinence from eating certain animals, and laws about birds and their nests. Do you mean soberly to suggest that a law code which is receptive to such legislative whims and caprices is in any way different from or superior to the laws of other people?"

To all this Philo replies as follows: "Yes, it is true as you say that there are two levels of law, the lower level which is the written law and the higher law which is the unwritten law of nature. You and I need to understand that

269

in the case of written laws there are some which are the product of tyranny; these laws contradict the law of nature. At the other extreme, there are certain laws which are so general and so little lacking in relevance that anarchy can result; such laws can hardly be reflections of the law of nature. But a written law which comprises justice and which by its nature is perpetual and immutable, which avoids the extremes of being cruel or inapplicable on the one hand, or irrelevant or loose on the other hand—such a written law actually is in conformity with the law of nature. Conformity with the law of nature does not mean identity with it, but it does mean that this reasonable law possesses a high validity beyond the caprice of time and place.

"If you are to understand the Law of Moses you must understand that it is indeed a written code, but it is a written code which—unlike any other—is in complete conformity with the law of nature. To understand more specifically what I mean we have to look at the nature of the Pentateuch. It begins, for example, with the creation of the world. I ask you a reasonable question, is there in the narrative of the creation of the world any *law?* I dare say not. We see then that the nature of the Law of Moses is such that it begins with a historical section which precedes the emergence of specific laws. This very circumstance should be sufficient to indicate that the Law of Moses is different at least in form from the law codes which operate among the Greeks.

"We need to understand why Scripture begins with the creation. It is to outline for us, through events of the past, that which is the daily contemporary experience of every person who has something of a mind and something of insight. Creation was begun originally not by God but by the wisdom of God, his logos. Man was fashioned originally out of pure immaterial substance, but when man gave way to the quest for material pleasures then man, as it were, fell and became partly immaterial and partly material. As a result, all men are composed of these two elements, the material and the immaterial, and the question which each human being faces is whether he will tend toward the immaterial or tend toward the material."

At this point, one of Philo's auditors may interrupt and say, "Philo, all of that is very interesting but I have read the Bible and I haven't seen that. Where in the Bible is all that related?"

To this Philo replies: "There are two aspects of Scripture. One aspect is the body of Scripture which is the literal text. That is all right for immature minds. But if you want to get into the soul of Scripture, then you must look beyond the literal and have recourse to allegory to acquire the true intent of the scriptural text. Allegory discloses to us that Adam is mind—any mind, any neutral mind; that is to say, a mind which is neither good nor bad. Eve is sense—perception. When mind joins with sense, nothing untoward need necessarily result, for the mind is able to get its perceptions only through the senses. The difficulty is that Adam and Eve encounter the serpent, pleasure, and when mind and sense turn toward pleasure, they turn toward bodily things. So, if you will look about you here in Alexandria, you will find the usual man with the usual five senses. Now to what does the usual man devote himself? To physical pleasure. Such a person is dedicated to materialism, and there really is not too much good that can come out of that person.

"Scripture goes on to tell us there was a series of three men who sought a better state of affairs than pleasure-seeking and who had a better kind of mind than Adam had. The first of these men was Enos, and he is the figure for the man who hopes."

At this point, one of the auditors, recognizably Palestinian, interrupted. He said to Philo, "Why do you associate Enos with hope?"

Philo replied, "Why, in the Bible it says, 'Enos hoped to call on the name of God.' "

The auditor replied, "In the Hebrew Bible there is nothing at all said about his hoping to call on the name of God. The text says that men *began* to call on the name of God."

To this Philo replied, "You must not limit interpretation to what is in the Hebrew Bible. The Greek Bible is equally inspired, and I assure you that if you will look in our Greek version you will find that Enos hoped.

"The second of the three was Enoch, which simply means the 'recipient of grace.' Enoch had the grace of God so that he was transferred; that is to say, his old reprehensible life was blotted out and was found no more. We see in Enoch, therefore, the symbol of the man who repents. Accordingly, hope for something better, coupled with repentance, moves us along the road toward the redeemed man.

"Now the third man in this series was a man named Noah. His name means either 'rest' or 'just,' and either translation will do, for we see in him a man who was calm, serene, and tranquil, as behooves a person who is just.

"The ascent of man begins as it were when hope, repentance and justice become part of a person's qualities. But these steps are just the initial steps by which an individual's redemption from materialism takes place. There

271

are certain gifted men whose fate is different from the ordinary man. Such gifted men can through God's grace inherit three qualities which are often to be associated with each other. These qualities have to do with attaining perfection. They are these: first, the ability to learn; second, natural endowment; and third, the practice of virtue. None of these graces ever appears singly, but always in connection with the other two, and we characterize the person who possesses them by that one of the three which predominates in him. These three graces are Abraham, Isaac, and Jacob. Some people make the mistake of thinking that Abraham, Isaac, and Jacob were merely historical people; they are much more than that. They are the three graces of whom the Greeks speak and they are, respectively, perfection attained by being taught, by natural endowment, and by practice.

"The individual who rises beyond hope, repentance, and justice can become an imitator of the ancestors of us Jews if he possesses the three qualities which respectively mark them off. Abraham is a man of worth who is perfected by being taught, and Isaac was perfected by nature, and Jacob by practice. Naturally, each of the patriarchs had some of the qualities of the other two, as I have indicated above."

At this point there was another interruption. "This thing that you are saying about the three types of perfection," said one of the auditors, "it seems I read that in the Nichomachean Ethics of Aristotle."

Philo nodded his head. "Yes, that is true. But if you will look there in Aristotle, he will tell you that only the first and the third have ever come to earth, for Aristotle denies that any individual was ever born perfect. That is because Aristotle knew nothing about Isaac, for that Aristotle met a Jew is a myth—Aristotle knew nothing about Isaac, for had he known about Isaac he would have known of an instance in which a man was born perfect.

"Now the sense in which the three patriarchs are graces is this. Every person who is a Jew either by descent or by his way of life shares in part their experience of beginning with specific endowments. But the sense in which the patriarchs are historical personages is somewhat different, and here you must give me your full attention.

"Abraham, Isaac and Jacob were what we call in Greek, *nomoi empsychoi kai logikoi,* which we might translate, laws made incarnate and vocal.[3]

"Does this phrase trouble you? Let me try to explain it. It is bandied about in our day by tyrants who pretend to be sage-rulers; they are not. They pretend to be living laws; they are not. But Abraham, Isaac, and Jacob were living laws. They were men who lived not by any written code but by the unwritten law of nature itself. There were no written codes in their days. Those things which they did became the laws which the people after them are enjoined to do. In fact, the Law of Moses is nothing other than the record of what Abraham, Isaac and Jacob did. Since the Law of Moses is the record of what they did and since they lived by the law of nature, anyone who observes the Law of Moses lives in conformity with the law of nature. Since the three lived by the law of nature and since someone observing the Law of Moses lives in conformity with the law of nature, then we can see that the purpose of the Law of Moses is to enable a person to live in conformity with nature. And it is not impossible to do, for Abraham, Isaac and Jacob did it long before the law was written down, and true Jews have been doing it since Moses recorded the Law.

"Here then"—Philo thumped on the desk for emphasis—"is the reason why Moses preceded the details of the Law with the various historical narratives. It was his purpose to demonstrate that the law which he would specify was in conformity with nature, and therefore he portrayed the lives of the founders of our race to show that his Law is the best possible imitation of the law of nature and in conformity with it. You know that when you move from Sparta to Athens the law changes; note that the Jews live all over the world but their Law never changes, the Jewish Law is the same wherever you are. Note that when a Greek tyrant comes to power he can abrogate the law in his region; the Jewish Law is eternal. Even in the mundane world of change and tyranny and war and so forth, even in this world where all written law is subject to caprice of time and place, the Jewish Law is immutable and everywhere identical. Therefore, it follows that it is superior to all mundane law and its superiority lies in the fact that it conforms with the law of nature. Finally, to repeat, anyone who lives by the Law of Moses lives by the law of nature."

One of the students shook his head. Philo said, "What is troubling you?"

The student said, "We were saying before you spoke at length of the fact that much of the Bible Law is irrelevant and seems petty. Now you come to tell us that it is in conformity with nature. How can that be?"

Philo smiled. "That is very easy. We must apply the allegory equally to the laws as to the narrative."

"How about circumcision?"

"The law of circumcision is a symbol. When a Jew circumcises himself, symbolically he puts off passion from himself. Since he has thus excised passion he is no longer subject to whims of sensual pleasure or material desire and thereby he is able so to regiment his desires that he controls them and thereby he lives by the law of nature."

"Do you mean to suggest that such laws are only symbols?"

Philo was troubled. "It is a fact," he replied, "that laws are primarily symbols. For example, we are forbidden to eat pork. Pork is the sweetest of meats; at least, so I am informed by those who have tasted it. We abstain from eating it, not because it is bad, but because it is so good. We train ourselves in curbing a pursuit of physical pleasure by foregoing the delicacy of pork. In that sense, pork is for us a symbol. And the other specific laws are symbols too.

"But," and here Philo's voice was raised, "they are also more than symbols. If they were only symbols, there might be justification for a person who knows the symbolic value to live by the value and to neglect or negate the symbol. That is what some of our half-renegade Jews here in Alexandria do.[4] They contend that since they know the meaning of the symbols they can do without them. While they are perfectly right in the symbolic value which they attach to the law, they make a very bad mistake in not observing the literal law."

One of the students pressed him a little further. "Don't you think, Philo, that you are carrying water on both shoulders when you uphold both the literal and the allegorical?"

Philo frowned. "Maybe I am. But that is the way it seems to me. I can tell you that I have no use for those who observe only the literal and see in the law only the literal command. Such people are stupid. Our Law is not a set of arbitrary musts. The Torah does not command; it suggests and admonishes.[5] But those who fail to observe the literal law because they know the symbolic value—it seems to me that they are making a bad mistake. Anyway, that is how I feel about it."

"How," asked one of the students, "do you explain the ability of Moses to record written laws so that they conform with the laws of nature?"

Philo smiled, "That is because of the outstanding kind of person Moses was. He was a prophet, priest, and king, and a legislator.

"I need not explain prophecy to you, since the explanation which you know from Plato is correct. It is, you will recall, that state of ecstasy in which the mind stands out from the body. I assure you, it is not like a dream, or insanity, or intoxication. Such a pure prophet was Moses—indeed, he became ultimately purely mind.

274

"It is his prophetic nature which made him a lawgiver superior to even the finest and most just pagan king.

"As a priest, Moses came both to love God and to be loved by Him as few others. Now before Moses became a priest he was instructed by divine oracles in everything that pertains to the rites of worship and to the sacred task of service. These included abstinence from food and drink and from sexual acts. Thereupon he went to the top of the highest and most sacred mountain in the region and remained there for forty days and nights receiving instructions in the mysteries of priesthood. Out of this instruction, he had stamped on his mind the immaterial form of the movable tabernacle with its equipment which later on Bezalel made out of material objects.

"If you have followed me, our elaborate Hebrew ritual and law was revealed by God through Moses and is in conformity with nature."

There was a moment's silence as his auditors considered his words. Then one of them spoke up. "Just what did you mean when you said Moses became pure mind?"

Philo smiled. "I thought you were going to ask me something different, that you were going to follow up on your question about aspects of the Torah which you said were either petty or foolish, and demand to know how these could have been revealed by the great Moses with what you imply is some relative imperfection. Perhaps that is the intent of your question. But let me answer both your question and the one I have myself raised.

"It is in the nature of things that reason has a double aspect. Each of us has had the experience of having some specific thought in our mind, but our speech or our pen has often, or perhaps always, failed to give utterance to our thought with exactitude and precision. Unuttered thought is related to uttered thought as a man is to his brother. Unuttered thought is pure, uttered thought never free from impurities.

"If we will apply this, we will understand the characteristics of the Jewish ritual. It was all revealed to Moses, or through Moses, and in the process of revelation his mind shaped the transmitted content with precision. But Moses, you will recall, had described himself, in the usual human fashion (Exodus 4:10), as lacking the gift of speech, and Aaron was designated to be his mouth. Now Aaron, the man who is the priest but not the prophet, is the brother of Moses; that is to say, Aaron utters imperfectly the thoughts which Moses conceives perfectly.[6] 'For Moses is mind at its purest, and Aaron is its word, and each has been trained to holy things, the mind to

275

grasp them in a divine manner and the word to express them worthily. . . .' [7]

"Since the commandments come from Moses, from pure mind, then they are the product of pure reason. Since the ritual is mediated through the priest, the specific requirements are those of uttered reason, rather than pure reason. Now Aaron does not distort Moses; he only falls a little short of interpreting him. However, when we apply allegory to the Aaronic requirements, we can revert, as it were, from the imperfect level of Aaron to Moses, to unuttered and therefore pure thought.

"Moreover, since Moses is purely mind, those laws which Moses has recorded through Aaron or through his own hand, are the products not only of unuttered reason, but of right reason—*orthos logos*. What Moses commands is reasonable, and right reason itself, detached from Holy Scripture, would inevitably arrive in a given problem, to that which Moses through Scripture enjoins.

"Scripture therefore is right reason. Accordingly, any one of us who gets a university education (that is, who like Abraham marries Hagar), and who proceeds beyond these routines studies into true philosophy (that is, supplants Hagar by mating with Sarah) can of his own thought arrive at the conclusions in which the Bible has anticipated him.

"Indeed, it is the experience of each of us who has a better than average mind that initially we mate with Hagar; as students we sometimes get so over-enamored of our college education that we progress no further; indeed, some of the deceived among us spend all their life at college, and never pass beyond Hagar. The truly wise among us, however, pass on to mate with Sarah."

The auditor with the foreign accent was a little horrified. "Philo, do you know what you are saying?"

Philo smiled benignly. "You are making the usual literal mistake of assuming that Hagar and Sarah are women. Do you seriously suppose that Scripture in telling us of Sarah's afflicting Hagar wants to trouble us with some petty narrative of feminine jealousy? No; it is not women who are spoken of,[8] but rather minds, the mind at the stage of the university education and the mind which has gone on to wisdom.

"In this latter sense, each of us who has a superior mind weds first Hagar and begets out of her only sophistry, but thereafter some of us go on to wed Sarah, out of whom God can graciously beget for us the joy of the sage which is symbolized by Isaac."

"You are hard to follow, Philo," said one of the auditors.

276

"No," said Philo, "not if you will keep the allegory straight. Of course every now and then I need to assign two related though different quantities to the same character, as I have just finished doing with Isaac. In his own right he is perfection by natural endowment; as the offspring of wisdom, he is joy. And since none of us begets joy, but rather receives it from God, it is manifest that not we, but God, is the father of the joy through the virgin mother wisdom."

The auditor shook his head. "You make it all the harder, Philo."

Philo looked sad. "Some of these things," he said, "are clearer when you read them than when you hear them."

But still another auditor spoke up. "Here is where I don't follow you, Philo," he said. "You say that right reason yields the same results as the Bible. Is that so?"

Philo nodded. "Yes, I said that. But I said more than that. I have said, too, that the Bible is a vehicle embodying records of revelation."

"Aha!" said the auditor. "Now I have you. If reason gets you to the same result as the Bible, then the Bible is in reality reason, and not revelation."

Philo smiled tolerantly. "You go far down the road to truth, but not quite far enough. The Bible is a history of revelations. But it is more than that. Manifestly, reason, when it rises above the obstacles of passion and sense, is pure. But the Bible not only contains a history of revelation, it is also an instrumentality for achieving continuing revelations. 'Israel' means 'one who sees God.' A Jew is not simply a person who possesses right reason. A Jew is one who rises to the climactic quality of receiving the vision of God. A Jew is one who sees God."

One of those present spoke up. "Sees God with his eyes?"

"Of course not," snapped Philo. "Only with the eyes of his higher mind. God is not discernible to the senses. The senses can see the effect of God, such as creation and the rule of the universe, as in the motions of the planets. But physical eyes do not see God. God is not knowable in the physical world."

The same questioner continued. "But to see God with the mind—that is in reality only to conceive God."

"No," said Philo. "You can speak of conceiving God as a mere intellectual abstract process. I am, however, talking about a moment of vivid experience; remote though it may be, it is nevertheless a specific and definite experience. More properly, however, we ought not to say that the eye of the higher mind sees God, since this would imply that the sight is the result of man's own

277

initiative; on the contrary, the proper way to put it is that God graciously appears to the eye of the higher mind." There was a moment of silence as his hearers pondered his words. Philo's voice was low, and it quavered with deep emotion. "That is the goal of all religious living; so to experience God is the true meaning of Judaism."

The voice with the accent interrupted. "Do you mean," he said indignantly, "that this experience of God occurs even in our day and age?"

"It does; indeed it must," said Philo.

"It cannot," replied his questioner. "What you are describing is the union of the prophet with God, and you know of course that prophecy ceased in the time of Ezra."

Philo looked shocked. "Where did you get that, my dear boy?" he asked.

"So I was taught in Palestine."

Philo shook his head. "I do not doubt your honesty, I doubt your accuracy. At any rate, we Alexandrians have a different view. For us it is impossible that prophecy should have ceased. Otherwise, what goal would there be to religious living? Moreover, my dear young man"—here Philo's voice reflected some embarrassment—"I know prophecy has not ceased. For if it had, how then would I have been able, from time to time, to experience it? And I attest that I have had this experience."

The Palestinian was moved by Philo's words, but hardly convinced even by his attestation, and there ensued a rather long discussion of the nature of prophecy of the kind which Philo had earlier intimated could be taken for granted. It seems to be often the case that the discussion of some minor point, believed safely traversed by the philosopher, becomes the focus of the attendant minds. We can leave off listening to Philo and his group, and summarize Philo's position.

The Bible is for Philo not alone a record of ancient deeds and ancient laws; it is much more than that: it is a living, contemporaneous vehicle of continuing revelation. A thing is true because it is in the Bible; but the truth of a thing is capable of corroboration by right reason. The record of revelation is a trustworthy one, for it discloses not only its own content, but gives the prescription whereby a pious person can pass through stages of religious ascent and, through God's grace, receive revelation too.

Such, then, is the Bible as the authoritative word of God for Philo. It is the rational, accurate, truthfully revealed and contemporaneously alive vehicle for religious living.

21

The Confrontation of Greek and Jewish Ethics: Philo, *De Decalogo**

THERE ARE TWO usual definitions of theology which, though related, are quite different, involving a distinction that goes back at least to the beginning of the nineteenth century. Let me phrase these as questions: Is theology merely a systematic inquiry into the tenets of religion? If yes, then theology, when it relates to the Bible or to the rabbinic literature or to Philo or to the Church Fathers, is an antiquarian pursuit. Or is theology, on the other hand, a living system which is obligatory on or commended to the modern communicant? Antiquarian analysis is a much safer pursuit than is the provision of on-going relevancy, for this latter is much more arduous.

Yet assuming that there could be some definition agreed on, so that there resulted some consensus about the premises, and assuming that it would be possible to collate the ethical mandates from the past and make them relevant for today, it would still be possible for wide differences of opinion to exist. This is so because the ancient ethical systems are partly attitude and partly programmatic, but necessarily they cannot remain programmatic for every age and every situation; the more complex society becomes, the less easy it is to adapt general ethical attitudes or ancient programs to specific modern needs.

The relevancy of raising the question of Jewish and Greek ethics could possibly be antiquarian. On the other hand it can stem from this important

* One of several papers read at a theological seminar at Hebrew Union College-Jewish Institute of Religion in March, 1967, this article appeared in *CCAR Journal*, 15 (January 1968): 54 ff.

consideration that, by and large, Jewish ethics historically was considered to be a divinely revealed mandate; normally, in our general thinking, we assume that Greek ethical theories are without a divine origin, and emerged, as it were, out of experience or out of speculative analysis. I think that I will be able to demonstrate that this latter is quite an oversimplification. But let me ask a question, just so we have a background question to shape our discussion: In what way is Jewish ethics markedly different from the ethical mandate that comes out of the French Bill of Rights, the rights of man, the American Bill of Rights, or out of the series of ethical thinkers who cannot properly be allocated to any specific religious tradition but who are secular? The confrontation of Jewish and Greek ethics long ago is a kind of forerunner to the problem of religious versus secular ethics today. We have, in the person of Philo, the result of the confrontation of these two systems.

I have selected the treatise *Concerning the Decalogue* for a number of reasons. First, as Philo's treatises go, it is relatively short; second, we are all interested in the Ten Commandments; third, the treatise lends itself, I believe, to the best introduction to the special topic that we are looking at, as it is handled in Philo's thought.

With respect to the external format, the essay is divisible into two parts, the first dealing with the first five commandments and the second with the last five. This division is significant only because it is found elsewhere, in other treatises of Philo, and also in IV Maccabees. This division sets into equilibrium, on the one hand, piety, which is man's obligation to God and, on the other hand, the virtues, which are the enumerations of man's obligation to his fellowman. Obviously, piety, man's relationship to God, must yield consequences, and these consequences are man's relationship to his fellowman. But if you divide the Ten Commandments in half, the fifth one would be, "Honor your father and mother," then you could ask, "How does that relate to God?" This is the one commandment that I think is worthwhile mentioning because, Philo, having decided to divide things into the typical two-part pattern, must strain a bit to justify his allocation. Here Philo's ingenuity enters in. Parents, insofar as they are procreators, are like God, and insofar as they are mortal, they are like men; the honoring of parents is kindred to honoring God. The limitation of the mortal lives of parents is a good transition to enable Philo to move to man's obligation to his fellowman. So, honoring one's parents is subsumed under piety to God.

Rather notably in this essay, when Philo comes to give an interpretation of the tenth commandment, he interprets, "You shall not covet," in pretty much the same way that some modern scholars have rendered it, namely by the word "desire." I think in English there is quite a margin of difference between "desire" and "covet"; "covet" is a stronger word, for it implies that aggressive action results from coveting, but that desire itself can be limited and contained. Philo moves from his use of "desire," into introducing the question, "What are the total passions of which desire is one?" In answer, there are four passions; in addition to desire, the other three are grief, pleasure, and fear. I mention this item so as to lead us into the specific discussion of our topic: What was there in the way of ethics in the Greek world and what was there in the Jewish world, and how did these things come to be equated with each other?

I ask you to accept, at least tentatively, the following as true. All of Philo's religious sentiments are Jewish, and hence, he believes in revelation. He believes in God, and he does not feel that he has to prove God's existence. So, too, he believes in prophecy. His explanation of his beliefs, of how things happen, is Grecian. When he wants to describe the phenomenon of prophecy, he gets this directly from Plato. I do not think that Plato ever contended that he himself has been a recipient of prophecy, for Plato is only describing how prophecy works. Philo will borrow the definition from Plato, but the contention in Philo that there is such a thing as prophecy is Jewish. (Only indirectly does Philo regard himself a prophet.)

As a consequence of this tendency to use Platonism and Stoicism to explain Jewish religious intuition, Philo's exposition of Jewish ethics is necessarily Stoic and Platonic; hence, the need to enumerate the passions as four. One thing you might notice is that he does not normally use the word "ethics." Like the Stoics, he uses the word "virtue." He speaks, in many places, of four cardinal virtues, as the Stoics did: justice, prudence, temperance, and bravery. Piety toward God wavers in his treatises between being a summary of the four cardinal virtues, and between being the impetus (the generic) out of which the others (the specific) ensue. (You can see, of course, that there is a great deal at stake, in the distinction as to whether piety and four virtues are a summary, or whether they are the source and subsequent derivation.) Philo accepts Stoic terms, Stoic mannerisms, and Stoic standards. In *Concerning the Decalogue,* he explains Jewish law in terms of Stoic requirements, and in the treatise which follows it, called *Concerning the Special Laws* (by "special laws" Philo means the specific Mosaic regulations which in the Bible come immediately after the Decalogue), Philo, still in Stoicism, regards these laws as only expansions of that which is adumbrated, already intimated, in the Decalogue. The Decalogue is, as it were, and to use an expression which Philo never uses, *roshay tayvot*,[1] and the other regulations are only the filled-in matter.

With respect to piety toward God, the substance of the first five commandments, you can ask the question: If the exposition of what is involved in them is Grecian, in what way does Philo associate piety with divine revelation? The answer can get to be a little complicated but such an answer must be given to you or we will not meet the mandate of our topic. I should therefore fill in some things which are not in the treatise and this I now propose to do.

One of the principles that Philo holds with the Stoics is that man is able to learn both data, in the sense of information, and also to learn himself. Learning one's self means not only the ability to give the traditional Greek list of the five senses, graded as to quality with sight highest and touch lowest, and the four passions, but to perceive that beyond this knowledge lies the question of man's inner control of sense and passion. Moreover, one must infer from these terms that it is possible to move from the world of sense perception into the world of concept. Thus, if I see this table, if I touch this table, if I hear this table by moving it, then I am in the realm of perception; perception is that which is achieved by the five senses. If, having seen and heard and touched, I am able in my mind to fashion an image of a table, then I am now in the realm of concept. You say, does this not sound like Plato and the world of ideas? Yes. An idea is that apprehension by the mind which is abstracted from the perceptions of the senses. Concept is the immaterial image, which arises after perception has done its work.

Let us imagine that there are two mathematicians who do not know each other but who have each decided to try to bisect an angle. If you remember this from your high school geometry, it can be done. If you get two competent and reasonable mathematicians, and set them on the problem, and if they use right logic and right method, they will come to the same end result. The fact that they come to the same conclusion implies that there is a body of universal knowledge which the mind can aspire to reach, and can actually reach, if only the mind is able to work with true logic. If the mind does not work with true logic, then it cannot get to concept, and to such universal knowledge. The Stoics had spoken of this universal knowledge. Jews had spoken of *ḥokmā*. When Jews ran into Greeks, probably as early as Ecclesiasticus, a grand equation was made wherein Greek wisdom, *sophia*, equalled *ḥokmā;* and since *ḥokmā* is found in the book of Proverbs, which is in Scripture, *hokmā* equals "Torah." The word which the Stoics preferred for the encompassing universal knowledge which a man would, by exercise and right reason, get to, is summarized in the word "logos." The equation needs to be extended so that "Torah" equals "logos," or vice versa.

There is no single, easy definition for "logos." The only thing we can be certain about is that the translation of John, "In the beginning was the logos and the logos was with God and the logos was Divine/God," should not be, "In the beginning was the Word, the Word was with God and the Word was God/Divine." "Logos" is not "a word," nor "the Word." Logos is not only reason; logos, indeed, is the whole complex of data that the reasoning mind can get to. Just as *hokmā* has an implicit separate existence (hypostasis), in that *hokmā* cries aloud in the streets, or builds a house in Proverbs, so logos has a separate existence. Logos then is not simply the capacity to reason, but is rather that goal of knowledge and the universal wisdom to which right reason can bring a person. On principle, any gifted person who learns data, who regiments his senses and his passions so that he avoids error, who uses right reason, can get to the pinnacle of living, which is to live simply by right reason. To live ethically implies both the comprehension of ethics as concepts, and also the resistance to the seductive or delusive capacities of the senses and the passions.

The religious question for Philo is: What is the relationship of a history of revelation to man's possible capacity to live by exalted right reason? The answer, which varies from time to time, would be found, normally, in two possibilities. One possibility, ignoring divine revelation, can suppose that certain men possess as gifts from God the traits by which these men, through learning, or practice (*askesis*), or intuition, or all of these, are enabled on their own to follow right reason to its ultimate destination of logos. But, on the other hand, God had pity on man, and therefore made it easier for him, with the result that man does not have to run the risk of relying on what might turn out to be faulty reason. Moreover, the second way implies there is a margin of difference between mere possibility and surety.

Consistent with these possibilities is Philo's allegorical explanation: Moses, the author of the Pentateuch, is the allegory for the logos. The logos, now in the sense of a body of wisdom, guides by means of its innate character. Moses does not command (this may shock you); he guides or exhorts, but he does not command, for "command" implies authority, but authority over a mind is irreconcilable with the freedom of the mind to learn.

Philo makes a distinction, which again is Stoic, between written logos and spoken logos. For the Stoics, speech is thought when it is uttered. Thought is speech when it is unuttered. Which is pure, thought or speech? We always manage not to say what we mean; hence thought is pure, whereas speech is impure thought. Moses is logos in the form of *thought,* and Aaron is logos in the form of *speech,* because Moses was tongue-tied and Aaron was his brother and was his mouth. The written requirements in the Pentateuch are on the level of Aaron, but he who knows allegory can penetrate into their profound meaning and get to the level of pure logos. Accordingly, if you observe the laws found in the Chumash on the literal level, without giving any thought to them, you are on the level of the mystery of Aaron, and while you are living by the logos, you do not *know* you are. But if you have become schooled, and inducted into philosophy and trained in it, then you live on the level of the mystery of Moses because you know what you are doing. Philo has scorn for those who live only on the level of Aaron; they are the mere literalists. Philo, of course, lives on the level of the logos, of the mystery of Moses, as one might reasonably expect. Now, do you want to live by the logos? Then you observe the particular laws, and you do so by coincidence. Do you want to live more deeply, indeed, deliberately, by the logos? Then study hard, and control your senses and passions, and learn, learn, learn. Learn to know not only the what of the Laws, but the profound why of them.

Shall we call this logos-theory merely Stoic? No, it is partially Stoic, but it is more than Stoic. It is thoroughly saturated with a Jewish background. What makes this wisdom wise? That its source is God. On the other hand, in speaking *analytically* about the logos, Philo will often give it an overtone as though it is merely the Stoic body of immanent wisdom which permeates the universe. And when it comes to defining Jewish ethics, Philo inevitably gives definitions that can be paralleled in and buttressed by recourse to the Stoics. In his use of the Stoic categories, Philo may put Jewish items into four Stoic categories, that is, the last five commandments into the four cardinal virtues, but that is only because his enumeration is basically Stoic. One could put it this way, that in Philo the Jewish and the Stoic ethics are interchangeable in their substance, however they differ in origin.

But let us revert to our question, what is the mandate for man respecting the virtues?

It is necessary here to make a correction, intimated above as necessary, of a prevailing view that Greek philosophy is simply a disinterested inquiry into the nature of things and that it was in some way an experiential matter.

Now, obviously experience entered into Greek law. For a good Stoic, what is law? Let me give you a definition. Law is that midpoint between tyranny and anarchy. Law is that which emerges when the monarch is a philosopher. It does not mean that he is a student of Philo or a student of Plato. What it does mean is that the king is able to regiment his senses and passions, to free his mind from the obstacles offered by the body, and to let his mind soar up into the logos, into the realm of ideas, and there encounter what the Stoics called, inheriting the term from earlier times and developing it, the "unwritten law of nature." Now we have to pause and talk a little bit about this unwritten law of nature.

If you are a good Platonist, this table before us, which could be chopped up and could be burned up, was made by somebody who started with an idea of a table in his mind; that idea is not subject to decay or destruction. Now, the better your craftsman is, the more nearly your table, made of wood, is an imitation of the immaterial, ideal table. The worse the craftsman, the less correspondence there is. The ideal table is perfect. Putatively, there is a body of law which is perfect, and that is the law of nature. It is inherent in the very essence of things that it must be unwritten, because whoever tries to write down a law is like a carpenter who tries to make a table: there is a gap between his achievement and the idea. The achievement is inevitably, in some degree, imperfect, and always inferior to that perfection which was in his mind when the artisan began. A philosopher-king is able to let his mind range into the realm of ideas to encounter there the law of nature, unwritten, and then he turns the law of nature into the best possible written specific statutes. If he is not a philosopher, he does not have this ability. If he is not a philosopher, the laws come out of his caprice, or out of the whims of his personality, not out of nature. If he is a strong, narcissistic person, the laws will be tyrannical, and not reflect nature. If he is a weakling who inherits the throne from his father, he will be a mollycoddle, and the end result will be anarchy, not true law. Hence, the true king is that philosopher who exceeds the rest of the populace in spiritual stature, as he often exceeds it in physical stature.

Now ask this question. Are the Laws of Moses the unwritten law of nature, or are they the imitation of the law of nature? In answer, they are written, so that they must be the imitation. Where, then, do you find the law of nature in the Bible? In Genesis. Abraham, Isaac, and Jacob were philosopher kings who, by virtue of the ability to live by nature, are exponents of the law of nature, and all that Moses did in the laws of Exodus,

285

Leviticus, Numbers, and Deuteronomy, was to write down there the record of the lives of Abraham, Isaac, and Jacob. If, therefore, you live by the Laws of Moses, the particular laws, you will live like Abraham, Isaac, and Jacob, and you will be living by the law of nature. If you are a dumb literalist, you will be doing it coincidentally, on the level of Aaron. If you are a student, then you will be doing it with knowledge, and therefore you will know what you are doing, and be on the level of Moses.

The Laws of Moses, according to Philo, are the best possible imitation of and substitute for the law of nature. They are that, as can be demonstrated by the circumstance that they are immutable and eternal. In Athens, the new king abrogates the laws of the preceding king, so the Athenian laws are never immutable. If you move from Athens to Sparta, the laws change, but the Laws of Moses are everywhere the same. While, then, the Laws of Moses belong in the category of written laws, they are the best possible approximation of the law of nature.

The Stoic, then, did not derive laws solely from experience, nor is the Stoic notion of an ideal king that of somebody who has tried X, Y, Z ways, and has said this one of them is the best. The ideal king is that person who has utilized philosophy as a discipline, so as to rise above appearance and to get to immaterial reality. The easy equation of philosophy as mere secularism emerging out of experience is a little bit unfair to the Greek tradition. If we make that corrective, that is enough for our present purposes.

Yet we want to press on to the question: Does Philo, equating Jewish ethics with the Stoic, really consider the Jewish mandates divine? To answer that we would have to give a resounding "yes." The fact that Philo can demonstrate their "validity" through the use of Plato or Stoicism, does not touch upon the issue: Does he consider them the products of revelation? He absolutely does. He can make more complicated the doctrine of logos by implying that God is so transcendent that God becomes immanent in the world only through logos; and he can thereby anticipate, and be parallel to to that tradition among all philosophical mystics, that God in his essence is unknowable and that it is only facets of God, such as the logos, that the mind can get to. In Philo, the mind cannot go beyond the logos to God. Logos is susceptible of synonyms, for it can be "Moses," or, elsewhere, "the High Priest," also an allegory for the logos. The logos is the first-born of God. The logos is the only begotten, as the Christian has it, of God. You can use these synonyms; on the other hand, I do not know of any passage in which he gives a definition of "logos." We give the definition, when we see how he uses "logos": The logos is the highest aspect of the godhead which the mind can get to.

Philo rejects the supposition that God is named Elohim (*theos* in Greek) or Adonoi (*kyrios* in Greek). God is nameless. For God, Philo usually uses the Greek expression *to on,* that which exists, a Platonic term. "That which exists" is, for Philo, an active idea. Philo at times tends to dissolve history, in that Moses is an omnipresent logos, transcending his allocation to that ancient period, between the Egyptian enslavement and the settlement in Canaan, and thereby Moses becomes, instead, the existential experience of every man; nevertheless, Philo has the vivid belief in God, and in Scripture as a product of God. Ofttimes when you read a bit and piece here and there of Philo, it sounds so excessively naturalistic, that people who read Philo in excerpt are often betrayed by his naturalism. He, indeed, naturalizes every miracle that I can think of. He believes in miracles, but he always explains them in ways in which they are not miraculous, so that he sounds like a naturalist, but he has a firm belief in God. The commandments, then, come from God, and the utility of philosophy is to explain how they come from God; only, Moses exhorts, he does not command.

To summarize at this point, Philo adopts the nomenclature of the Greeks respecting ethical formulation, and he makes equations, with the result that the Jewish ethics and the Greek tend to become virtually identical. But he insists on the superiority of the Jewish formulation, and he concedes that gifted persons can conceivably get to the goal without the formulation, but those who can are very few. Hence, you need Moses. But you need him so as to achieve the ethical goal, you do not need him to know the ethical content.

Since Philo was a Greek Jew, and Paul was also a Greek Jew, I want to introduce something else for a contrast, because it may give a little more dimension to what we are talking about. In Paul, there is the contention, first, that righteousness cannot be achieved by abiding by the law; second, the law can be an obstacle to righteousness. Third, there is a very curious passage (Gal. 3:19) that the Mosaic Laws were ordained by the angels, and angels is a plural. Now what does this latter mean? There is destined to be a perpetual disagreement over the passage between secular students of the history of religion and most pious Christians. In another passage, in I Corinthians 11:10, Paul gives the mandates to women to keep the head covered "because of the angels." A reasonable explanation of "angels" is "demons"; the word is a euphemism. The law is the product of demons? Yes, as is repeated by second-century gnostics. Fourth, the transition from sinfulness to righteousness is something that man cannot work out on his own. This is able to come about only through the action of God who can transform man; it can come because the logos, Christ, died on the cross, and thereby atonement was made for man's sinful nature. The transition from sin to righteousness was made through this an act of grace on the part of God, and not because man did, or could do, anything to merit it. The supposition that man can merit righteousness supposes that man can observe laws and that there is something valid in their observance. This supposition tends to negate God's grace, for if grace is that which comes freely from God, then, works implies that man can earn grace, and hence grace is nullified. Paul raises the question, should sin increase in quantity so that God's grace can increase, and there Paul takes a clear stand against this. If men do not earn righteousness, does grace come to everybody? No. It comes to those called, those predestined for it.

Is there in Philo any reflection of such suppositions that the Laws are the product of a second-rate revelation, or the product of revelation by demons, or that man cannot observe the Law, or that grace alone saves, and that grave is meted out through divine election? Almost none at all!

I have raised the issue about Paul for still another reason, because there is an implication which you can run into among your Christian colleagues from time to time, depending on how strongly Lutheran or Calvinistic they are. For some such Christians the whole realm of ethics is ruled out as a religious matter. In different ages, when vested interests began to arise, and various aspects of social problems emerged, there were reflections in Christian thought of different values invested in grace, predestination, and the like. Some distortion could arise. For example, if God decides whether you are to be rich or poor, and he picks you to be rich, and he picks your neighbor to be poor, should you help out your neighbor? To do that, you are interfering with God's predestination. There are on record those who distort Calvin into a sanction for social unconcern, and argue against a state concern, because if God had intended "those people" to be well off, he would have made them well off. Or, if God had intended black men to be free and to have equal opportunity, he would have created them that way, and for a preacher to get up and advocate equal rights is to usurp God's prerogative. Or, it could be used in behalf of special interests. If a church owns a red light district, you as a minister must not speak out against it. Or, when you get the movement around the 1890s, the Social Gospel, which interpreted Christianity as a reform movement, then economic conservatives could cite Calvin or Luther or Augustine or Paul and say that social reform has nothing to do with religion.

There is often a dimension, then, in which Christians say that preachers should keep out of politics, which is different from that in which Jewish congregants say that rabbis should keep out of politics. What Jewish congregations mean is, "It is not good for us Jews to take the lead." That is, Christians can one-sidedly, but honestly, urge a traditional theological sanction for inaction, but Jews cannot.

Philo insists that a person can choose; he insists that a person can observe the Law; he does not liquidate, as Paul does, repentance, this because in the Pauline system man can do nothing. There is no echo in Philo of age old Christian debate: Does a man at least have the choice to qualify himself for grace? Augustine said no and Pelagius said yes and Pelagius was voted to be a heretic. There is nothing in Philo that frees the person from that moral responsibility, which is implicit in choice. Man, according to Philo, can choose to observe the Laws and can achieve the observance of them. And man can take those steps to advance to the logos. Grace is restricted to the mystic vision, as proved by *ophthe* ("was seen"), the Greek passive which renders the passive *va-yēra* of Genesis 12:1; man can prepare himself to receive the divine vision, but Genesis 12:1 uses the passive to teach that it is God's grace which determines who of the self-prepared receive it, and who do not.

Now what is it that we have encompassed? Philo's exposition of Jewish ethics is Grecian. His explanation of how the ethics is defined is Grecian. His bill of particulars is often Grecian. Yet he never abandons the Jewish assumption that the Laws are literally the product of revelation. I concede that when he gets through rationalizing how revelation works, you may say that it is no longer revelation; that is why I find it necessary to emphasize that Philo does believe the Laws are products of revelation.

There are a half-dozen passages in this treatise that I think you would all be well advised to look at sometime. When Philo speaks about respect for father and mother, he is very eloquent. When he talks about idolatry, he lacks the uncharitableness of the Epistle of Baruch which is added to the book of Jeremiah in the Greek translation. When he talks about the Sabbath, it is really not in terms of those who worry about pressing an electric button, or something like that. For him, the Sabbath is that day in which you indulge in wisdom, and wisdom is where you separate the mind from the body, so that the mind can go up and commune with God. The Sabbath is really a spiritual essence in this most high-minded treatise.

You ask: Does Philo throw some light for us on our theological problems? That is why I began with the formulation, What are we looking for? Are we looking for an arrangement and analysis of what is in the ancient documents? That is only antiquarianism.

Are we looking for formulas? Even the ancient documents cannot give us specific programs. My two older sons and I are inevitably divided, completely divided, on what to do about Vietnam, even though we talk from the same religious context. Honest people can interpret a common mandate in diverse ways. Respecting Jewish theology, I wonder whether we are not talking about a mandate for our people based on a supposition of revelation which a naturalistic age has queries about. How good it would have been had Philo argued that Jewish ethics was different even in substance from the Stoic, and proved it! How good it would be if we could contend that Jewish ethics surpasses the secular, and prove it! I guess what characterizes the C.C.A.R. is that its members are 90 percent naturalistic and 10 percent theistic, and it is searching for a mandatory theology which it desires should be 100 percent theistic, and no percent naturalistic. How one gets out of this dilemma, I do not know. If I knew the way, I would tell you. Maybe to see the problem is in itself something of a virtue; maybe. I am not sure. It is a little too comforting to tell one's self that the answers are less cogent than are the questions.

22

Parallelomania *

I ENCOUNTERED THE term "parallelomania," as I recall, in a
French book published about 1830, whose title and author I
have forgotten,[1] in a context in which certain passages in the Pauline
Epistles and in the Book of Wisdom seem to have some resemblance were
being examined, along with the consequent view that when Paul wrote the
Epistle to the Romans, a copy of the Book of Wisdom lay open before
him, and that Paul in Romans copied generously from it. Three items are
to be noted: (1) that some passages are allegedly parallel; (2) that a direct
organic literary connection is assumed to have provided the parallels; and
(3) that the conclusion is drawn that the flow is in a particular direction,
namely, from Wisdom to Paul, and not from Paul to Wisdom. Our French
author disputes all three points: he denies that the passages cited are true
parallels; he denies that a direct literary connection exists; he denies that
Paul copied directly from Wisdom, and he calls the citations and the inferences "parallelomania." We might for our purposes define "parallelomania"
as that extravagance among scholars which first overdoes the supposed similarity in passages and then proceeds to describe source and derivation as if
implying literary connection flowing in an inevitable or predetermined direction.

The key word in my essay is "extravagance." I am not denying that
literary parallels and literary influence, in the form of source and derivation,

---

* The Presidential Address delivered at the annual meeting of the Society of Biblical
Literature and Exegesis on December 27, 1961, at Concordia Theological Seminary, St.
Louis, Missouri, this article appeared in *Journal of Biblical Literature,* 31 (1962): 1–13.

exist. I am not seeking to discourage the study of these parallels, but, especially in the case of the Qumran documents, to encourage them. However, I am speaking words of caution about exaggerations about the parallels and about source and derivation. I shall not exhaust what might be said in all the areas which members of this Society might be interested in, but confine myself to the areas of rabbinic literature and the Gospels, Philo and Paul, and the Dead Sea Scrolls and the New Testament. That is to say, my paper is a series of comments primarily in the general area of the literatures relevant to early rabbinic Judaism and early Christianity.

An important consideration is the difference between an abstract position on the one hand and the specific application on the other. Thus, in the case of passages in Samuel-Kings and Chronicles, the concession that parallel passages do exist falls short of determining whether the Chronicler borrowed from the author of Samuel-Kings or vice versa. That determination rests on inherent probabilities which emerge from close study. Similarly, Matthew may have borrowed from Mark, or Mark from Matthew; and still similarly, John may be later than and a borrower of the Synoptic tradition, or earlier and in some way a source for, or completely different from, the Synoptists. Hence, it is in the detailed study rather than in the abstract statement that there can emerge persuasive bases for judgment. Most of us would, I think, come to the view that the Chronicler borrowed from Samuel-Kings, and not vice versa, this because of clear phenomena in the texts. But elsewhere the phenomena may not be quite so clear. Thus, in the question of the chronological relation of John to the Synoptists, Erwin Goodenough [2] and William F. Albright [3] have adduced two different bases for dating John early instead of late. I would term these bases as abstract rather than applied. Goodenough restricts his argument to the Christology, arguing that the high Christology of John is not only no proof of John's lateness, but conceivably an indication of its earliness, for in Paul too there is an advanced Christology. Albright, in the quest of some relationship between Jesus and the Qumran community, argues that there is no reason to suppose that the Jesus who spoke one way in the Synoptics could not have spoken another way in John. Abstractly, both views are right. Yet when all the factors in the gospel problems are weighed, the decision would seem to be that although John abstractly could have been the earliest, detailed study would incline to the conclusion that it is the last of the gospels.

Abstractly, Qumran might have influenced the New Testament, or abstractly, it might not have, or Talmud the New Testament, or the Midrash Philo, or Philo Paul. The issue for the student is not the abstraction but the specific. Detailed study is the criterion, and the detailed study ought to respect the context and not be limited to juxtaposing mere excerpts. Two passages may sound the same in splendid isolation from their context, but when seen in context reflect difference rather than similarity. The neophytes and the unwary often rush in, for example, to suppose that Philo's *nomos agraphos* and the rabbinic *torah she-be'al pe* are one and the same thing, for unwritten law and Oral Torah do sound alike.[4] But Philo is dealing with a concept of the relationship of enacted statutes to what the Greek philosophers call pure law, the law of nature, while the rabbis are dealing with the authoritative character of explanations to, and expansions of, the Pentateuch. It turns out from detailed study that the two similar terms have no relationship whatsoever. In this case we have not a true parallel, but only an alleged one.

Moreover, when we deal with rabbinic literature, the Gospels, the Epistles, the Pseudepigrapha, and Philo we are in an area which we can momentarily describe as post-Tanak Judaism. This is the case even if the final canonization of the hagiographa is later than Paul's Epistles, and is the case if one will rise above nomenclature and be willing for purposes of discussion to regard Paul's writings as an expression of a Judaism. If, accordingly, all these writings are post-Tanak Judaism, then obviously the Tanak has some status and influence in all of them. What could conceivably surprise us would be the absence of Tanak influence from this literature, not its presence. Furthermore, since all this literature is Jewish, it should reasonably reflect Judaism. Paul and the rabbis should overlap, and Paul and Philo and the Qumran writings and the rabbis should overlap. Accordingly, even true parallels may be of no great significance in themselves.

In the variety of the Judaisms, as represented by terms such as Pharisees, Sadducees, Qumran, Therapeutae, it is a restricted area which makes each of these groups distinctive within the totality of Judaisms; it is the distinctive which is significant for identifying the particular, and not the broad areas in common with other Judaisms.

There is nothing to be excited by in the circumstanace that the rabbis and Jesus agree that the healing of the sick is permitted on the Sabbath. It would be exciting, though, if rabbinic literature contained a parallel to the "Son of Man is lord of the Sabbath." The mote and the beam do not surprise us in appearing in both; certain criticisms of the Pharisees should reasonably appear in both.

293

For the rabbis and Philo to agree that Noah's righteousness is relative and lower than that of an Abraham or a Moses reflects simply the close study of the Tanak and hence the ascription of some pregnant meaning to a pleonastic work or syllable. Since Genesis describes Noah as righteous "in his generations" we should not be overwhelmed at discovering that the rabbis and Philo unite in inferring from these words a reduced admiration for Noah's righteousness. That Scripture is as a source common to Philo and the rabbis is quite as reasonable a conclusion as that Philo drew the item from the rabbis, or the rabbis from Philo.

These varieties of Judaism, then, are bound to harbor true parallels which are of no consequence. The connections between two or more of these Judaisms is not determined by inconsequential parallels.

Furthermore, each of us operates within certain biases, and since I have one about Christianity, I must expose it here. It is that I regard early Christianity as a Jewish movement which was in particular ways distinctive from other Judaisms. This distinctiveness is an intertwining of events in, and of theology about, the career of Jesus, whether we can recover that career or not, and the histories of his direct disciples and of later apostles, and what they believed and thought. Only by such a supposition of such distinctiveness can I account to myself for the origin and growth of Christianity and its ultimate separation from Judaism. If, on the other hand, the particular content of early Christianity is contained in and anticipated chronologically by the Dead Sea Scrolls and anachronistically by the rabbinic literature, then I am at a loss to understand the movement. While I hold that Mark was a source utilized by both Matthew and Luke, I am not prepared to believe that the writers of Christian literature only copied sources and never did anything original and creative.

In the case of Paul and the rabbis, let us assume that at no less than 259 places, Paul's Epistles contain acknowledged parallels to passages in the rabbis. Would this hypothetical situation imply that Paul and the rabbis are in thorough agreement? No. Is it conceivable that despite the parallels, Paul and the rabbis present attitudes and conclusions about the Torah that are diametrically opposed? Yes. Then what in context would be the significance of the hypothetical parallels? Surely it would be small. I doubt that as many as 59, let alone 259 parallels could be adduced. It was right for the scholarship of two hundred and a hundred years ago to have gathered the true and the alleged parallels. Today, however, it is a fruitless quest to continue to try to find elusive rabbinic sources for everything which Paul wrote. His first and second Adam are not found in the rabbis, the mediation of the angels at Sinai is not found in the rabbis, and his view that the *nomos* is superseded by the advent of the Messiah is not found there. To allude, as some have done, to Paul's use of Scripture as rabbinic exegesis is to forget that Philo and the Qumranites were also exegetes; it is to overlook some elementary issues in chronology. I don't believe that Paul bore the title "Rabbi" or that there is any genetic connection between the specific content of his Epistles, or the theology in them, and that of rabbinic literature. Abstractly, it is conceivable that Paul had nothing of his own to say, and that his achievement was that he was only an eclectic. But this seems to me to break down at two points. First, no rabbinic parallels have been found to that which in Paul is Pauline; and secondly, it took Dupont-Sommer's emendations [5] of the Qumran Scrolls to have them contain pre-Pauline Paulinism. I for one am prepared to believe that Paul was a person of an originality which went beyond the mere echoing of his predecessors or contemporaries. I am prepared to believe that Paul represents more than a hodgepodge of sources. I find in his epistles a consistency and a cohesiveness of thought that make me suppose that he had some genuine individuality. I admit that I am not a partisan of his views, any more than I am of those of Philo. But I hold that he had a mind of high caliber, and an inventiveness of high order. And even were the 259 hypothetical parallels present, I should want to inquire whether they are significant or merely routine.

Indeed, I should insist on proceeding to the next question, namely, what is the significance in the context of Paul's Epistles of these parallels. To distort just a little, I would ask this question, What is the use that Paul makes of those parallels which he allegedly has borrowed?

Paul's context is of infinitely more significance than the question of the alleged parallels. Indeed, to make Paul's context conform to the content of the alleged parallels is to distort Paul. The knowledge on our part of the parallels may assist us in understanding Paul; but if we make him mean only what the parallels mean, we are using the parallels in a way that can lead us to misunderstand Paul.

I am not prepared to suppose that Philo of Alexandria had to go to his mailbox at regular intervals, learn by letter what the rabbis in Palestine were saying, and then be in a position to transmute the newly received data into philosophical ideas. Again, I am not prepared to believe that there was a bridge for one-way traffic that stretched directly from the caves on the west bank of the Dead Sea to Galilee, or even further into Tarsus, Ephesus, Galatia, and Mars Hill. While I am prepared to join in speculations that John the Baptist had some connection with Qumran, I will not accept it as proved without seeing some evidence for it; and I have been considerably surprised at an essay given before this society that speculated on why John had disaffiliated from Qumran.

The various Jewish movements, whether we are satisfied to call them groups or sects or sectarians, make sense to me only if I conceive of them as simultaneously reflecting broad areas of overlapping and restricted areas of distinctiveness. The phrase "restricted areas" is a surface measurement, for its extent could well have been small, but its depth tremendous. Where the literatures present us with acknowledged parallels, I am often more inclined to ascribe these to the common Jewish content of all these Jewish movements than to believe in advance that some item common to the scrolls and the gospels or to Paul implies that the Gospels or Paul got that item specifically from the scrolls.

In dealing with Qumran and Ephesians, K. G. Kuhn, in "Der Epheserbrief im Lichte der Qumrantexte," [6] after noting certain parallels which cannot come from a common biblical source, points to what he terms *Traditionszusammenhang*. The existence of a community of postbiblical tradition reflected now in Qumran, now in Philo, now in rabbinic literature, now in the New Testament, seems most reasonable, especially if one will emend the word into the plural, *Traditionenzusammenhang,* so as to allow for diversities among the aspects of tradition, as exemplified, for example, by the distinctions between rabbinic midrash and Philo's.

If we are, as I believe, justified in speaking of traditions in plural, then we may call to mind a distinction made a century ago between the so-called Hellenistic midrash and the rabbinic. The former term has been used to describe materials found in Philo, Josephus, various apocrypha and pseudepigrapha, and the fragments preserved in Josephus and Eusebius. On the one hand, it is true that the Greek civilization represents a cultural and religious complex different from the Hebraic and Jewish; on the other hand, when Greek civilization penetrated Palestine and when Jews moved into the Greek dispersion, the Greek civilization began to penetrate the Jewish, evoking both a conscious rejection and also an acceptance and adaptation, whether conscious or unconscious. The term "Hellenistic Jewish" is often better to describe certain doctrines or ideas than the bare term "Hellenistic." But here exists one confusion that I doubt will ever be cleared up. It is this: when we describe something as Hellenistic, are we speaking about the language in which an idea is expressed, or are we alluding to some demonstrable difference between a Jewish and a Greek idea? It seems to me that a Greek idea could receive expression in mishnaic or Qumran Hebrew, and a Jewish idea in *koine* Greek. Or does the term "Hellenistic Jewish" merely describe the geography of a writing? It seems to me that a work written in Greek could have been composed in Palestinian soil, or one written in Hebrew or Aramaic in the Greek Dispersion. Granted that language and ideational content can point to a great probability as to the place of origin, we go too far when we move from the probability to a pre-determined inference. Therefore, at one and the same time I could assert that plural aspects of post-Tanak traditions marked the various Judaisms and also that these plural traditions do not always lend themselves to ready separation into neat categories. Hence, Qumran can in principle share tra-ditions with the rabbis, with Philo, and with the New Testament, and on the one hand, Qumran can share certain traditions with the rabbis but not with Philo, certain traditions with Philo and not the rabbis, and certain traditions with the New Testament but not with the rabbis and Philo. And Qumran can be alone in certain traditions.

In the matter of parallels, we could conceivably be justified in speaking of rabbinic versus Hellenistic midrash, if we abstain from assuming that no communication took place, and providing we remain prudent in isolat-ing in some given literature that individuality which is the hallmark of it. For Ephesians and Qumran to echo each other has a definite significance; that Ephesians has a Christology lacking in Qumran is even more signifi-cant, for it gives us the hallmark of the Christian character of Ephesians. Kuhn is quite right in telling us that "überhaupt gibt es zur Christologie . . . von Qumran keinerlei Parallelen."

It would seem to me to follow that, in dealing with similarities, we can sometimes discover exact parallels, some with and some devoid of signifi-cance; seeming parallels which are so only imperfectly; and statements which can be called parallels only by taking them out of context. I must go on to allege that I encounter from time to time scholarly writings which go astray in this last regard. It is the question of excerpt versus context, which I have touched on and now return to.

Let me lead into this by a related matter, for thereafter the danger in studying parallels only in excerpts can become clearer. Over a century ago the Jewish historian Graetz identified Jesus as an Essene, and in the subsequent decades there was almost as much written on the Essenes as there has been in the last decade. The earliest literary source on the Essenes is Philo's treatise entitled "That Every Good Man is Free," wherein Philo illustrates a theme by his description of the Essenes. That theme is that the life of *askesis* is both commendable and viable for attaining perfection. A second essay by Philo, "On the Contemplative Life," argues that still another way to perfection, that of contemplation, is commendable and viable, and is illustrated by the Therapeutae. Indeed, at the beginning of the essay on the Therapeutae Philo hearkens back to his "That Every Good Man is Free."

One cannot understand Philo's intent fully without some recourse to Philo's other writings. It is not methodologically sound, in view of the preservation of so much of Philo's writing, to study the material in isolation on the Essenes in "That Every Good Man is Free." The person who immerses himself in Philo necessarily goes on to note that *askesis* is symbolized recurrently by Jacob and contemplation by Abraham; a third way to perfection is intuition, symbolized by Isaac.

I have to state that my studies in Philo lead me to regard him as an apologist, and a preacher, and to have no great confidence in the reliability of his reports on either the Therapeutae or the Essenes. In the case of the latter I suspect we deal with Philo's third-hand knowledge and not his direct contact on any intensive basis, for Philo was an Alexandrian whose known visits to Palestine turn out to number exactly one. A study of Philo discloses, for example, that he can say of Abraham's father Terah that the name means "to spy out odor," and that Terah only asked questions but never got to knowledge, and that Terah is the character whom the Greeks called Socrates. Hence, I find myself somewhat disinclined to take Philo's historical statements too seriously. Moreover, he tells us that the meaning of Abraham's marriage to Hagar is that Abraham went to college, and then he proceeds to deny that Hagar and Sarah are historical characters. Accordingly, my skepticism increases about his reliability. Indeed, when I consider the apologetic tendencies, and concomitant distortions, in both Philo and Josephus, I find myself taking what they say with elaborate grains of salt. Josephus tells us that the Essenes were Neo-Pythagoreans. Indeed, he makes philosophers out of all Jews, equating the movements with Greek philosophical schools. To my mind, we encounter in Josephus not precision but pretension.

I do not trust what Philo and Josephus tell about the Essenes. About six years ago I wrote that to identify the Qumran community with the Essenes is to explain one unknown by another. I should phrase it a little differently today. I would never try to identify the Qumran community by the Essenes, but I incline to some willingness to identify the Essenes by the Qumran community.

If it is foolhardy to take without sifting a long parallel from Philo's "That Every Good Man is Free," how much more foolhardy is it to take out of context a sentence from one of his laborous allegories and use it for comparison. Wilfred Knox's cautious listing of passages in Philo which have some echoes in Paul seems sounder to me than Gerald Friedlander's view that Paul had necessarily read Philo.

Harry Wolfson and Louis Ginzberg have recorded many passages which presumably reflect parallels between the rabbis and Philo. Inasmuch as the overlappings in the varieties of Judaisms would reasonably suggest that parallels would appear, it is striking that most of the paired passages which these two cite are actually not parallels, but are instead statements of considerable difference. I have discussed this at length in my book, *Philo's Place in Judaism,* and I need not here repeat myself. There I contend that Wolfson and Ginzberg suppose that parallels, both the true and the alleged, mean that Philo drew on the rabbis, as though there was no creativity in the Alexandrian Jewish community. I would only suggest that if a Wolfson, who wrote a magnificent two-volume book, *Philo,* [7] could be mistaken so often about parallels, it is not prudent for the mere amateur to rush into excerpts from Philo.

What shall we make of the five immense books which constitute the Strack and Billerbeck *Kommentar zum Neuen Testament aus Talmud and Midrasch?* [8] Let us grant that it is a useful tool. So is a hammer, if one needs to drive nails. But if one needs to bisect a board, then a hammer is scarcely the useful tool. Four major errors in the use of Strack and Billerbeck, caused by its construction, mar its usefulness. The first is to be stated as follows. When Luke, presumably of Roman origin, appends editorializing comments to Mark, then it is scarcely likely that rabbinic passages can serve as persuasive parallels or, more importantly, as the direct sources for such editorializing. Strack-Billerbeck list such rabbinic parallels, and indeed, do so for Paul, James, the Johannine literature, the Pastorals, and so on. The impression thereupon exists that the unfolding Christian literature, even after Christendom became Gentile in the Dispersion in the second century, still owes some immediate debt to the rabbinic literature, even in passages emerging from Babylonia in the fifth century. If it is retorted that I am addressing myself not to the value of Strack-Billerbeck but to its misuse, then I must reply that the manufacturer who shapes a hammer to resemble a saw bears some responsibility for the misuse of the tool. I would charge therefore that Strack-Billerbeck is shaped as though its compilers were out of touch with New Testament scholarship.

Secondly, Strack-Billerbeck misleads many into confusing a scrutiny of excerpts with a genuine comprehension of the tone, texture, and import of a literature. One recalls the proposal that in the verse, "Let the dead bury the dead," we should understand that mistranslation has occurred, and that the first "dead" really was the "place," *metā,* for *mētayā;* so that the verse should read, "Let the place bury the dead." One can go on thereafter to cite biblical and rabbinic requirements about the burial of unclaimed bodies, and thereby miss the intent, and the deliberate bite, in the Gospel passage. Rabbinists have sometimes assumed that a Gospel pericope was lifted bodily from Gemara. Elsewhere I have expressed the opinion that rabbinic scholars have assumed that a mastery of the Talmud confers automatic mastery of the Gospels.

I would state here that New Testament scholars devoid of rabbinic learning have been misled by Strack-Billerbeck into arrogating to themselves a competency they do not possess. Strack-Billerbeck confers upon a student untrained and inexperienced in rabbinic literature not competency but confusion. The list of indiscretions by New Testament scholars in rabbinics, or by rabbinic scholars in New Testament, would be a long one. I allude here to errors in scholarship and not to pseudo scholarship. By this latter I have in mind the distorted evaluation of rabbinic Judaism as merely dry and arid legalism—it is never dry *or* arid, but always dry *and* arid; or a judgment such as Friedlander's that what is good in the Sermon on the Mount is borrowed from Jewish sources,[9] and what isn't, isn't very good. I am not implying that scholars are without the right to make value judgments. I am only suggesting the lack of value in many value judgments, when these emerge from an acquaintance merely with excerpt instead of with the intent, and the nuances, of a literature.

Third, in the major sins of Strack-Billerbeck is the excessive piling up of rabbinic passages. Nowhere else in scholarly literature is quantity so confused for quality as in Strack-Billerbeck. The mere abundance of so-called parallels is its own distortion, for the height of the pile misleads him who reads as he runs to suppose that he is dealing with sifted material. The distortion lies also in the circumstance that quantity lends a tone of authority all too often submitted to. The counterbalance is notably absent, the qualifying is withheld, and the pile acts as an obstruction to seeing what really should be seen. If Philo can undergo mayhem by study in excerpt, then this is mild compared to what rabbinic literature studied only in Strack-Billerbeck undergoes. And lest my statement here seems to be some Jewish provincialism, I must hasten to say that I am paraphrasing what was said about the competency of Ferdinand Weber's *Theologie der alten Synagogue* and Wilhelm Bousset's *Religion* by a Presbyterian named George Foot Moore.[10]

The fourth and crowning sin of Strack-Billerbeck involves a paradox. On the one hand, they quote the rabbinic literature endlessly to clarify the New Testament. Yet even where Jesus and the rabbis seem to say identically the same thing, Strack-Billerbeck manage to demonstrate that what Jesus said was finer and better. I am a religious liberal and to the best of my knowledge a student free of conscious partisanship in dealing with the ancient past. Somewhat like Claude Montefiore,[11] I am impelled to admire some statements attributed to Jesus more than similar statements of certain rabbis, and at other places the statements of certain rabbis more than those attributed to Jesus. Scholarly impartiality, achieved by many Christian scholars in this Society, is not a characteristic or a goal of Strack-Billerbeck. Why, I must ask, pile up the alleged parallels, if the end result is to show a forced, artificial, and untenable distinction even wthin the admitted parallels?

It is scarcely cricket to pile up Strack-Billerbeck sheer irrelevances, as they do, in connection with the admirable injunction in Matthew 5:43–48, not to hate one's enemies. Strack-Billerbeck concede that parallels are here lacking, yet they manage to conclude that Judaism actually teaches the hatred of enemies, almost as a central doctrine. Strack-Billerbeck carefully omit such Gospel passages as Matthew 23, which to any fair-minded reader, such as a man from Mars, would prevent the characterization of the Gospels as expressive of love and only love. Christianity shared with other versions of Judaism both the ideal of the love of one's fellow-men and also a hostility to the out-group. What else should one reasonably expect? If love was distinctively a Christian virtue, absent from Judaism, what happened to it when the Church Fathers dealt with fellow Christians who disagreed with them? I think, for example, of Tertullian's dealing with Marcion. Unparallel parallels which feed a partisan ego scarcely represent good scholarship, whether the dabblers are Christians or Jews. How should a serious student assess the statement of a modern writer that "in many ways the New Testament is the reassertion of the authentic Old Testament tradition over against the rabbinic distortion of it"? [12] Sober scholarship and partisan apologetics are too quite different matters.

The various literatures relevant to Judaism and Christianity are so bulky and so diverse and so complex that no one person can master them all and the secondary scholarship in full thoroughness. This has been the case for at least a century and a half or ever since modern scientific scholarship arose. The discovery of the Dead Sea Scrolls has provided an addition to the relevant literature, this in the last twelve or thirteen years. Since the scrolls are in Hebrew, the first people who worked in them were, naturally, Hebraists, not New Testament scholars whose milieu has been Greek. Sometimes the Hebraists have been masters of biblical Hebrew, and not of the mishnaic; and sometimes the Hebraists have failed to display a deep comprehension of the problems inherent in New Testament scholarship. Sometimes New Testament scholars have made forays into the scrolls as if they are listed in the Muratorian fragment.

If ever there was a time when interdisciplinary partnerships were called for, this should have been the case when the scrolls emerged to notice. Instead, the scrolls have been at the mercy of extreme individualists, especially on the part of those who have ascribed to them some special, indeed, unique relationship to early Christianity. When the scrolls first came to light, there were flamboyant statements made about them. Let me paraphrase four of them: (1) the greatest discovery in the history of archeology; (2) all the mysteries about the origins of Christianity are now solved; (3) everything that has even been written about Judaism and Christianity must now be rewritten; and (4) the scrolls, sight unseen, are a hoax.

The individualism has prompted a good many theories, most of them competently assembled in H. H. Rowley's very able article in the *Bulletin of the John Rylands Library*.[13] There can be no doubt that the scrolls captured the imagination of the general public. They also spawned some of the most spectacular exhibitions which I have ever encountered. If I pick out one to mention, it is only because it is typical of a certain lack of restraint. I allude to the work of a British scholar, the author of many works on Jewish history, who began his essay on the scrolls by saying that the difficulty in the problem of the scrolls stemmed from the fact that up to the time of his writing, no historian had approached the scrolls. Quite modestly, this British scholar offered himself for the task. His theory wins by a length in my opinion the race for the most preposterous of the theories about the scrolls.

Edmund Wilson was the first popularizer to titillate the general public about the scrolls. Mr. Wilson has written both literary criticism and fiction —and one can be uncertain as to just where to classify his book, *The Scrolls from the Dead Sea*.[14] He makes the contention that New Testament scholarship, even the liberal scholarship, has shied away from the scrolls, out of fear of theological positions being upset. This was in May, 1955. In 1954 I was invited to be part of a panel at the December meeting of the Society on the scrolls and the New Testament. I was not able to accept the invitation, but I still keep Franklin Young's telegram inviting me because it predates Mr. Wilson's libel on New Testament scholars.

Since I am a New Testament specialist, and Jewish, I hope you can take it at face value that no theory about the scrolls, moderate or extreme, will step on my theological toes. It was not my theology which Mr. Wilson offended, but whatever learning I had acquired. New Testament scholars, far from shying away from the scrolls, have possibly been guilty of going overboard about them.

The vaunted novelties which the scrolls were alleged to contain did excite me at one time, but always in prospect. When I acquired my copies, this excitement receded, for I learned that those things which might have made the scrolls exciting were not and are not there. As the scrolls relate to early Christianity, they are notable for the absence of concrete, recognizable history, and this may possibly be pointed up in the following way. In my judgment, the scriptural books and fragments are of infinitely greater value than the sectarian documents and the Hodayoth, and I for one would willingly trade in the sectarian documents and the Hodayoth for just one tiny Qumran fragment that would mention Jesus, or Cephas, or Paul. Until such a fragment appears, I shall continue to believe, respecting the scrolls and early Christianity, that they contribute a few more drops to a bucket that was already half-full.

With the passing of months and of years, we have come to a better perspective on the scrolls. In the light of that perspective perhaps many here will agree with me that the scrolls reflect the greatest exaggeration in the history of biblical scholarship. To speak of exaggeration is to imply that there is a basic substance. I am not denying utility and worth to the scrolls. But I do not hesitate to express the judgment that they are not nearly so useful and worthy as was initially claimed.

Further, respecting interdisciplinary partnership, virtually all of us have loyalties which we neither can nor should deny. I for one have no scruples at stating that I am Jewish and a rabbi. There is an affirmative sense in which in context one can speak of Jewish scholarship or of Christian scholarship. At the same time, there are other contexts in which scholarship needs other descriptive adjectives. Where we deal with documents from long ago, it seems to me that the ideal is sound scholarship rather than unsound, accurate rather than inaccurate, objective rather than partisan.

Someday some cultural historian might want to study a phenomenon in our Society of Biblical Literature. Two hundred years ago Christians and Jews and Roman Catholics and Protestants seldom read each other's books, and almost never met together to exchange views and opinions on academic matters related to religious documents. Even a hundred years ago such cross-fertilization or meeting was rare. In this, our ninety-seventh meeting, we take it as a norm for us to read each other's writings and to meet together, debate with each other, and agree or disagree with each other in small or large matters of scholarship. The legacy from past centuries, of misunderstanding and even of animosity, has all but been dissolved in the framework of our organization. Would that humanity at large could achieve what has been achieved in our Society.

It is proper that the Society of Biblical Literature should be host to differences of opinion, and even acute ones. We do not want to arrive at some pallid unanimity, but rather to be the market place in which vigorously held viewpoints, freely expressed, vie with each other for acceptance. When one recalls the occasional fervid debate in this Society, it is notable that the issues have been primarily scholarly, and never to my recollection denominational. This is as it should be.

In scholarship, full accuracy and full depth are an ideal occasionally approached but never quite realized, certainly not by any one person. The realization comes the nearest to the ideal not in an individual, but in our corporate strivings, as together we seek always to know more, and always to know better.

It seems to me that we are at a junction when biblical scholarship should recognize parallelomania for the disease that it is. It is time to draw away from the extravagance which has always been a latent danger and which the scrolls have made an imminent and omnipresent one.

It would be a real achievement if biblical scholarship today were to be characterized by perspective and direction, with the older theories reassessed, and our collective learning broadened and deepened.

23

Genesis 4:26b *

THE HALF-VERSE with which this paper deals has in it no unusual words and it presents no great problem in translation.
The ensuing summary of exegesis of the verse might be subtitled, a history
of reading difficulties into a text.

The verse, after telling that a son Enos was born also to Seth, states that
"then there began the calling on the name of Yahwe." The awkwardness of
the translation stems from the Masoretic Text, where we encounter 'az
huḥal, a hophal of ḥll, meaning "to begin."

The difficulty in our half-verse is scarcely in its meaning, but rather in
its implication. First, since Genesis 4:4 had described Cain and Abel as
bringing offerings to Yahwe, the suggestion in our verse that only in the
time of Seth did the worship of Yahwe begin can perhaps point toward
contradiction; modern literary analysts have suggested that two variant
traditions of the earliest worship of Yahwe are discernible within Genesis 4.
Second, the half-verse, whatever it may mean, is perhaps in surface contradiction with Exodus 6:3 which states that the name of Yahwe was made
known only in the time of Moses. The half-verse is in conflict with Exodus
3:14. Third, somewhat similarly, haggadic embellishments in postbiblical
times credited the patriarch Abraham with the momentous discovery of the
existence of the one true God, and our half-verse, if interpreted naturally,
would be in contradiction to that distinctive haggadic motif.

The ancient versions reflect translations which both raise textual questions and which have themselves spawned secondary and tertiary develop-

* This article first appeared in *Hebrew Union College Annual,* 32 (1961): 19–29.

ments. These flower in that exegesis which we moderns are prone to label fanciful. But we shall see that even the most sober and pedantic among modern scholars have succumbed to the far-fetched and the overly ingenious.

Our first field to survey is that of rabbinic exegesis. Targum Onkelos renders our half-verse: "Then men *profaned* the name of God in their prayers."[1] The Palestinian Targum (Pseudo-Jonathan) proceeds to read the verse as though a missing direct object for *liqro* to be understood: men profaned the name of God by calling *men and idols* by divine names. (Rashi to the verse rephrases the content of the Palestinian Targum, stating more specifically that the giving of divine names to men and idols profaned the name of God.)

Still other bits of rabbinic exegesis are worth noting. One interpretation states that this passage is one of three in which the particle *'az* introduces an account of rebellion.[2] Another view contrasts the fate of Israel, for whom God provided dry land out of the sea, with that of Enos's generation, upon whom God sent a flood which turned the land into sea. This was not the same as Noah's flood, for this one covered only a third of the earth's surface. Again, the wickedness of the generation of Enos was such that the Shekhinah, which at Cain's murder of Abel had moved from the first heaven to the second, now moved further from earth, from the second to the third heaven. Enos's name, we are assured, in early sources means "sickness" or possibly "weakness." A narrative relates that Enos was asked some questions by his neighbors about his ancestors. In his answer, Enos alluded to Adam's having been fashioned out of dust. Finding that his replies elicited skepticism, Enos himself fashioned an image from dust, and when Enos blew into it, a demon entered, giving the image life. The neighbors promptly declared this "golem" to be their god and they believed in it.

All this exegesis is in keeping with the supposition that *huhal* must mean profane. By and large the earlier of the rabbinic sources seem by inference to exclude Enos himself from the charge of idolatry. But Maimonides, writing in the twelfth century, extends that transgression to include even that worthy.

It is to be noted that insofar as such exegesis or legend is tied to the verse, the bond rests in taking both *'az huhal* and the phrase *qara' b'shem yhvh* out of their usual and natural meaning. But, on the other hand, medieval Jewish interpreters of the more literal and rational disposition, such as Ibn Ezra and Sforno, did not succumb to the traditional fancies. Ibn Ezra not only assures us that *huhal* must mean "began" and not "profaned," but he proceeds to give a grammatical analysis in his own terminology to show that "profane" is ruled out.[3]

It is to be observed that Ibn Ezra and Rashi are here not harmonizable. The Jewish tradition subsequent to them, to which we shall return, inherits both the fancies of Rashi and the literal view of Ibn Ezra.

Our second avenue is the Septuagint and its derivatives. After relating the birth of Enos, the text tells us, "He (*houtos*) hoped to call on the name of the Lord God." Three things are to be noted: (1) the emphatic *houtos*, he; (2) the rendering, *hoped*; and (3) the Lord *God*. It is recalled that *yhwh* was rendered by *kyrios* and *'elohim* by *theos*; did the Septuagint read *yhvh 'elohim*?

The Septuagint translators took the crucial word as coming from the root *yhl*, to hope or await. To the question whether a reading different from the Masoretic Text lay before the translators we shall return presently.

As was the case with Jews in the rabbinic tradition, for whom exegesis and legend were concomitant, this Greek rendering begat Graeco-Jewish marvels of development. In Philo and those influenced by him or by his atmosphere, a striking "midrash" is to be found. The identification of Enos, man, with hope became in Philo's hands a means of pointing to man's distinction over animals; the latter are without hope, but man is not. On an even grander scale, Philo sets forth a view of what we might today call the existential meaning of Scripture. Genesis is for Philo a record of the progress of the soul to perfection. The story of creation in Genesis 2 is somewhat equivalent in his thought to man's "fall," for such is the import of man's being a mixture of dust and of spirit. Philo proceeds, then, to set forth how man can rise. He gives us two triads of biblical characters who, allegorically, represents aspects of man's endowments. The second triad consists of Abraham, Isaac, and Jacob. Allegorically these "Patriarchs" are qualities, indeed graces, and not men, and they are respectively, ability to learn, the intuitive capacity, and training (*askesis*). But preliminary to these qualities is the progressing soul's need to possess inner serenity, for which Noah is the allegory. Inner serenity is attainable through repentance, for which Enoch is the symbol. But repentance, in turn, needs to be preceded by hope —for which Enos is the symbol. So Enos, Enoch, and Noah are the first triad.[4] Could this wondrous exegesis even have developed without the Septuagint rendering of *huḥal* by *hoped?*

Though the elaborateness of Philo's construction is not always echoed in patristic writings, they not infrequently allude to Enos as "hope." So the *Recognitions* of Pseudo-Clement (IV, xii), where Philo's Enos and Enoch seem to have become telescoped.

In Eusebius (*Praep. Ev.* vii, 8) the Philonic interpretation of Enos is alluded to most vividly, and even developed some further. Eusebius tells us:

> I think we ought to receive the history of the Hebrews from among the learned of the Hebrews and not from any other source. As the story holds among them, from the beginning before the Flood, from the first creation of mankind and for the following generations there have been a certain number of righteous men beloved of God; one of whom "hoped to call upon the name of the Lord God." Now this shows that to none but the Creator of all things he [Enos] gave the title both of the Lord and God [5] of the universe. For he was persuaded that not only by creative power He well and orderly disposed the whole, but also, like the lord as it were of a great city, was the ruler of the whole, and dispenser, and master of the house, being at once Lord, King, and God. The first to lay to heart the idea and name of this being . . . was the godly man of whom I speak, and who in place of all substance, and title, and abundance . . . "hoped to call upon the name of the Lord God," . . . having procured Him for a treasure to himself of blessings both of soul and body. In consequence of this it is recorded that he was the first to be called among the Hebrews a "true man." At all events he is named Enos, which is "true man," by a well applied appellation. ". . . So Enos

is recorded as the first of the beloved of God among the Hebrews, since he first hoped" . . . proving the truly rational faculty of the soul to be capable of knowledge and of understanding the true worship of the Godhead; the first of which would be a proof of the true knowledge of God, and the second of his hope in the God whom he knew.

The third avenue is led into through Aquila, as preserved in Origen.

Aquila presents two major and two minor deviations from the usual Septuagint reading. Of the major, *houtos* is absent, giving way to *tō,* "then." "Hoped" is restored to "began." Where the Septuagint read *epikaleisthai tō onomati,* Aquila reads *kaleisthai* [6] *en onomati;* the differences between the two senses may or may not be sharp. Subsequent Latin renderings uniformly take *epikaleisthai* as active in sense, but *kaleisthai* as passive, and I am not completely sure that the distinction is tenable. Thus the Septuagint would mean, "This one hoped to invoke the name of God"; while Aquila is rendered, "then there began the being named (*vocari*) in the name of God" (as for example, Yehonathan, or any man's name which is theophoric).

Whether the differences are really susceptible of the delicate distinctions is unnecessary for us to decide. Hugo Grotius accepts the distinction between Septuagint and Aquila as valid, and prefers the sense of Aquila, though indicating that Septuagint can also be accepted. He cites that Cyril had interpreted our verse in the Septuagint to mean that men were named with the name of God; he tells us that this overtone is exactly what Aquila was driving at; and he informs us that Irenaeus favored this sense also. If it should be demurred that "to be named in the name of God" is without specific meaning, then we shall see that subsequent commentators go further and specify what Aquila seems only to imply.

Skipping to Luther's age, Luther rendered our passage: "Zu der selbigen Zeit fing man an zu predigen von des Herrn Namen." Note the *predigen.*

In a book called *Recognitio,* published in 1550, which discusses Greek and Hebrew textual variants, written by an Augustinian priest Eugubinus, we get the following comment, which I paraphrase: *'az huhal* means, "then began"; it refers to time and not to a person. So too Aquila rendered the Hebrew. I do not know why the Septuagint renders it, "this one hoped"; nor is any reason known among us to explain the cause. The text has not become corrupt, for we observe that Gregory Nanzianzus alludes to this passage in this way: "Concerning Faith, Abraham was considered just for his faith. Concerning hope, Enos first hoped to call on the name of the Lord." Perhaps we should single out Eugubinus for special praise in that his inability to explain an uncertainty did not lead him into far-fetched conjectures.

Augustus Pfeiffer, in his *Dubia Vexata* [7] allocates his chapter xvii to our passage. Systematically he gives four numbered paragraphs posing the problem, and then he solves it. As to the problem part, first he cites the Septuagint, declaring that "hoped to call" is senseless, for *huḥal* is a passive and therefore may not be rendered by the active "hoped." Second, he cites the rendering in the Targum, Rashi, etc., conceding that *huḥal* may really mean profane but, nevertheless, profaned is impossible in this passage, because it is joined with *liqro;* that meaning would be possible, he says, only if we read *huḥal miqra.* Third, he cites the very many who interpret the passage (Theodoret, Chamierus, Bertramus) in the sense of being named in God's name. But we should need the *niph'al, le-hiqqare,* rather than the *qal, liqro.* Grotius had solved the problem in this latter way and had cited Genesis 6:2, the *b'ne elohim,* as an example of being named with God's name. But in Genesis 6:2 the fallen angels are *b'ne elohim* not *b'ne yhvh,* so that one Calovius had castigated Grotius for the suggestion. Fourth, Bellarminus had supposed that our passage meant that some finer and more sublime religion had been instituted, namely, that the monastic state had begun, while Jacob Boulduc had transformed Enos and his group into Carthusians. So far the problem.

Then Pfeiffer sets forth the solution. The true meaning of the half-verse is that it signalizes the solemn introduction of public exercises of invoking God, and of the whole divine cult.

We learn from Samuel Nelson's *Anti-Deistic Bible,* [8] which I have consulted in a German translation from the English—the date of publication of the German is 1766—that there are three differing interpretations of our half-verse. First, our verse implies that in those days men began *more often* to call upon the name of God and to visit those places where his worship was practiced; second, men began to give themselves divine names and impiously to term themselves divine; third, the offspring of Seth began at that time to separate themselves from the destructive practice of the Cainites and to dedicate themselves to the worship of God. A footnote adds a fourth explanation, attributed to one Teller: men incorporated the name of God in the names which they gave their children so as to separate them from the evil Cainites.

Among modern Jewish scholars, those who work within the framework of liberal suppositions do not reflect the earlier interpretations. But a sampling can indicate that the traditional exegesis has remained alive among traditional scholars. We recall that Rashi and Ibn Ezra had gone in different directions.

Samson Raphael Hirsch, in his translation,[9] renders "Damals fing man an im Namen Gottes zu verkünden." Yet his comments disclose some unhappiness about the rendering. He mentions that the verse could possibly be translated, "Then men began to profane the name of God." But he concludes, poignantly, that the rendering by Rashi is not just.

Hirsch wants his readers to know of an interpretation by his teacher, Bernays, which is, he asserts, certainly the correct one. In Abraham's time the *qara b'shem* was meritorious, for it was the rediscovery of God, a reversion to a better time, coming after God's name had been completely forgotten. The *qara b'shem* of Enos came at the beginning of man's falling away; first in the evil time of Enos did it become necessary to proclaim the name of God, for antecedently the situation had existed which Jeremiah 30:34 described as fated to return, when no one would need to be instructed in the knowledge of God. Hence, Enos marks descent; Abraham ascent. Hirsch goes on to state that *qara b'shem* means more than call or preach; it means a complete devotion and submission to the divine will.

Herbert S. Goldstein, in *Bible Comments for Home Reading*,[10] hearkens back to the putative flood of the days of Enos. Goldstein tells us that it reached from the Atlantic to Gibraltar and then to Asia Minor, causing the Mediterranean sea to divide Europe from Africa. Then, as though to justify this midrashic comment by natural science, Goldstein adds: "This would harmonize with the scientific account of a big partial flood covering one third of the world." Goldstein gives no reference to his source for the "scientific account." His comment on *qara b'shem* follows Rashi: "They gave appellations to God's created objects. They thought that by revering His servants or officials, they were honoring Him. This would be true," concludes Goldstein, "if God were not omnipresent."

311

Solomon Goldman, *The Book of Human Destiny*,[11] paraphrases as follows: It was in the days of Seth's son Enos that men acquired some conception of the Deity and learned to pray. In his notes Goldman says, "For this interpretation cf. Kimḥi; Luzzatto. Some scholars interpret it to mean that the Four Letter Name was first heard of then." [12]

Joseph Hertz, the late Chief Rabbi of the British Empire, accepts the translation along the lines of Ibn Ezra, but in his notes he suggests an alternate, "Once again men began to call upon God under the name, Lord, which seems to have been forgotten among the descendants of Cain." [13] This rendering Hertz ascribes to one Hoffman, probably David Hoffman, a fine scholar whose attack on the Graf-Wellhausen hypothesis is an unhappy and atypical sample of the man's true learning.[14]

But these renderings and interpretations need scarcely apologize to the scientific scholars. Kalisch, in *Genesis*,[15] rejects the view of Clericus that then men began to call themselves by the name of God; he also rejects the Targum and the Septuagint. He states that he "cannot repress a feeling of astonishment that these simple and clear words should have suffered so many forced and often strange interpretations, since we need only take them in their obvious sense in order to arrive at a perfectly satisfactory idea." In contrast with the physical form of worship, sacrifice, displayed by Cain and Abel. " 'men began to invoke the name of the Lord,' either in private prayer or in public supplication . . . The first descendant of Seth advances a decided and bold step towards the realm of spirituality . . . he boldly opens the portals of the purest religion."

In Keil and Delitzsch [16] we get the assurance that Enos etymologically means "weak," "faint," "frail," and "designates man from his frail and mortal condition," as contrasted with "the pride and arrogance displayed by the (*sic*) Canaanitish family." They cite from Oehler that the name of God signifies in general "the whole nature of God, by which He attests his personal presence in the relation into which He has entered with man, the divine manifestation, or the whole of the revealed side of the divine nature, which is here turned towards man. They conclude, finally, that the Cainites [17] . . . were laying the foundation of this world: the . . . Sethites began . . . to found and erect the kingdom of God."

The best discussion of the passage, so we are told by Gunkel,[18] is that offered by Dillmann.[19] It is therefore worth noting some of the things which Dillmann says. The word "Enos," according to Dillmann, derives from the root meaning "to be weak"; Dillmann suggests that weakness describes man in contrast with God. He quotes Ewald approvingly to the effect that the intent of the passage is that man learned to distinguish more strictly between man and God. That is, in the time of Enos, or already at the time of his birth, man began to call with the name of Yahwe, that means, not merely to name or make use of this name, but to *call upon,* that is, worship him also. Dillmann records a disagreement with Clericus and Ilgen who had thought that the phrase meant to use a theophoric name. But *liqro,* says Dillmann, in quoting Knobel, "applies properly to prayer to Yahwe . . . possibly also to the proclamation of his name, as in Isaiah 12:4." He cites Luther, to "preach of the name of the Lord."

His digression over, Dillmann reverts to Knobel. The expression *liqro b'shem* "is used also of the Yahwe worship generally, designating that worship as a whole by one of its principle parts." Dillmann proceeds:

> Man's knowledge of God is assumed to have been from the beginning (see chapter 2:16), but the solemn adoration of public worship must have had a beginning at some special time; and if we compare how the present formula recurs in chapters 12:8, 13:4, 21:33, 26:5 . . . not only can there be no longer any doubt as to its meaning, it will also be recognized that we have here a notice of the first beginnings of the true religion, whose continuation is afterwards traced in the line of Seth, Shem, Abraham. But with the author [of the verse] the conception of true religion attached itself to the name of Yahwe, hence this formula of his. The finer distinction between essence and name, thing and expression, found in Exod. 3:13 ff., 6:3, is not made by him.

It is entirely consistent with the narrative of C—the symbol by which Dillmann meant what we would usually call J—that the public worship of Yahwe should have begun in the third generation of men. But, says Dillmann, it is apparently less in agreement with verses 3–5, where Cain and Abel are already represented as offering sacrifices. But this latter beginning was only an isolated prelude, and the proper purpose of 26b is to tell us where and when the worship of Yahwe originated.

While modern scholarship handles the alleged double tradition within Genesis 4 by dividing it into two J sources, such a division was not in Dillmann's mind. The distinction he drew between the approach of Cain and Abel and that of Enos is the difference between an isolated interlude and a public proclamation. Dillmann describes the rabbinic view which interprets *huhal* as profaned, as a perverse understanding.[20]

Dillmann tells us furthermore that the reading in consonantal texts was *zhhl,* and that the reading *'az huhal* is connected with the interpretation of the Targum. Perhaps this is not clear. But Wellhausen and Skinner clarify it for us.

Skinner, in the *ICC Genesis,* also cites this supposed consonantal text. The emphatic position in which the Septuagint put the pronoun *houtos* shows that our text originally read *zeh hēhēl,* "this one began." I have not found anyone who says so explicitly, but the point seems to be that under the influence of rabbinic exegesis, a desire to reduce the stature of Enos resulted in a change from *zeh hēhēl,* "this one began" into *'az huhal,* "then there began." We get from Skinner a restoration of the supposed right text on the basis, in part, of the rendering of the Septuagint, buttressed by the Targum, even though the Septuagint and the Targum are hardly in good accord with each other! Parenthetically, Skinner notes only part of Aquila's deviation from Septuagint.

Driver, does not deign to note either the Septuagint or targumic renderings of the verse.[21] His treatment is laconic, as if to imply that there are no difficulties. His comment is limited to noting that in 4:26b we are given a "parallel line . . . in contrast to that of Cain . . . and under Enos the public worship of Jehovah is stated to have been introduced."

Gunkel opposes a view of Eerdmans which would regard Genesis 4:25–26 as an interpolation from some late quasi-professional hand.[22] He finds it a usual thing for the ancients to trace the beginnings of their worship to earliest antiquity. The verse is in conflict, Gunkel assures us, with Exodus 3:14 and 6:2; we have no knowledge, he adds, of the basis on which the author attributes the first worship to Enos. We have here very old reflections about the antiquity of Yahwe worship; the impression of the verse, that the worship of Yahwe is older than Moses and the people of Israel, is quite correct. He cites extra-biblical names (*Azrijau* and *Jaubidi*) as relics of the non-Israelite worship of Yahwe. He adds that the immemorial antiquity of the name of Yahwe does not exclude the possibility that only at Moses' time did He become revealed as the national God of Israel.

Furthermore, he continues, this section is very important for source analysis. In earlier sections the source from which this material was drawn uses *elohim;* the Cain-Abel sage, which uses Yahwe, could not have stood in this same source. Gunkel uses J_e for the symbol of this Seth-lineage source, and J_j for the Cain-Abel source. That is, there is no true E source in Genesis 1–11. For *'az huhal* Gunkel therefore reads with the Septuagint, zeh hēhēl, with Wellhausen and against Eerdmans.[23]

Qara b'shem, according to Gunkel, is in general a term of divine worship. In a setting of polytheism, it is understandable that the particular God needs to be called on by a specific name, as at the beginning of many Psalms and even in modern prayers.

Simpson, *Early Tradition of Israel,*[24] allocates 4:25 and 26b to J1; 26a, he allocates to J2, as ". . . presumably derived from a genealogical tradition more developed than known to J1." In his notes to the passage in *The Interpreter's Bible* I, *ad loc.* Simpson urges that we follow the Septuagint. We would render: "He was the man who began the call upon the name of the Lord."

And finally, Mowinckel assures us that the E code is indeed found in Genesis 1–11; in his context, he adverts to a circumstance which we have already noted, that Septuagint reads *kyriou tou theou.*[25]

It is not impossible, says Mowinckel, that the original may have been *"b'shem elohim . . . Kyriou* may have been inserted." Hence, we *do* have E even prior to Genesis 15.[26]

To end where we began, the difficulty is not in the obscurity of the verse, but in its clarity. The Septuagint is an interpretation, not a translation. Had the scientific scholars recognized this elementary consideration, they would never have seriously proposed their emendations.

Does the verse clash with other verses? As in the Midrash we find Abraham's age of recognizing the Deity given variously as one, three, ten, and forty-eight, so Scripture ascribes the beginning of the worship of Yahwe both to Enos and to Moses; the rabbis take Genesis 12 and 15 as the basis for ascribing the true priority to Abraham. Of course, the verse clashes.[27]

But why emend the text?

The Haggada Within Scripture *

* This article first appeared in *Journal of Biblical Literature,* 80 (1961): 105–122.

T HIS ESSAY MAY seem to some an effort to drive still another nail into the coffin of the Graf-Wellhausen hypothesis, but that would be an indirect result rather than a deliberate purpose. So as not to be misunderstood, I should state a truism which unhappily seems to need frequent restatement in our day, namely, that to abandon the Graf-Wellhausen hypothesis is not the same as rushing into the comforting arms of an orthodoxy, authentic or neo.

The Graf-Wellhausen hypothesis emerged from phenomena in Scripture, not from the caprice of scholars. Were the phenomena not present in Scripture, the hypothesis would not have been put forward. Since they are present, the Graf-Wellhausen hypothesis was an effort to account for the phenomena. That effort could have been right or it could be wrong; or, to say this more judiciously, it could have been adequate or inadequate. It came into the public arena of biblical scholarship out of the curiosity and the learning and the *Zeitgeist* of respected and respectable scholars, who still have much to teach us.

It is scarcely necessary to recapitulate in other than broad terms the main objections to the Graf-Wellhausen hypothesis. A Hegelian view of history dominated its originators; they presumed that religious developments (that is, evolution) necessarily follow a prescribed pattern, as though de-

I record my deep gratitude to my friend and colleague, the late Dr. Julius Lewy, for both a critical reading of this essay, and for certain references found in the notes. Needless to say, the opinions in this chapter are my own, and not necessarily Dr. Lewy's.

velopment is rectilinear; they appear to have assumed that once a religious idea was expressed, it emerged to obliterate those ideas which it encountered; and it rested on a painstaking analysis of strata alleged to exist in what for the adherents was the proper unit, the Hexateuch rather than the Pentateuch.

Since the adherents worked largely prior to, but essentially divorced from archeology, both artifacts and also the tremendous yield of linguistic data and texts, their primary tool was literary analysis. Most of us have used, or at least seen, the text published with the various layers distinguished either by the font prescribed for the printer or else by the use of many colors, as in the Polychrome Bible.

In the past two decades there have risen to prominence theories of oral tradition which can necessitate a rethinking of what a stratum or a document might imply. Explanations which allude to cultic legends have attracted attention. One scholar, Ezekiel Kaufmann, has suggested that P is the oldest rather than the youngest stratum. Two scholars, Volz and Rudolph, have denied that there was ever an E document.

It can be appropriate, therefore, for still another suggestion to put forth. But the context for what I here propose must not fade from view: The explanations offered emerge not from caprice, but from phenomena in the text. Whether an explanation seems right and gains acceptance, or seems wrong and fades into a mere footnote in a book like Pfeiffer's *Introduction to the Old Testament*[1] in no way makes the phenomena in the text disappear. The explanations may vary, the phenomena remain constant.

If a personal word is not out of order, what I here set forth emerges from a return to Tanak[2] studies rather than from an unbroken preoccupation with them. The disadvantage may lie in the recession from one's memory of the details, especially the tiny ones, of the exercises in source analysis which I once did. Perhaps, though, to leave Tanak alone and then return to it presents some advantages. Before reverting to Tanak studies, I did considerable work in New Testament, rabbinics, apocrypha and pseudepigrapha, and in Philo. The phenomena in these literatures unquestionably array themselves in particular ways in the mind of the student, and thereafter he can find himself perhaps unduly influenced by them. Yet perhaps even in missing some occasional trees in the Tanak, he might feel that now he sees the forest better than he did.

Several near axioms in the study of the literary history of the Tanak have periodically bothered me. Two of these I mention here.

One is R^{JE}. This symbol stands for the hypothetical editor, compiler, or whatever one calls him, who combined the J and the E accounts. Pfeiffer tells us that "this redactor was no mere hack writer."[3] Yet when I read Pfeiffer's description of the four methods allegedly used by this redactor, to me the epithet "hack" rushes to the tip of the tongue, for Pfeiffer makes him at best only a copyist. Pfeiffer attributes to him four methods: preserving intact valuable stories; omitting a story found in one source through the inclusion of the same story from the other; giving one story in full and supplementing it from the other source; or reproducing two stories, making the identical appear to be reports of successive incidents. None of these four implies a viewpoint or any creativity. Lods,[4] on the other hand, attributes to R^{JE} no brilliance, no originality, and no profundity of thought. How come such diverse judgments?

But with what do we deal in R^{JE}? Were there two divergent documents, J and E? Did R^{JE} sit at a desk, copying now from J, and now from E, adding a phrase here and there? A hack such as Tatian did this with four Gospels, but by Tatian's time these Gospels were virtually canonized; why should a Hebrew Tatian have spent time blending two accounts, but without himself having any discernible motive or viewpoint? To me, this whole matter of R^{JE} makes no sense.

But the phenomena of blending are present, at least if for the moment we accept that doublets imply divergent sources. Yet suppose that R^{JE} was a writer, not a redactor, and that he had before him one account, not two, and suppose that he rewrote the one account, though supplementing it both by utilizing extant older material, and also by creating new material? To me it makes sense to conceive of someone who rewrites something older and does so for a purpose; the mere copyist seems to me inhuman, and an impossibility.

But suppose Volz and Rudolph[5] are right, and there was never an E code? What happens to R^{JE}? Then we could no longer speak of blended documents, but of a source that underwent rewriting; we would deal not with two documents, but with two stages, or more, of the one document.

The second near axiom troubles me even more. On at least twelve occasions in the annual teaching of the same course, I have stated that Genesis 1:1–2:4 is P, and 2:4 ff is J. From at least Philo on, the dissimilarity in these two accounts has been public property. Assuming that a priestly editor inserted this J account into a P framework, then was this P editor completely oblivious to the dissimilarity so clear to modern scholars? Was he less perceptive, less intelligent, than we? How is it that we can see what he was blind to? Must I not try to understand this putative blindness on his part and to explain it, at least to myself?

That important line of research which begins with Gunkel and extends into the modern Scandinavians such as Nyberg, Mowinckel, and especially Engnell has properly alerted us to oral tradition.[6] Yet I sometimes have the feeling that some exponents of oral traditions so stress the oral that they forget that their pursuit is what lies behind documents which are written; and while one can overlook their scorn of literary critics, it seems a little more difficult to forgive their scorn of written documents.

Does oral tradition remain constant and unchanged within the oral stage? Such is the implication of the modern oralists. Are the men who transformed the oral into the written mere recorders? Again, this is the implication of the oralists. I have myself written enough, and taught enough students who have written, to believe that no one ever wrote without having a viewpoint or a purpose. The latter may not be so marked as to constitute what in New Testament studies is called a *Tendenz*,[7] but I find it a priori impossible to believe that a writer can abstain from letting at least some tiny facet of his personality enter in.

From a different viewpoint, I confess to becoming weary of a typical Ph.D. exercise: the discovery of the sources alleged to exist in documents. Stated absurdly, the premise behind such studies, now that scientific biblical scholarship is at least 160 years old, seems to be that nobody ever wrote anything: he only copied sources. There has been a spate of studies embracing source and derivation: What Philo tells, he got from the rabbis; what Jesus taught, he got from the rabbis; what Paul taught, he got from the rabbis (or the Wisdom of Solomon). What New Testament teaches is derived from the Dead Sea Scrolls. It is certainly legitimate to ask, are there discernible sources behind this document. But the issue is prejudiced when the question is put, What are the sources behind the document? And when the searcher for the sources forgets the particular document allegedly containing a source, the student has embarked on an egregious tangent!

An oblivion to the text itself seems to me the greatest defect in present-day biblical scholarship. I say this at the same time that I express the view that the Graf-Wellhausen set of documents is incorrect.

The hypothetical documents, J, E, D, and P, as most usually they are called, are the result of the discernment in the text of doublets or triplets and of contradictory narratives. On the supposition that a single writer would scarcely repeat himself, or flagrantly contradict himself, these phenomena were explained as resulting from the blending together of different sources.

To illustrate beyond the creation accounts, Abraham's sojourn in Egypt (Genesis 12:9–20) is J, while the account in 20 is E; that Beersheba (21) means "seven" is J, but "oath" is E; the first expulsion of Hagar in Genesis 16 is J; that in 21 is E.

Is a theory of diverse documents, written as suggested in the case of the Graf-Wellhausen hypothesis, or oral sources the only conceivable explanation? I do not think so. Rather, there exists an easier, simpler explanation.

A good approach to the explanation presently to be offered begins with postbiblical Judaism on the one hand and the Gospels on the other hand. From the latter, let us take three individual items. First, Mark relates that Jesus was baptized by John, Matthew appends to the narrative that John would have prevented him, while Luke relegates the matter to a subordinate clause; John omits it entirely, possibly deliberately. The apocryphal Gospel of the Hebrews [8] provides a brief scene of Jesus and his mother discussing whether or not he should go to be baptized. Do we deal in these accounts of the same thing with divergent and multiple sources? Next, the so-called rejection in the synagogue at Nazareth discloses that Mark attributed to Jesus an inability to work miracles, a motif altered by Matthew from *could not* to *did not do,* and absent from Luke; Luke, however, has transposed the position of the rejection so that it comes virtually at the beginning of the events, rather than almost midway, as is the case with Matthew, and a third of the way as in Mark. Moreover, Luke portrays Jesus as citing events about Elijah and Elisha which have in common a benefit wrought for a gentile. The incident at Nazareth is not found in John. Again, have our authors utilized divergent sources? Third, the money-changers incident occurs in Mark on what seems to be the second day of Jesus' entry into the Temple; Matthew allocates the event to the first day, this in a prolonged account, while Luke relates the event very briefly, yet adds that Jesus was daily in the Temple teaching, thus greatly de-emphasizing the narrative itself. In John, the incident is found, not as an event of Passion Week, but in the second chapter. Were the sources multiple?

In view of these divergencies, which can be multiplied by countless other examples, how much fixity can be attributed to Gospel tradition, whether it is oral or written? Does the *Tendenz* of the evangelist in any way affect his allocation of this material, or his manner of relating it?

I have cited from the apocryphal Gospel of the Hebrews to suggest that while canonization can act to crystallize tradition, it does not fix it beyond change. If illustration is needed, consider the narrative in Genesis 12:10–20 of Abraham's sojourn in Egypt. Philo so recasts the account as to depict a base king guilty of the grossest disregard to regulations of hospitality. Josephus embellishes the account by relating that Abraham went to Egypt to convert or be converted by the Egyptian priests, and coincidentally taught them mathematics, which they in turn taught the Greeks. The rabbis embellish the story by having an angel present in the bedroom to administer beatings to Pharaoh when his lust prompts him to make advances toward Sarah. The narrative in Genesis 12:10–20 in no way explicitly states or implicitly suggests that Sarah's virtue was not violated; to the contrary. But all these embellishments unite in the conclusion that her virtue was unsullied.

Or, to take another example, the early history of Jacob is that of a deceiver who takes from his brother both the *beracha* ("blessing") and the *bechora* ("primogeniture"), so that Esau says of him, Did they call him Jacob because he, as now, has "Jacobed" me twice? But how do the postbiblical narratives treat these incidents? In them Jacob is the righteous hero—the pious scholar of soft voice—while Esau is the villain whose strong hands impel him to horrendous sins of violence.

Such exegesis, when it is narrative, is called by Jews "haggada"; the word means "narration," a term used in contradistinction to "halaka," the term for legal matters. Haggada, in short, is the fanciful retelling of tales.

The acquisition of the status of canonicity not only did not impede haggada, but spurred it on, even to the point where the haggada contradicted facets of the content of the canonical.

The bare incident of Genesis 12:10-20 relates that Abraham took Sarah to Egypt, passed her off as his sister; she was taken to Pharaoh's harem, and, postprandially Yahwe wrought a plague on Pharaoh and the latter sent Abraham away. In Genesis 20, Abimelech similarly takes Sarah to his domicile. But now Elohim appears to Abimelech in a dream, warning him that he may die because of this married woman. We are told explicitly that Abimelech did not approach her. Indeed, Abimelech defends his having Sarah with him on the grounds that he understood her to be Abraham's sister. Elohim attests to Abimelech's purity—a strange attestation, for are sisters to be considered as readily available? [9]—and advises Abimelech to restore Sarah to Abraham, for the latter is a prophet who could pray on behalf of Abimelech. What Abraham is to pray for is not yet clear; that comes at the very end of the story: Abraham prays that the sterility of the Philistine women be cancelled, for the Deity had brought about the sterility.

What embellishments do we see? The random plague of Pharaoh becomes now the plague of sterility; the Deity has intervened, and Sarah's virtue is unimpaired. Not only has Abraham not committed a prevarication, but he is a prophet. Abraham was not lying; Sarah was his half sister.

Were we to find this story in Genesis Rabbah instead of Genesis 20, we would promptly recognize it as a haggada based on Genesis 12:10-20.

As for the Hagar story, Genesis 16 relates that after Hagar became pregnant, she was disrespectful to Sarah. At Sarah's bidding Abraham permitted her to send the maid away. An angel of Yahwe found Hagar in the wilderness, and assured her that her offspring would be the progenitor of a mighty people.

Neither Sarah nor Abraham appears admirable in this account.[10] Rabbinic exegesis rescued them. So too, Philo escaped from his embarrassment at their character by means of his allegory. He states that Scripture has no intention of portraying two women in a domestic quarrel. Rather, when Abraham married Hagar, the meaning is that Abraham went to college. Hagar represents the encyclical studies, while Sarah is true wisdom.

The second story of the expulsion of Hagar tells us that Ishmael is now born, and is guilty of some misconduct toward or with Isaac—the text here fails us—and that is why Sarah is indignant. Abraham is, properly, distressed at Sarah's demand that Hagar be expelled. At this juncture Elohim advises Abraham to hearken to Sarah, for Ishmael is to be the progenitor of a great people. This time Abraham gives Hagar bread and wine to take with her into the wilderness. She puts Ishmael on her shoulder. (The P chronology establishes, as the rabbis noted, that Ishmael was a lad of sixteen, but the rabbis inform us that Ishmael was smitten with a disease that shrank him to the size of a babe.) When the water gave out, Elohim was true to his promise to Abraham, and he provided water for Hagar.

In this second version, it is Ishmael who evokes Sarah's displeasure, not Hagar; Abraham is distressed, rather than compliant; and it is Elohim who responsibly decides what is to be done and how.

Again, this is exculpating material which is familiar to us from the Midrash.

There is a third version of the patriarch and his wife. It is related of Isaac that he told Abimelech that Rebekah was his sister. In this version the king does not take the patriarch's wife to his harem; one wonders why the fib. The truth of the relationship is revealed to Abimelech not by the Deity, but by his looking out the window and seeing Isaac and Rebekah *in flagrante delicto*. Some scholars have taken this version to be the oldest of the three stories. I doubt this. To my mind the narrator, having named his Philistine king Abimelech, simply retold the story. In this version, the Deity is not needed, for Abimelech is not lustful; now no plagues are required, for it is only to Isaac that Rebekah belongs. Indeed, the rebuke of Abimelech to Isaac states simply: one of the people might have lain with her—but didn't.

Or, why did Jacob go to Paddan-aram? [11] Genesis 27 motivates the trip through Esau's threat to kill Jacob. But Genesis 26:34 has told us that Esau married two Hittite girls, thus embittering Rebekah and Isaac; accordingly, Rebekah, in 27:46, expresses anxiety that Jacob may also marry a Hittite, so that Isaac in 27:1 tells him not to marry a local girl, but to go east and get a proper wife. This latter version is termed P, while the former is JE. I do believe that there was a P code; I am not sure that this is in reality P. But without regard to labels, haggada has again entered in to recast an older account in terms favorable to the patriarchs.

Why must this rewritten account of Jacob's motive in going east for a wife be P? The analysts ascribe Genesis 24 to J—usually J^2. There underlies this latter account the same viewpoint which supposed that Jacob must go east to marry, namely, that a good Jew should not marry, as it were, out of the faith. But in those early times where were there Jewish girls? The narrators solve this problem by having Abraham, Isaac, and Jacob all marry girls from the east. (They seem oblivious about Jacob's eleven sons and they allow Joseph to marry an Egyptian!) Are these eastern wives history or haggada?

To move to the Joseph story, there are variations as to whether it was Reuben or Judah who alone among the brothers had some sense of conscience; and whether it was at Judah's suggestion that Joseph was sold to Ishmaelites, or, instead, rescued and kidnapped by Midianites. Are these variant traditions, or a story and a haggada? Reuben in Genesis 35:22, a story begun but not finished, had an affair with Bilhah, Jacob's concubine, earning Jacob's scolding in Genesis 49:3–4. Why then retain him as a hero, especially in the time when his tribe had died out? What is more natural than to make Judah the hero in place of Reuben? And is it not intended as an accolade that Judah takes the initiative, admirable in the situation, of saving Joseph by selling him into slavery, whereas Reuben passively returned to the pit to find it empty? No, the Judah passages are a haggada on the Reuben passages; they are not a separate source.

Similarly, the account in Genesis 34 of Dinah and Shechem is "composite." In one aspect, Dinah has been raped, but Shechem proposes to marry her. Obliged by Dinah's brothers to be circumcised, Shechem is killed, along with his father, by Simeon and Levi, and for this action Jacob rebukes them. In the other aspect, Dinah has been seduced, not raped, by Shechem. The latter's father seeks out Jacob, proposes marriage, and indeed, subsequent intermarriages; he is told that circumcision is a necessary preliminary. Every male in the city was circumcised; thereupon the sons of Jacob slew them all and plundered the city. The second account is termed E, indeed E^2; the former is J.

To my mind the relationship is the reverse, that the older aspect is that of seduction, of a dignified marriage proposed through the father, and of a destruction of an entire populace by all of Jacob's sons. I take this earlier account to be a late anti-Samaritan passage. As for the other account, it is a series of corrections, calculated to soften what would otherwise necessarily be a harsh judgment. Seduction becomes rape; the proposal of marriage is made by Shechem rather than, properly, by his father; the slain are only Shechem and his father, not the whole city; the slayers are only two of the brothers, Simeon and Levi, conforming to Genesis 49:5–7; and Jacob rebukes them for their deed.

Lastly, for our purposes, we may turn to the so-called E account of the revelation of the divine name in Exodus 3:6–15. A parallel account in Exodus 6:3 is attributed to P. To J is attributed Genesis 4:26b, against whose natural meaning the ancient versions struggle desperately; this verse attributes to Enos the initial knowledge of Yahwe's name. The translations of Genesis 4:26 (Targum Onkelos, Pseudo-Jonathan, and the Septuagint) attempt to deprive Enos of the credit for the discovery of the divine name, for by the time of translations it was a standard Jewish haggada, found in the Midrash, Josephus, and Philo, that it was Abraham who had made the momentous discovery.[12]

The passage Exodus 3:13–15 can be ascribed to some ancient document only by ignoring the high good humor of the haggadic passage. The "I am who I am" is simply a good-natured pun, the humor of which has escaped the long-faced grammarians who have disputed whether *ehye* in verse 14, "ehye sent me," is a qal or a nif'al; or a Gressmann who dutifully cites Wellhausen that the third person, not the first, is *erwartet*. A wag could write "I am sent me"; an ancient source scarcely. The wag was indulging in his very early times in the by now age-old pursuit of giving a supposed etymology of "Yahwe," and has done so almost as well as modern scholars.

A point to be stressed is that a tradition which includes the ascription of the discovery of God to Enos, Abraham, and Moses is thereby reflecting its living quality. And if one replies that these items are contradictory of each other, then notice how in Genesis Rabbah the age of Abraham at his discovery of Yahwe is given variously as one, three, ten, or forty-eight. Moreover, the ten plagues—the dividers into J and E are pushed to say that the E "narratives have evidently in some cases been abbreviated or omitted"— grow in miraculous nature through haggada within Scripture, and then in number in rabbinic exegesis from ten to fifty to two hundred.

The Chronicler reflects a haggadic approach to Samuel-Kings; but even within Samuel-Kings haggada is present.[13] This is the case not only with the pro- and anti-monarchy sentiments attributed to the man Samuel, but haggada can be illustrated typically from two quite separate stories. First in I Samuel 24, while Saul is defecating in a cave, David cuts off a part of Saul's skirt.[14] This legend, or version of a legend, was told to create laughter (as was the legend that David brought a dowry of a hundred Philistine foreskins to Saul!); a haggadist, with a deep hostility to Saul, here retold the story found in 26; there David, with Abishai, steals into Saul's encampment and makes off with his spear and canteen. Second, in David's slaying of Goliath (an act done really by Elhanan, II Samuel 21:19; see the Chronicler's harmonization, I Chronicles 20:5), a legend told that David, as yet unknown to Saul, came to the front lines to visit his brothers, and then slew Goliath. After David's fame as a musician had become legendary, a haggadist recast the beginning of the Goliath incident: Saul was prone to melancholy (a haggadic strand consistently disparages Saul), so that David was brought to court so as, by his lyre, to lull Saul into moments of normalcy; so David was already known to Saul.

We deal not with sources blended, but with haggadic recastings of a single source.

Sometimes the recasting converts a secular story into a religious story. Such is the case with the rollicking account of Ehud in Judges 3:12–30, and of Samson, the consorter with prostitutes, in Judges 16:1–3. When once Samson is made a battler for Yahwe, he acquires from a haggadist a wondrous birth, as in 13:2–25. Indeed, the haggadists so work in Joshua-Judges as to try to persuade us that conquest and settlement were two separate stages; but simultaneously Scripture gives us a picture of slow penetration and conquest in Judges 1:1–2:5. In Joshua we read of an easy and total conquest under Joshua's leadership (with a temporary setback only at Ai); but passages in the Pentateuch gives us the haggada that the true conquerer is the hornet.

The usual disquisitions on E (and P) tell us that these sources increase the miraculous elements in J, and increase the theological. Such is the bent of haggada. But it is haggada, not documents. While P is to be regarded as a document (but embodying a considerable amount of older material), E never was a saga and never was an extended document.

Was J a document? Was it a saga? To the first question the answer is no. To the second, if we mean a long, connected document, the answer is again no. If by the symbol J we mean a level of narration relatively free from theological interpretation, and in that sense "secular," then J was a group of early legends and myths. In very early form, such a group included an account of the origin of circumcision in Moses' time, the truncated narrative in Exodus 4:24–26. This is treated in a totally different way by a haggadist in Genesis 17 who traces circumcision to Abraham. The Eden traditions—the etiologies—may be termed J, in a loose sense.

But J never was a long, connected document. If we will exclude the brief Isaac material (Genesis 25–26), the very ancient story of Tamar (Genesis 38) and the account of Dinah (Genesis 34), Genesis falls into four major parts, the last three of which are the traditions, respectively, about Abraham, Jacob, and Joseph; the first would lend itself to subdivision into Adam and Noah. But a survey of the supposed J accounts in these four segments would lead necessarily to the conclusion that this J was never a unified document. If it was, how account for the character of Jacob in Segment III and his totally different character in Segment IV? Does the honored Jacob in the Joseph cycle exhibit any affinity with the deceiver in the Jacob cycle? Of course not. If one says in rebuttal that the Jacob of the Joseph cycle is the reformed character Israel found at the end of the Jacob cycle, then this is tantamount to conceding that the Joseph cycle lacks the primitive quality which J ought to possess by the mere description which the scholars give of J as a saga.

An open-minded appraisal of the Jacob cycle must recognize that at its kernel lies a folk tale of incalculable antiquity.[15] It is the story of a clever deceiver, whose exploits delighted and tickled the risibilities of generations ancient beyond measure. But subsequent generations began to have reservations about the moral character of the supposed ancestor. One haggadist tries to divert from Jacob as a deceiver by having us suppose that his name means "ankler." Another haggadic aspect intervenes into the narrative to "nationalize" Jacob and Esau. Rebekah has two *nations* in her womb; *nations* will serve Jacob (Genesis 27:29) and Esau will also, though not forever (Genesis 26:40).

In the Jacob cycle we can see a folk character of low moral attributes who needed to be transformed from a mere ancestor into a respected ancestor, and from a respected individual to a national symbol. Since I have no great quarrel with the P Code, I am content to use this symbol; but in my own teaching of the Jacob cycle I speak, not of J and E, but of primitive "secular" elements, of "respected ancestor" materials, and of "nationalizing" materials.

The nationalizing is evident in the Abraham cycle (Genesis 12:2–3; 15:5,

18). But what is absent from the Abraham cycle is material primitive enough to be called J. Genesis 12:1-9 is a tendentious account; God gave the Hebrews Palestine through his gift of it to Abraham. Genesis 12:10-20 is the nearest thing to a J-type story; its purpose is to relate the source of Abraham's wealth. Genesis 13 is part and parcel of Genesis 18-19, to which we come in a moment. Genesis 14 relates the military prowess of Abraham (He conquers four eastern kings with 318 "home-trained" soldiers; that the data conforms with what archaeologists can tell us about the nineteenth or sixteenth pre-Christian century in no way alters the necessary conclusion that in its present form the chapter is a late haggada).[16] Genesis 15—supposedly the first appearance of E in Genesis—is haggada, an expansion of Genesis 12:1. (The ancient rabbis tell us this in the form of stating that the incident described in Genesis 15 occurred in Ur!) Genesis 16 is the work of the "nationalizer," explaining the kinship of the Hebrews and the dwellers in wilderness (Genesis 16:9 is a gloss to account for the two versions of Hagar's expulsion). Genesis 17 is P's account of the origin of circumcision, now a covenant symbol.

Genesis 13:18-19 is an elaborate and sophisticated account. Since Abraham lived long, long ago, it must have been at the time of the vaunted destruction of the four cities, Sodom, Gomorrah, Admah, and Zeboiim; our account mentions only the first two. Abraham is brought into relationship with these cities through his nephew Lot,[17] and he is made to intervene and to bargain with the deity on behalf of pure justice. The story grew by the addition of a story giving the etymology of Isaac's name, infelicitously ascribing a lie to Sarah (Genesis 18:15); the "P" account (Genesis 17) salvages her reputation by ascribing the laughter to Abraham, a laughter not denied in this haggadic recasting and hence not fibbed about. Genesis 20, as mentioned above, is a haggadic retelling of Genesis 12:10-20. Genesis 21:1-7 is a P summary; 8-21 is, to repeat, a retelling of Genesis 16; 22-33 is the etymology of Beer-sheba, whether *seven* (29-30) or *oath* (31). (Another haggadist tells it about Isaac, Genesis 26:15-33.)

Genesis 22:1-19, in which is discerned a preachment against child sacrifice, is in its present form embellished by making a didactic tale into the story of a man who withstood a test.[18] (The rabbis embellish the account into a Joblike narrative; and they increase the test from this one incident to a total of ten.)

Genesis 22:20-24 belong with Genesis 24. Genesis 23 tells of Sarah's death —Abraham graciously bought her burial place even though Yahwe had previously given him the land. Genesis 22:20–24 and Genesis 24 convert and old, old story of a marriage arrangement into an account of how Isaac managed to marry within the fold. The haggadist is at his best here, for the narrative is first-rate. The nationalizer's hand is present in 24:60. The P editor tells us (Genesis 25:20) that Isaac was forty when he married Rebekah; the rabbis note that Rebekah was three; they reflect no apparent surprise at this age which they ascribe to her. Genesis 25:1–18, the conclusion of the Abraham material, reflects the nationalizer.

As this survey suggests, virtually the only primitive aspect of the Abraham material is the supposition, coming from later times, that he dwelled in primitive times. He is not the folk character that Jacob is, in need of transformation into respectability. He is, except for Genesis 12:10–20, respectable at all times. There is a relative sophistication in the Abraham material, this emphasized by both the succeeding Jacob stories and the preceding Adam-Noah stories.

The proliferation in the scholarly literature of exponents to accompany code symbols, yielding J^1, J^2, J^3, and E^1, E^2, E^3 and the like, are in their own way testimony to the absence of persuasive evidence that Genesis is only a pedestrian amalgam of some ancient source or sources. We shall presently need to consider the difference between the viewpoint argued for herein and the more traditional view. But for our immediate purposes the recognition is essential that the four cycles do not present that kind of unified, cohesive material of the same kind and level which could reasonably lead to conceiving of J as a long, connected saga, stretching from Genesis 2 into Joshua or even further.

The material in the Adam-Noah cycle has lent itself to a usual interpretation which is dependent on the supposition that the author (whether single or plural) of the P code was a complete moron. The aspersions of the P writer are many and invariably wrongheaded, but they have never been this explicit. Preliminary to any comment on the Adam-Noah cycle J material imbedded in P is the question of P's procedure. It is fairly universally conceded that P starts on a broad canvas: Creation and the origin of mankind, and then a gradual narrowing of the focus to only Israel. If P apparently decided on this course, and was bent on amplifying his framework by adding extant material, what sorts of material could there have conceivably been available to him? He might have borrowed from the Babylonians and gone from cosmogony into theogony, but his theological premises of monotheism barred such a step. Rather, he chose a series of etiological legends which have a common base in that they explain the origin of human ways and institutions, not the origins of God. Thus, man is the result of Yahwe's fashioning, trees of his planting. Men die, but mankind learns; hence the two trees, of life and of knowledge, were available, but man ate of learning, not of immortality. Woman—so kindred to man—came from man's rib. Animals received names because man gave the names to them. Why is a serpent legless? Why does woman travail in childbirth? Why must man toil for his livelihood? Why are clothes worn even beyond any need for protection? How did earth get populated, and how did the trades and occupations develop? What prompts murder, and how do men regard the murderer?

Are these not etiologies whose relationship is to mankind, not to the Hebrews in particular? What other kind of material would P have introduced, once it was his decision to introduce material? For Lamech he found a poem available; for other persons or events he called on folk tales. Are these folk anecdotes of the same level as the Abraham material? Of course not. Then were they part of the same saga? Of course not. Rather, these tales were the floating property of men, and introduced as such with editorializing more prone to exclusion than to inclusion. Explicit myth has been winnowed out of these stories except at one point. Genesis 6:1-7, the union of the sons of the gods with women, somehow escaped the pruning scissors, and its presence suggests that P might easily have provided a whole spate of mythological ancedotes. Whether P drew on oral or written sources is a matter merely for conjecture; what is certain is that he was highly selective in the bits and pieces which he utilized.

The so-called narrative of the flood reveals its advanced character when it is contrasted with the Gilgamesh epic. The P editor felt called on to annotate it rather than simply reproduce it, probably because he was dealing with a written document which he was winnowing. He recognizes that men live under laws; so he attributes a revelation of a limited number of laws to Noah. Since P, through using the flood, has gotten the world depopulated, he must now account for the repopulation, through Noah's three sons; he pauses to tell only that Hamites are slaves. Having cited the genealogies of nations in Genesis 10, he resorts to a legend to account for a world divided into nations speaking different languages, reaching his climax in a pun on babel and balal. And having succeeded in telling how humanity came to be divided into nations and tongues, he is ready to address himself to his prime topic, a particular nation and tongue.

The so-called J materials in the Adam-Noah cycle are the result of a

sophisticated use of comparatively naïve materials. They can scarcely be regarded in the same light as the folk tales of Jacob, or the novelette of Joseph,
or the didactic tales about Abraham.

Yet a question can be raised about P. Respecting the Abraham and Joseph
materials there is very little of the so-called J that P need have objected to.
There is little in these two cycles he could not have believed in. The question,
then, is this, did P believe this assembly of etiological tales? Did he believe
creation took place as he himself described it, or as J described it? Was he
aware of contradictions, discrepancies, anomalies, and the like? And if he
was not, shall we term him a moron?

A factor which is relevant to the discipline of Bible study is the resiliency
of the religious mind. A Tatian could blend together four gospels which
modern scholars prefer to print in parallel columns; these days they limit the
parallel columns to three, ruling John to be too distant. Once one spoke of
a harmony of the Gospels, today one speaks of Gospel parallels. Yet Tatian
wove all four together. Do we not all know Old Testament scholars who are
opaque to problems so clear to the rest of us in New Testament, and rabbinics scholars unable to discern, let alone confront, problems in the Tanak?
Do we not all know of biblical archaeologists who are blind to the textual
and literary problems of Scripture? This, in general, is what I mean by the
resiliency of the religious mind.

Did P believe the folk tales he interpolated into his *Grundschrift?* Of
course he did, for he read and understood them in the light of his own beliefs, and for him Genesis 2:4 ff. was not out of accord with Genesis 1.

But here the interjection might be made that I have described the haggadic materials in the Tanak as reflecting correction as well as embellishment, refinement as well as elaboration. It could be supposed that I am here
contradicting myself.

Such is not the case. It is phenomena in Scripture which I am describing,
and these phenomena are there. What needs to be clear is a peculiarity in
the literary methods of the biblical authors. I shall initially describe it as a
disinclination to expunge. Just as Genesis 6:1–7 attests to the deliberate
winnowing out of the mythological materials, so too Genesis 35:22a under-
scores the disinclination to expunge. Here we have the beginning of a
narrative known to some redactor in a longer version. The amount told us
is no more than that in absence of Jacob, Reuben lay with Bilhah, his
father's concubine, and Israel heard of it. Any reading of this verse is its
own persuader that something has begun which is not fully narrated; moreover, Genesis 49:4 discloses that the incident was in circulation. Why did

the redactor not retell the whole story? And if he was going to expunge, why expunge the end, but retain the beginning?

The redactors turn out to have counterbalanced the disinclination to expunge by adopting what we may call a process of neutralizing by addition. The haggadic item once added, meant to the redactor that that which he was emending had the same meaning as that which was the result of the emendation. The Abraham of Genesis 20 thus determines the character of the Abraham of Genesis 12:10–20. The disenchantment with kingship of I Samuel 8 means to the haggadist that all of Samuel-Kings reflects this disenchantment.

The P editor could set forth his own religious calendar in Leviticus 23 and still reproduce the discrepant calendars in Exodus 23:14–19 and 34:21–24, for he understood these calendars as in accord with the revised and precise list he was himself devising.

In this same fashion, the author of Jubilees in rewriting Genesis provides a calendar of a pentacontad type completely at variance with the solar-lunar calendar of P. This freedom on the part of Jubilees has led an occasional scholar to suppose that Jubilees must be as old or older than P; this view is based on the wrong premise that canonicity produced rigidity.

Reverting to the Tanak the redactor could and did object to this or that. But this way of handling the objectionable was to append something, a verse or an incident, or a new version, but without removing that which bothered him. The redactors of the Pentateuch did not feel that need which the Chronicler felt to create a new work; nor to create, as did the Church, a series of Gospels, instead of one redacted and reredacted Gospel. (Tatian who combined the four is described by Eusebius as an Assyrian; perhaps something in the Semitic psyche accounts for Tatian's being a combiner rather than the author of a new eclectic and selective gospel.)

Were these haggadic additions oral before they were written? Quite possibly. What is important to recognize, however, is that when they were written down, it was not disinterested writing, not mere automatic copying.

No writer ever writes without some purpose. The Scandinavians and the Dibeliuses go far astray in disregarding in surviving literary documents the personality, interests, and motives of the writer.

By redactor I have not meant to imply a person who worked on the totality of a writing; it might have been one single item which he added in the margin of his text, or included on a piece of parchment sewn on to his scroll. The haggadist was that person who felt the need to embellish or modify. By a redactor I mean a writer who either recorded an oral haggada which became his by conviction, or else gave birth to his haggada when his pen touched paper.

Such stages of redaction seem to me not only truer to the genre of Scripture; but the theory of the blending of diverse sources is an invitation to the improbabilities which mark the pages of so much nineteenth-century scholarship. The premise of blended sources leads to the conceit that the sources involved can be disentangled, and that, by and large, they are blended together in equal quantity. As a result, a disentangler feels the need to end up with two or more self-contained entities. No such obligation rests on him who searches for haggadic additions; and hence he is free from the absurdity of those analyses which ascribe 1a, 2b, 3c, 4a to J; 1b, 3ab, and 4b to E.

Moreover, if a scriptural chapter is recognized as containing both ancient tradition and also subsequent haggadic expansion it is unnecessary to strive, as do some few archeologists,[19] to attribute historical reliability even to the haggadic elements. Nineteenth-century scholarship was too skeptical of that reliable history coincidental to Samuel and Kings. Some scholars of the past decades have been too credulous of the haggadic elements which encase the reliable history. And for the Pentateuch they bring criteria for fixing historical accuracy which overlook the unhistorical genre of the literature.

The haggadic tendency makes of Scripture a literature which grew by accretion. This seems to me exactly the way in which literary reflection of a live religious tradition would grow. From the oral to the written, and from the book to canonicity, and from canon to midrash, represents a continuous process.

In the first Christian century this midrash took two major turns (along with some minor ones). One midrash resulted in Mishnah and Gemara, *The* Midrash, and the targumim; then Saboraim and the Gaonim and then philosophers, Aristotelian and Neo-Platonic. The other resulted in Gospels and Epistles, and ultimately a New Testament; there were in addition Apostles, Fathers, and Ante-Nicene Fathers, and Post-Nicene Fathers, and then philosophers, Aristotelian and Neo-Platonic.

The Graf-Wellhausen hypothesis remains the point of departure for scientific biblical scholarship. This is the case not because its answers are right, but because they have reflected an awareness of the right questions. Scripture remains; the hypotheses come and go. For the Graf-Wellhausen hypothesis to merit the high accolade of being the point of departure implies the need to depart from it.

25

On Canon *

WHEN THE INVITATION came to participate in this panel, and I reverted to the usual standard books, and the newer ones, I discovered that a rather good consensus exists among scholars of all viewpoints respecting the Pentateuch and the Prophets, and slightly divergent theories about the Hagiographa, which either accept Jamnia 90 or else suggest some alternative. In sum, however much as this or that scholar deviates in some particular, the consensus about the history of the canon of the Hebrew Old Testament seemed rather fully established.

I concentrate here, not on the history of the canon, but on canon in the Jewish tradition and its significance to someone who is both a loyal adherent of that tradition, but also something of a modern scientific scholar and also a modern religious man. Accordingly, my short paper is divided into three parts.

First, from the standpoint of the Jewish tradition, the Jewish inquiry into the *history* of the canon is a reflection of the general trend of biblical scholarship. The great name in the specific Jewish inquiry could possibly begin with Elijah Levita, who was born near Nuremberg in 1468 and died in Venice in 1549. Under the patronage of Aegidius of Viterbo of the Augustinian Order, he wrote, between 1509 and 1522, a series of books on Hebrew grammar. His work on the text, rather than on canon, *Massoret ha-Massoret,*

* This paper was read before the Society of Biblical Literature in December, 1965, along with papers by the Roman Catholic Roland E. Murphy and the Protestant Albert C. Sundberg, Jr.; the three papers appeared together in *Catholic Biblical Quarterly* 27 (1966): 189–207.

was published in 1538; a year later a second edition appeared, with some parts translated into Latin by Sebastian Münster. The book, influential on Christian Hebraists, underwent frequent reprinting, and frequent translation, as into German in 1772, and into English in 1867.

Subsequent to this book, those Jews who in any way have participated in the trends of Western European biblical scholarship used Levita and his successors, and, of course, the modern scholars.

Second, and turning away, though, from the question of the history of the canon, it may be in order to speak a few words on what I shall call quasi-canonical. What I have in mind is the position of sanctity and authority of the rabbinic literature in Judaism. This literature has served Jews almost as if it were inherently blended into Scripture, and almost equal to it in sanctity and authority. It was through the interpretive norms of the rabbinic literature that Jews derived their understanding of the contents of Scripture; the body of interpretation, to which the name "Oral Torah" was given, was both authoritative in its influence, and no less than the determining factor in the shaping of subsequent Judaism. While Jews, on developing a historical sense, inquired into the origin of the various aspects of rabbinic literature, and in the nineteenth century set forth theories about the origin of this or that rabbinic work on a scientific rather than traditional basis, the rabbinic literature was uniformly accepted as co-authoritative with Scripture in a way that calls for a term such as "quasi-canonical."

When the sect of Karaites arose in the eighth century, its thrust was in the direction of reverting to Scripture, of asserting the Jewish equivalent of *sola Scriptura,* and of denying the validity of the accrued rabbinic appendixes to Scripture. Because of this biblical "centralism," the sect received its name of Karaites, which we can translate "biblists." One can, indeed, put it this way, that the Karaites rejected the quasi-canonical status of the rabbinic literature. Again in the nineteenth century when Reform Judaism emerged, an attitude toward rabbinic literature both similar to and yet distinct from that of the Karaites arose. Reform Judaism denied the binding authority of the rabbinic halaka as religious requirement, but Reform, as a child of the study of the "history of religions," could not and did not deny that the rabbinic literature and the rabbinic developments had had both ongoing consequence and also a shaping factor in the emergence of its inherited Judaism and its projection for the future. Hence, both Karaism and Reform Judaism denied the quasi-canonical character of the rabbinic literature, though one

336

must say that the Karaites did so out of hostility while the Reformers did so with considerable, but not with unbroken, affection.

Turning now to the third part, let me lead into it by saying that I am simultaneously a loyal adherent of Judaism and also something of a modern scientific scholar. As a loyal adherent, I have no wish to create meaningless upheavals. As this relates to the canon of Scripture, I would never dream of suggesting for divine worship that the scriptural lessons which form the traditional readings, be altered or amplified so as to include books which did not get into the canon. Elsewhere in the divine service, however, as for example, when Reform Jews read the "praise of great men" from Ben Sira at the memorial service on Yom Kippur, I am quite happy for such random selective insertions. With respect, then, to the ongoing practice in my own tradition, I am quite content to let the ancient canon determine the synagogue practice.

As a student, however, I must persist in regarding canon as a logical development, but also as one determined by fortuitous circumstance. If I may put it in this way, suppose that canon had waited for the sixth Christian century instead of being fixed in the first or early part of the second, a quite different collection would have been made, and if somehow or other canon were to become open in the twentieth century, I would be among those who would vote to exclude Esther, and I think that there are a number of suggestions for inclusions that I would make, such as IV Maccabees. I must confess that I cannot share in those theories which attribute to the generations that formed the canon an insight which was truly divine, nor can I acquiesce in the proposition which I frequently read that the canonical books simply by being canonical possess values which exceed those of the noncanonical. My point here is not that as a student I must give attention to Jubilees as well as to Genesis, for I take that to be self-evident; rather, my point is that in the subjective matter of value, as a modern free student would interpret value, canon is in itself no guarantor of value. Canon only reflects the sanctity which a given era chanced to assign to a given number of books.

The implication of this position is that there is a possible tension between the assessments of authority and sanctity made at a given period by the tradition, and the assessments that a modern, free scholar would make. I would not hesitate to describe this position as untraditional. I would rather be straightforward, though, and suggest this kind of position, rather than to resort, instead, to what seems to me to be a deviousness, or to something perilously close to intellectual dishonesty, such as strained exegesis, especially the allegorical. The recourse to such imported meanings seems to me a device by which to continue to sanctify that which the very adoption of allegory or of strained exegesis implies is not essentially and truly sacred.

I raised this issue in my book, *The Hebrew Scriptures* (New York, 1963, pp. 4–5), in a somewhat different way. I said there, "To regard the Tanak [Old Testament] as sacred is reasonable, but its sanctity ought to be impressed on us by study, rather than assumed beforehand." By its very nature, the term canon implies that we are completely assured of the sanctity of a given aggregate of materials, even before we have looked at them.

Canon, moreover, seems to imply that all the books that achieved a place on the approved list are of similar, or comparable or interchangeable sanctity. Perhaps, in a given tradition, one section may be, as it were, *primus inter pares:* the Pentateuch, I would judge, is among Jews in this situation, in relation to the Prophets and the Hagiographa. There is, however, among Jews a sense of an abiding equality in all the books that got into Scripture. Nevertheless, I wish I could believe that the Book of Joshua is as ethically motivated as the Book of Jonah, but I cannot believe that this is the case. I cannot believe that the Book of Chronicles matches the Books of Amos and Jeremiah. I cannot believe that the Book of Proverbs has the profundity of the Book of Psalms. Whenever I chance to make the gradations for my own comprehension of the values in the canonical books, I find myself encountering comparisons, and then I move on to distinctions which to me are tremendous. It is not that I believe that I am barred from understanding how it was that Ezekiel or Daniel got into the canon; it is that I do not find them speaking to me in the same clarity that II Isaiah speaks. I often speculate on the fate of Obadiah, had it appeared in Scripture only in that portion which one might say lies buried in the Book of Jeremiah, and had not reached the accidental eminence of being its own book.

What all this amounts to is the double statement that first, not everything that has come to the canon possesses for someone as subjective as me a full value, and second, there are writings which chanced not to get into the canon, and indeed, some books so late as not to have been eligible for the ancient canon, that do speak to me.

It also seems inescapable to me that just as there was a precanonical period, so for the modern religionist there has to be a postcanonical period. Yielding to no one in my love of the Hebrew Scriptures, and also of the Greek Jewish

Scriptures, canon for me is neither a guarantor nor a security of relevancy, or of relevant sanctity. All the canon, all of it, is illuminating to me and, in a certain sense, to use an old word, a *hodogete,* something which leads one along the way. But canon is neither the sole guide nor the complete guide. Canon is an incident, and no more than that. The books themselves are in part much more important, and in part much less important than the act of canonization.

Abbreviations

BA, *Biblical Archaeologist*

BZAW, *Bleischift Zeitschrift auf Wissen-schaft*

HTR, *Harvard Theological Review*

HUCA, *Hebrew Union College Annual*

ICC, *International Critical Commentary*

JBL, *Journal of Biblical Literature*

JJS, *Journal of Jewish Studies*

JTS, *Journal of Theological Studies*

JQR, *Jewish Quarterly Review*

MGWJ, *Monatsschrift für Geschichte und Wissenschaft des Judentums*

NTS, *New Testament Studies*

RHR, *Revue d'Histoire des Religions*

Chapter 3

1. Karl Popper, "Has History Any Meaning?" in Hans Meyerhoff, ed., *The Philosophy of History in Our Time* (New York, 1959), p. 307.

Chapter 5

1. *Commentary*, 3, No. 6 (June, 1947): 27–34. Review of Milton Steinberg, *Basic Judaism* (New York, 1947).

2. W. D. Davies, *The Setting of the Sermon on the Mount* (New York, 1964), p. 437.

3. Passages in the preexilic prophets are on the surface anti-ritual. Scholars dispute the import of these passages, some interpreting them as denying the efficiency of ritual, but others interpreting them as criticism of misguided ritual. The latter view characterizes the traditional view, which reads Amos 5:21 as follows: "I hate, I despise *your* festivals," that is, *your* deviations from God's way. Even those interpreters who would regard the prophetic passages as anti-ritual would concede that the Hebrew Scriptures lack the directness of antithesis which the New Testament provides.

4. George Foot Moore properly notes the almost total absence of "repentance" in Paul's Epistles.

5. Philadelphia, 1963.

Chapter 10

1. See Henry Cadbury, *The Peril of Modernizing Jesus* (New York, 1937).

2. An initial difficulty ensues from the circumstances that books deemed apocryphal in certain religious traditions are accepted as canonical in others; Catholics accept as canonical books such as I and II Maccabees. Protestants in general regard as apocryphal those books which have not survived in Hebrew; the Catholic "canon" includes books which were preserved only in Greek.

3. See J. Guttmann on Klauser's *Jesus of Nazareth,* in *MGWJ* 75 (1931): 250 ff., and Solomon Zeitlin, "Studies in the Beginnings of Christianity," *JQR,* 14 (1923–24): 111–139.

4. These are the best-known rabbinic works. Equally important are the Midrash and the Tosefta.

5. W. Bousset, *Die Religion des Judentums in neutestamentlichen Zeitalter* (Berlin, 1903); a second edition, edited by Gressmann, is called: *Die Religion des Judentums im späthellenistischen Zeitalter* (Tübingen, 1926).

6. Felix Perles, *Bousset's Religion des Judentums in neutestamentlichen Zeitalter kritisch untersucht* (Berlin, 1903).

7. W. Bousset, *Volksfrömmigkeit und Schriftgelehrsamkeit* (Berlin, 1903).

8. George F. Moore, *Judaism in the First Centuries of the Christian Era,* 3 vols., (Cambridge, 1927–30).

9. It is thus meaningless when W. F. Howard, *Christianity According to St. John* (Philadelphia, 1946), tells us again and again that the background is Jewish, not Greek. Conceding for a moment that the statement is correct, the insistent question is, what specific type of Jewish background? But cf. below the discussion of the motive in labelling a doctrine Jewish or Greek.

10. See Jacob Mann, "Rabbinic Studies in the Synoptic Gospels," *HUCA,* 1 (1924): 324–25; and Ludwig Blau, "Early Christian Archaeology from the Jewish Point of View," *HUCA,* 3 (1926): 169–70.

11. On *Maaseh Bereshith* and *Maaseh Merkabah,* see the section in Gershom Scholem, *Major Trends in Jewish Mysticism* (New York, 1946), pp. 39–78, 140.

12. Hermann L. Strack and Paul Billerbeck, *Kommentar zum Neuen Testament aus Talmud und Midrasch,* 5 vols. (1922–1955).

13. B. J. Bamberger, "The Dating of Aggadic Materials," *JBL* 68 (1949): 115–123.

14. A. Marmorstein, *The Old Rabbinic Doctrine of God,* 1 (London, 1927): 45 ff; and "Philo and the Names of God," *JQR,* n.s., 22 (1932): 295 ff. There intervened a protest against Marmorstein's first statement by Finkelstein in *JQR,* n.s., 20 (1930): 363; Marmorstein's second is a rejoinder to Finkelstein.

15. A striking example of such procedure is W. D. Davies' greatly erudite *Paul and Rabbinic Judaism* (London, 1948).

16. Saul Lieberman, *Hellenism in Jewish Palestine* (New York, 1950).

17. Max L. Margolis, *The Story of Bible Translations* (Philadelphia, 1917), pp. 35–36.

18. See Ralph Marcus, "Jewish and Greek Elements in the Septuagint," in *Louis Ginzberg Jubilee Volume* (New York, 1945), pp. 227–45.

19. Louis Ginzberg, *The Legends of the Jews* (Philadelphia, 1925), 5: viii.

20. Harry A. Wolfson, *Philo,* 2 vols. (Cambridge, 1947). This author goes to the point of denying entirely any hellenization beyond surface in Philo. But see Erwin R. Goodenough, *By Light, Light* (New Haven, 1935).

21. See D. W. Riddle, *Paul, Man of Conflict* (Nashville, 1940); R. M. Hawkins, *The Recovery of the Historical Paul* (Nashville, 1943); and John Knox, *Chapters in the Life of Paul* (New York, 1950).

22. Arthur C. Drews, *The Christ Myth* (London, 1910).

23. See William Fairweather, *Jesus and the Greeks* (Edinburgh, 1924); H. A. Kennedy, *St. Paul and the Mystery Religions* (New York, 1913); S. Angus, *The Mystery Religions and Christianity* (New York, 1925). Another sample of divergent use of the same material is G. H. Gilbert, *Greek Thought in the New Testament* (New York, 1928), which admits the presence of Greek ideas but deplores them.

24. Plato, *Gorgias*, 493a.

25. Wolfson, *Philo*.

26. F. Weber, *Jüdische Theologie auf Grund des Talmud und verwandter Schriften* (Leipzig, 1897).

27. See Mary E. Andrews, "Paul, Philo and the Intellectuals," *JBL*, 53 (1934): 150–66.

28. Joseph Klausner, *From Jesus to Paul* (New York, 1943).

29. Eg., Frank C. Porter, *The Mind of Christ in Paul* (New York, 1932), pp. 18 ff.

30. The outstanding German names are K. L. Schmidt, *Der Rahmen der Geschichte Jesu* (Berlin, 1919); Martin Dibelius, *Die Formgeschichte des Evangeliums* (Tübingen, [1919] 1933); Rudolf Bultmann, *Geschichte der synoptischen Tradition* (Göttingen, [1921] 1931). In America such studies were pursued by D. W. Riddle, *The Gospels, Their Origin and Growth* (Chicago, 1939) and S. J. Case, *The Evolution of Early Christianity* (Chicago, 1914) at Chicago. An excellent summary of the results and methods is to be found in a book by a Catholic author, L. J. McGinley, *Form-Criticism of the Synoptic Healing Narratives* (Woodstock, Md., 1944), written not in approval of form criticism, but in some effort to show either its inadequacy or irrelevance. McGinley's summary is excellent.

31. Paul Fiebig, *Die Gleichnisreden Jesu im Lichte der rabbinischen Gleichnisse des neutestamentlichen Zeitalters* (Tübingen, 1912).

32. Asher Feldman, *The Parables and the Similes of the Rabbis* (Cambridge, 1924).

33. D. W. Riddle, *Jesus and the Pharisees* (Chicago, 1928).

34. A watershed in the history of the liberal scholarship, affecting the tone of its treatment of Judaism is to be discerned in the period comprising Strack-Billerbeck (see note 12) and Moore's *Judaism in the First Centuries of the Christian Era* (see note 8). Before them the liberal scholarship was not free from condescension or even an outright sneer at Judaism; for example, F. Weber's *Jüdische Theologie auf Grund des Talmud und verwandter Schriften* (Leipzig, 1897), or G. B. Stevens' *The Theology of the New Testament* (New York [1902] 1947), and even the writings of the famous historian Edward Meyer. Against this background the Jewish dictum that higher criticism is the higher anti-Semitism is to be considered a just reaction. But the reappraisal which was indicated in the books of a Christian, Robert Travers Herford (*Pharisaism, Its Aim and Its Method* [New York, 1912], and *The Pharisees* [New York, 1924]), has crucially altered the tone of scholarship and, by freeing Jews from a need of defensiveness, has encouraged them to make substantial contributions, even in the field of New Testament; see the superficial study by Thomas Walker, *Jewish Views of Jesus* (London, 1931), and the distinguished study by Gösta Lindeskog, *Die Jesufrage im neuzeitlichen Judentum* (Uppsala, 1938).

35. Of the former, a good example is Joseph Klausner; of the latter, an attitude attributed to Harry Emerson Fosdick. Rabbis named treatises after the first significant word is the treatise; their discussion of festival regulations accordingly is called "Egg"; Fosdick was reported in the *Yale Daily News* of October 13, 1948, by coincidence Yom Kipper, as having declared that Jesus was interested in the essentials of religion while the rabbis

were interested only in an egg! The published version of the lecture, in *The Man from Nazareth* (New York, 1949), indicates that the undergraduate reporter did not listen with both ears. He misunderstood Fosdick's intent and spirit; but Fosdick's words lack precautions against such distortion.

36. Nazis, with obvious motive, denied that Jesus was a Jew; some scholars, without such motive, have made the serious but absurd suggestion that Greek, not Aramaic, was the language of Jesus.

37. Julius Wellhausen, *Einleitung in die drei ersten Evangelien* (Berlin, 1905); F. Burney, *The Poetry of our Lord* (Oxford, 1925); C. Torrey, *Our Translated Gospels* (New York, 1936).

38. Three considerations combine to form the usual view that the author of Matthew was a "Jewish" Christian: (1) early church tradition declares it was written in Hebrew (Aramaic); (2) Old Testament quotations are abundant; (3) the Gospel sets up a kind of legalism. Too little notice has been taken in the scholarly world of the objections of Kenneth Clark, "The Gentile Bias in Matthew," *JBL*, 66 (1947): 165–72, to the usual view; it is really time for it to be abandoned.

39. R. Reitzenstein, *Die hellenistichen Mysterienreligionen* (Leipzig, 1910); *Poimandres: Studien zur griechischägyptischen und frühchristlichen Literatur* (Leipzig, 1904); F. Cumont, *The Oriental Religions in Roman Paganism* (Chicago, 1911); W. L. Knox, *St. Paul and the Church at Jerusalem* (Cambridge, 1925); *St. Paul and the Church of the Gentiles* (Cambridge, 1939); *Some Hellenistic Elements in Primitive Christianity* (London, 1944); P. Wendland, *Die hellenistisch-römische Kultur in ihren Bezeihungen zu Judentum und Christentum* (Tübingen, 1912); principally Nock's *Conversion* (London, 1933). Also see principally Erwin R. Goodenough's *By Light, Light,* which despite some occasional overstatement is a landmark which points toward the fullest knowledge of the meaning of Hellenistic Judaism. In it one finds a rarity in scholarship: the utilization of the significant Hermetic literature, overlooked and ignored despite a fine translation in a good edition in four volumes by Walter Scott, *Hermetica* (Oxford, 1924–36).

Chapter 11

1. 2d ed. (New York, 1970), pp. 163–75.

2. Originally titled *Die Formgeschichte des Evangeliums* (Tübingen, 1919), pp. 4–5. Here are Dibelius' words: "Eine Gemeinde unliterarischer Menschen, die heute oder morgen das Weltende erwartet, hat zur Produktion von Büchern weder Fähigkeit noch Neigung, und so werden wir den Christengemeinden der ersten zwei oder drei Jahrzehnte eine eigentlich schriftstellerische Tätigkeit nicht zutrauen dürfen."

3. *HTR*, 16 (1923): 81–92.

4. *JBL*, 75 (1956): 19–26.

5. Chicago, 1936.

6. Hans Lietzmann, *Der Menschensohn* (Freiburg and Leipzig, 1896).

7. Wilhelm Wrede, *Das Messiasgeheimnis in den Evangalien* (Göttingen, 1901). The real clue to the "secrecy" is the need to emphasize the disciples' blindness.

Chapter 12

1. Walter Lock, *ICC, The Pastoral Epistles* (New York, 1924), pp. 8–9, begins by stating that "The exact reference is uncertain." He goes on to suggest two possibilities, of which the explanation along the lines of gnosticism is his second and that of the "Rabbinical Haggada" is his first.

2. Lock points especially to *Adv. Haer.* I. 30, as an example of profitless discussions. I Timothy 1:4 is paraphrased in Iraneus' preface, apparently there directed against Valentinus, as in Tertullian (*Praescr.* 7 and 33).

3. Spence, in *Ellicott's Commentary on the Whole Bible,* 8: 253–54, reads as follows to Titus 1:14: "*Not giving heed to Jewish fables.*—Such as we now find embodied in the Talmud (See Note on I Tim. 1:4). The oral law and traditional interpretations and glosses had, to a great measure, obscured the original simple text. The Israelite of the time of St. Paul, trained in the stricter Jewish schools, was taught that the way to win the approval of the Most High was through the observance of countless ceremonies and the practice of an elaborate ritual." When we look back to the note on I Timothy 1:4 in Spence's remarks, we read as follows: "These fables were, no doubt, purely Rabbinical. It was said in the Jewish schools that an oral Law had been given on Sinai, and that this Law, a succession of teachers had handed down . . . Genealogies in their proper sense, as found in the Book of the Pentateuch, and to which wild allegorical interpretations has been assigned. Such purely fanciful meanings had been already developed by Philo, whose religious writings were becoming at this time known and popular in many of the Jewish schools. Such teaching, if allowed in the Christian Church, St. Paul saw would effectually put a stop to the growth of Gentile Christendom."

The view that Paul wrote the Pastorals—rejected by virtually all modern commentators —finds support for solving the allusion as talmudic, often more judiciously than the helter-skelter words of Spence, by coupling our two passages with Titus 3:9: "But avoid stupid controversies, genealogies, dissensions, and quarrels over the law, for they are unprofitable and fruitless." See J. R. Dummelow, *A Commentary on the Holy Bible* (New York, 1911), where we are told that the allusion means "not Gnostic stories of emanations and aeons, but idle Jewish legends and genealogical claims. . . ." Burton Easton, who rejects the Pauline authorship, says of Titus 3:9 (*The Pastoral Epistles* [New York, 1947], p. 104): "The explicit mention of the Law may be due to a desire for a Pauline coloring." Lock, who abstains from committing himself clearly on the authorship, merely cites Ambrosiaster and Jerome on genealogies, but says nothing about the Law. Another rejector of Pauline authorship, Morton Dibelius, *Handbuch zum Neuen Testament,* Vol. 13, *Die Pastoral Briefe* (Tübingen, 1931), makes no comment on Titus 3:9, but discusses 3:8–11 as a discussion of the Pastor's ideal piety contrasted with the heretically inclined.

4. The only notice they take is on I Timothy 6:4 (Vol. 3: 655), to which they have a cross reference from Titus 3:9. They point to several references to show that *zeteseis* and *logomachiai* were found in the Jewish academies too. None of these references, however, impinge on myths or genealogies.

5. Dibelius, p. 10.

6. The passage, in the judgment of my colleague Professor Alexander Guttmann, whose valuable assistance I gratefully acknowledge, is a strictly haggadic layer. It focuses on three biblical worthies, Abraham, Samson, and David, the names of whose mothers are not supplied by the biblical text. These names are here supplied, after which the question of the utility of the information is queried; to this the laconic response is made, "For replying to the *minim* ('heretics')."

Dibelius comments that the word "myths" in combination with genealogies prohibits understanding the allusion to descent from Abraham, for neither Paul nor a Pseudo-Paul would have termed Abrahamic descent as a "myth." He cites the authority of G. Kittel (*Zf. für neutestamentliche Wissenschaft*, 20 [1921]: 49 ff.) that postexilic Judaism harbored genealogical speculations which under some conditions could involve "heresy." Dibelius continues: "Dass in diese Diskussionen auch Christen verflochten wurden, zeigt Baba Batra 91a. . . . Aber in den Past kann man eine Polemik gegen solche Spekulationen nur finden, wenn man wegen Titus 1:10; 1:14 eine Art von Judasimus für das wesenlichste Element der hier bekämpften Ketzerei hält" (tr.: That in such discussions Christians were also involved is shown by Baba Batra 91a. . . . One can discover such a polemic against such speculation in the Pastorals only if one considers Titus 1:10; 1:14 an aspect of Judaism as the likeliest element in the heresy here opposed).

Another comment of Dibelius is worth citing (p. 42): "Finally, any form of asceticism or any peculiar sanctification of a day could be called Judaism by the Christians."

7. *Judaistic Christianity*, pp. 132–137.

8. Hort (see note 7), pp. 134 and 137. On this former page Hort discusses and discards a theory of Weiss which would identify these errorists with the Essenes. On page 130, Hort declares himself in favor of Pauline authorship of the Epistles. On page 135 Hort cites from Polybius ix, 1:4 an assertion that Polybius has been pursuing an "austere" narrative, rather than enticing his reader by "the genealogical way." This latter phrase, according to Hort, refers to Greek historians whose histories of earlier times were full of mythologies of early legends; on this, see below the citation from Colson, note 10. Hort goes on to show that "Philo divides the Pentateuch first into history and law, and then subdivides the history into creation and 'the genealogical,' of which, he says, part refers to the punishment of the impious, part to the honor of the righteous. . . . He uses the term in no depreciatory sense. . . . Now if Philo could apply this term to the historical part of the Pentateuch, it would *a fortiori* be applicable to the rank growth of legend respecting the patriarchs and other heroes of early Mosaic history. . . ."

It is to be noted that Hort is arguing not from evidence, but from logic—and it seems rather poor logic. It would seem also to reflect an acquaintance with Philo via excerpt rather than intensive study, and, furthermore, one wonders how much genuine personal reading Hort ever did in Midrash, Jubilees, and Philo. The documentation which Hort supplies for his comment of the Haggada is limited to a reference to a chapter in Schürer, *History of the Jewish People in the Time of Jesus Christ* (English translation [Edinburgh, 1872]). George Foot Moore does not mention Hort in his article, "Christian Writers on Judaism," *HTR* 14 (1921): 197–254; the words there relating to Bousset would well apply here: "Bousset never conceived his task as a historian; it was not Judaism as a religion, but Judaism as the background, environment, source and foil of nascent Christianity that he has in mind. . . ."

9. F. H. Colson, *JTS* 17 (1918): 265–71. Kittel, "Die Genealogiai der Pastoralbriefe" (*Zf. für Neutestamentliche Wissenschaft* 20 [1921], 49–69) devotes much of his essay to the question of proper methodology required to identify the malefactors. He proposes to make good an alleged deficiency: "Nur ein Gebiet ist bisher im Verhältnis recht wenig zur Veranschaulichung herangezogen worden: die Talmudische Literatur" (tr.: Only one domain has hitherto been drawn on, in rather restricted relationship, for clarification: the talmudic literature). Kittel goes on to describe various genealogies among Jews (such as in Genesis and Chronicles), and comes to concentrate on the *yuhasin* ("genealogies") as in Pes. 62b, of the Rabbis, and other preoccupations along this line in the talmudic literature. He gives us much data, but little relevancy; and, on the side of methodology, I believe that he gives much more attention to suppositions about the background than he does to the text itself. Of Hort and Colson he says not one word.

10. Colson, p. 269 (see note 9). Colson continues: "I venture to think that on one point at least my view meets the facts better than Dr. Hort's. For when Dr. Hort suggests that the writer attacks the frivolities of the Haggada, he overlooks the fact that the writer of 2 Timothy is apparently a Haggadist himself." The allusion is to the mention of Jannes and Jambres. "It would seem strange that one who saw such danger in Haggadic legend should write thus. But it is quite intelligible that one who cherished Haggadic lore should strongly object to seeing it treated on a par with heathen myths." Colson adds in a footnote: "Indeed such a feeling may perhaps lie behind the phrase 'Jewish myths.' 'You apply the term "myths" with all its evil associations to our venerable traditions.'" This last sentence of Colson's is not crystal-clear.

11. Burton Easton, *The Pastoral Epistles* (New York, 1947), pp. 87–88. Easton holds the Epistles to be pseudonymous. Respecting Hort's view he says (p. 112): "The nature of the endless genealogies should never have been in doubt; Irenaeus quotes this verse in the first sentence of his *Heresies*. . . . It is therefore quite impossible to identify the 'genealogies' with legends about the pedigrees of the patriarchs, Rabbinic haggadas . . . or Philo's own allegories. Such productions were often futile and wearisome, but they were academic speculations of the learned, which could by no stretch of the imagination endanger the Church's general harmony."

12. Colson, pp. 267–68.

13. See E. Klostermann, *Markus, Handbuch zum Neuen Testament,* 3 (Tübingen, 1926): 1.

14. *Encyclopaedia Biblica,* 2: 2521.

15. Ernest Colwell, *John Defends the Gospel* (Chicago, 1936).

16. Floyd V. Filson, *The Interpreter's Bible,* 10 (New York, 1951–57): 336–38, says: "As applied to Christ, it means to think of his lowly life and shameful crucifixion as proof that he was disowned by God and so should be rejected by men. Paul once regarded Christ in this way; that was before he became a Christian, when he was still sinfully persecuting Christ's followers. But now (*nun*) since we have become Christians, we regard him thus no longer, for he was sent of God to save men." Filson is ostensibly supplying the "exegesis"; in the "interpretation" by Read, just below the exegesis, we read that the RSV, in rendering the phrase "from the human point of view" succeeds in disposing "of various speculations concerning his meaning which were left open by the KJV, 'though we have known Christ after the flesh.' It disposes of the suggestion that Paul was speaking of his estimate of the Christ as the Jewish Messiah. Equally impossible is the idea that Paul refers to his knowledge of the earthly life and deeds of Jesus. . . . The statement means just what it says. All false ideas about him were gone. . . . To regard Christ from a human point of view means to lay emphasis on externals, to think of him merely in relation to his own time, to become immersed in such personal details as are emphasized in some biographies. These may be interesting but they do not really matter. . . . This does not mean, as has been suggested, that Paul was indifferent to the earthly life and teaching of Jesus, and that he depended upon the Spirit for all he knew."

Rudolf Bultmann, *Theology of the New Testament,* 1 (English translation), Kendrick Grobel, trans. (New York, 1951–55), p. 237, terms the phrase "according to the flesh," as *"an existence or an attitude* not as natural-human, but *as sinful"* (his italics). He reverts to the passage, page 238; insofar as I understand him, Bultmann first is suggesting that "according to the flesh" can possibly modify the verbs in the sentence, rather than the nouns; "but this decision means nothing for the sense of the total context, for a 'Christ regarded in the manner of the flesh' is just what a 'Christ after the flesh' is."

The problem can be pursued through endless writers, as I have done, but with little yield; some commentators glide over the passage as though it were not there; others seem to me to talk around it. In sum, Weizsäcker seems to me to have been on the right track

(*The Apostolic Age of the Christian Church*, trans. from the 2nd rev. ed., 1:142; originally, *Das apostolische Zeitalter der Christliche Kirche*, Freiburg i.B., 1892) in saying: "Paul was expressing his judgment on the value of the earthly life of Jesus, in contrast with His present rank." So, too, Henry Carré, *Paul's Doctrine of Redemption* (New York, 1914), p. 140, declares that the passage "means that the earthly historical Jesus had no vital significance for him." See also in Hans Lietzmann, *An die Korinther* (*Handbuch zum Neuen Testament*, 9 [Tübingen, 1949]), 125–26, the interesting and probably likely view that the passage reflects the contentions between "disciples" who had known Jesus and "late-comers," such as Paul, who had not known him. The passage would mean: "Wenn ich auch, wie es ja der Fall ist, Christus einst persönlich gekannt habe, so mache ich jetzt davon keinen Gebrauch" [If I too, as is indeed the case, once knew Christ personally, now I make no use of that]. Martin Dibelius, in *Paul*, edited and completed by W. G. Kümmel, trans. Frank Clarke, pp. 54 ff. (originally, *Paulus* [Berlin, 1951]) declares that the verse is "first of all a repudiation of the view of all those who relied on connections, even on personal connection with Jesus. . . . It is therefore a . . . probable inference . . . that Paul had never seen in earthly form the one he portrayed. . . . The Lord who had been raised up to God . . . was more real and more binding than the historical connection with Jesus. We may ask whether . . . the historical life of Jesus had any effect on him. . . . If he had any discussion with a man like Stephen, it would have concerned the coming salvation and the resurrection, not the paltry, trifling incidents . . . in the life of Jesus. . . . Earthly connections, even connections with the historical Jesus, were no longer of any account."

17. The German "Fabeln" carries the import better than does the English myth. "Myth" has too great an overtone which connotes false or unhistorical. I would not suggest that the Pastor would regard details, such as the Synoptics, as unhistorical. It is their triviality or their irrelevance which he is underscoring, and not their falsity. Somewhat congruently Philo is moved to deny (at least momentarily) the literalness of narratives in the Pentateuch, such as Sarah's quarrels with Hagar, as at the end of *Congress;* allegory, having given Philo a satisfactory measure of spiritual significance, can also prompt him to disregard the details of the narrative.

18. Such as Clement of Alexandria and Origen.

19. See George Salmon, *A Historical Introduction to the Study of the Books of the New Testament* (London, 1892), pp. 31–35.

20. See "Bible Canon," No. 11: "Controversies about Separate Books," in *Jewish Encyclopedia*, 3 (New York, 1902), pp. 148–49.

21. See my *Philo's Place in Judaism* (Cincinnati, 1956), pp. 29–35.

22. It is unlikely that Kings was canonical when Chronicles was written; the manner in which the Chronicles used Kings is, however, another illustration of how traditional material can be used to serve a *Tendenz,* and how similar material can be variously presented.

23. See note 3, Easton's comment, and note 6, Dibelius', on the desire for a Pauline coloring.

24. The Tübingen school alerted scholarship to the presence of *Tendenz* in ancient books, but it often failed to identify the *Tendenz* accurately and persuasively, partly because of its bondage to Hegelianism. In my *Genius of Paul* (New York, 1958), I set forth what I believe to be a more prudent statement of the true *Tendenz* in Acts; and I set forth there a view of Mark, which, if correct, has some very radical implications for both Gospel study and also for early Christian history. I have adumbrated some of this material on Mark in *A Jewish Understanding of the New Testament* (Cincinnati, 1956).

25. *Haer.,* II. i. 57.

26. A. B. Davidson, *Epistle to the Hebrews* (Grand Rapids, 1950).

Chapter 13

1. Hans Lietzmann, *Der Menschensohn,* 1896, pp. 93–95.

2. Mark is not simple Gospel; it bristles with problems. The theory of an Ur-Mark, an edition prior to the canonical Mark, seems to me unmistakably correct. I believe, too, that after Ur-Mark was rewritten to yield the present Mark, it underwent some minor interpolations, such as 14:28 and 16:7.

3. This conclusion, among others, is found in Wilhelm Wrede, *Das Messiasgeheimnis in den Evangalien* (Göttingen, 1901). The German title of Albert Schweitzer, *The Quest for the Historical Jesus,* is *Von Reimarus zu Wrede.* Both in its own terms but especially in its position in Schweitzer's study, Wrede's views have been of great influence in subsequent scholarship.

On whether or not Jesus was understood in his own time, see the excellent study of Morton Enslin, "Twixt the Dusk and the Daylight," *JBL,* 75 (1956): 19–26.

4. See my *Genius of Paul* (New York, 1958), pp. 163–75, and "Myths, Genealogies and Jewish Myths and the Writing of Gospels," reprinted in this volume, Chapter 12.

5. Matthew 20:28 regards the request as unseemly, and makes the mother of the two the requester.

6. I am tempted to regard 8:29–30 as an interpolation from the same hand that inserted 14:28 and 6:7. We must note that Peter's so-called confession entails no sequel and apparently no consequences. It would hence appear that Peter understands what Christ means but completely fails to understand that teaching of Jesus which supposedly ensues immediately on that understanding. In *The Genius of Paul,* pp. 146 and 166, I set forth some of the other peculiarities in the Gospels and Acts which relate to Peter.

7. In the usual Jewish view, the Messiah was to be of Davidic ancestry. This Jewish view is reflected a number of times in the Gospels: Mark 10:48 and 11:10 and in the genealogies in Matthew 1 and Luke 3 and elsewhere. A Christian transformation was to regard the Christ as "preexistent," and hence antedating even Abraham ("Before Abraham was, I am," John 8:58; but see John 7:40–43). Modern Western canons of logic would find intolerable certain inconsistencies which seem not to have bothered the ancients, see my "The Haggada Within Scripture," this volume, Chapter 24.

8. In Mark, the supposed Jewish objection to Jesus is his claim to be the Christ, while the Roman objection is to his being "King of the Jews" (Mark 15:2). The mocking of Jesus on the cross in 15:32 brings the two titles together. Dangerous as it is to conclude too much from laconic passages, it would seem that Mark distinguishes in his mind between the religious and the political.

9. Matthew 27:11–14 seems to suppose that Jesus is denying it as if it were a false allegation; John 18:33–37 recounts the incident with emphasis on "my kingship is not of this world."

Chapter 15

1. *Judaism and St. Paul,* p. 188.

2. *Ibid.,* pp. 180–81.

3. *Ibid.,* pp. 1–129.

4. In *By Light, Light: The Mystic Gospel of Hellenistic Judaism* (New Haven, 1935), and in many subsequent writings.

5. *By Light, Light,* pp. 76–77 and elsewere in passing.

6. Pages 370–413.

7. London, 1955.

8. See for example, J. Dupont, *Gnosis: La Connaissance religieuse dans les épitres de Saint Paul* (Louvain, 1949).

9. *IJS,* 2 (Cambridge, 1950), pp. 97–98.

10. *The Genius of Paul,* reprint (New York, 1970), pp. 61–66.

Chapter 17

1. IV: 197–254.

2. In Div. 2 Vol. 2: 90–125, in the English translation.

3. In my "Parallelomania" reprinted in this volume, Chapter 22.

4. New York, 1958.

5. The full title is *Primitive Christianity in Its Contemporary Setting* (New York, 1956).

6. Two volumes (New York, 1951 and 1955).

7. Göttingen, 1941. It has not been translated into English.

8. Göttingen, 1921, and thereafter. The translation into English, *The History of the Synoptic Tradition* was published in Oxford, 1963.

9. Israel Abrahams, in *Studies in Pharisaism and the Gospels,* 2nd ser., "The Yoke" (Cambridge, 1917), pp. 4–14.

10. The virtual abandonment of eschatology is an example. See, C. H. Dodd, *The Parables of the Kingdom* (London, 1948), and Martin Werner (Eng. trans.), *The Formation of Christian Dogma* (New York, 1957), especially pp. 31–119.

11. The seventh (Matt. 5:43–48) is likewise intended as a scriptural quotation; the "quoted" passage simply is absent from Scripture.

12. See my *Philo's Place in Judaism* (Cincinnati, 1958).

Chapter 18

1. All his books were published in Cincinnati.

2. *The Israelite,* July 7, 1865, p. 428. All further references to Wise's series are documented in the text.

3. Albert Schweitzer, *The Quest of the Historical Jesus,* ignores the deists in general, and the British deists in particular. See Maurice Goguel, *Jesus the Nazarene, Myth or History,* English translation (1926), p. 2, note 4.

4. See note 3.

5. Bruno Bauer, *Kritik der evangelischen Geschichte der Synoptiker* (Leipzig, 1841–1842).

6. Wise's skepticism at that time (1865) extended to the question of "Jewish-Christianity": "If the cradle of Christianity was in Alexandria, the Jewish-Christians were proselytes of a later date" (*The Israelite,* July 7, 1865, p. 12). Commenting in the same issue of Wislicenus' discussion of the genealogy of Jesus, Wise says:

It is strange that after the admission that we know of Jesus only what we learn from the Gospels, which are as good as no source, the author should maintain to

know anything sure regarding Jesus. Nothing is sure, not even that he existed.
Jesus might have been a dramatical fiction, invented for religious mysteries.

Where Wislicenus denies that Jesus was born in Bethlehem, declaring that "it was
historically known and could not be denied that Jesus was from Nazareth," Wise comments: "Nothing could be *historically known* concerning Jesus, as nothing is *historically
known* about him today" (*The Israelite,* August 11, 1865, p. 36).
Wise was prepared at that time to extend his skepticism to the point of denying that
John the Baptist had ever lived. Wise, discussing the baptism of Jesus, comments on the
mention of John in Josephus:

> It (the baptism) might be a historical fact, if the following doubts did not exist.
> 1st. Did Jesus exist, or is he a dramatical fiction, invented for religious mysteries
> of days long before Paul? 2nd. Did John exist? The passages regarding him in
> Josephus are spurious. If John and Jesus were real personages . . . then there
> is no evidence of their having had any acquaintance with each other, outside
> of the New Testament, and this can not be used as a historical text at all (*The
> Israelite,* August 11, 1865, p. 45).

As to the words which the Gospels attribute to Jesus, Wise says:

> There is not the slightest evidence in record that he existed, much less that he
> made a speech. Nothing is more common to ancient chronographers than to in-
> vent speeches for their favorite heroes and put them conveniently in their mouths
> (*The Israelite,* October 27, 1865; see items in a similar vein in the issues of
> November 3rd, 17th, and 24th of the same year).

7. *Das Judentum und seine Geschichte* (Breslau, 1864). See my *We Jews and Jesus*
(New York, 1965), pp. 64–66.
8. *Geschichte der Juden.* On Graetz in this connection, see my *We Jews and Jesus*
(New York, 1965), pp. 61–66.
9. See Caspar René Gregory, *Canon and Text of the New Testament* (New York,
1907), p. 262: "The Council of Nicea in 325 does not appear to have determined anything about Scripture."
10. See the convenient table in James Moffatt, *An Introduction to the Literature of
the New Testament,* p. 213.
11. See Adam Fyfe Findlay, "Jewish Christian Gospels," in his *Byways in Early Christian Literature* (Edinburgh, 1923), pp. 33–78.
12. See Jacob Z. Lauterbach, *Rabbinic Essays* (Cincinnati, 1951), pp. 514–30.
13. "John's Gospel can hardly be counted in this direction. He is a dogmatic writer
and no biographer. He shaped the biography of Jesus, and wrote speeches for him, to express John's dogma of Alexandrian Christianity, as it originated [*note here the change
in Wise's viewpoint*] in the second century. . . . We know of those corresponding passages, that they were copied and translated from a Hebrew or Aramaic work, which
existed in the second half of the first century" (*The Israelite,* July 30, 1869).
14. On this hoary problem, see Charles A. H. Guignebert, *Jesus* (English translation
by S. H. Hooke) (London, 1935), pp. 96–104.
15. Wise here has a footnote: "See Rashi to Exodus 1:16."
16. One needs to say that Wise's interpretation of the transfiguration, Mark 9:2–13,
is as extreme an example of "rationalistic" interpretation as that which he himself had
scorned. The dependency of the passage in Mark on the *Phaedon* is new to me; David

Friedrich Strauss, *Life of Jesus,* English translation by George Eliot (London, 1892), pp. 545–46, note 19, finds a similarity in Plato's *Symposium,* 523 B ff., suggestive.

17. I discuss this in *The Genius of Paul,* pp. 173–174.

18. "Chapter headings!"

19. Wise continues: "If Jesus had been asked the question of crusades against infidels, pyres for hereties [sic!] and unbelievers, persecution and torture for schismatics and Jews, exceptional laws and oppression for dissenters and heathens, inquisitions and auto-da-fees [sic!] in the name of the church; he would have turned aside with a shudder in his veins and exclaimed, 'Ye are ripe for the kingdom of Satan'" (*The Israelite,* December 3, 1869).

20. Cincinnati, 1880, pp. 255–68.

21. Cincinnati, 1874.

22. English translation *Ha-toren* (New York, 1922), p. 414. Klausner was taken to task by Armand Kaminka (*Ha-toren,* August, 1922) for the sentiments quoted. A partial translation of Kaminka's sharp criticism is to be found in *HTR* 16 (January, 1923): 100–103.

23. I record my thanks to Rabbi Albert G. Minda for giving me his file on this affair. It is a good collection of clippings from the days and weeks after Wise's sermon. An account of the matter can be found in the *Review of Reviews,* 73 (1925): 203, and in the *Christian Century,* 42 (1925): 26.

Chapter 20

1. Harry Wolfson, *Philo* (Cambridge, 1947).

2. A view with which the name of Erwin R. Goodenough is associated and which I also hold.

3. This rendering is by Erwin Goodenough, *By Light, Light* (New Haven, 1935), p. 128. The phrase occurs in Philo's *De Abrahamo.*

4. *De Migratione Abrahami,* pp. 89–93.

5. *Moses,* 2:51.

6. *Deter.,* 38 ff.

7. *Mutation,* 208.

8. *Congressu,* end.

Chapter 21

1. This Hebrew expression is equivalent to "topic headings," that is, broad clues, not developed exposition.

Chapter 22

1. A. T. S. Goodrick, *The Book of Wisdom* (New York, 1913), p. 405, apparently attributes the phrase to Menzel, *De Graecis in libris Koheleth et Sophiae vestigiis,* p. 40. Goodrick gives neither the place nor the date of publication. Perhaps it is P. Menzel; cf. Charles, *Apocrypha and Pseudepigrapha of the O.T.,* i: 533.

2. "John a Primitive Gospel," in *JBL*, 64 (1945): 145–85.

3. In his essay in *The Background of the New Testament and its Eschatology*, William David Davies and David Daube (eds.) (Cambridge, 1955), pp. 153–71.

4. See Isaac Heinemann, "Die Lehre vom Ungeschriebenen Gesetz in Jüdischen Schrifttum," *HUCA*, 4 (1927): 149–72.

5. See *The Dead Sea Scrolls*, trans. by E. Margaret Rowley (London, 1952), and the various critical assessments.

6. *NTS*, 7 (1960): 334–46.

7. Cambridge, 1947.

8. 1922–1955. Index volume, 1961.

9. See Gerald Friedlander, *The Jewish Sources of the Sermon on the Mount* (London, 1911).

10. "Christian Writers on Judaism," in *HTR*, 14 (1921): 197–254.

11. See, especially, *Rabbinic Literature and Gospel Teachings* (London, 1930).

12. Fuller, in G. Ernest Wright and Reginald Fuller, *The Book of the Acts of God* (New York, 1957), p. 209.

13. Vol. 44 (1961): 119–56.

14. New York, 1955.

Chapter 23

1. Kasher, *Torah Shelemah*, 2 (New York, 1953): 342. Note 159 invites attention to variant readings in Onkelos, since Kimchi apparently had seen a literal text. But virtually all traditional Jewish commentators interpret the *huḥal* as meaning "profane."

2. The rabbinic material is reproduced conveniently in Kasher, *Torah Shelemah, ad loc.*

3. Ibn Ezra seems to be terming the form a *pu'al*, whereas we should call it a *hoph'al;* Ibn Ezra's term probably means simply passive. Somewhat less than clearly he adds what seems to be a clinching point that if the word meant profane then the noun would be nearer the verb. Exactly what this last means is not certain; the super-commentaries to Ibn Ezra interpret his comment to signify that were the meaning profane, then the word *liqro* would be superfluous. In the absence of a better explanation of this uncertainty of Ibn Ezra, we may as well accept this incongruent explanation. Much clearer than his words is his intent to offer a second and final reason for insisting that *huḥal* means "began."

4. See especially *De Abrahamo*, beginning.

5. We recall that the Septuagint had rendered *yhvh* here by "Lord God."

6. Rosenmüller, *Scholia in Vetus Testamentum* (Lipsiae, 1821), reproduces Aquila with *kalein* in place of *kaleisthai*. He mentions that Clericus (1733) had preferred the sense of "named with the name of God."

7. Dresden, 1679, pp. 55–57.

8. Samuel Nelson, *Die Antideistische Bibel* (Erlangen, 1766).

9. *Uebersetzung und Erklärung des Pentateuchs*, 3rd ed. (Frankford, 1883).

10. New York, 1928–35.

11. Philadelphia, 1949, II, 2.

12. *Ibid.*, p. 731.

13. *The Pentateuch and Haftorahs, Genesis* (New York, 1929), p. 41.

14. David Hoffmann, *Jeschurun, Monatsscrift für Lehre und Leben im Judentum*, ed. J. Wohlgemuth, 2 (Berlin, 1915): 503.

15. *Historical and Critical Commentary on the Old Testament* (London, 1858), pp. 153–55.

16. *Biblical Commentary on the Old Testament,* Vol. 1. *Pentateuch,* trans. James Martin (Edinburgh, 1891): 119.

17. The German reads *Kainitischen.* How did the translator and the proofreaders, forgivably, slip? Such minor errors are inevitable in ancient and even modern scribes.

18. *Genesis,* 5th ed. (Göttingen, 1922).

19. *Genesis,* trans. W. B. Stevenson (Edinburgh, 1897).

20. Cited in Stevenson's translation (see previous note).

21. *The Book of Genesis* (New York, 1904), p. 71.

22. See note 18.

23. Eerdmans, *Alttestamentliche Studien* 1 (Giessen, 1908): 81.

24. Oxford, 1948, pp. 495–96.

25. *The Two Sources of the Predeuteronomic Primeval History* (JE) *in Gen. 1–11* (Oslo, 1937), pp. 44–61.

26. On the issue of E, Volz and Rudolph, first to my knowledge suggested that E is an error of the analysts, and the E was not a narrator. In my article, "The Haggada Within Scripture," (Chapter 24), I go beyond them in repudiating E.

27. In "The Haggada Within Scripture," I present a view, which I believe to be unanticipated, about the variant forms of scriptural tradition.

Chapter 24

1. Robert H. Pfeiffer, *Introduction to the Old Testament,* rev. ed. (New York, 1948).

2. Tanak (which Jews pronounce *tanach*) stems from the abbreviations of the three divisions, *T*orah, *N*ebi'im, and *K*'tubim, of the Hebrew Scriptures. "Tanak" seems to me a more desirable term than "Old Testament," which Jews could object to, or "Bible," which Christians could object to if limited to Old Testament.

3. Pfeiffer, p. 283.

4. Adolphe Lods, *Histoire de la litterature hébraïque et juive depuis les origines jusq'à la ruine de l'etat juif (135 après J. C.)* (Paris, 1950), pp. 323–27.

5. Paul Volz and Wilhelm Rudolph, *Der Elohist als Erzähler ein Irrweg der Pentatechkritik, BZAW,* 63 (1933). They repudiate E not so much as a code, but as a *narrator* comparable to J. In Volz's portion of the monograph, he gives four objections to the usual source analysis (pp. 14 ff.): (1) A writer copying from two parallel narratives—here and there a word, or a half-sentence, or a sentence—is a scholarly artifice, not a reflection of real life. (2) The criteria for determining the source divisions rest on improper criteria. (3) The Pentateuch should be approached like other scriptural books, and not unlike them. If so, tiny repetitions, contradictions, etc. are discernible as glosses; longer such items represent J's use of divergent materials, all brought into J's long narrative; extensive items of this kind represent an edition of the long narrative, or of this narrative's being put into a new *Verband.* (4) The source analysts destroy the artistic beauty of the unified account.

Neither Volz nor Rudolph, however, supplies any positive hypothesis to replace the repudiation of E as a narrator. Martin Noth, *Überlieferungsgeschichte des Pentateuch,* pp. 22 ff., scarcely meets the challenge of Volz, but simply hews to the old line that parallel materials must necessarily mean parallel sources.

6. See Eduard Nielsen, *Oral Tradition* (Chicago, 1954), especially pp. 11–17. Hermann Gunkel, *Einleitung in die Psalmen* (various editions), emphasized "Form-Criti-

cism"; Sigmund Mowinckel (English translation), *The Psalms in Israel's Worship* (New York-Nashville, 1962), their cultic use.

7. *Tendenz* as an explanation of textual phenomena is, of course, not unknown in OT scholarship. To my knowledge, however, it was never raised to the critical eminence which NT scholarship is associated with F. C. Baur and the Tübingen school. I contend in *The Genius of Paul*, pp. 146–48, that the Tübingen school correctly noted that there is *Tendenz* in Acts of the Apostles, but Hegelianism blinded them from a proper characterization of it.

See the edition edited by M. R. James, *The Apocryphal New Testament* (Oxford, 1953), p. 16.

9. See Hildegard Lewy in *Orientalia*, 10 (1941): 211 on the practice in Nuzian society whereby a man could live with his sister in concubinage and yet not be averse to having her marry someone else, this in consideration of a sum of money. But the Nuzi theory, advocated by Ephraim Speiser, has been denied by David Freedman, "A New Approach to the Nuzi Sistership Contract," in *Journal of the Ancient Near Eastern Society of Columbia University*, 2 (1970): 77–85.

10. The bevahior of Sarah and Abraham conforms with the treatment of slave girls such as Hagar. See Codex Hammurabi, p. 145, and S. R. Driver and John G. Miles, *The Babylonian Laws*, 1 (1957): 305.

11. That he went eastward, and not south or west, reflects group historical memory, as of Haran. The issue is not where he went, but the motivation which the Tanak supplies for his going.

12. See "Genesis 4:26b," Chapter 23, this volume.

13. A full assessment of the succession of Deuteronomic writers is deliberately withheld here, out of considerations of space. I deal with the subject in my *The Hebrew Scriptures* (New York, 1963), 420–24. In brief, if it is just to label Job, Proverbs, and Ecclesiastes as wisdom literature, then the D writings can be put into this same loose category. The D writers represent neither the priesthood nor the prophets, despite friendliness to both, but are rather sages-teachers who inferred lessons, and taught them, from Israel's history. So strong in D is didacticism that while it is proper to credit the D writers with more accurate history than scholars did at the turn of the century, it is improper to make secular historians of them. Especially suspect are the fortuitous appearances of prophets, named or unnamed; and a more reliable history of prophecy can be written solely from the literary prophets (all of whom except Isaiah the D writers neglect) than from coalescing them with the accounts of prophets, including Elijah and Elisha, in Samuel and Kings. Moreover, it can be suggested, though the connection cannot be traced, that the post-Tanak descendants of the late P writers are the Sadducees and of the late D writers the scribes-Pharisees-rabbis.

14. The cutting of the skirt had symbolic force, as Julius Lewy notes, *RHR*, 9 (1934): 31. My comments are on the late setting of the anecdote, Saul in a cave, and not on the significance of the ancient symbol.

15. Professor Julius Lewy had the opinion that the stories may well have been current among Western Semites in Mesopotamia already in the nineteenth and eighteenth century.

16. Historical memory could be called on to reproduce in the Abraham material recollections of these early times. Thus a conformity to early historical conditions could emerge, to be blended with a late sophisticated assessment, of the patriarch. The conformity to early historical conditions does not in itself establish the historicity of the particular narrative. Scholars, in an eagerness to trace the background of a text, have often been neglectful of the text.

The ascription to Abraham of having given a tithe to a priest at Salem is not so much historical as a lesson taught by example. As yet there were no Israelite priests; as yet

Jerusalem was not Israelite. But if Abraham could offer a tithe at Salem, the precursor to Jerusalem, to the precursor of the Aaronites, how much the more should his descendants! Moriah of Gen. 22 became identified in II Chron. 3:1 and in the rabbis with Mount Zion, for where else would the patriarch have offered a ram? Note that in Gen. 14 the author is careful to tell us that Melchizedek was a priest, not of the *ba'al* but of the vague *el elyon*. That is, the author of this didactic section skillfully avoids the pits which he might have fallen into.

17. The nationalizer ascribes the origin of Ammon and Moab to an incestuous relationship (19:28); rabbinic exegesis in part condemns Lot's daughters, and in part, with Josephus, praises a motive ascribed to them of wishing to repopulate the world. See my *Philo's Place in Judaism* (Cincinnati, 1956), p. 69, note 303.

18. In its present form the accentuation in Gen. 22 is on Abraham's character rather than on the incident. This seems to me to represent a deviation, through accretion, from a simpler state in which the events, climaxing in the desisting from the act of child sacrifice, were the principal focus. An even more ancient folk tale may underlie the account; see Hildegard Lewy, in *Symbolae Hrozny* (1950), p. 353, note 106.

19. The archaeologists have often been the victims of popularizers. Occasionally an archaeologist has made statements which, taken from context, have been misconstrued. This latter was the experience of my intimate friend, Nelson Glueck, who learned to his dismay that there was being attributed to him a quasi-fundamentalism which his colleagues knew was remote from him; curiously, he was unjustly attacked from quite a different quarter on the basis of phrases lifted out of context from his *Rivers in the Desert* (New York, 1959). Wright's sober study, "Is Glueck's Aim to Prove that the Bible is True?," *BA*, 22 (1959): 101–8, should now set the record straight. It may also clarify for literary analysts the position held by responsible archaeologists. See also Nelson Glueck, "The Bible and Archaeology, in *Five Essays on the Bible* (New York), p. 66: "Although there is much which can be archaeologically confirmed, there is much more which cannot and need not and never will be historically substantiated." I do not hereby imply that archaeologists will, or should, espouse the viewpoint in this essay; I only suggest that this viewpoint is in full potential harmony with archaeology.

index

357

index of scriptures

Samuel Sandmel is Distinguished Service Professor at the Hebrew Union College—Jewish Institute of Religion. He was ordained as a rabbi at the Hebrew Union College (1937) and received his Ph.D. (1949) from Yale University. His many previous books include *A Jewish Understanding of the New Testament, We Jews and Jesus, The First Christian Century, The Genius of Paul,* and *The Hebrew Scriptures.*

This manuscript was edited by Sandra Yolles. The book was designed by Donald R. Ross. The type face for the text is Linotype Granjon designed by George W. Jones about 1928; and the display face is Cheltenham designed by Bertram Goodhue in 1896.

The text is printed on (*to be determined*) paper and the book is bound in Columbia Mills' Fictionette cloth and Process Material's Elephant Hide over binders' boards. Manufactured in the United States of America.